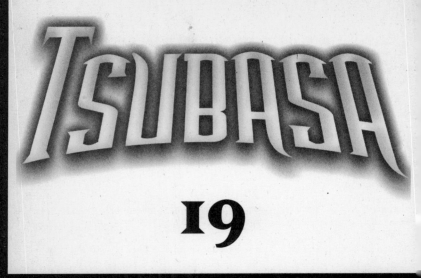

TSUBASA

19

CLAMP

TRANSLATED AND ADAPTED BY
William Flanagan

D BY

ward

DEL REY

BALLANTINE BOOKS • NEW YORK

Tsubasa, volume 19 is a work of fiction. Names, characters, places, and incidents are the products of the author's imagination or are used fictitiously. Any resemblance to actual events, locales, or persons, living or dead, is entirely coincidental.

A Del Rey Manga/Kodansha Trade Paperback Original

Published in the United States by Del Rey Books, an imprint of The Random House Publishing Group, a division of Random House, Inc., New York.

Publication rights arranged through Kodansha Ltd.

First published in Japan in 2007 by Kodansha Ltd., Tokyo

ISBN 978-0-345-50579-8

Printed in the United States of America

www.delreymanga.com

9 8 7 6 5 4 3 2 1

Translator/Adapter—William Flanagan
Lettering—Dana Hayward

Contents

Tsubasa crosses over with *xxxHOLiC*. Although it isn't necessary to read *xxxHOLiC* to understand the events in *Tsubasa*, you'll get to see the same events from different perspectives if you read both series!

Honorifics Explained

Throughout the Del Rey Manga books, you will find Japanese honorifics left intact in the translations. For those not familiar with how the Japanese use honorifics and, more important, how they differ from American honorifics, we present this brief overview.

Politeness has always been a critical facet of Japanese culture. Ever since the feudal era, when Japan was a highly stratified society, use of honorifics—which can be defined as polite speech that indicates relationship or status—has played an essential role in the Japanese language. When you address someone in Japanese, an honorific usually takes the form of a suffix attached to one's name (example: "Asuna-san"), is used as a title at the end of one's name, or appears in place of the name itself (example: "Negi-sensei," or simply "Sensei!").

Honorifics can be expressions of respect or endearment. In the context of manga and anime, honorifics give insight into the nature of the relationship between characters. Many English translations leave out these important honorifics and therefore distort the feel of the original Japanese. Because Japanese honorifics contain nuances that English honorifics lack, it is our policy at Del Rey not to translate them. Here, instead, is a guide to some of the honorifics you may encounter in Del Rey Manga.

-san: This is the most common honorific and is equivalent to Mr., Miss, Ms., or Mrs. It is the all-purpose honorific and can be used in any situation where politeness is required.

-sama: This is one level higher than "-san" and is used to confer great respect.

-dono: This comes from the word "tono," which means "lord." It is an even higher level than "-sama" and confers utmost respect.

-kun: This suffix is used at the end of boys' names to express familiarity or endearment. It is also sometimes used by men among friends, or when addressing someone younger or of a lower station.

-chan: This is used to express endearment, mostly toward girls. It is also used for little boys, pets, and even among lovers. It gives a sense of childish cuteness.

Bozu: This is an informal way to refer to a boy, similar to the English terms "kid" and "squirt."

Sempai/Senpai: This title suggests that the addressee is one's senior in a group or organization. It is most often used in a school setting, where underclassmen refer to their upperclassmen as "sempai." It can also be used in the workplace, such as when a newer employee addresses an employee who has seniority in the company.

Kohai: This is the opposite of "sempai" and is used toward underclassmen in school or newcomers in the workplace. It connotes that the addressee is of a lower station.

Sensei: Literally meaning "one who has come before," this title is used for teachers, doctors, or masters of any profession or art.

-[blank]: This is usually forgotten in these lists, but it is perhaps the most significant difference between Japanese and English. The lack of honorific means that the speaker has permission to address the person in a very intimate way. Usually, only family, spouses, or very close friends have this kind of permission. Known as *yobisute*, it can be gratifying when someone who has earned the intimacy starts to call one by one's name without an honorific. But when that intimacy hasn't been earned, it can be very insulting.

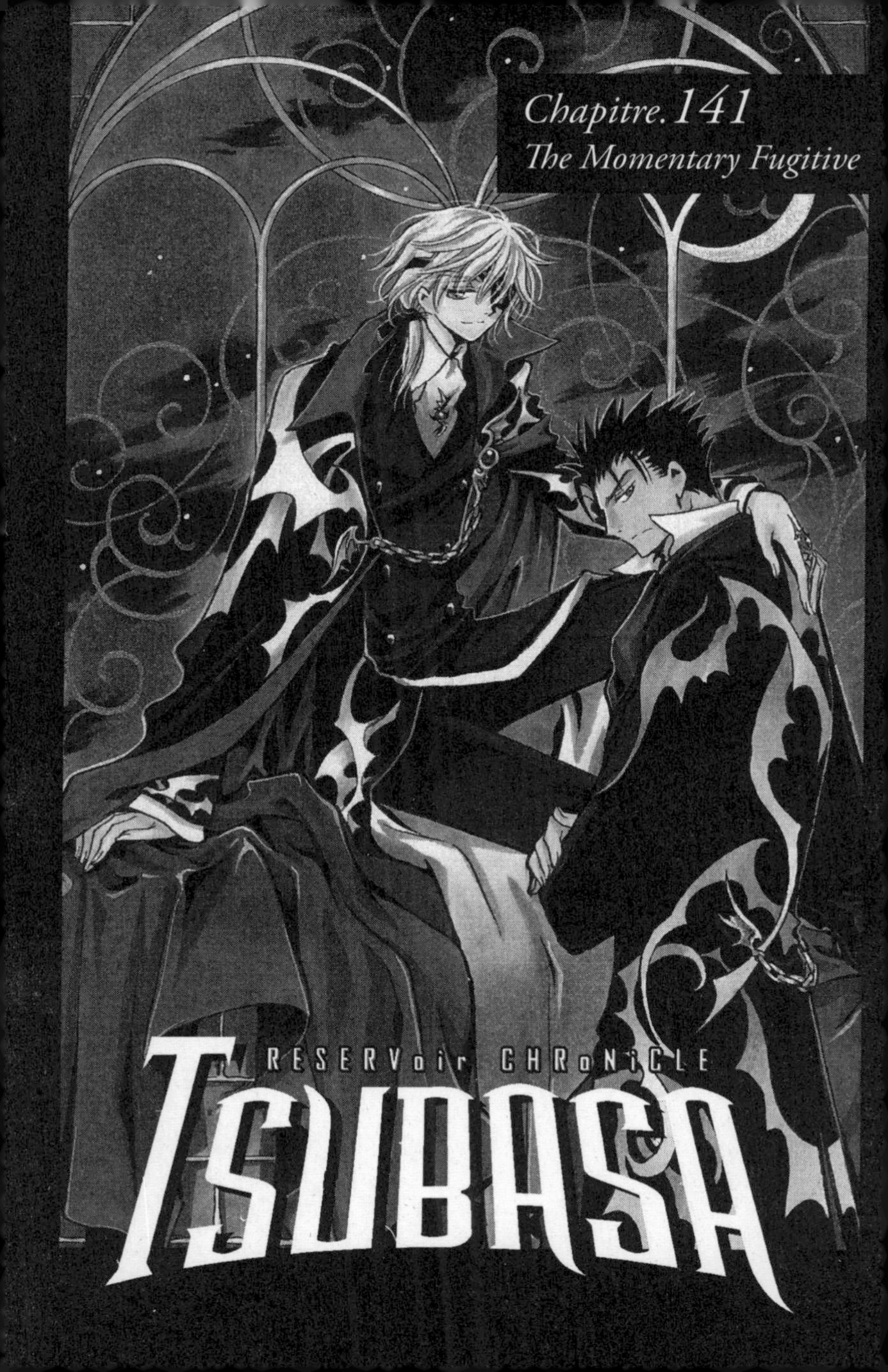
Chapitre. 141
The Momentary Fugitive
RESERVoir CHRoNiCLE
TSUBASA

ツバサ

RESERVoir CHRoNiCLE

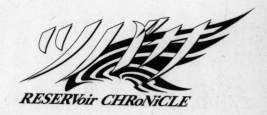

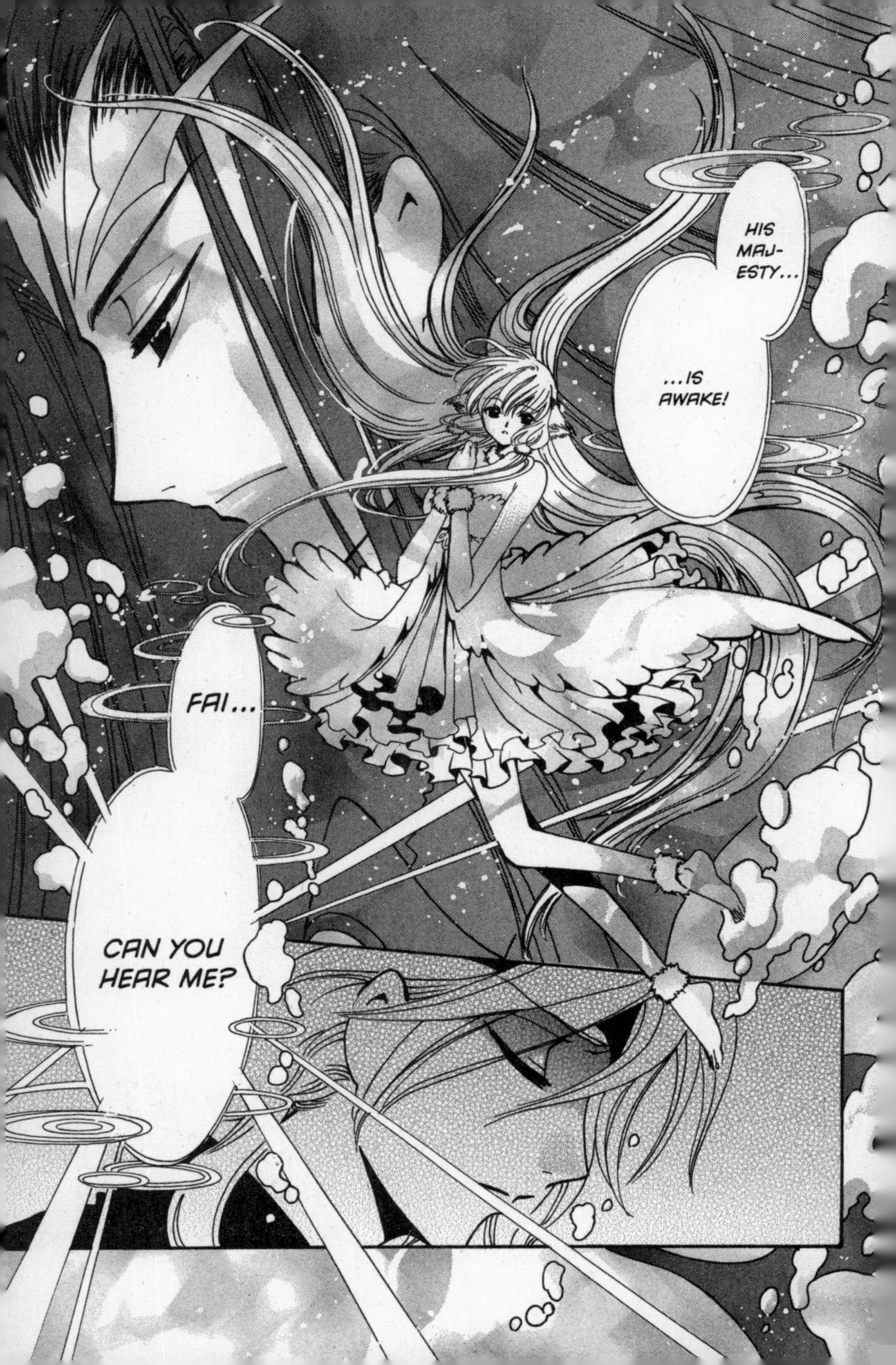
HIS MAJ-ESTY...
...IS AWAKE!
FAI...
CAN YOU HEAR ME?

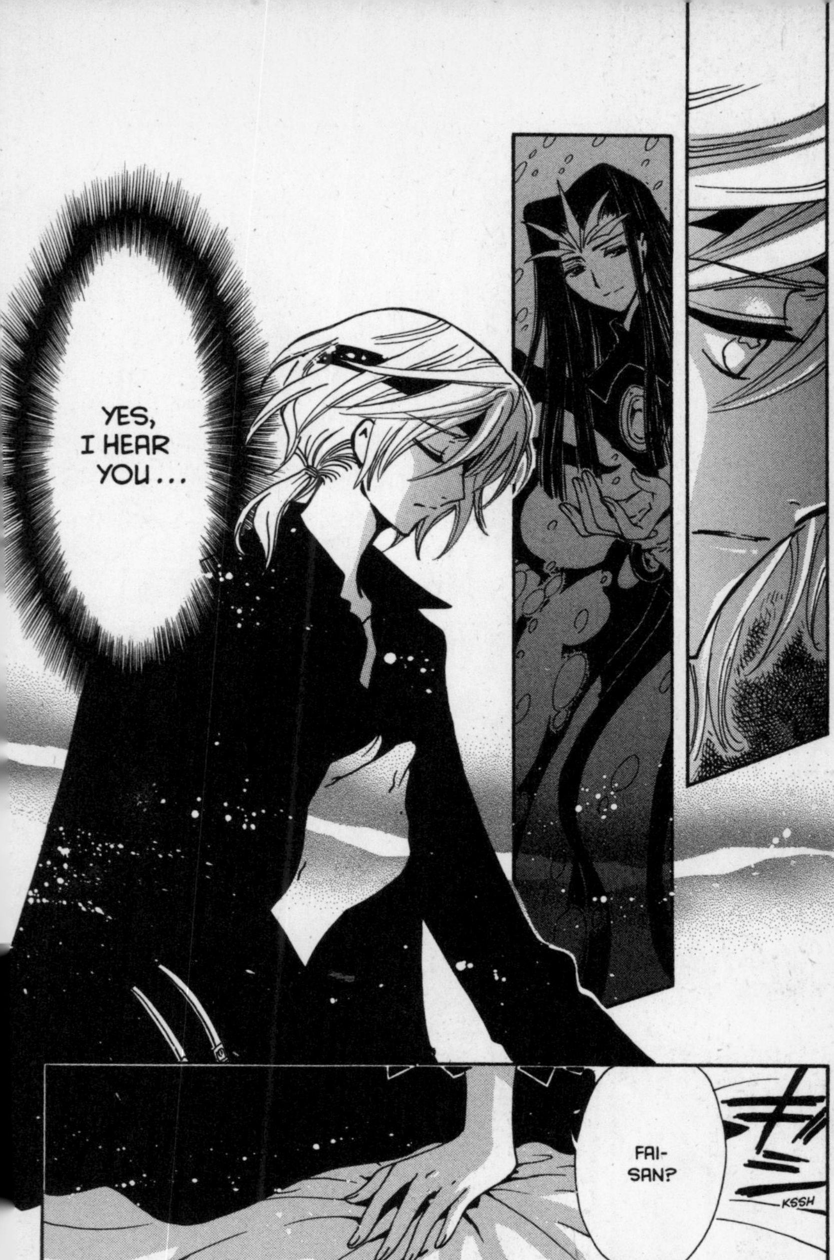
YES, I HEAR YOU...
FAI-SAN?
KSSH

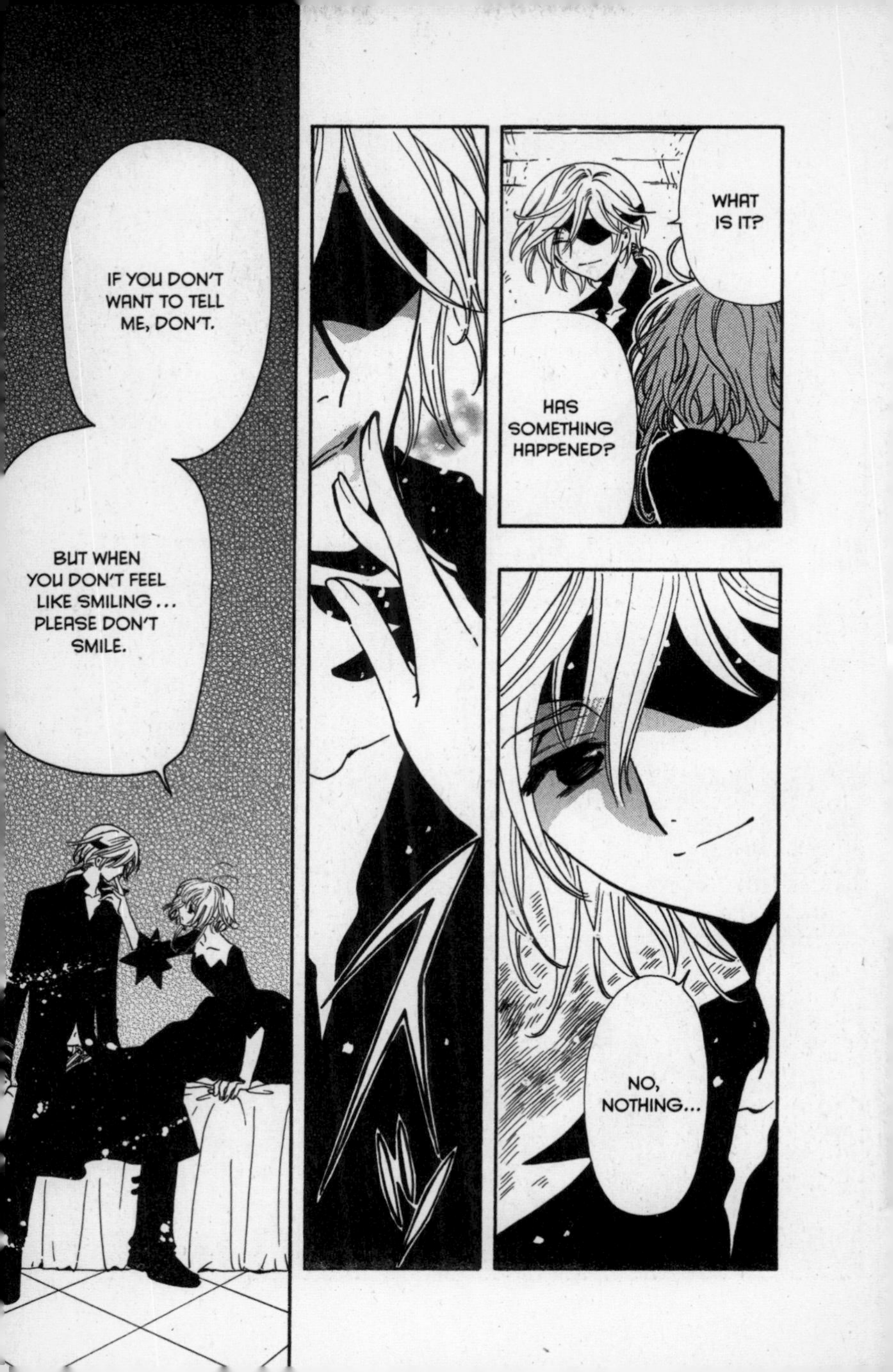
WHAT IS IT?
HAS SOMETHING HAPPENED?
NO, NOTHING...
IF YOU DON'T WANT TO TELL ME, DON'T.
BUT WHEN YOU DON'T FEEL LIKE SMILING... PLEASE DON'T SMILE.

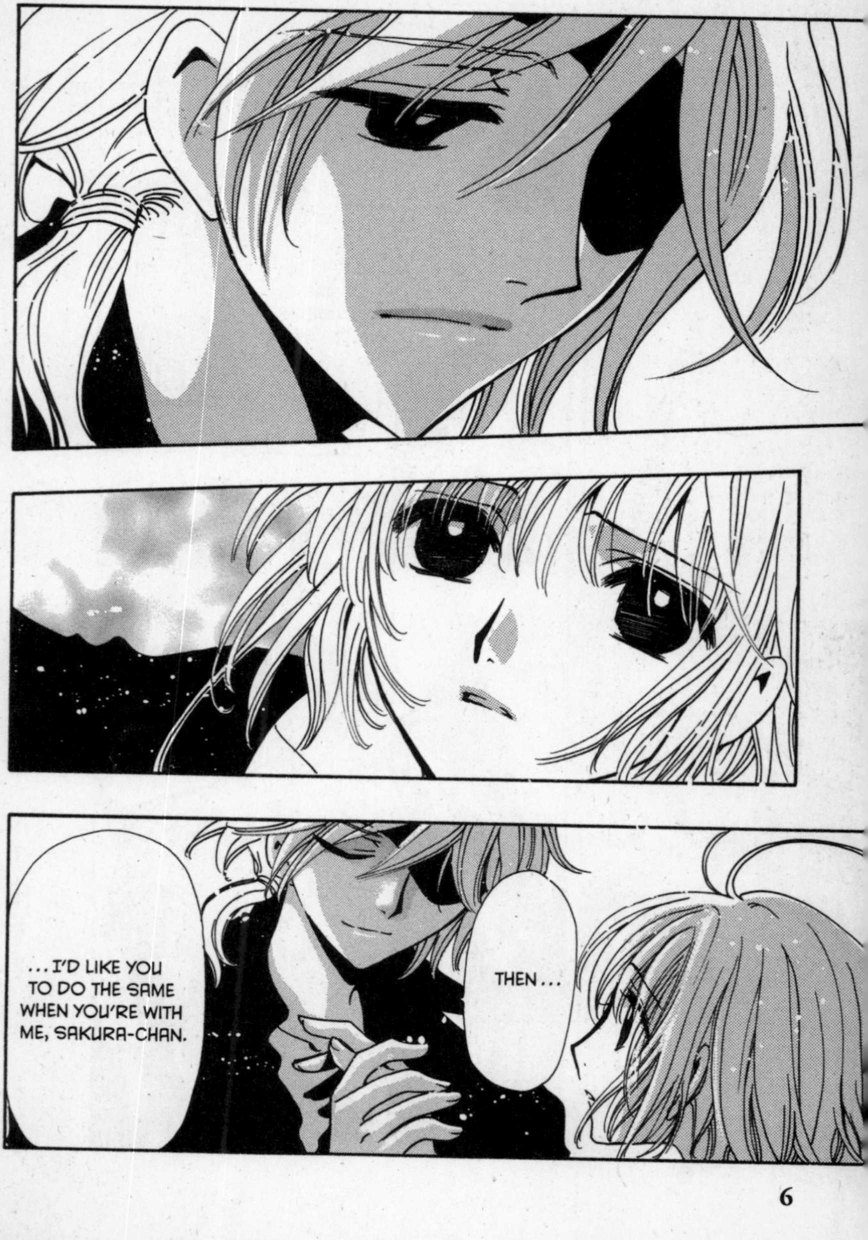
THEN...
...I'D LIKE YOU TO DO THE SAME WHEN YOU'RE WITH ME, SAKURA-CHAN.

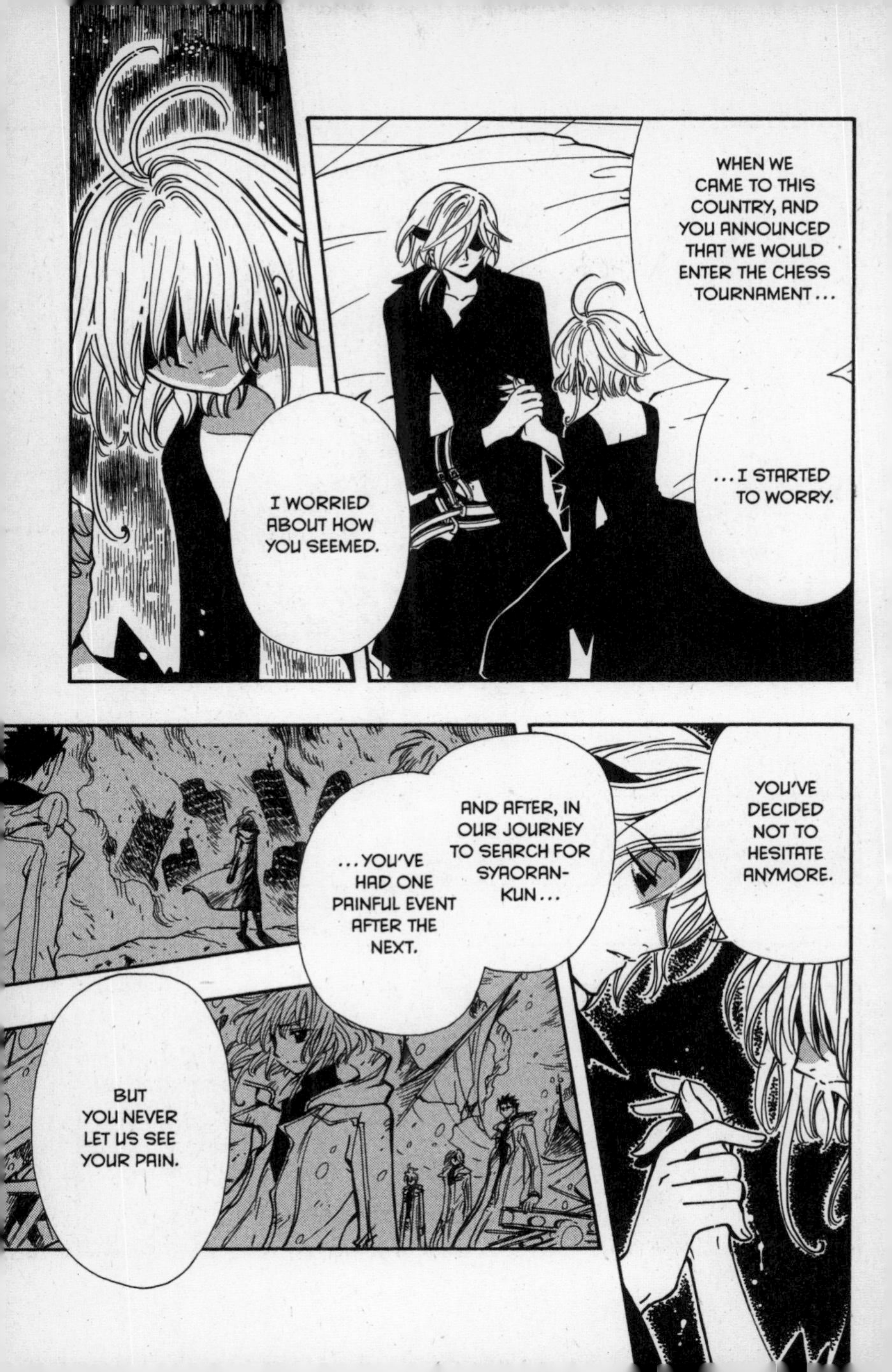
WHEN WE CAME TO THIS COUNTRY, AND YOU ANNOUNCED THAT WE WOULD ENTER THE CHESS TOURNAMENT...
...I STARTED TO WORRY.
I WORRIED ABOUT HOW YOU SEEMED.
YOU'VE DECIDED NOT TO HESITATE ANYMORE.
AND AFTER, IN OUR JOURNEY TO SEARCH FOR SYAORAN-KUN...
...YOU'VE HAD ONE PAINFUL EVENT AFTER THE NEXT.
BUT YOU NEVER LET US SEE YOUR PAIN.

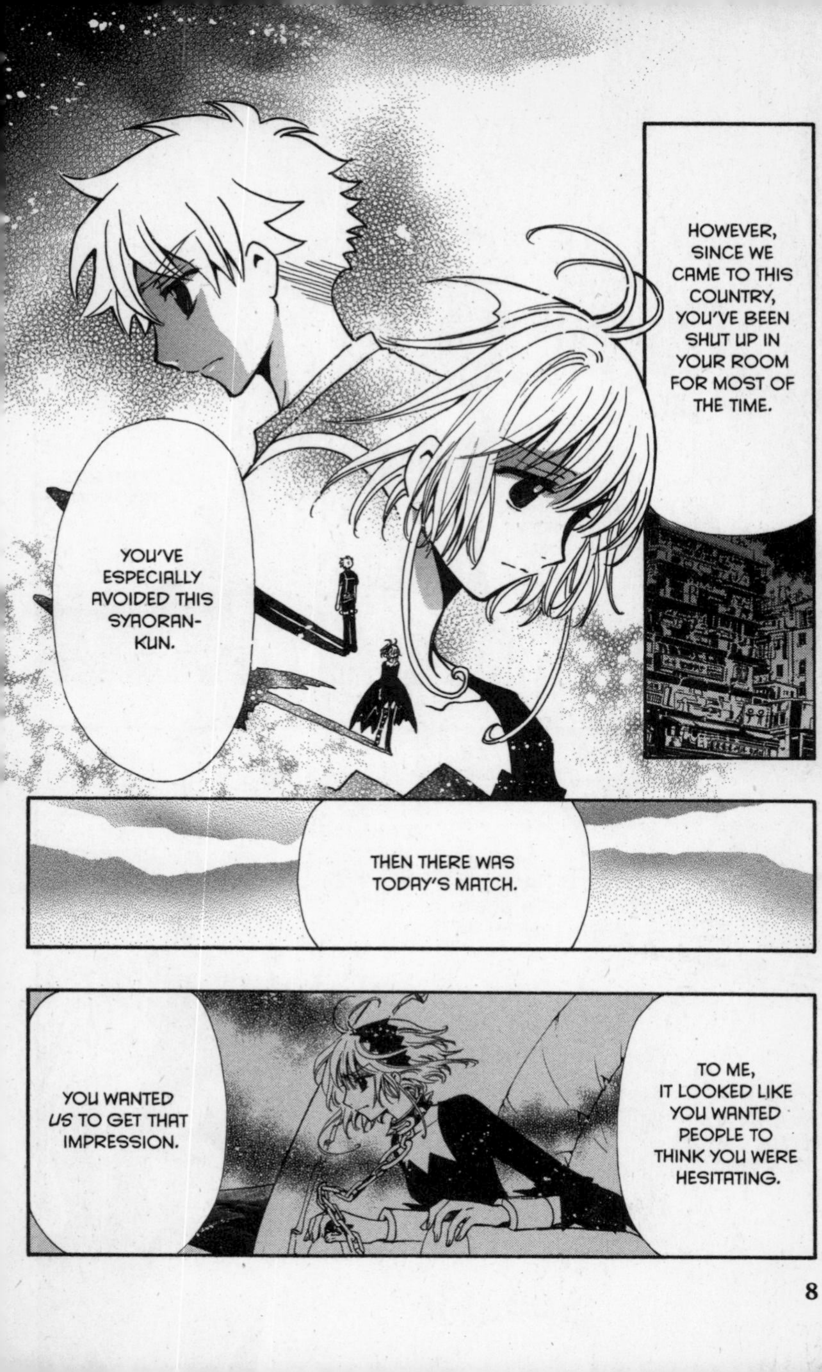
HOWEVER, SINCE WE CAME TO THIS COUNTRY, YOU'VE BEEN SHUT UP IN YOUR ROOM FOR MOST OF THE TIME.
YOU'VE ESPECIALLY AVOIDED THIS SYAORAN-KUN.
THEN THERE WAS TODAY'S MATCH.
TO ME, IT LOOKED LIKE YOU WANTED PEOPLE TO THINK YOU WERE HESITATING.
YOU WANTED *US* TO GET THAT IMPRESSION.

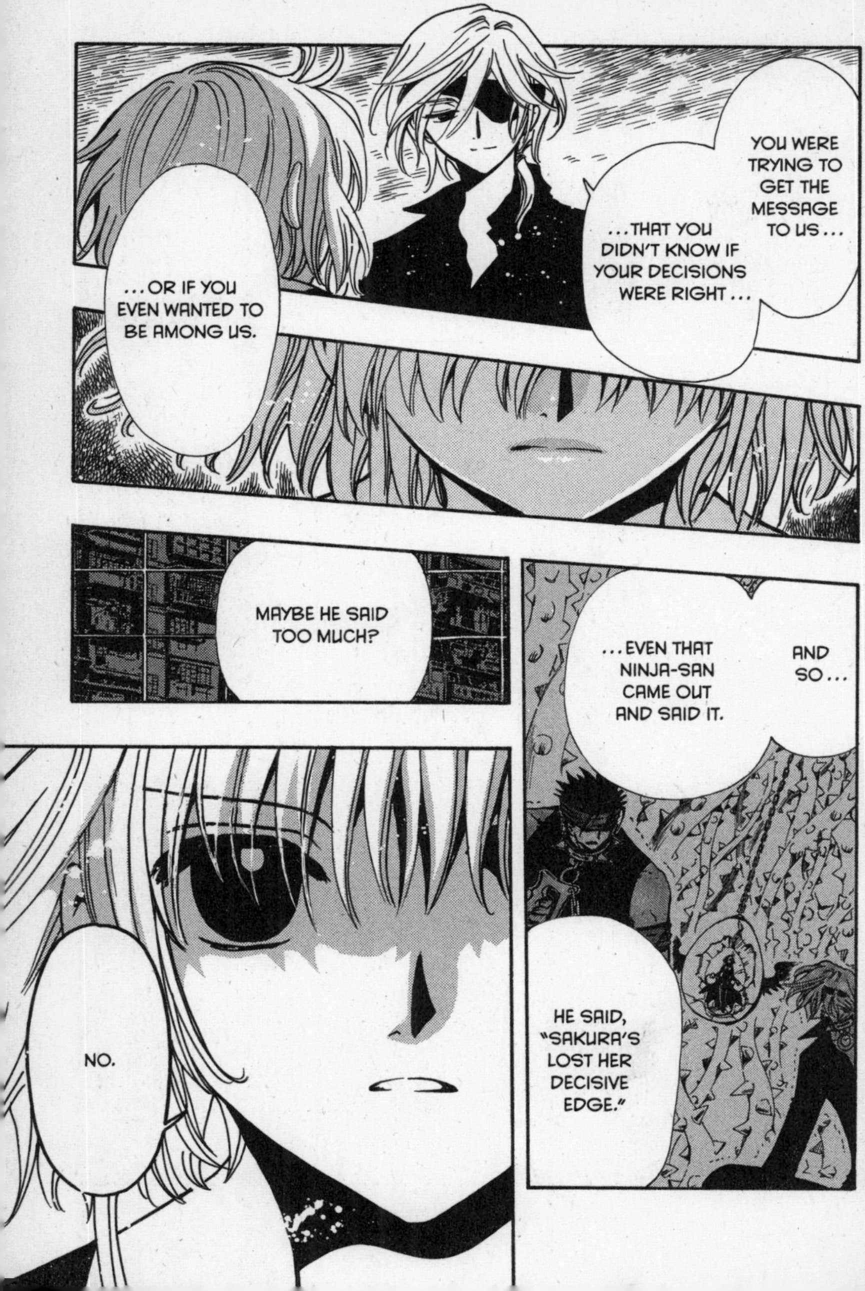
YOU WERE TRYING TO GET THE MESSAGE TO US...
...THAT YOU DIDN'T KNOW IF YOUR DECISIONS WERE RIGHT...
...OR IF YOU EVEN WANTED TO BE AMONG US.
AND SO...
...EVEN THAT NINJA-SAN CAME OUT AND SAID IT.
HE SAID, "SAKURA'S LOST HER DECISIVE EDGE."
MAYBE HE SAID TOO MUCH?
NO.

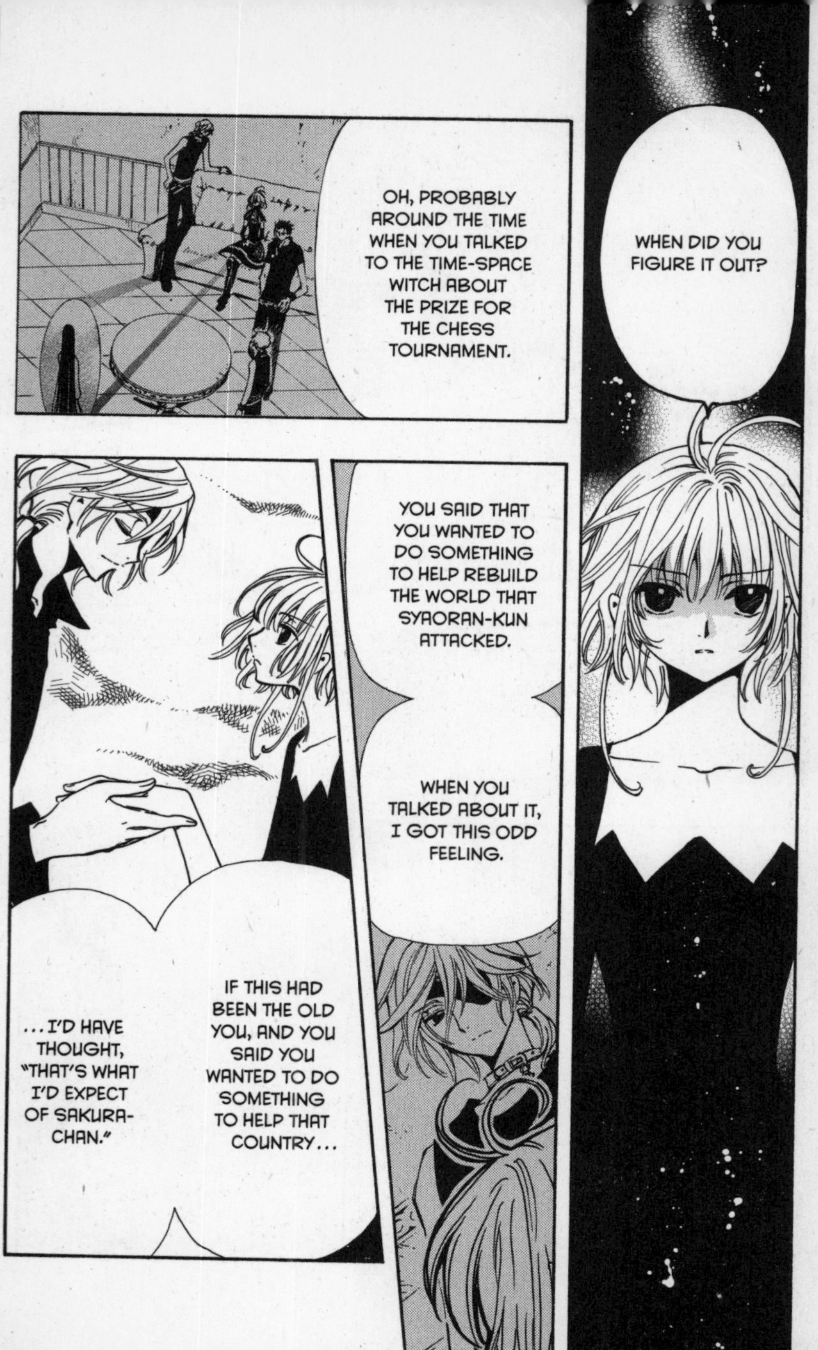
WHEN DID YOU FIGURE IT OUT?
OH, PROBABLY AROUND THE TIME WHEN YOU TALKED TO THE TIME-SPACE WITCH ABOUT THE PRIZE FOR THE CHESS TOURNAMENT.
YOU SAID THAT YOU WANTED TO DO SOMETHING TO HELP REBUILD THE WORLD THAT SYAORAN-KUN ATTACKED.
WHEN YOU TALKED ABOUT IT, I GOT THIS ODD FEELING.
IF THIS HAD BEEN THE OLD YOU, AND YOU SAID YOU WANTED TO DO SOMETHING TO HELP THAT COUNTRY...
...I'D HAVE THOUGHT, "THAT'S WHAT I'D EXPECT OF SAKURA-CHAN."

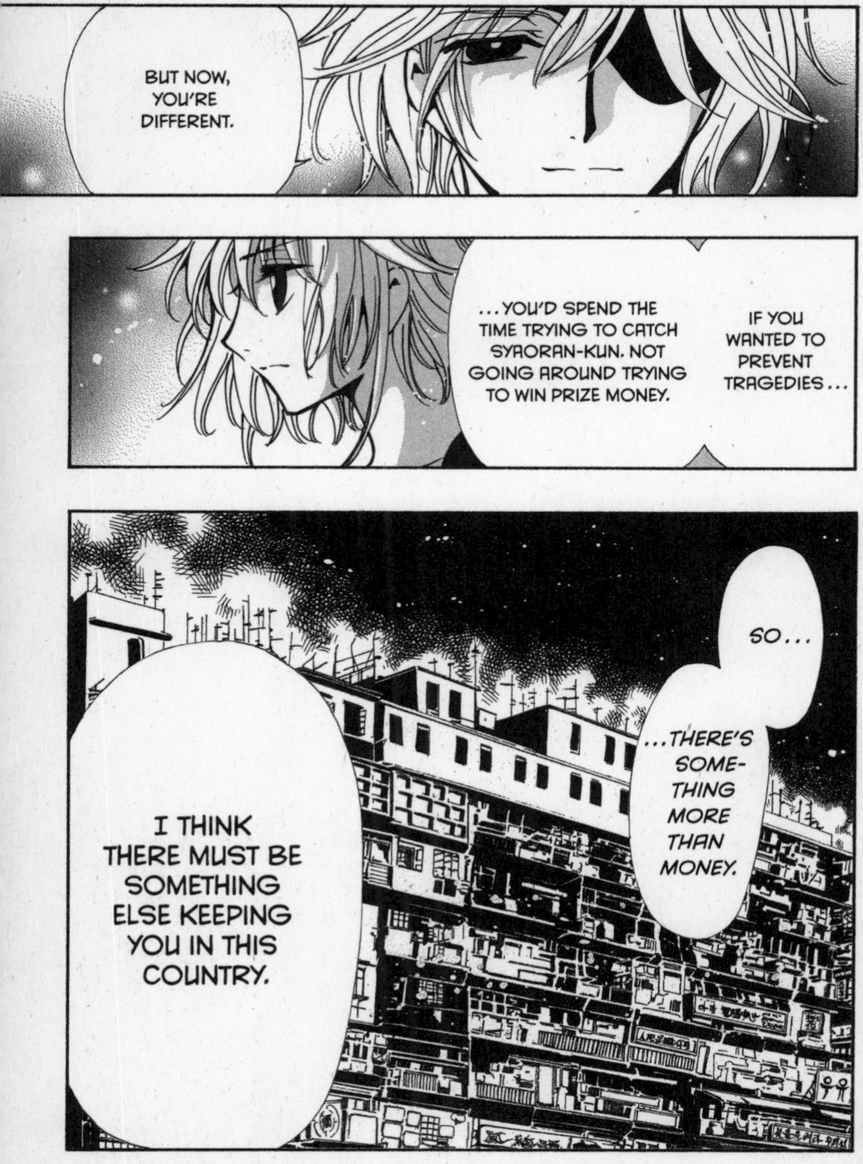
BUT NOW, YOU'RE DIFFERENT.
IF YOU WANTED TO PREVENT TRAGEDIES...
...YOU'D SPEND THE TIME TRYING TO CATCH SYAORAN-KUN. NOT GOING AROUND TRYING TO WIN PRIZE MONEY.
SO...
...THERE'S SOME-THING MORE THAN MONEY.
I THINK THERE MUST BE SOMETHING ELSE KEEPING YOU IN THIS COUNTRY.

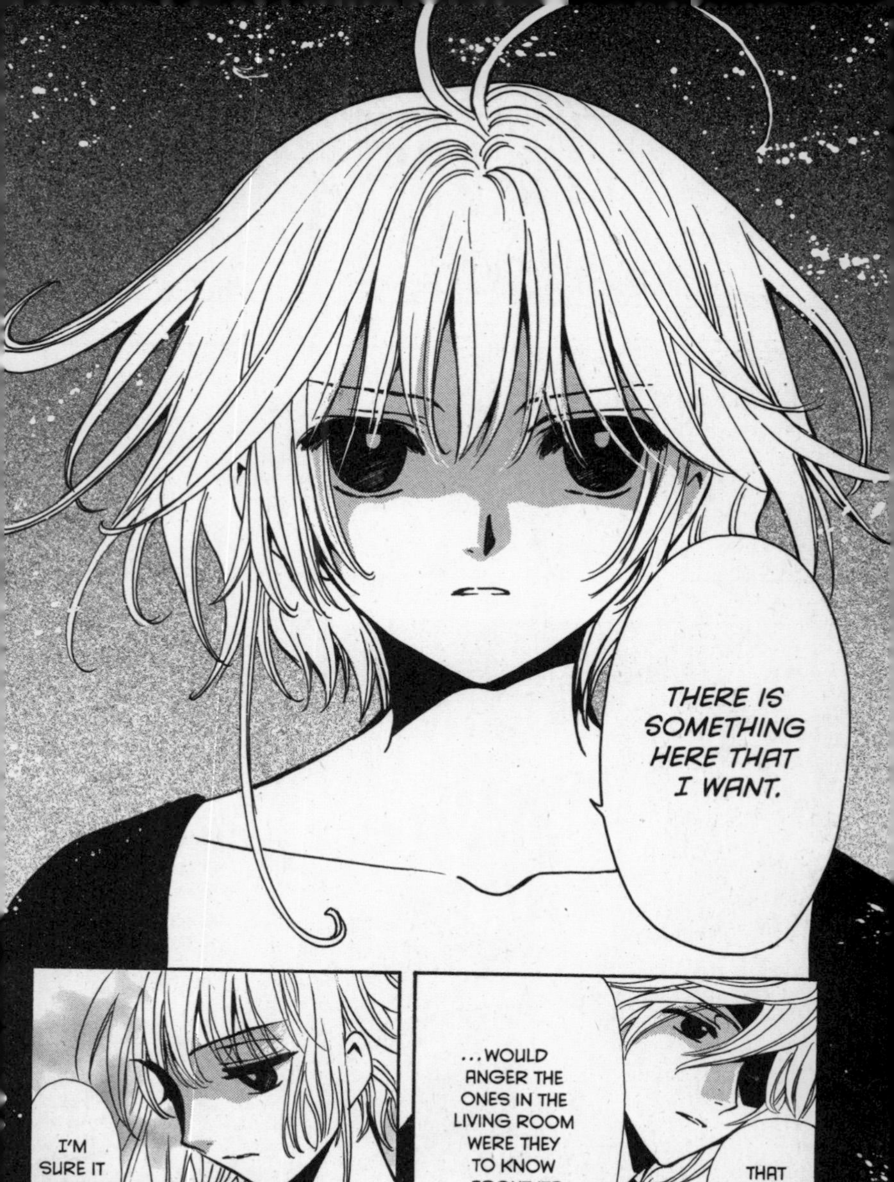
THERE IS SOMETHING HERE THAT I WANT.
THAT SOME-THING...
...WOULD ANGER THE ONES IN THE LIVING ROOM WERE THEY TO KNOW ABOUT IT?
I'M SURE IT WOULD.

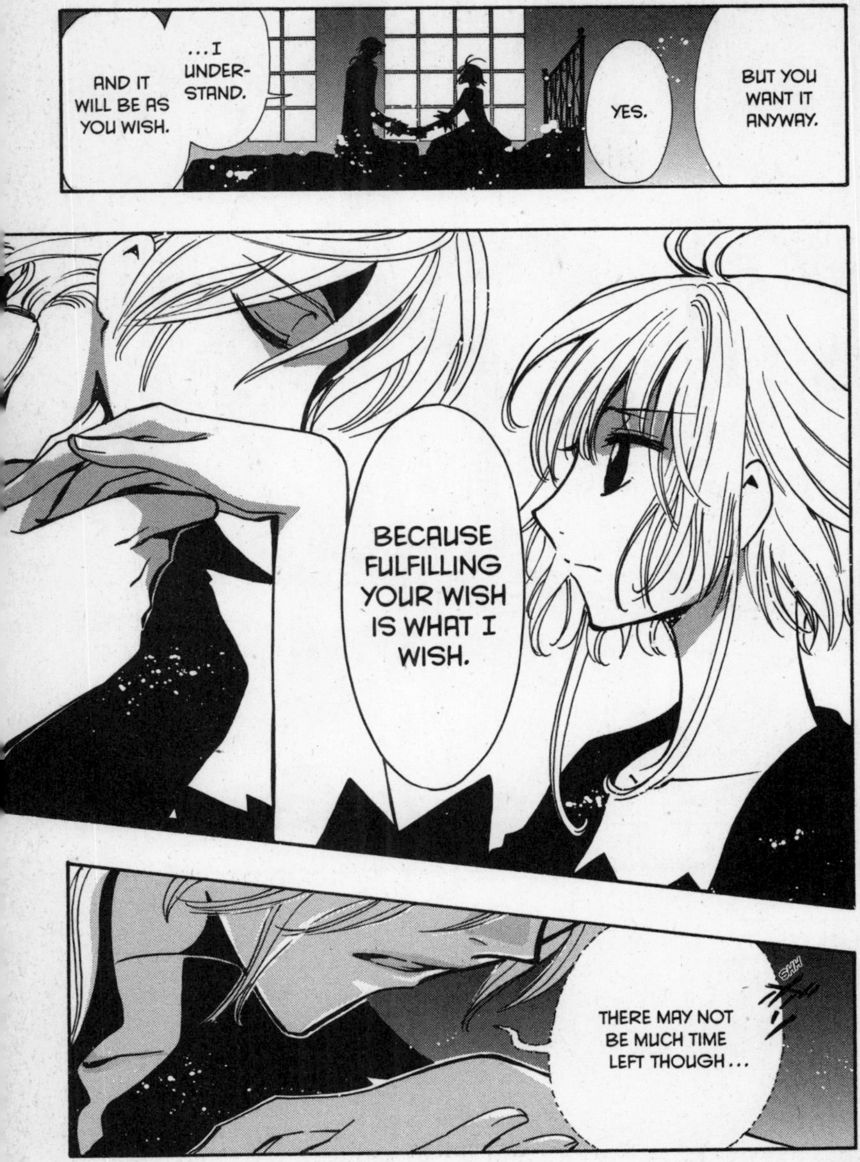
BUT YOU WANT IT ANYWAY.
YES.
...I UNDERSTAND.
AND IT WILL BE AS YOU WISH.
BECAUSE FULFILLING YOUR WISH IS WHAT I WISH.
SHH
THERE MAY NOT BE MUCH TIME LEFT THOUGH...

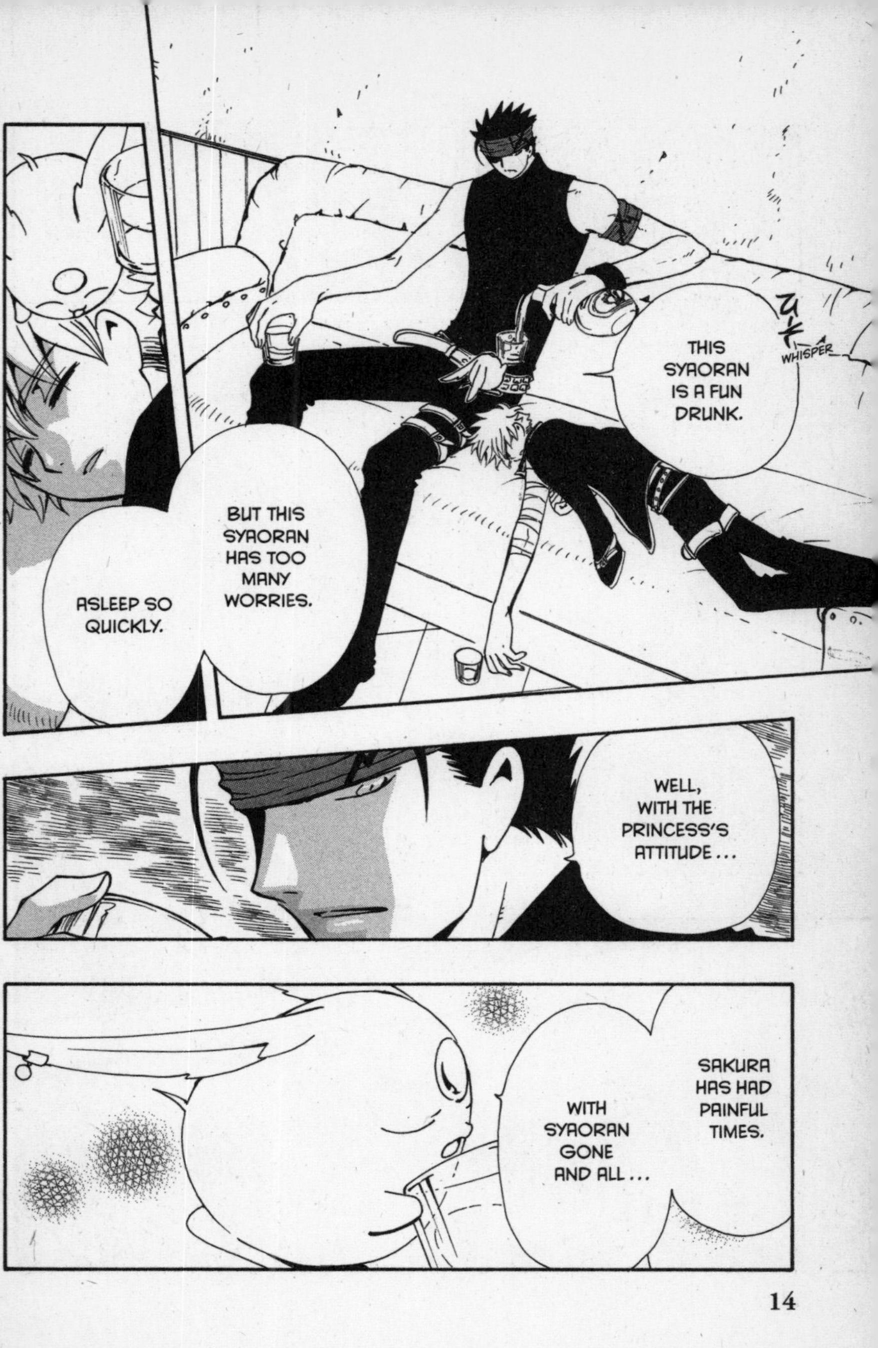
WHISPER
THIS SYAORAN IS A FUN DRUNK.
BUT THIS SYAORAN HAS TOO MANY WORRIES.
ASLEEP SO QUICKLY.
WELL, WITH THE PRINCESS'S ATTITUDE...
SAKURA HAS HAD PAINFUL TIMES.
WITH SYAORAN GONE AND ALL...

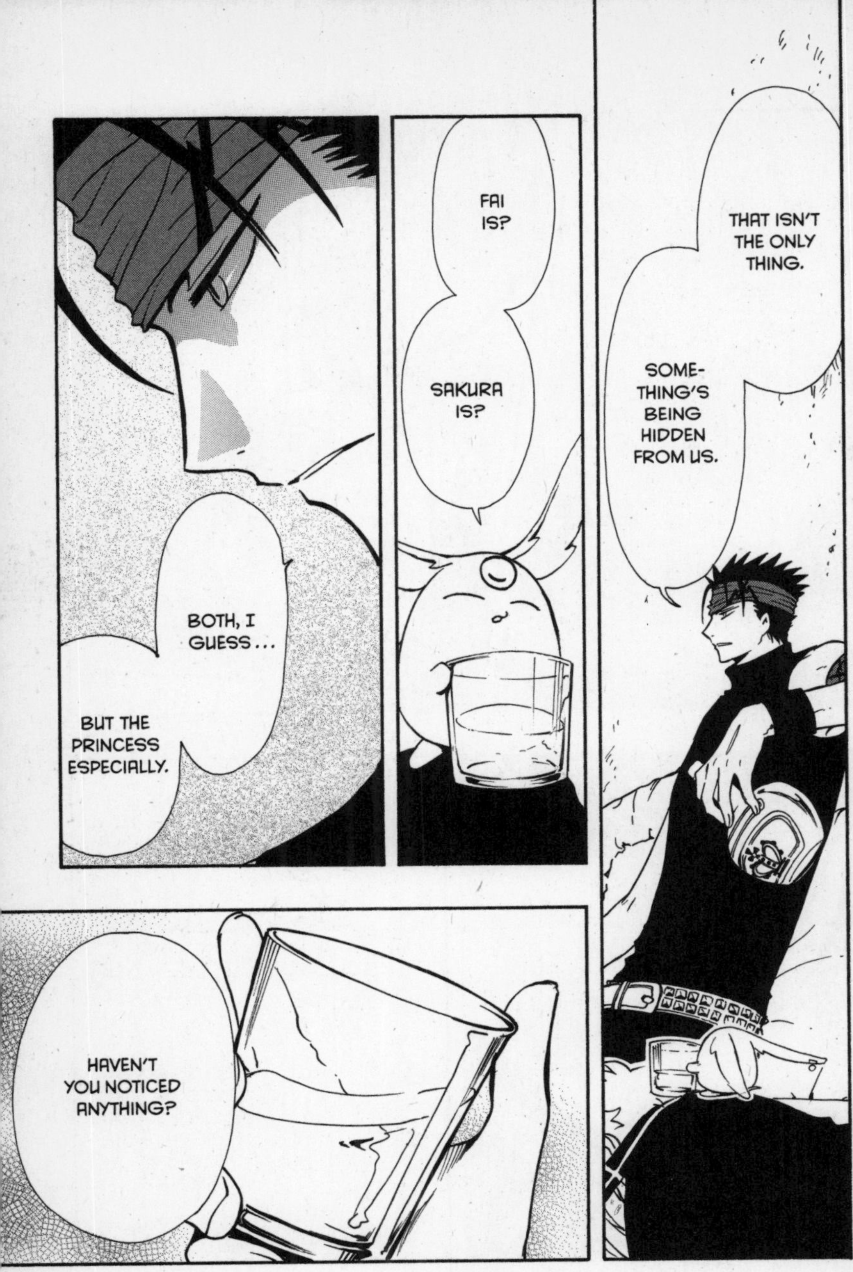
THAT ISN'T THE ONLY THING.
SOME-THING'S BEING HIDDEN FROM US.
FAI IS?
SAKURA IS?
BOTH, I GUESS...
BUT THE PRINCESS ESPECIALLY.
HAVEN'T YOU NOTICED ANYTHING?

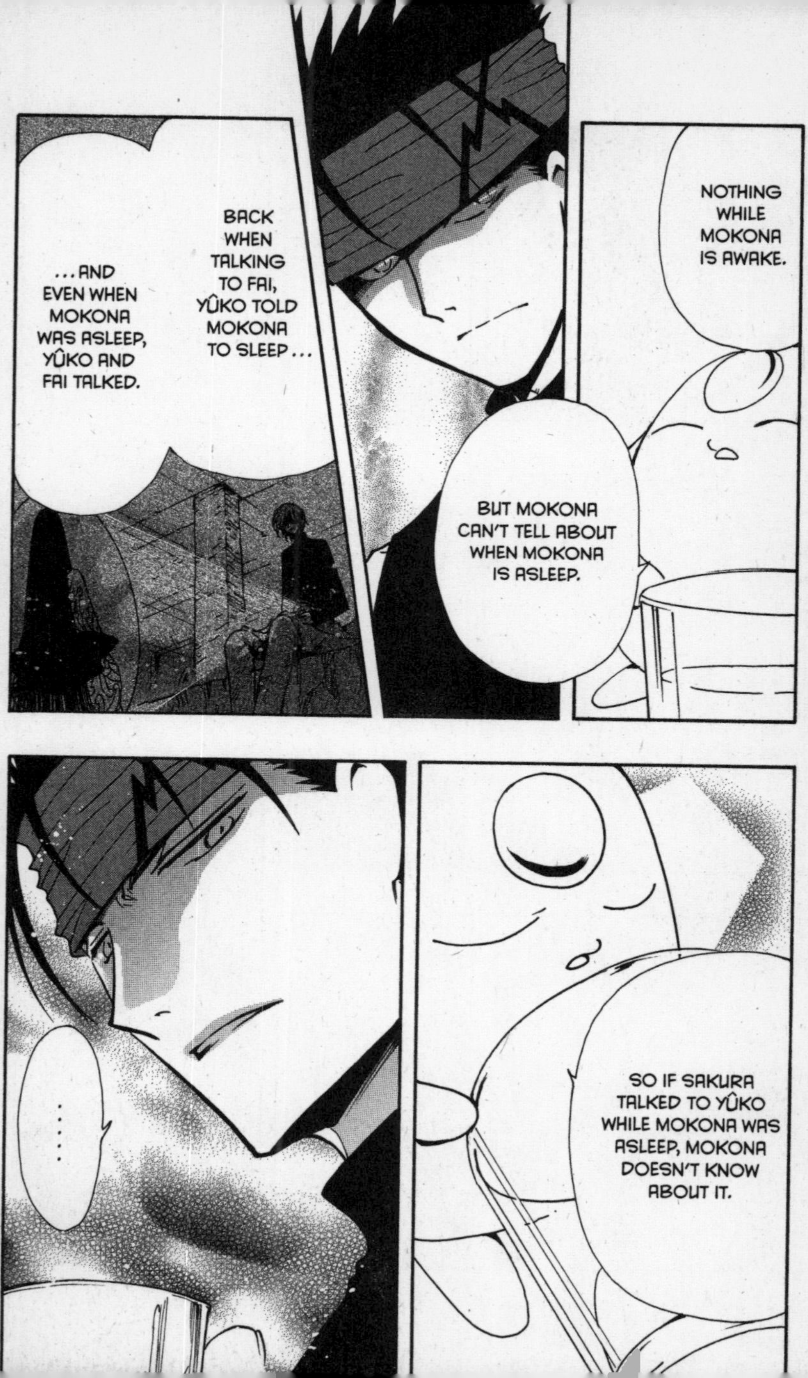
NOTHING WHILE MOKONA IS AWAKE.
BUT MOKONA CAN'T TELL ABOUT WHEN MOKONA IS ASLEEP.
BACK WHEN TALKING TO FAI, YÛKO TOLD MOKONA TO SLEEP...
...AND EVEN WHEN MOKONA WAS ASLEEP, YÛKO AND FAI TALKED.
SO IF SAKURA TALKED TO YÛKO WHILE MOKONA WAS ASLEEP, MOKONA DOESN'T KNOW ABOUT IT.
.....

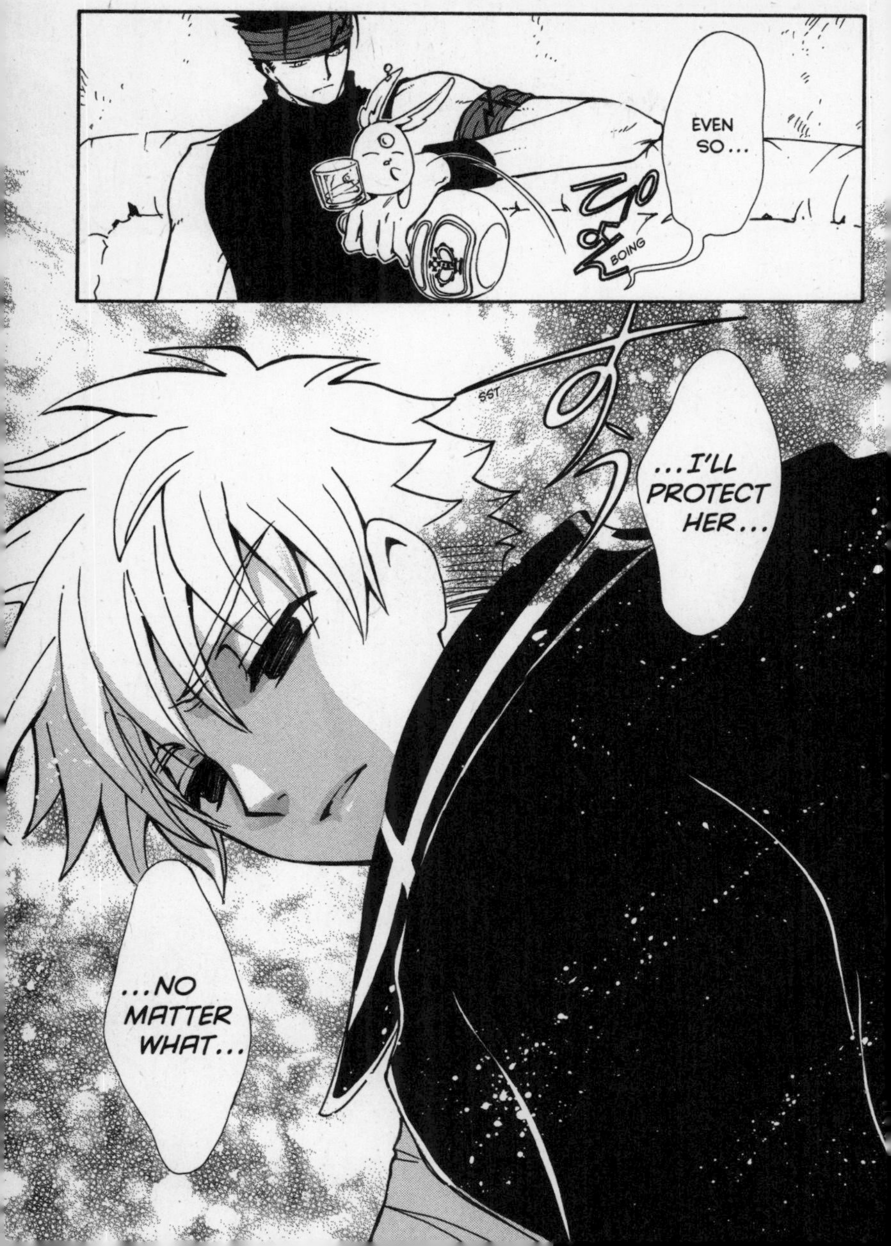
EVEN SO...
BOING
SST
...I'LL PROTECT HER...
...NO MATTER WHAT...

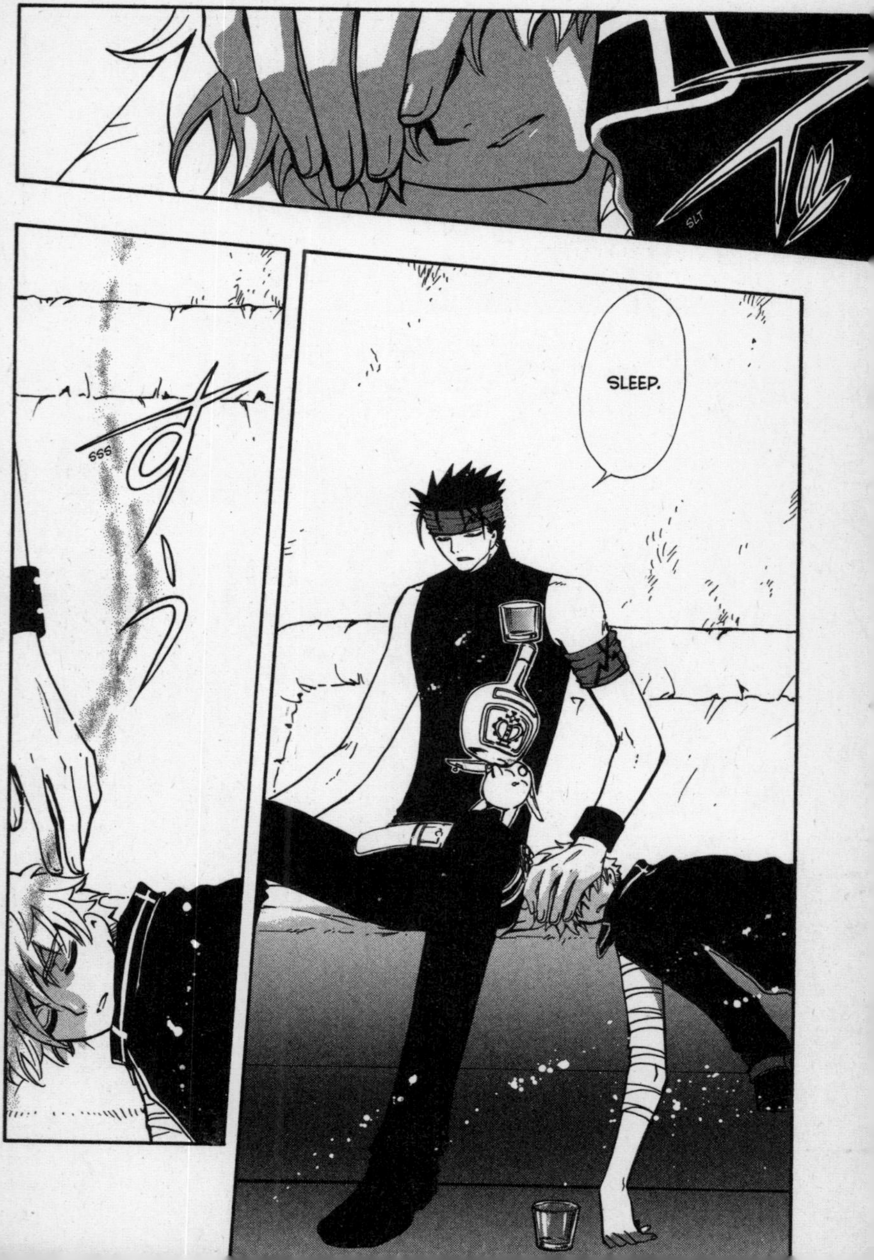
SLT
SLEEP.
SSS

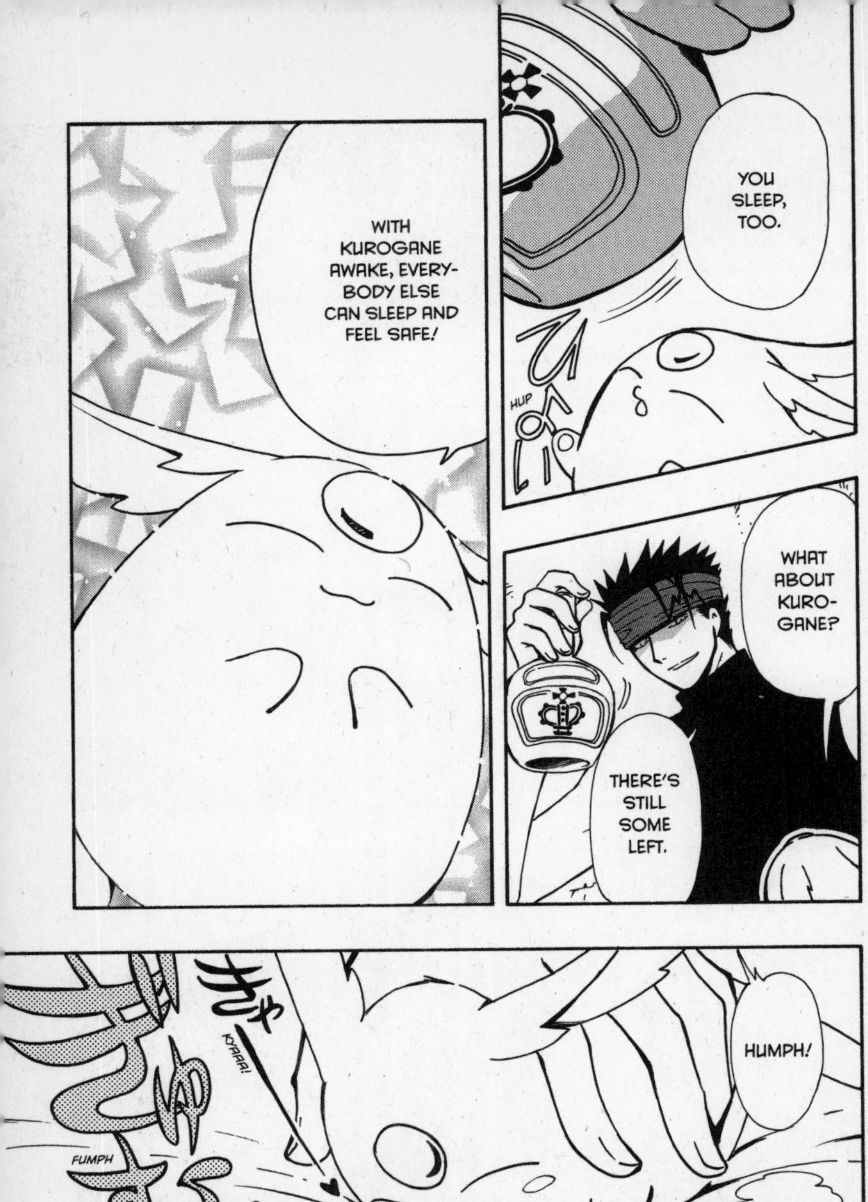
YOU SLEEP, TOO.
HUP
WHAT ABOUT KUROGANE?
THERE'S STILL SOME LEFT.
WITH KUROGANE AWAKE, EVERYBODY ELSE CAN SLEEP AND FEEL SAFE!
HUMPH!
KYAAA!
FUMPH

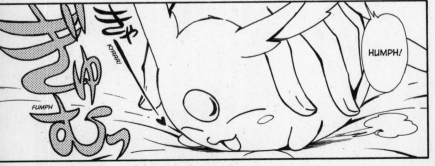

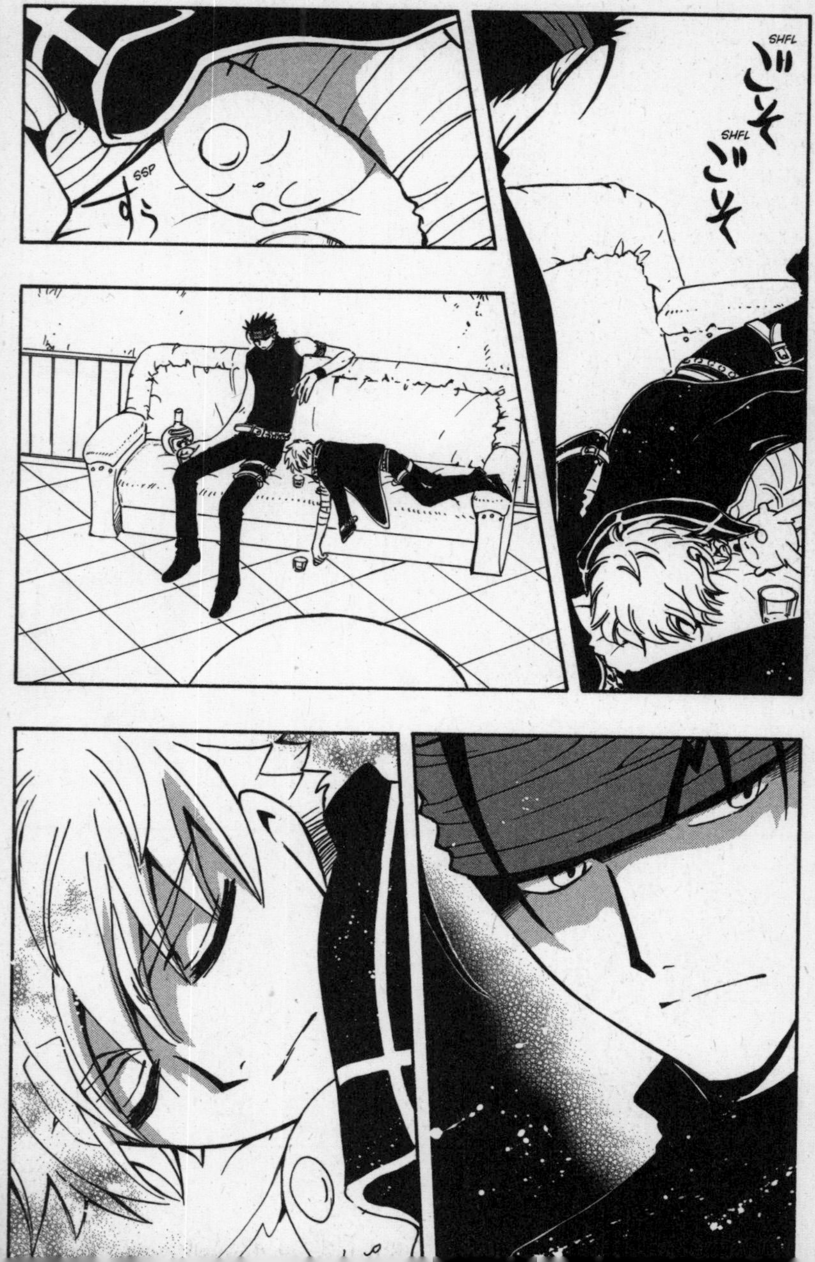
SHFL
ごそ
SHFL
ごそ
SSP
すぅ

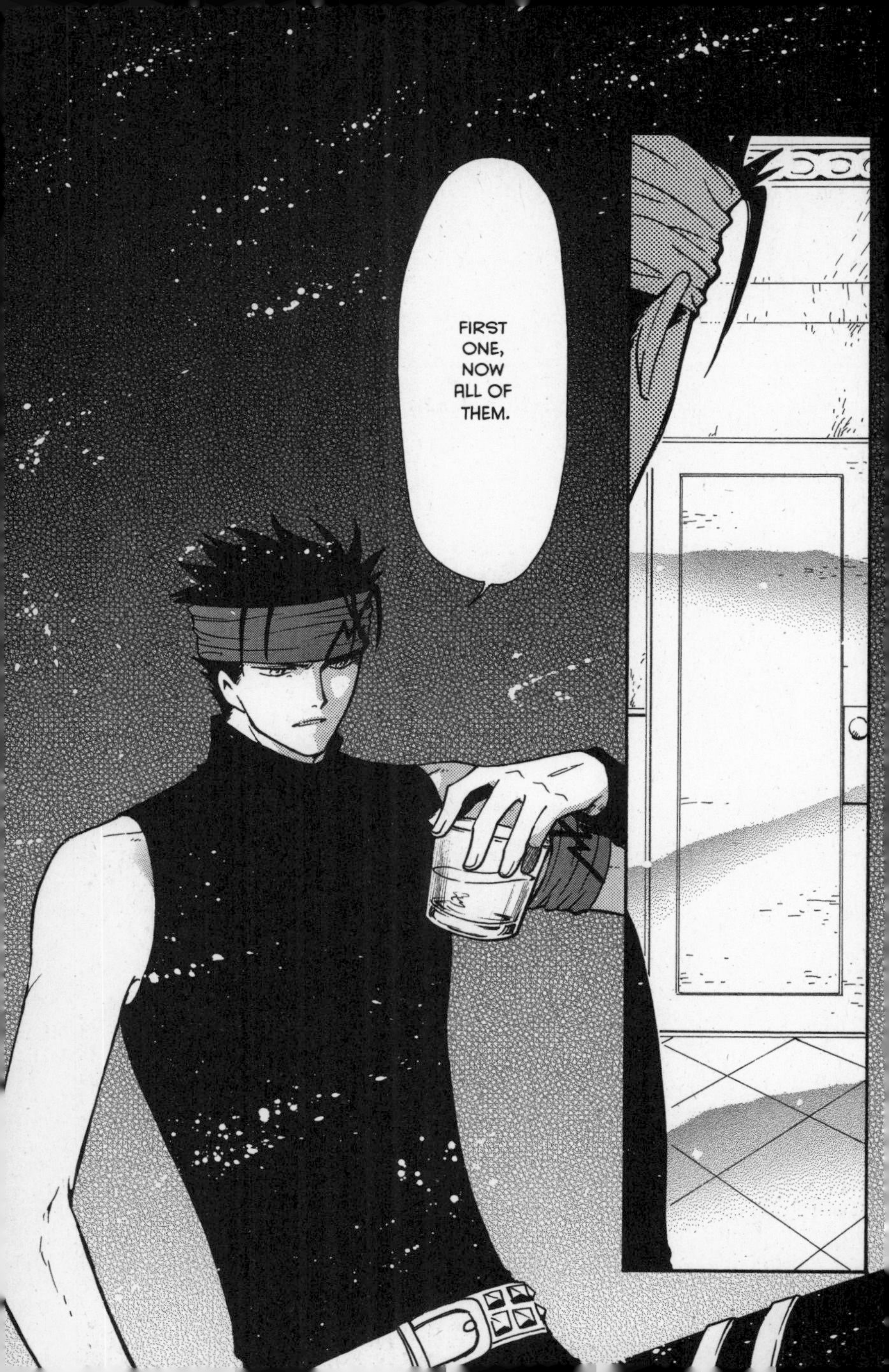
FIRST ONE, NOW ALL OF THEM.

ツバサ
RESERVoir CHRoNiCLE

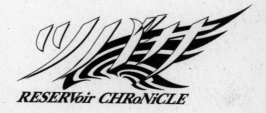

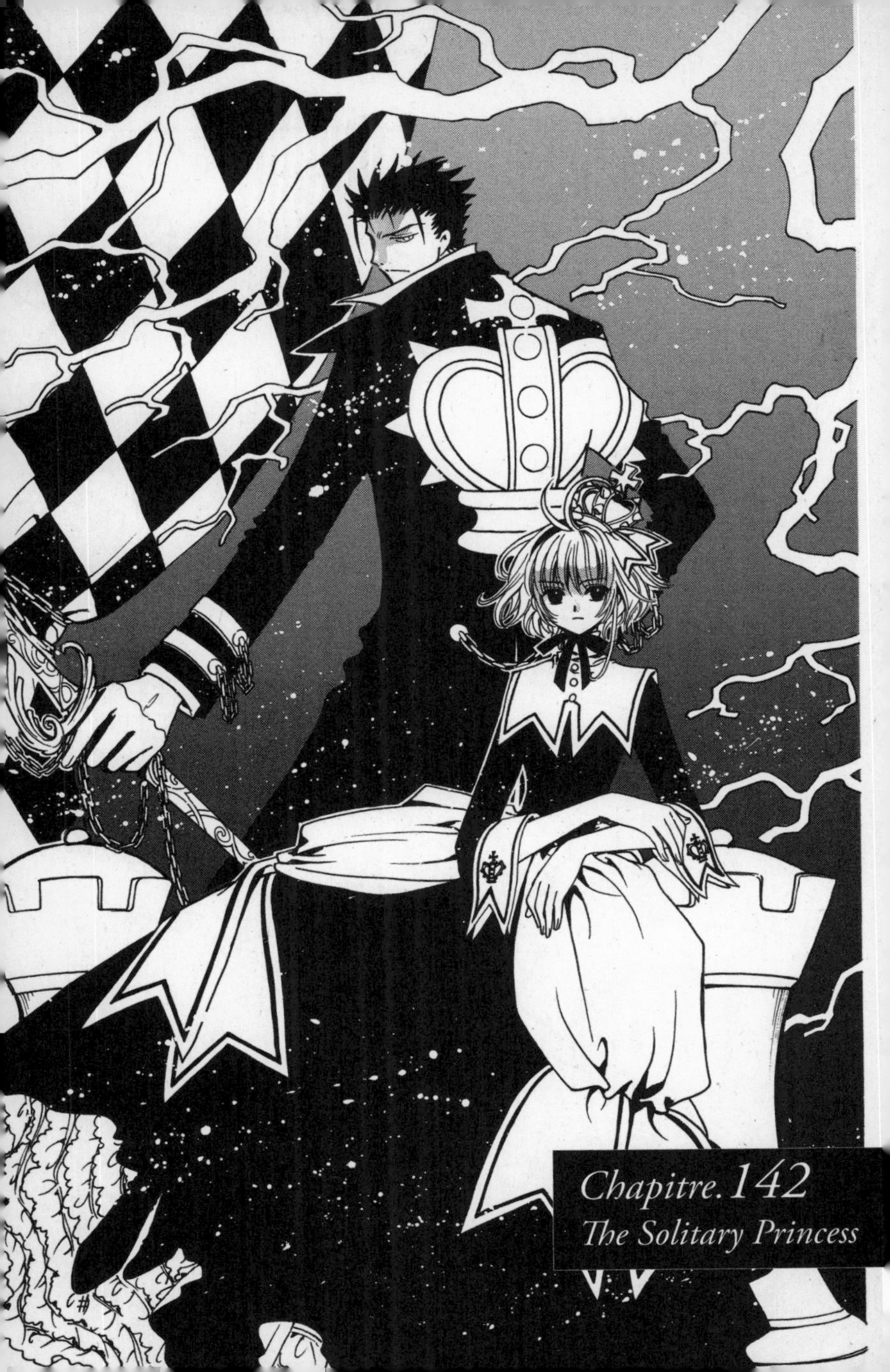
Chapitre. 142
The Solitary Princess

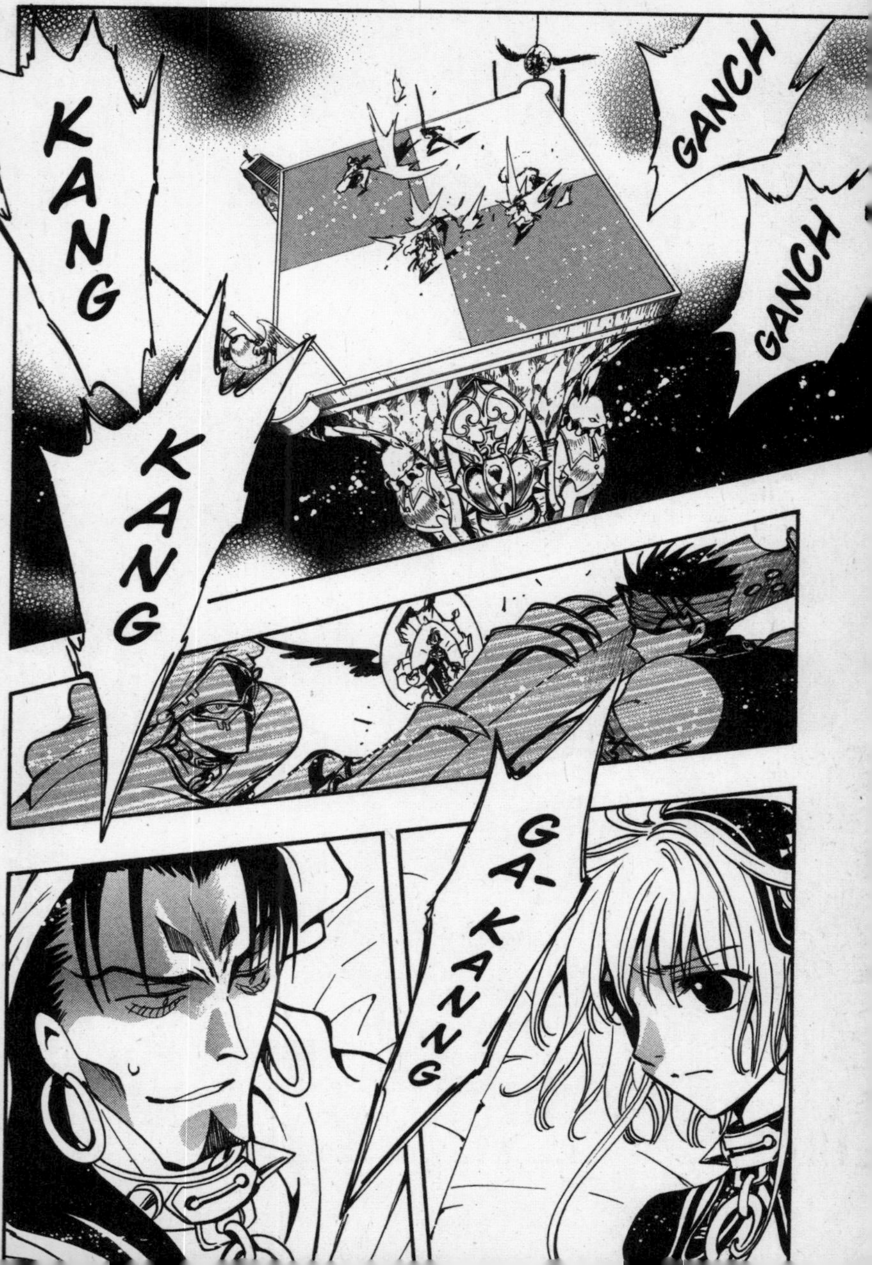
GANCH
GANCH
KANG
KANG
KANG
GA-KANNG

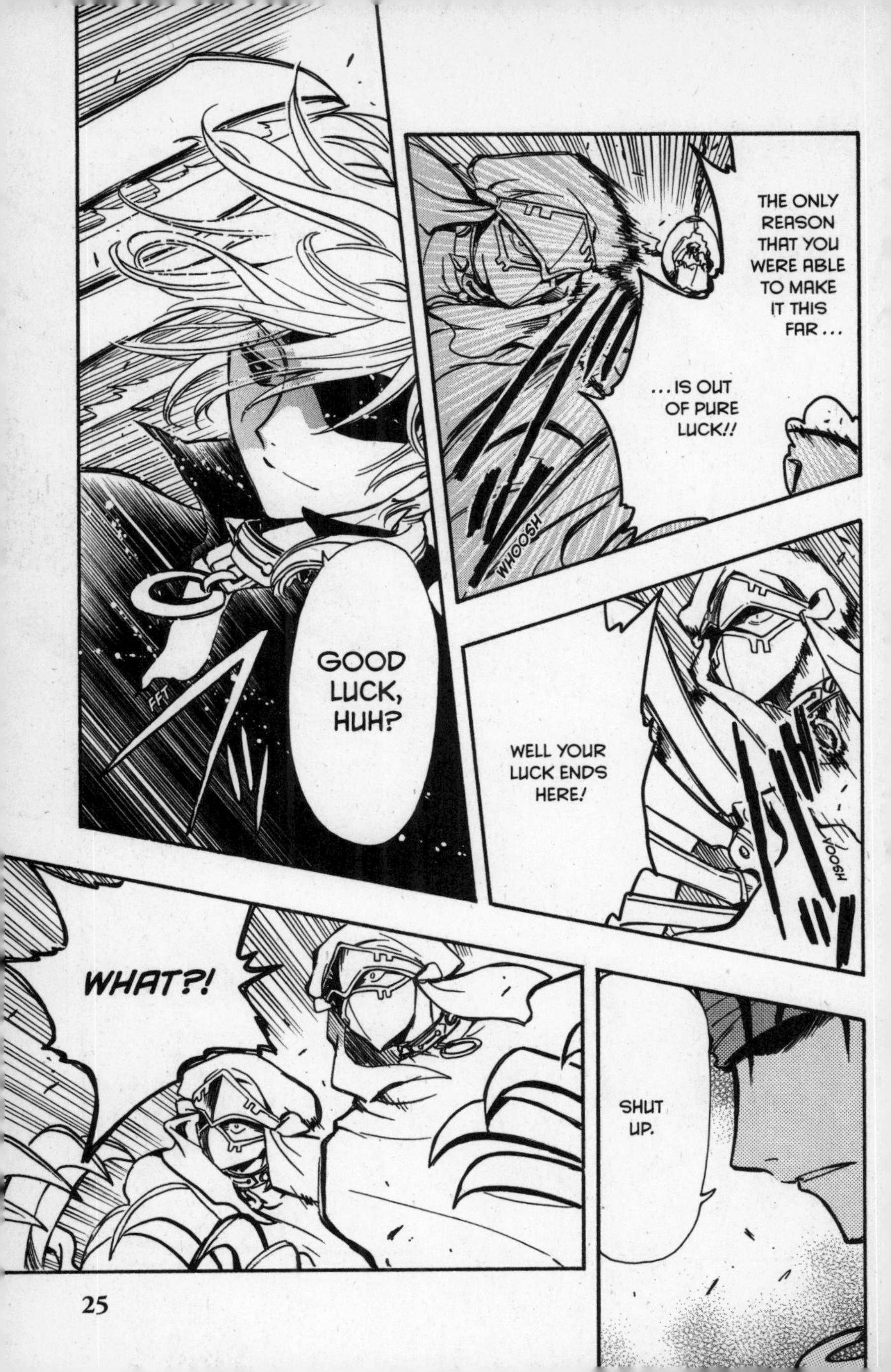
THE ONLY REASON THAT YOU WERE ABLE TO MAKE IT THIS FAR...
...IS OUT OF PURE LUCK!!
WHOOSH
WELL YOUR LUCK ENDS HERE!
WHOOSH
GOOD LUCK, HUH?
FFT
SHUT UP.
WHAT?!

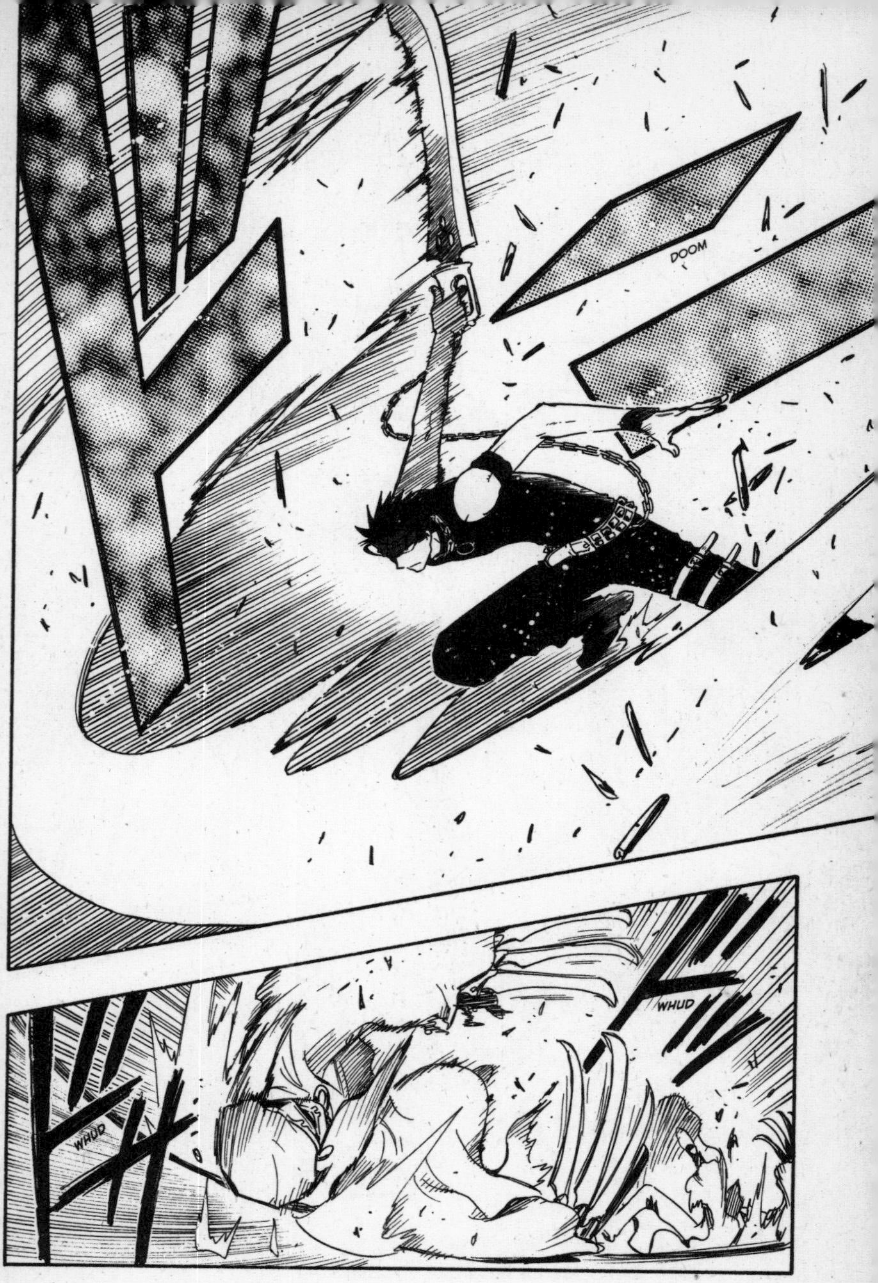
DOOM
WHUD
WHUD

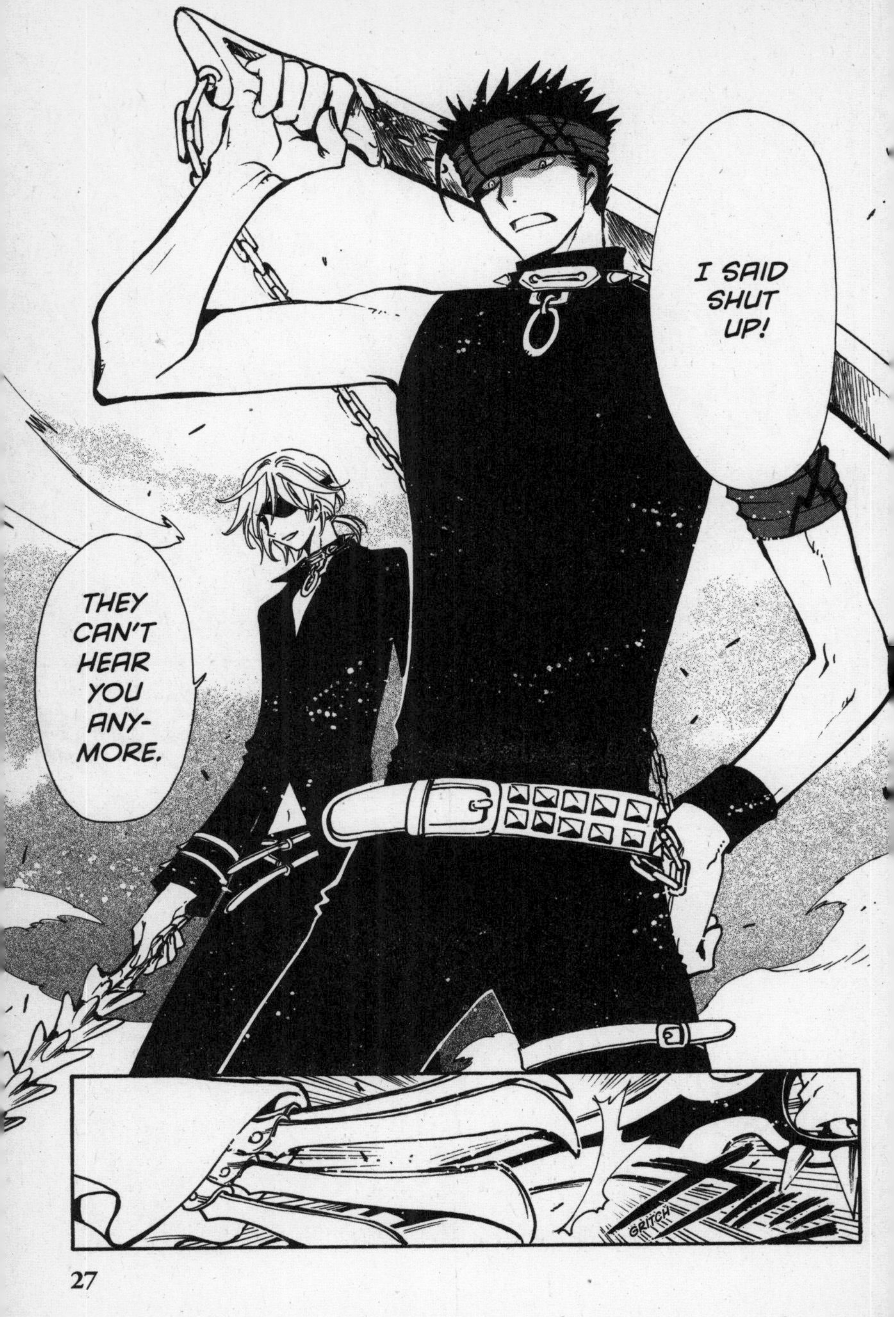
I SAID SHUT UP!
THEY CAN'T HEAR YOU ANYMORE.
GRITCH

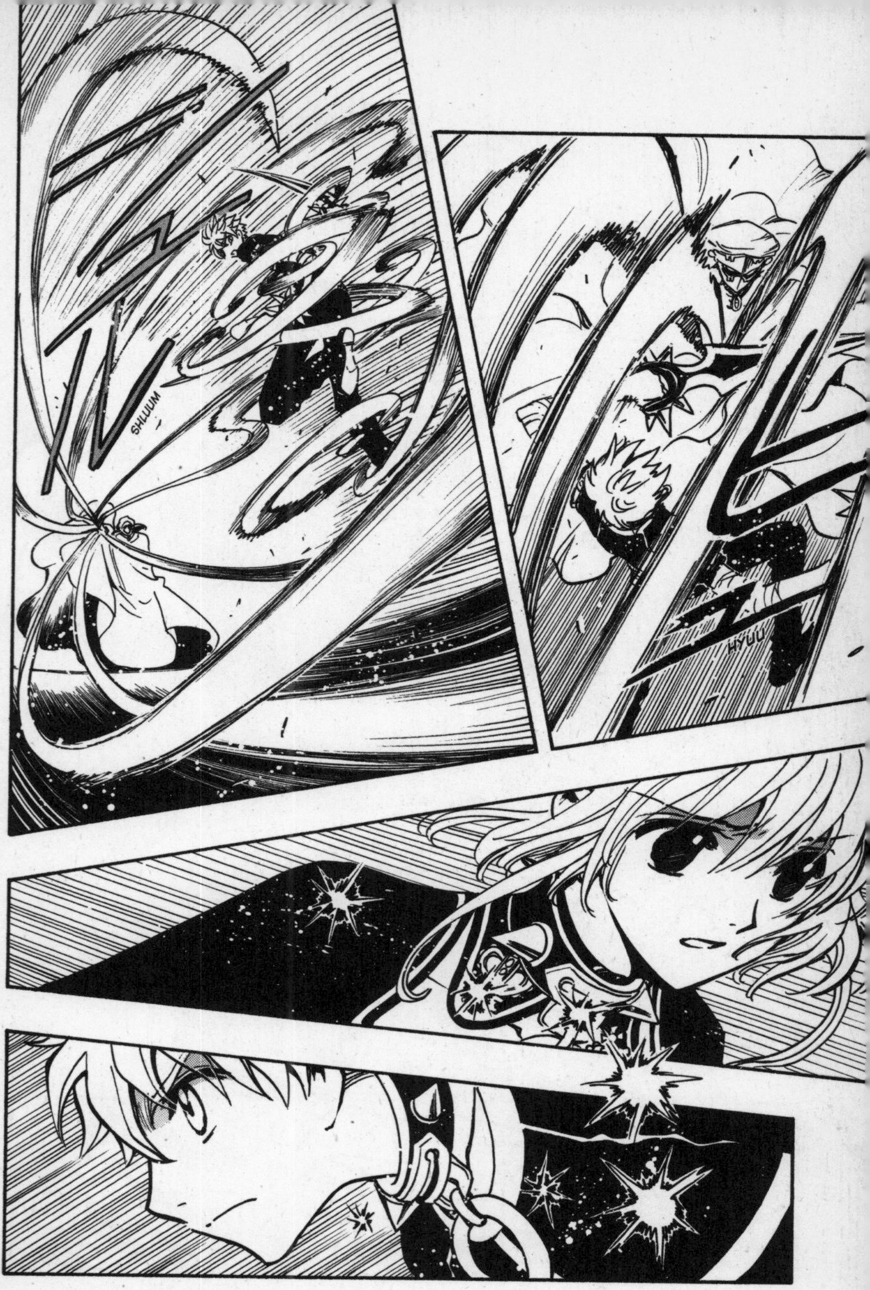
HYUU
SHLUUM

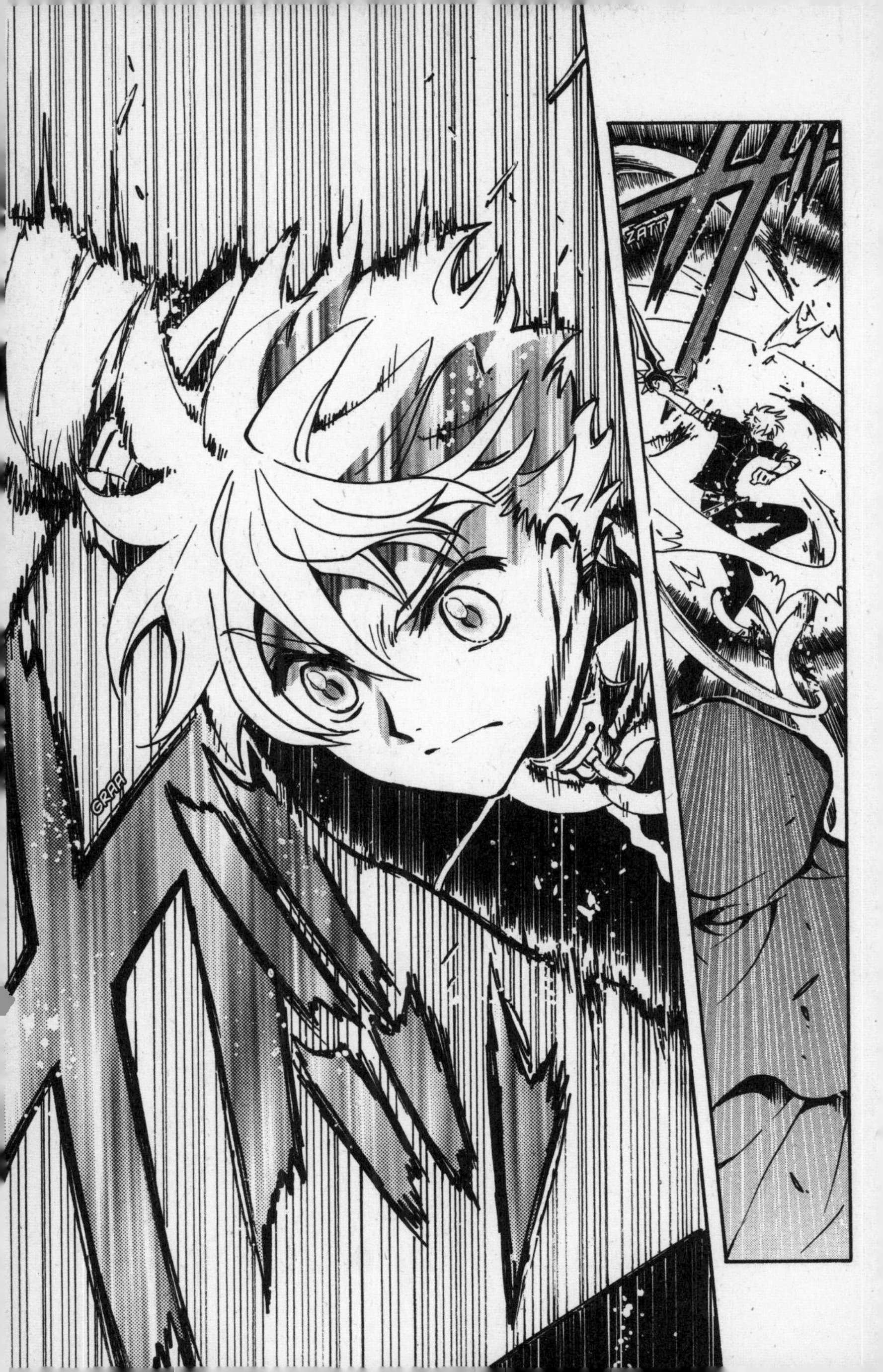
ZATT
GRAA

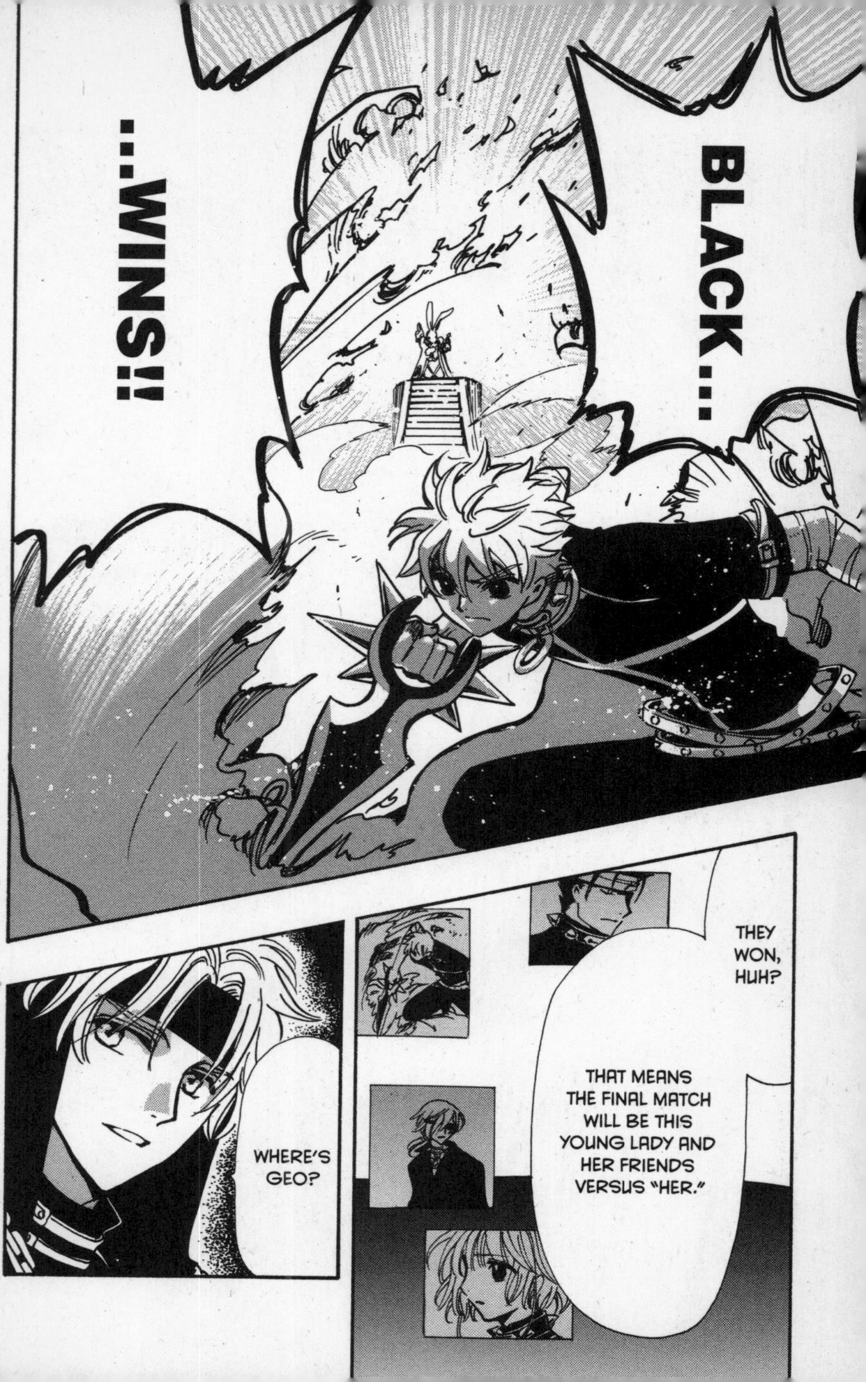
BLACK...
...WINS!!
THEY WON, HUH?
THAT MEANS THE FINAL MATCH WILL BE THIS YOUNG LADY AND HER FRIENDS VERSUS "HER."
WHERE'S GEO?

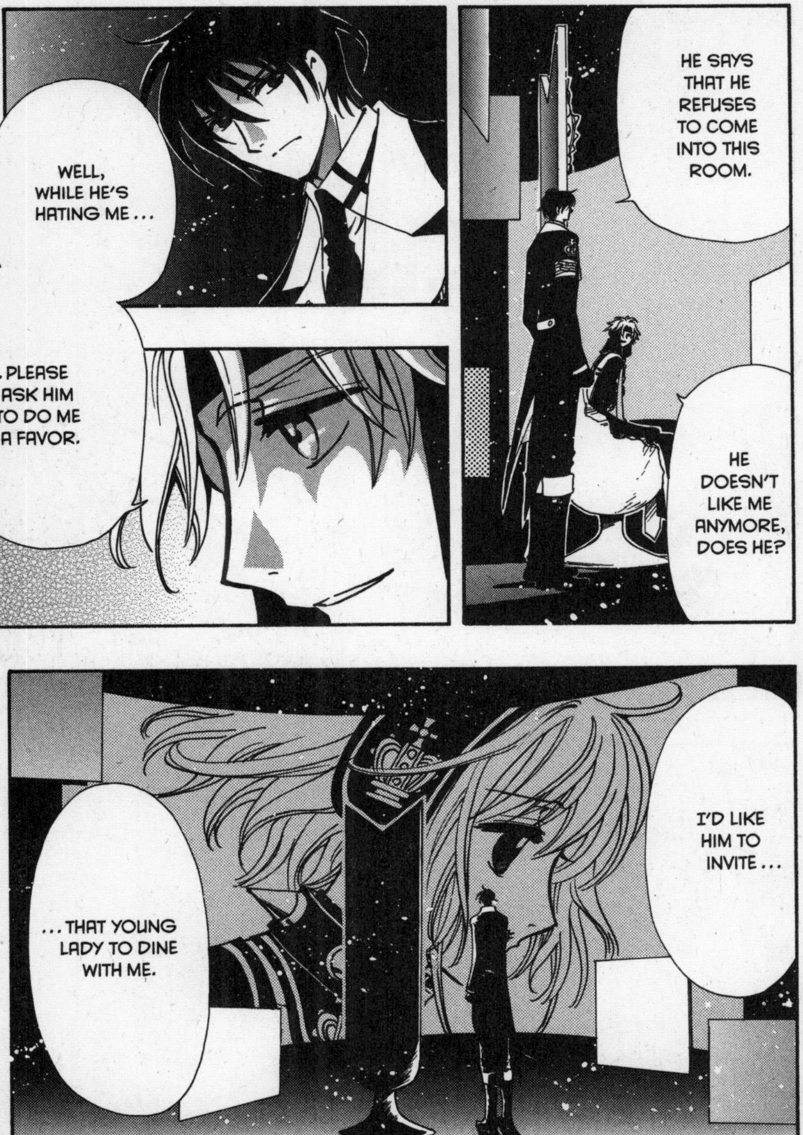
HE SAYS THAT HE REFUSES TO COME INTO THIS ROOM.
HE DOESN'T LIKE ME ANYMORE, DOES HE?
WELL, WHILE HE'S HATING ME...
...PLEASE ASK HIM TO DO ME A FAVOR.
I'D LIKE HIM TO INVITE...
...THAT YOUNG LADY TO DINE WITH ME.

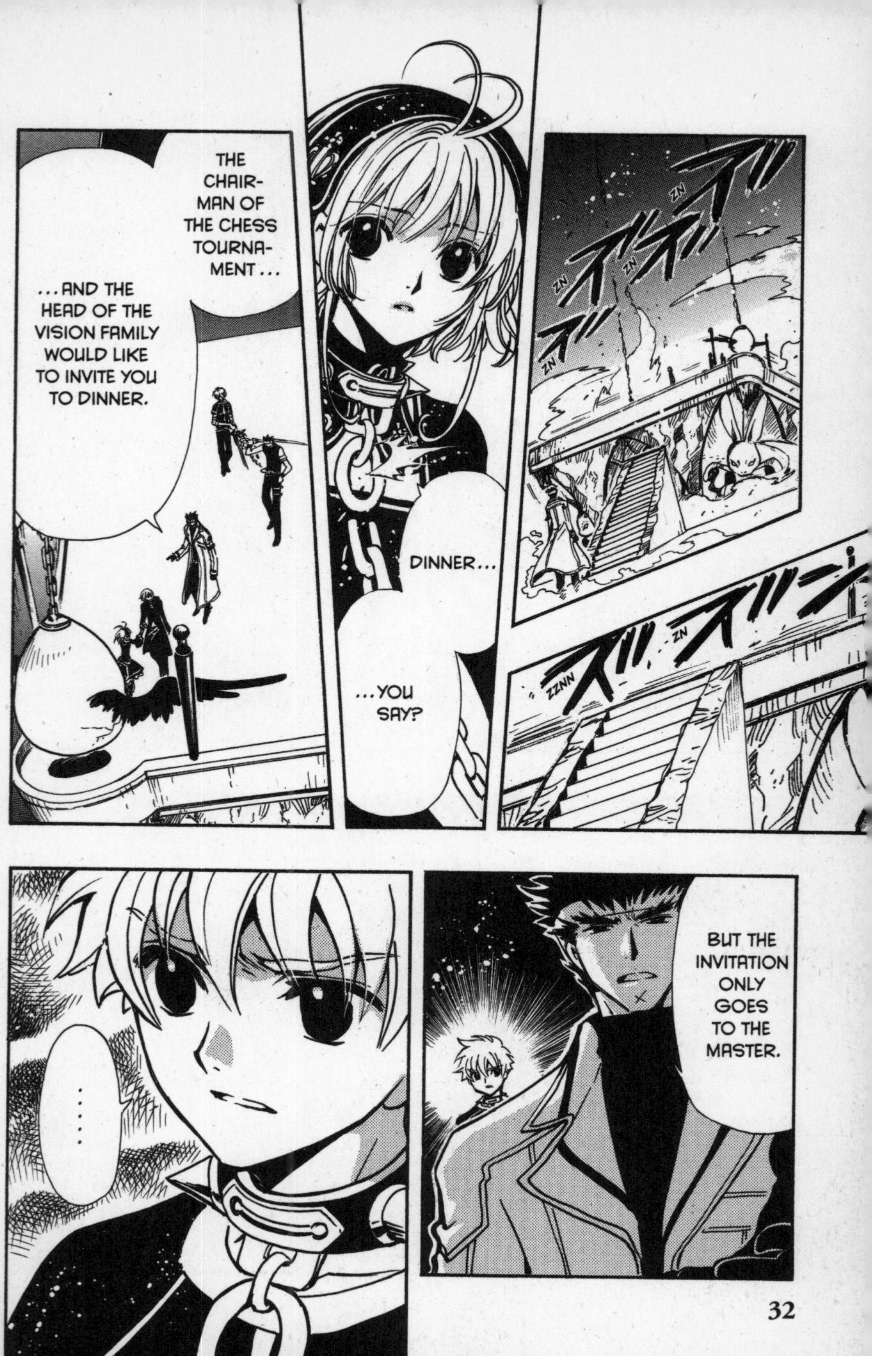
ZN
ZN
ZN
ZN
ZZNN
ZN
DINNER...
...YOU SAY?
THE CHAIRMAN OF THE CHESS TOURNAMENT...
...AND THE HEAD OF THE VISION FAMILY WOULD LIKE TO INVITE YOU TO DINNER.
BUT THE INVITATION ONLY GOES TO THE MASTER.
......

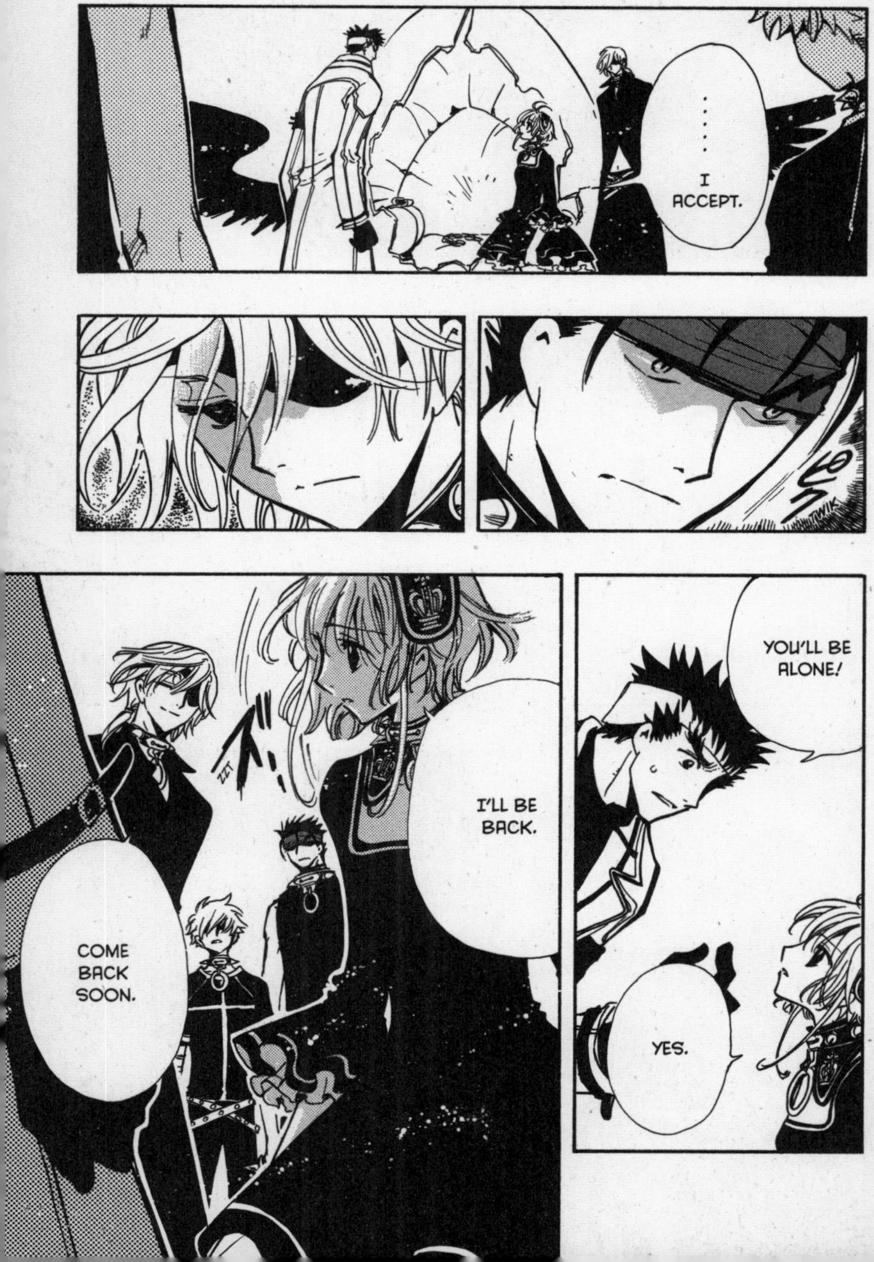
.....
I ACCEPT.
TWIK
YOU'LL BE ALONE!
YES.
I'LL BE BACK.
COME BACK SOON.

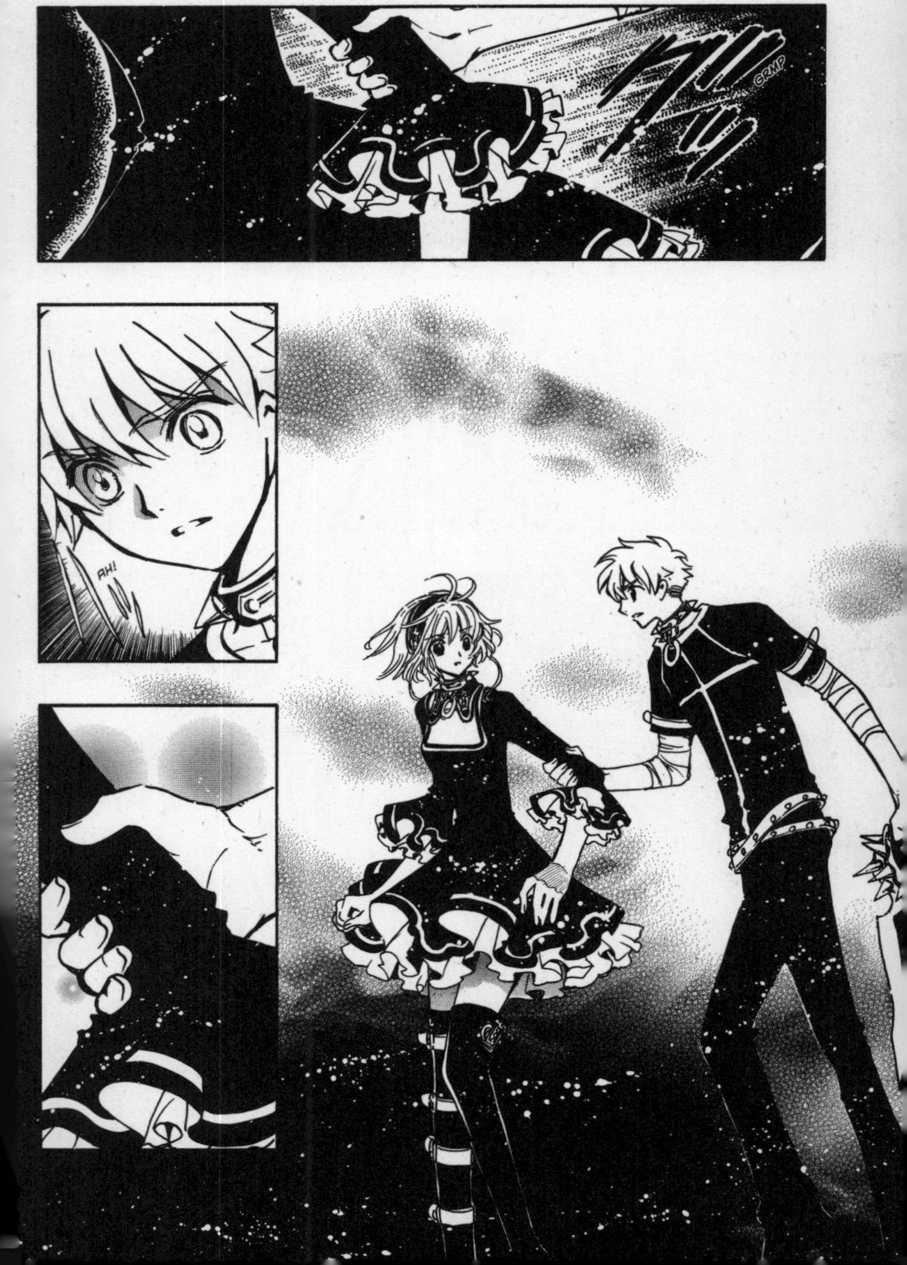
GRMP
AH!

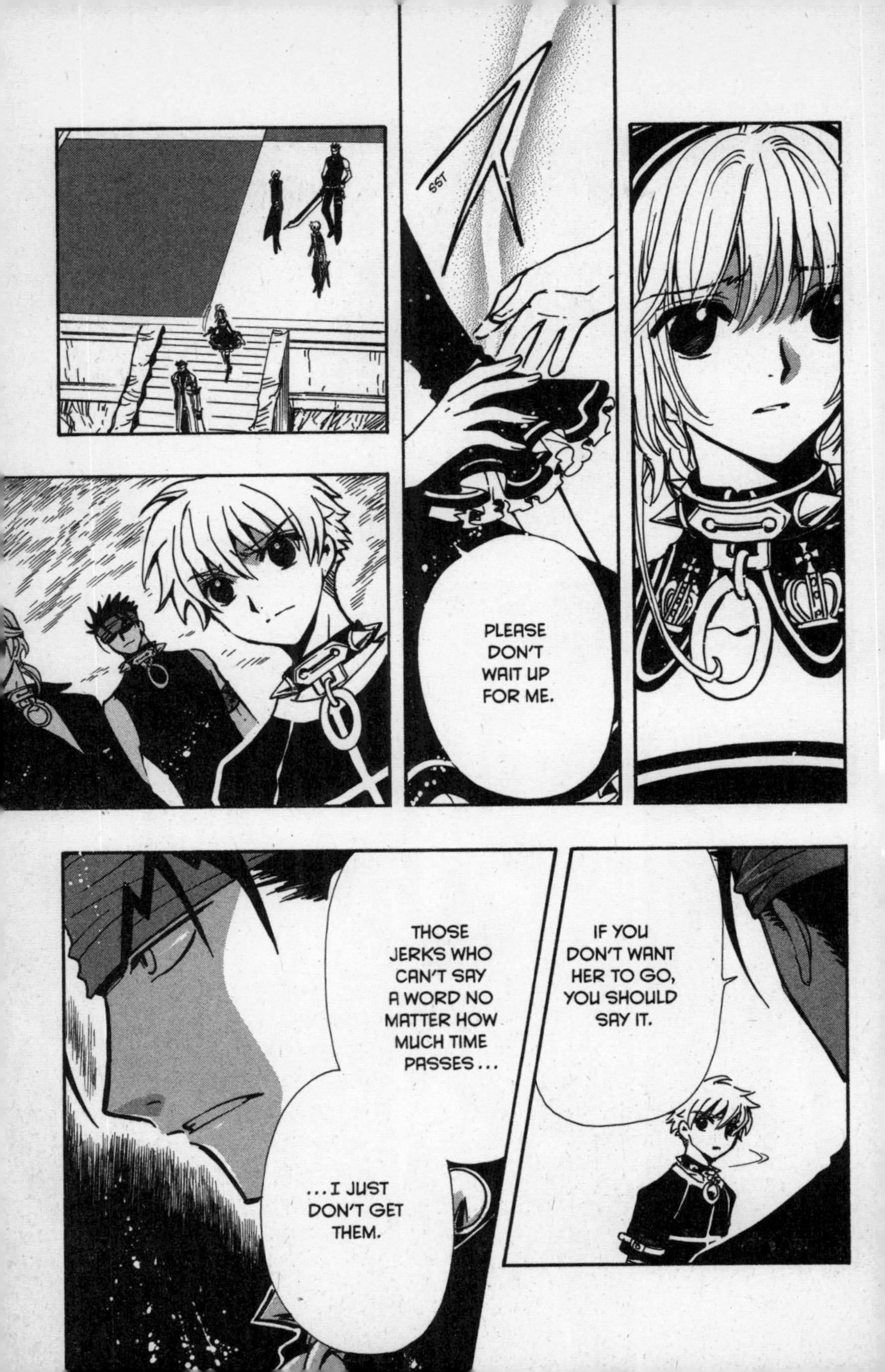
SST
PLEASE DON'T WAIT UP FOR ME.
IF YOU DON'T WANT HER TO GO, YOU SHOULD SAY IT.
THOSE JERKS WHO CAN'T SAY A WORD NO MATTER HOW MUCH TIME PASSES...
...I JUST DON'T GET THEM.

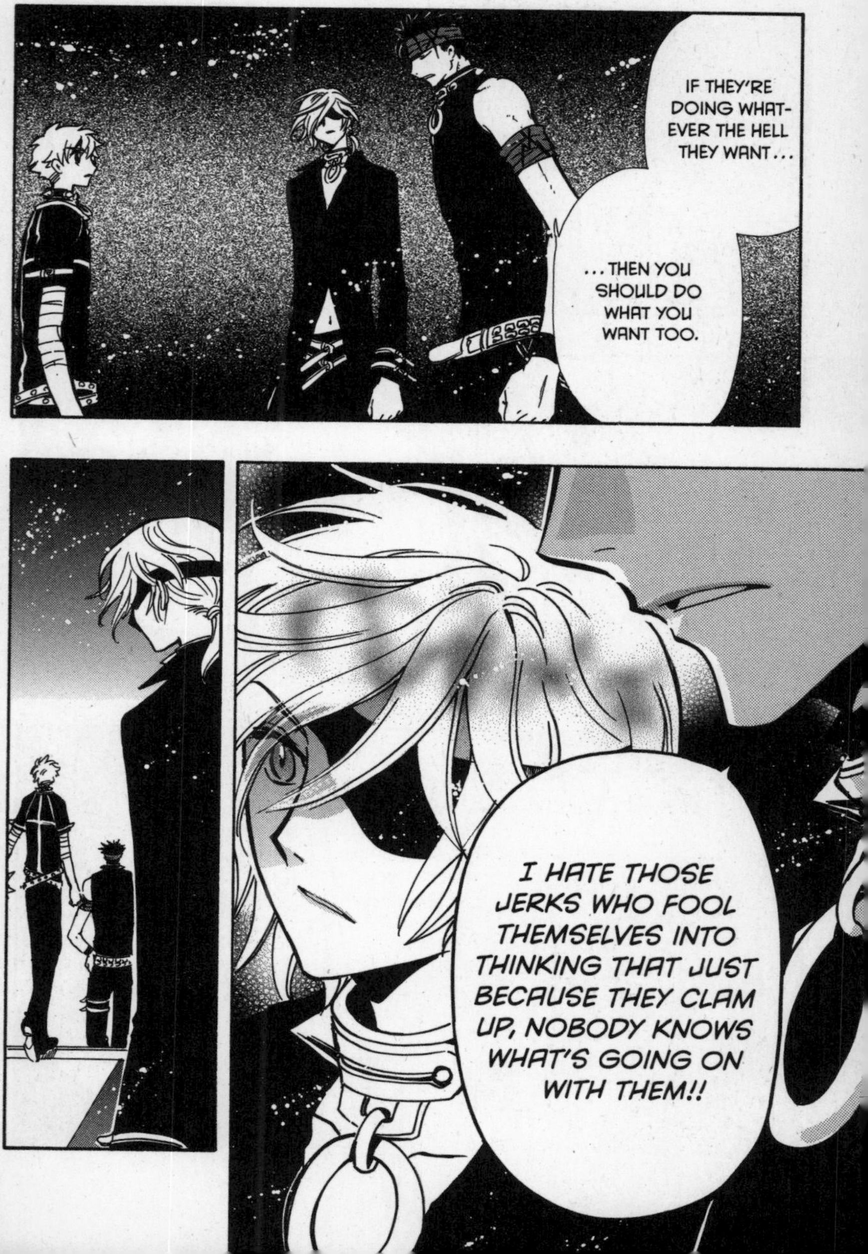
IF THEY'RE DOING WHAT-EVER THE HELL THEY WANT...
...THEN YOU SHOULD DO WHAT YOU WANT TOO.
I HATE THOSE JERKS WHO FOOL THEMSELVES INTO THINKING THAT JUST BECAUSE THEY CLAM UP, NOBODY KNOWS WHAT'S GOING ON WITH THEM!!

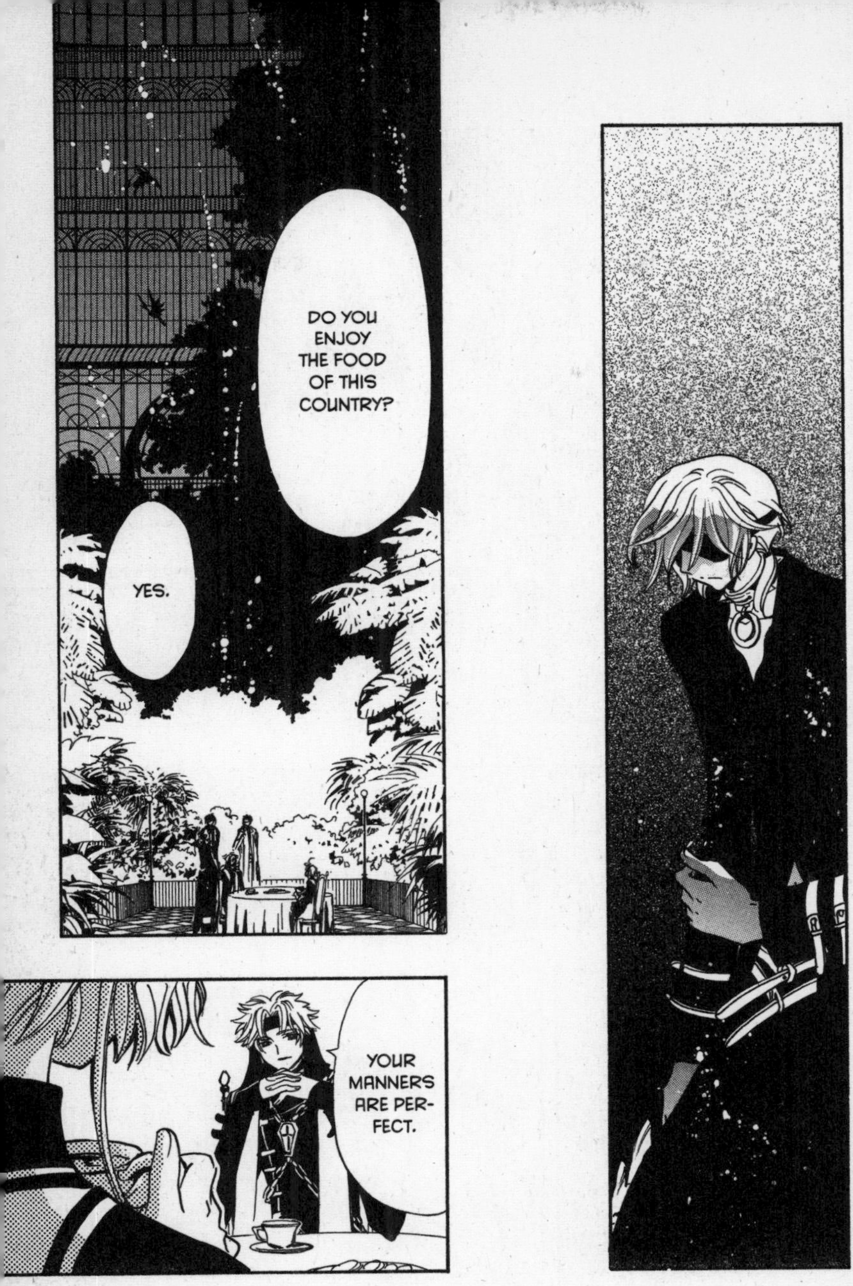
DO YOU ENJOY THE FOOD OF THIS COUNTRY?
YES.
YOUR MANNERS ARE PER-FECT.

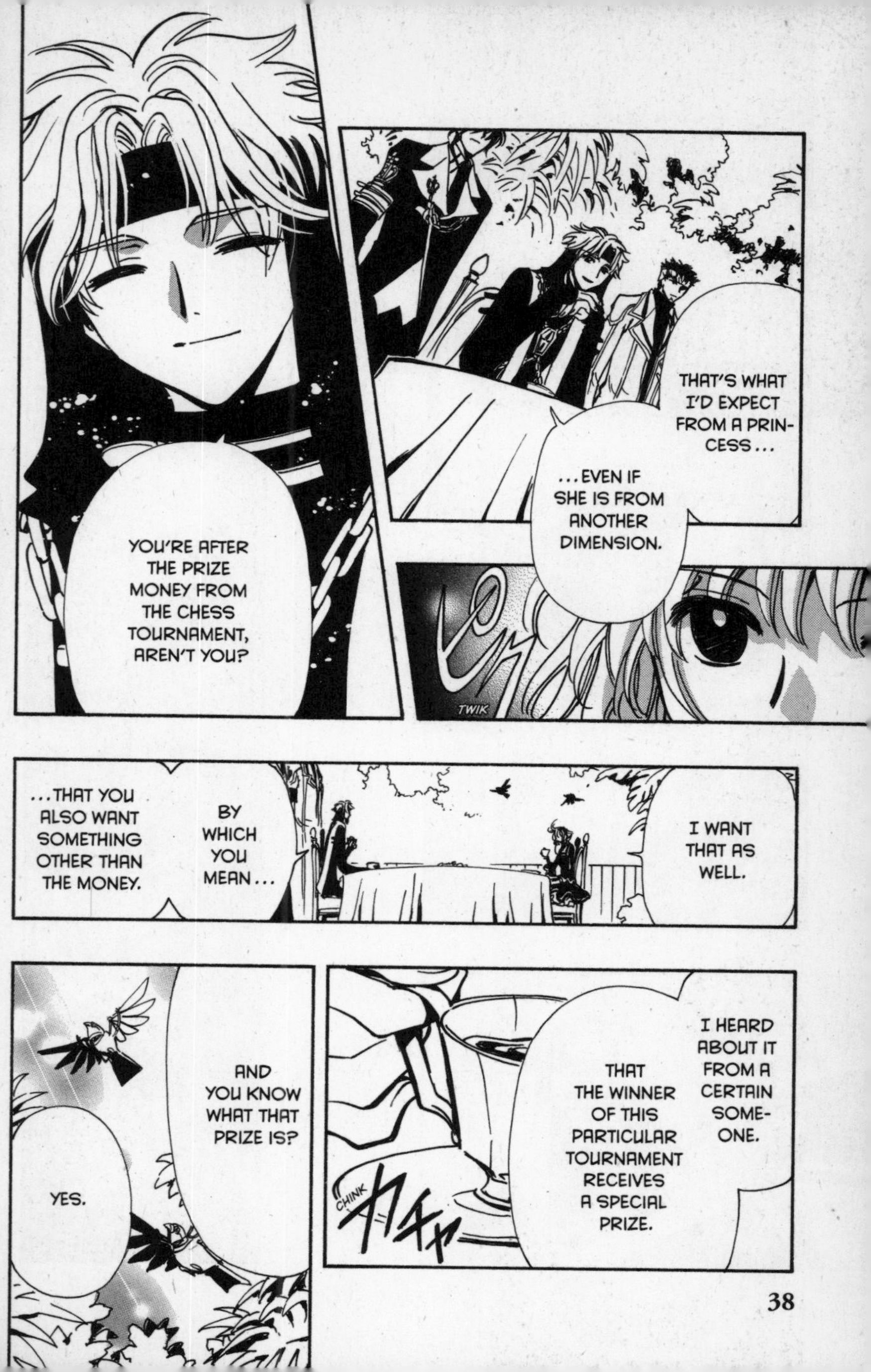
THAT'S WHAT I'D EXPECT FROM A PRINCESS...
...EVEN IF SHE IS FROM ANOTHER DIMENSION.
TWIK
YOU'RE AFTER THE PRIZE MONEY FROM THE CHESS TOURNAMENT, AREN'T YOU?
I WANT THAT AS WELL.
BY WHICH YOU MEAN...
...THAT YOU ALSO WANT SOMETHING OTHER THAN THE MONEY.
I HEARD ABOUT IT FROM A CERTAIN SOMEONE.
THAT THE WINNER OF THIS PARTICULAR TOURNAMENT RECEIVES A SPECIAL PRIZE.
CHINK
AND YOU KNOW WHAT THAT PRIZE IS?
YES.

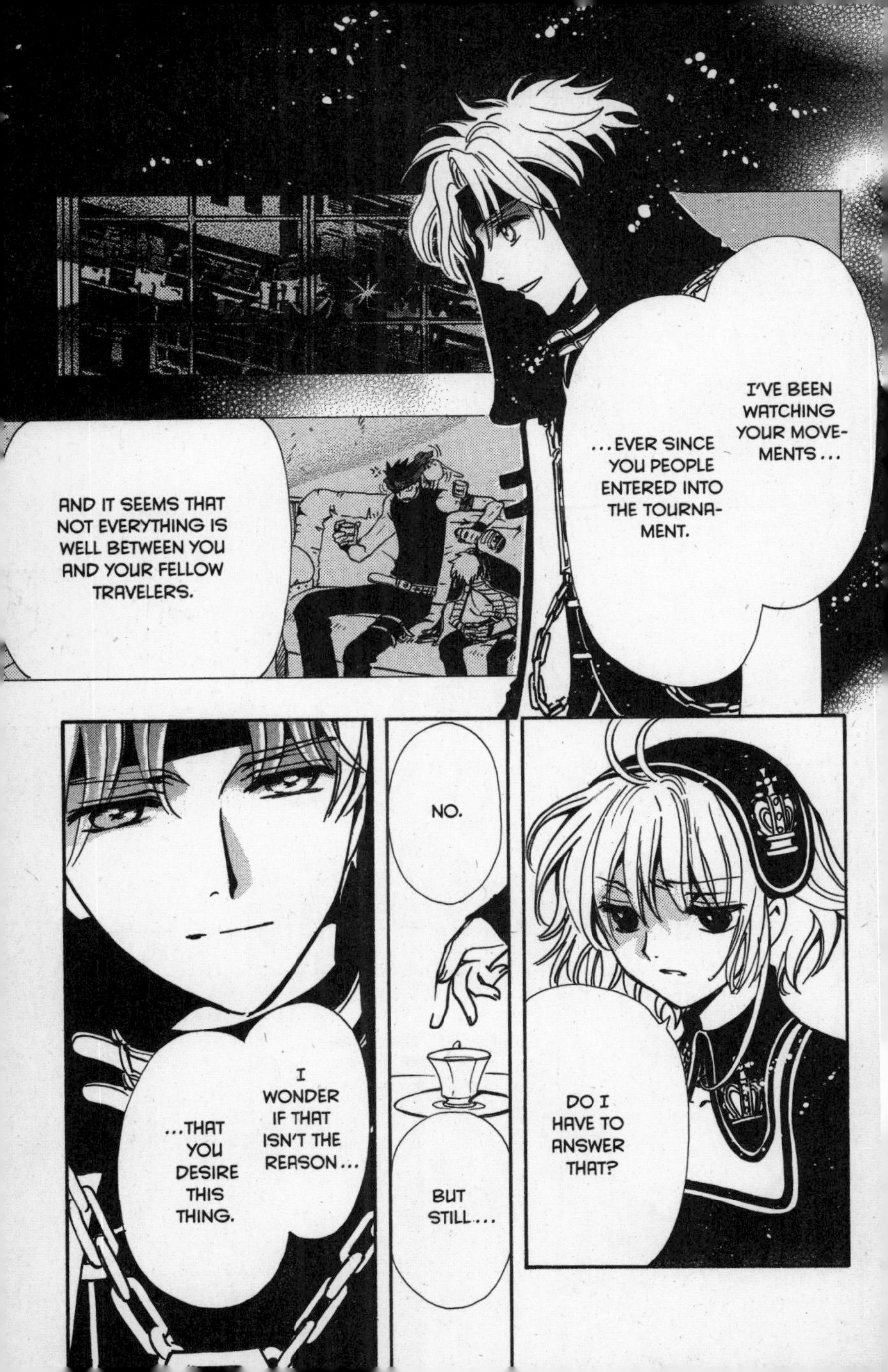

I'VE BEEN WATCHING YOUR MOVEMENTS...
...EVER SINCE YOU PEOPLE ENTERED INTO THE TOURNAMENT.
AND IT SEEMS THAT NOT EVERYTHING IS WELL BETWEEN YOU AND YOUR FELLOW TRAVELERS.
DO I HAVE TO ANSWER THAT?
NO.
BUT STILL...
I WONDER IF THAT ISN'T THE REASON...
...THAT YOU DESIRE THIS THING.

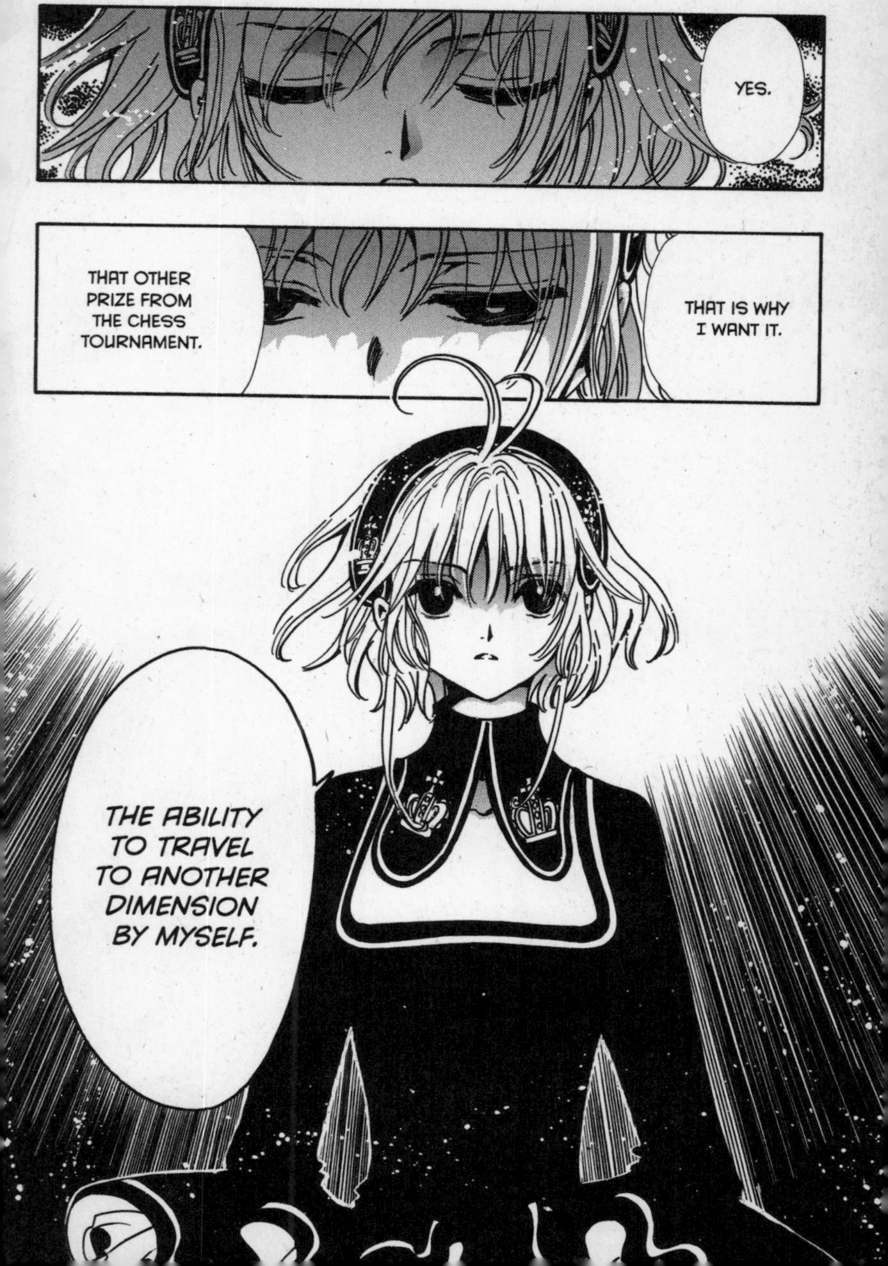
YES.
THAT IS WHY I WANT IT.
THAT OTHER PRIZE FROM THE CHESS TOURNAMENT.
THE ABILITY TO TRAVEL TO ANOTHER DIMENSION BY MYSELF.

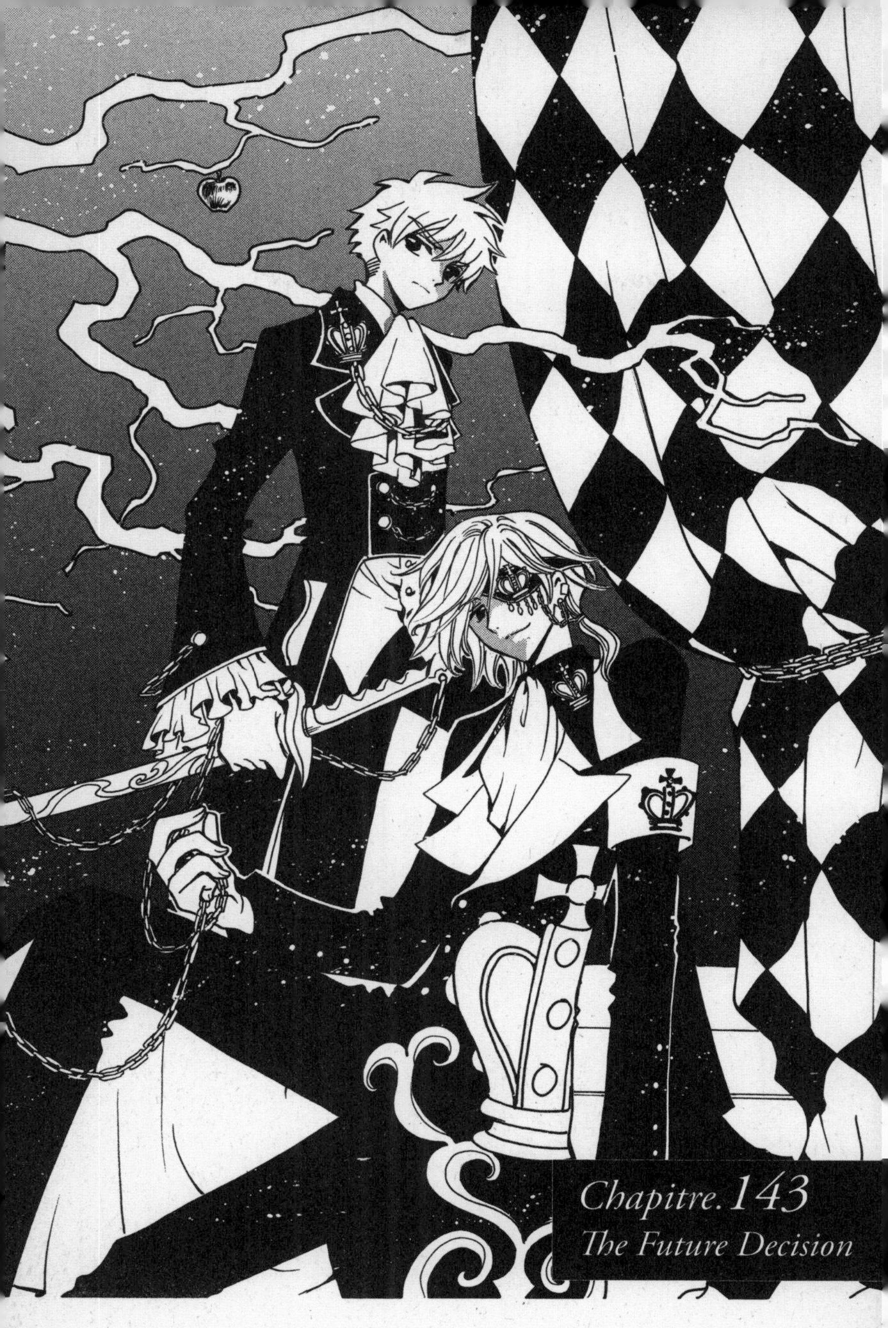

Chapitre.143
The Future Decision

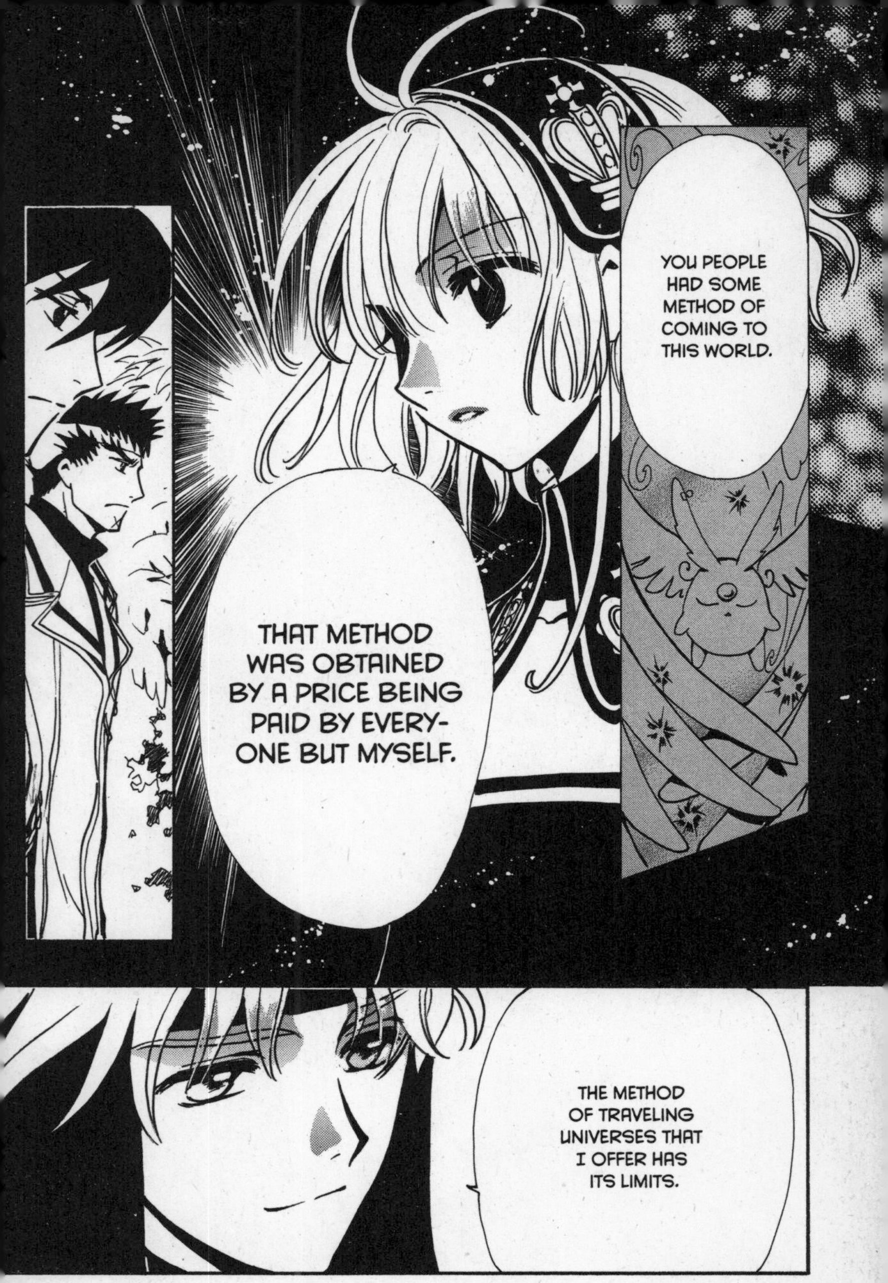
YOU PEOPLE HAD SOME METHOD OF COMING TO THIS WORLD.
THAT METHOD WAS OBTAINED BY A PRICE BEING PAID BY EVERY-ONE BUT MYSELF.
THE METHOD OF TRAVELING UNIVERSES THAT I OFFER HAS ITS LIMITS.

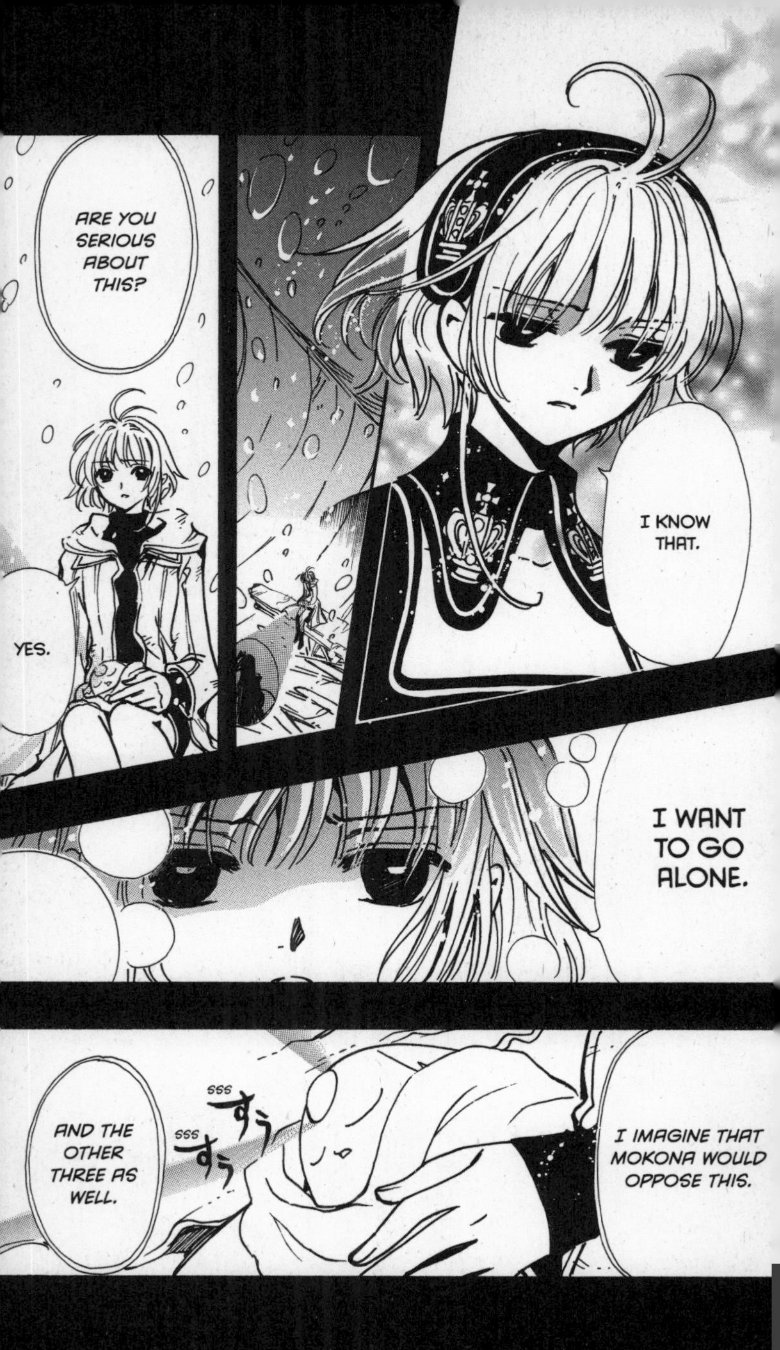
I KNOW THAT.
ARE YOU SERIOUS ABOUT THIS?
YES.
I WANT TO GO ALONE.
I IMAGINE THAT MOKONA WOULD OPPOSE THIS.
SSS すう
SSS すう
AND THE OTHER THREE AS WELL.

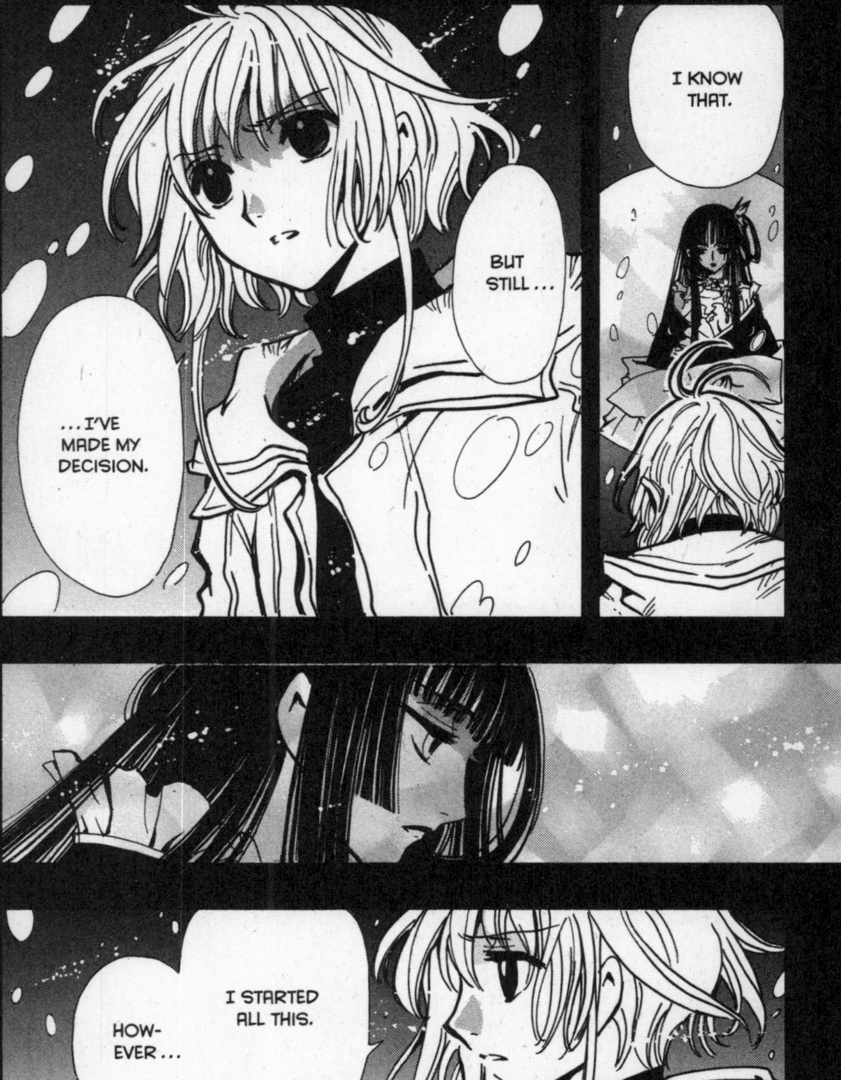
I KNOW THAT.
BUT STILL . . .
. . . I'VE MADE MY DECISION.
I STARTED ALL THIS.
HOW-EVER . . .

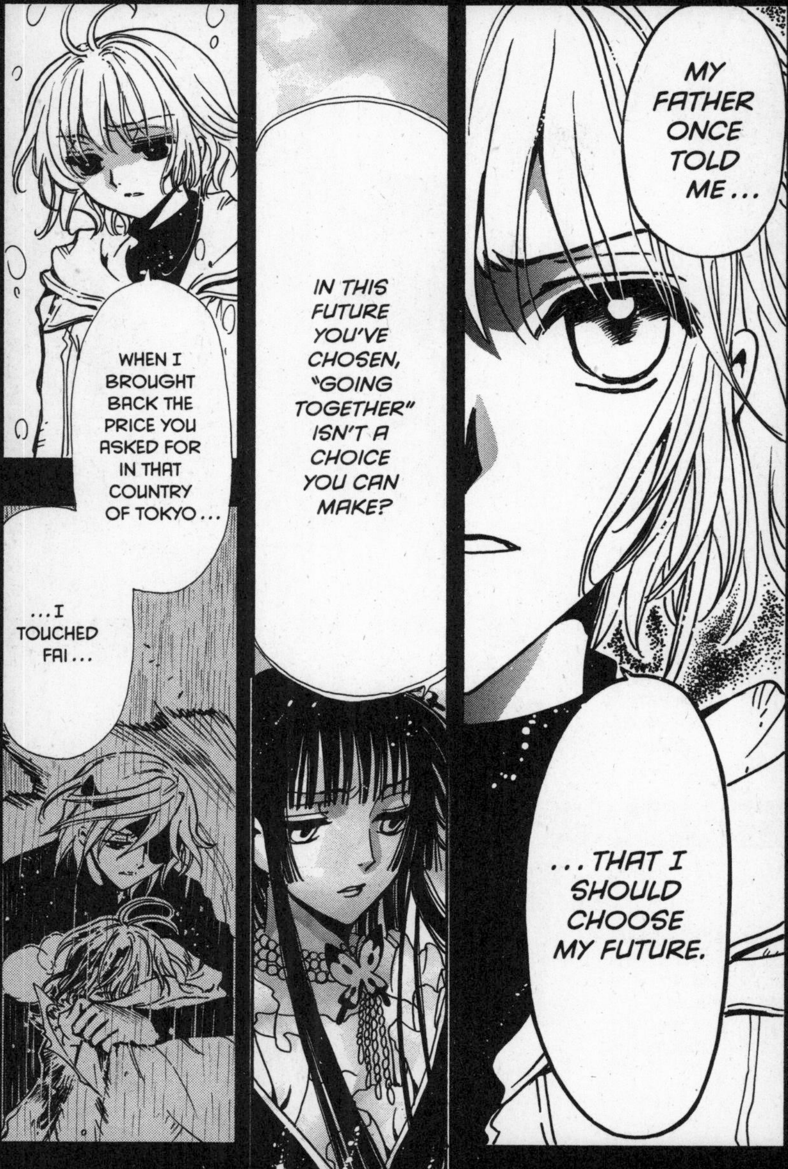
MY FATHER ONCE TOLD ME...
...THAT I SHOULD CHOOSE MY FUTURE.
IN THIS FUTURE YOU'VE CHOSEN, "GOING TOGETHER" ISN'T A CHOICE YOU CAN MAKE?
WHEN I BROUGHT BACK THE PRICE YOU ASKED FOR IN THAT COUNTRY OF TOKYO...
...I TOUCHED FAI...

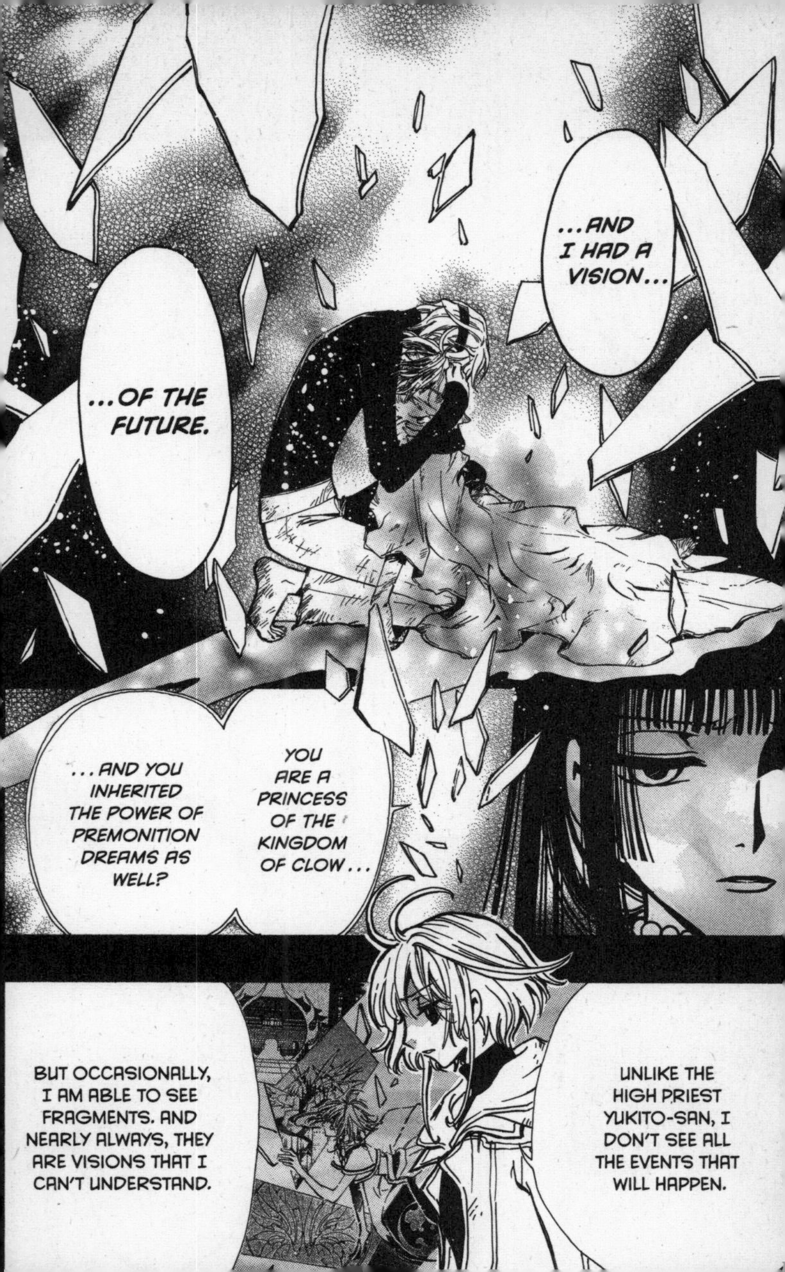
...AND I HAD A VISION...
...OF THE FUTURE.
YOU ARE A PRINCESS OF THE KINGDOM OF CLOW...
...AND YOU INHERITED THE POWER OF PREMONITION DREAMS AS WELL?
UNLIKE THE HIGH PRIEST YUKITO-SAN, I DON'T SEE ALL THE EVENTS THAT WILL HAPPEN.
BUT OCCASIONALLY, I AM ABLE TO SEE FRAGMENTS. AND NEARLY ALWAYS, THEY ARE VISIONS THAT I CAN'T UNDERSTAND.

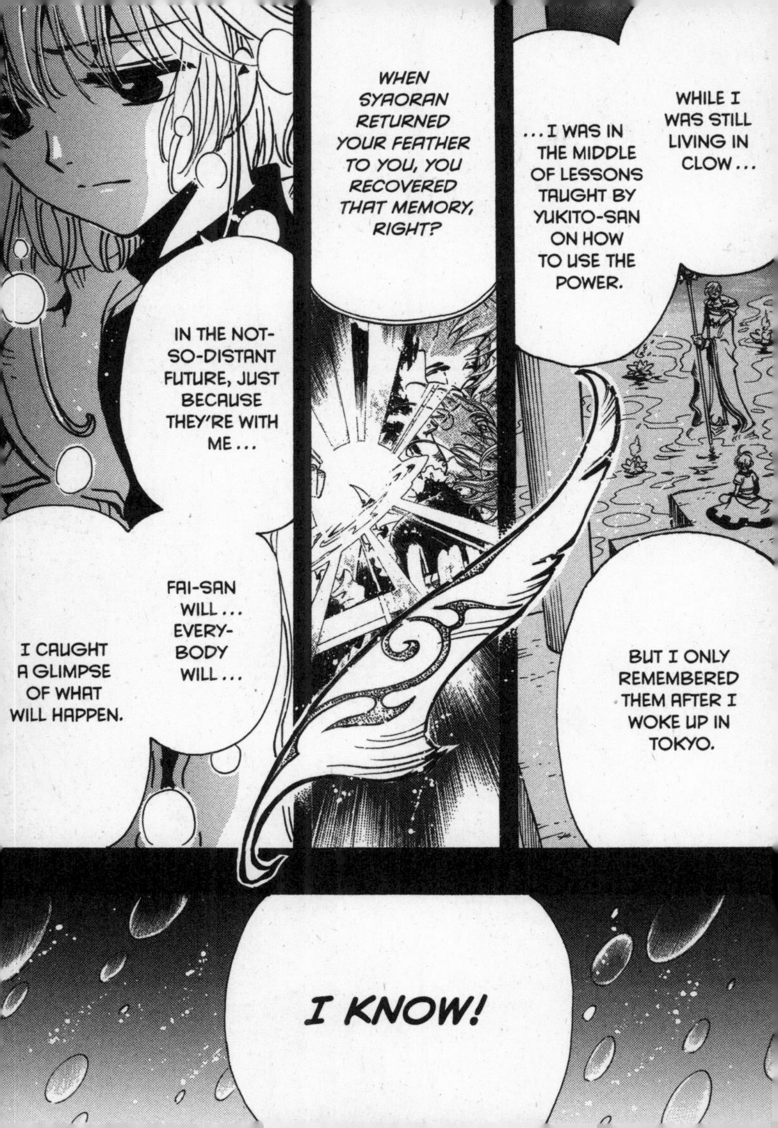
WHILE I WAS STILL LIVING IN CLOW...
...I WAS IN THE MIDDLE OF LESSONS TAUGHT BY YUKITO-SAN ON HOW TO USE THE POWER.
BUT I ONLY REMEMBERED THEM AFTER I WOKE UP IN TOKYO.
WHEN SYAORAN RETURNED YOUR FEATHER TO YOU, YOU RECOVERED THAT MEMORY, RIGHT?
IN THE NOT-SO-DISTANT FUTURE, JUST BECAUSE THEY'RE WITH ME...
FAI-SAN WILL... EVERY-BODY WILL...
I CAUGHT A GLIMPSE OF WHAT WILL HAPPEN.
I KNOW!

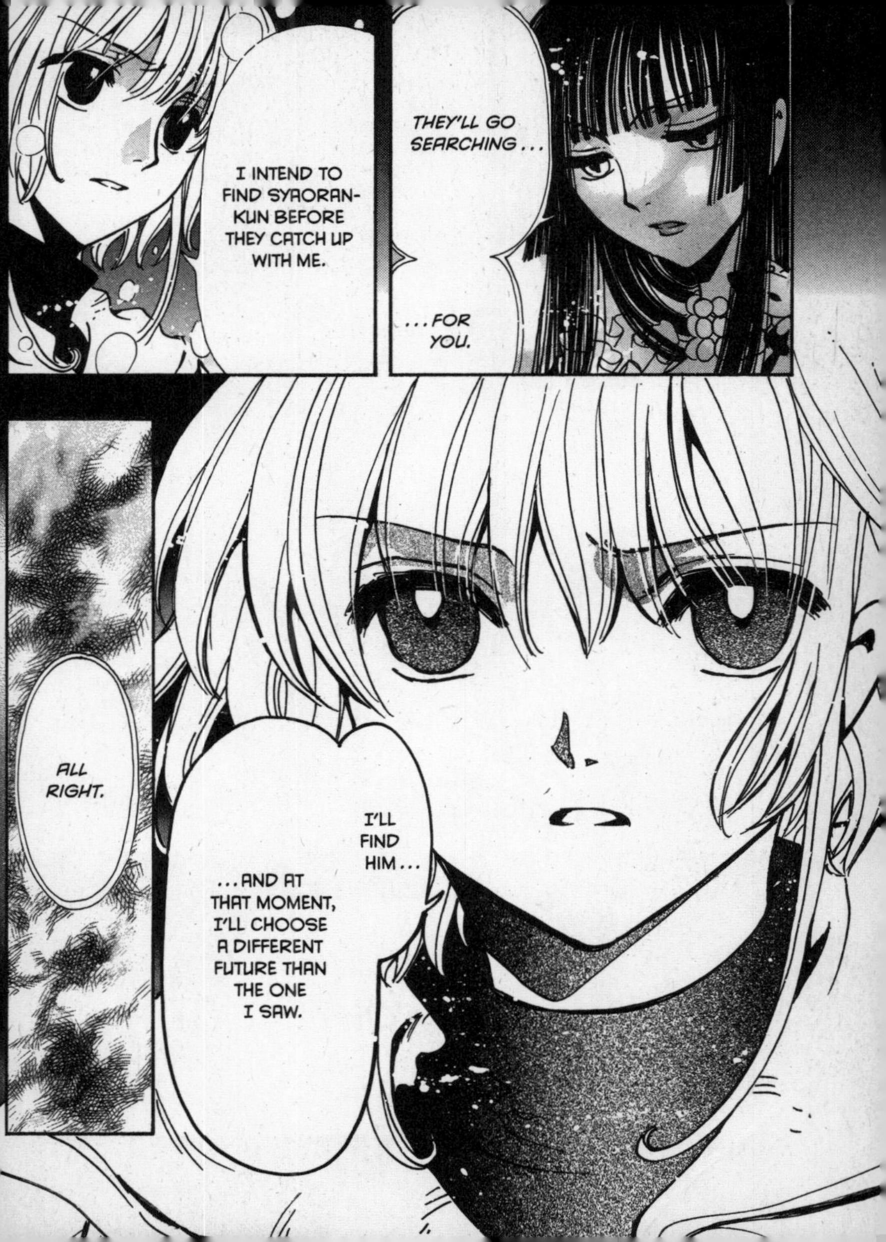
THEY'LL GO SEARCHING . . .
. . . FOR YOU.
I INTEND TO FIND SYAORAN-KUN BEFORE THEY CATCH UP WITH ME.
I'LL FIND HIM . . .
. . . AND AT THAT MOMENT, I'LL CHOOSE A DIFFERENT FUTURE THAN THE ONE I SAW.
ALL RIGHT.

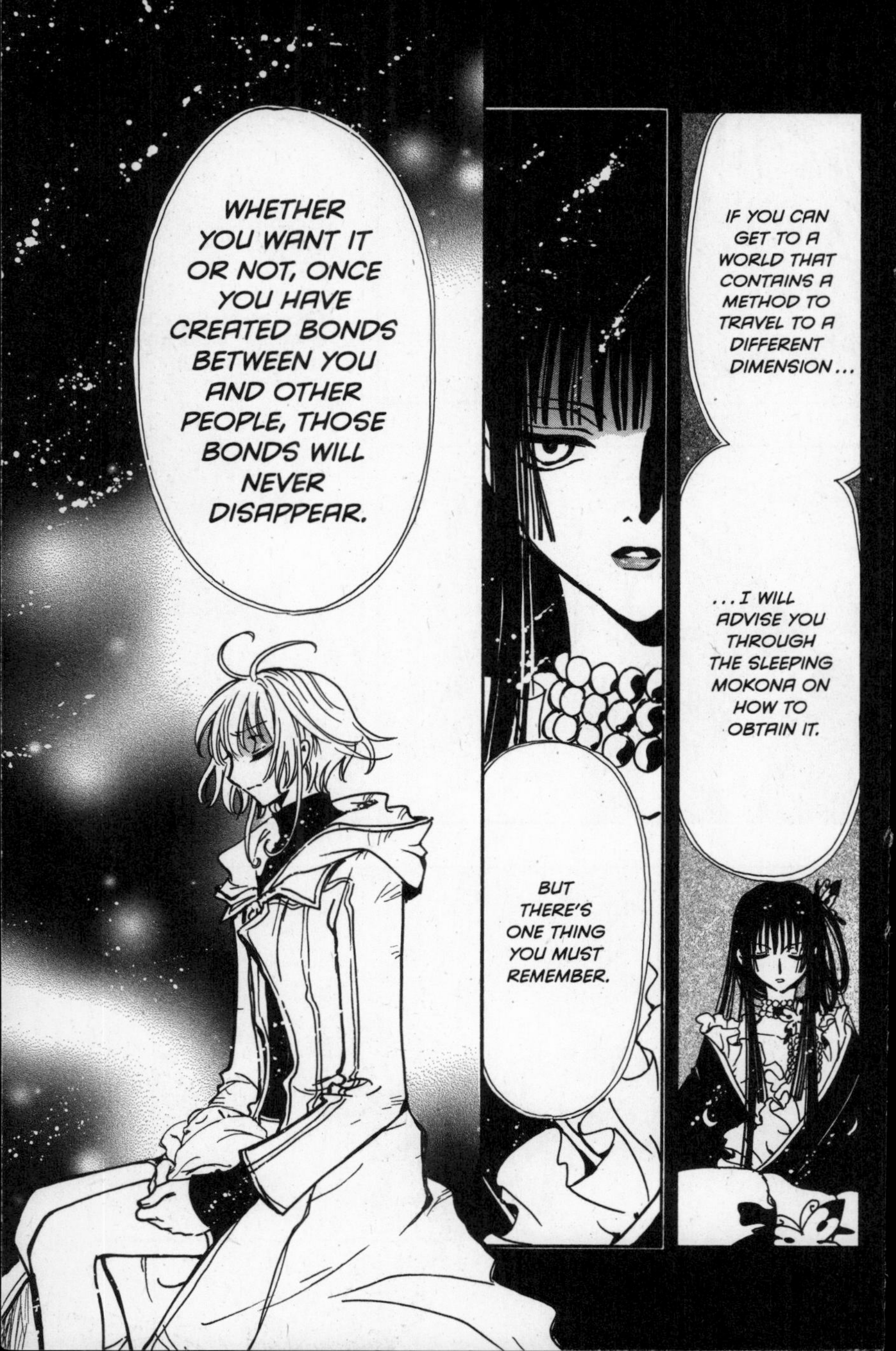
IF YOU CAN GET TO A WORLD THAT CONTAINS A METHOD TO TRAVEL TO A DIFFERENT DIMENSION...
...I WILL ADVISE YOU THROUGH THE SLEEPING MOKONA ON HOW TO OBTAIN IT.
BUT THERE'S ONE THING YOU MUST REMEMBER.
WHETHER YOU WANT IT OR NOT, ONCE YOU HAVE CREATED BONDS BETWEEN YOU AND OTHER PEOPLE, THOSE BONDS WILL NEVER DISAPPEAR.

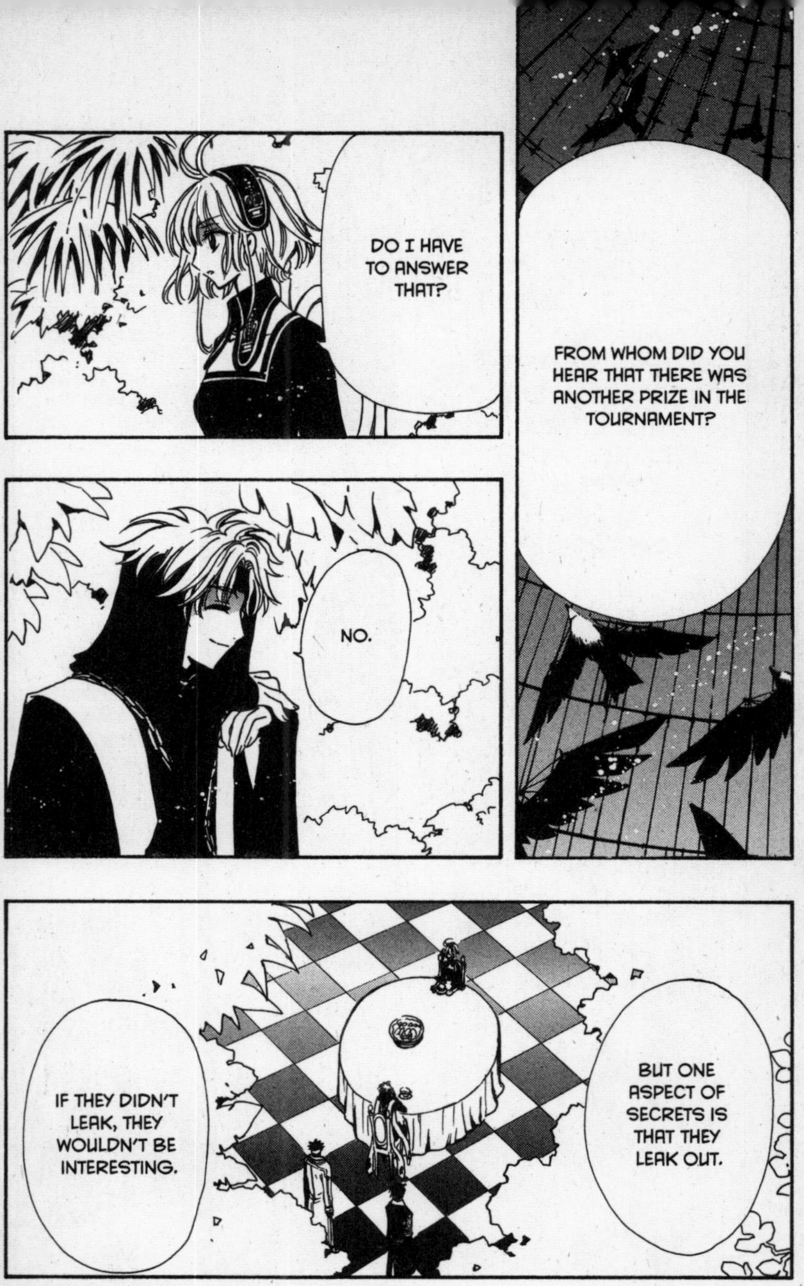
FROM WHOM DID YOU HEAR THAT THERE WAS ANOTHER PRIZE IN THE TOURNAMENT?
DO I HAVE TO ANSWER THAT?
NO.
BUT ONE ASPECT OF SECRETS IS THAT THEY LEAK OUT.
IF THEY DIDN'T LEAK, THEY WOULDN'T BE INTERESTING.

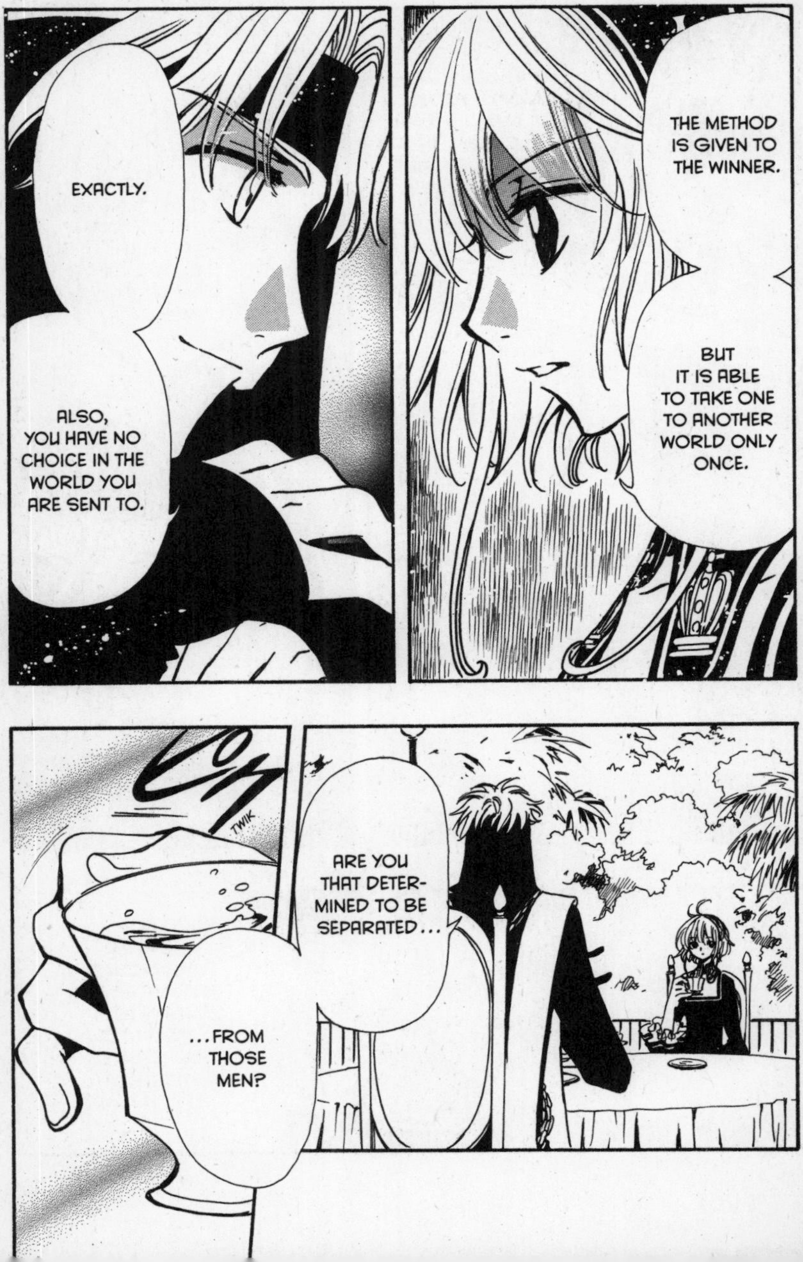
THE METHOD IS GIVEN TO THE WINNER.
BUT IT IS ABLE TO TAKE ONE TO ANOTHER WORLD ONLY ONCE.
EXACTLY.
ALSO, YOU HAVE NO CHOICE IN THE WORLD YOU ARE SENT TO.
ARE YOU THAT DETERMINED TO BE SEPARATED...
...FROM THOSE MEN?
TWIK

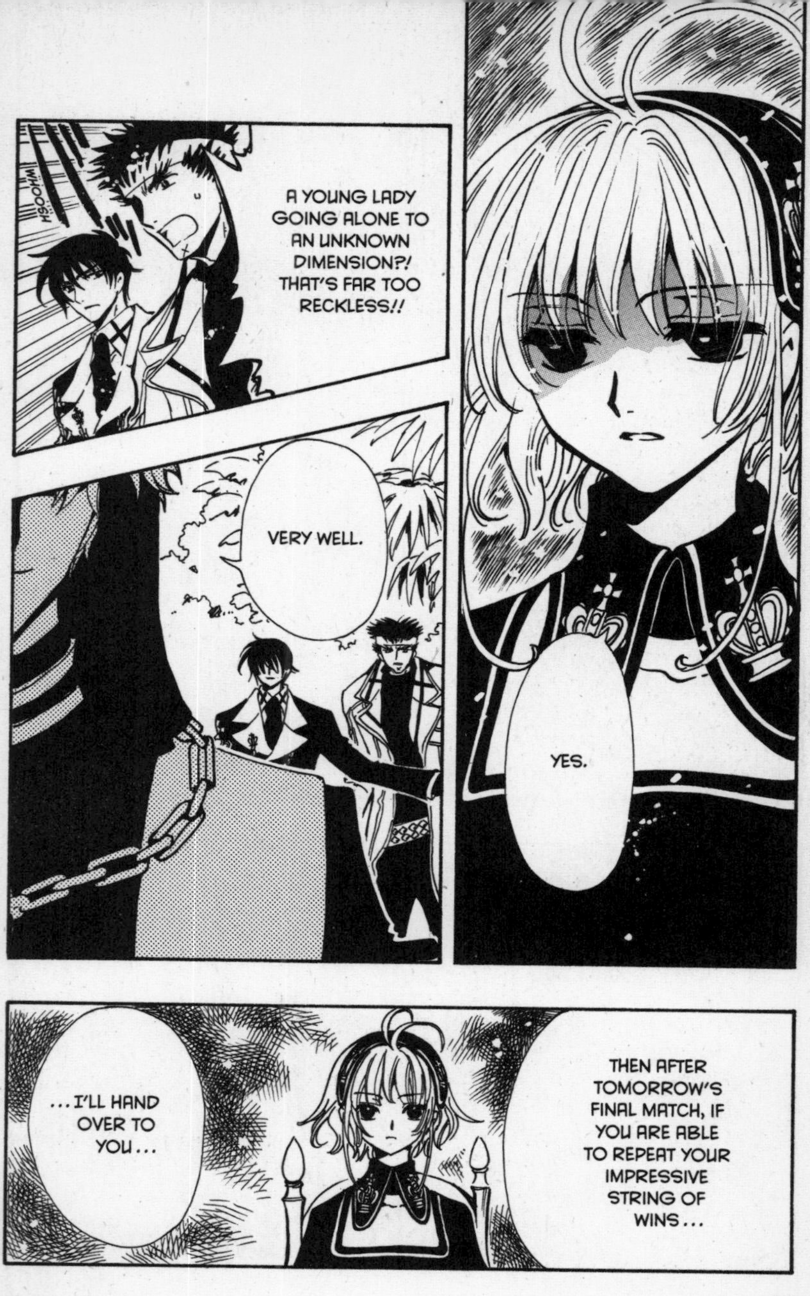
YES.
WHOOSH!!
A YOUNG LADY GOING ALONE TO AN UNKNOWN DIMENSION?! THAT'S FAR TOO RECKLESS!!
VERY WELL.
THEN AFTER TOMORROW'S FINAL MATCH, IF YOU ARE ABLE TO REPEAT YOUR IMPRESSIVE STRING OF WINS...
...I'LL HAND OVER TO YOU...

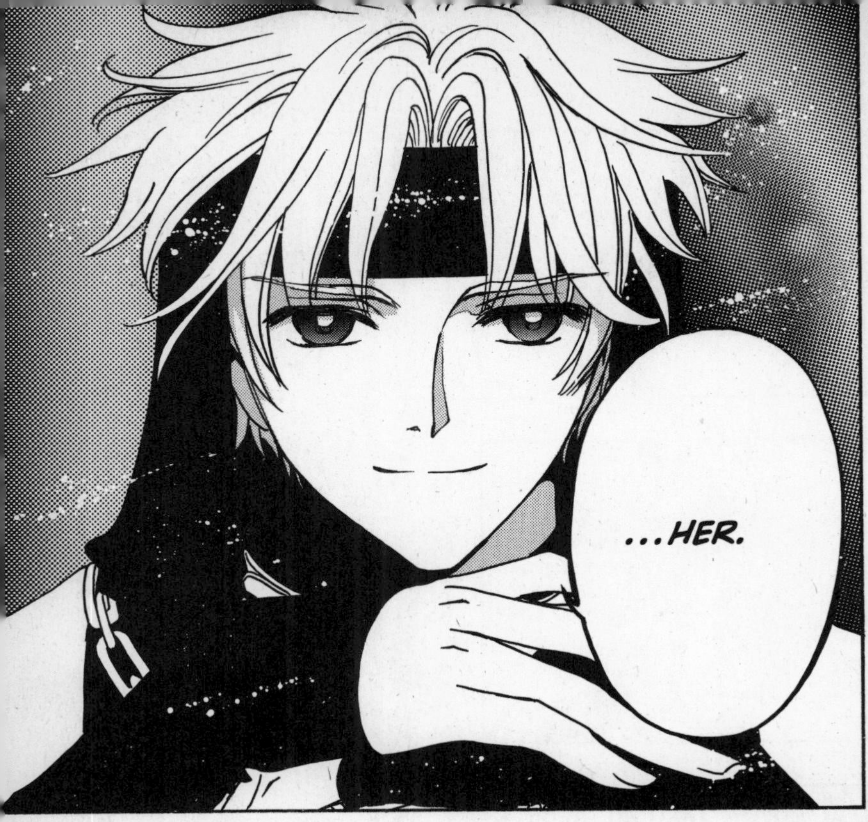
...HER.
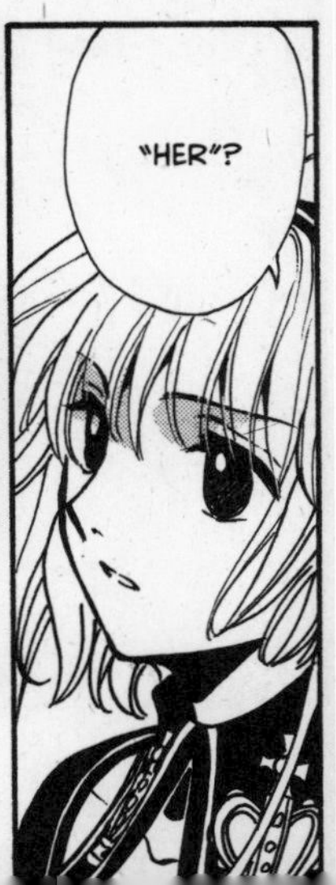
"HER"?
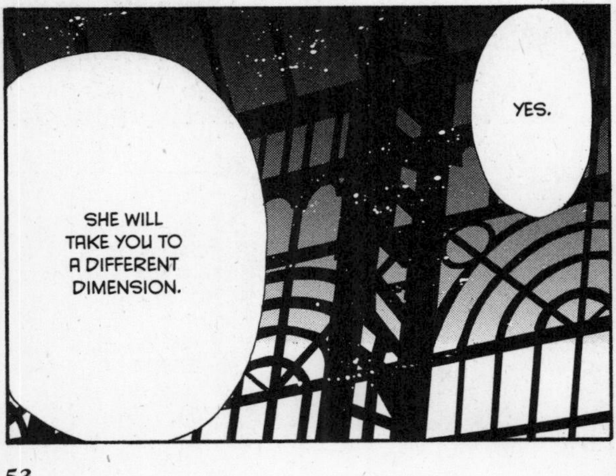
YES.
SHE WILL TAKE YOU TO A DIFFERENT DIMENSION.

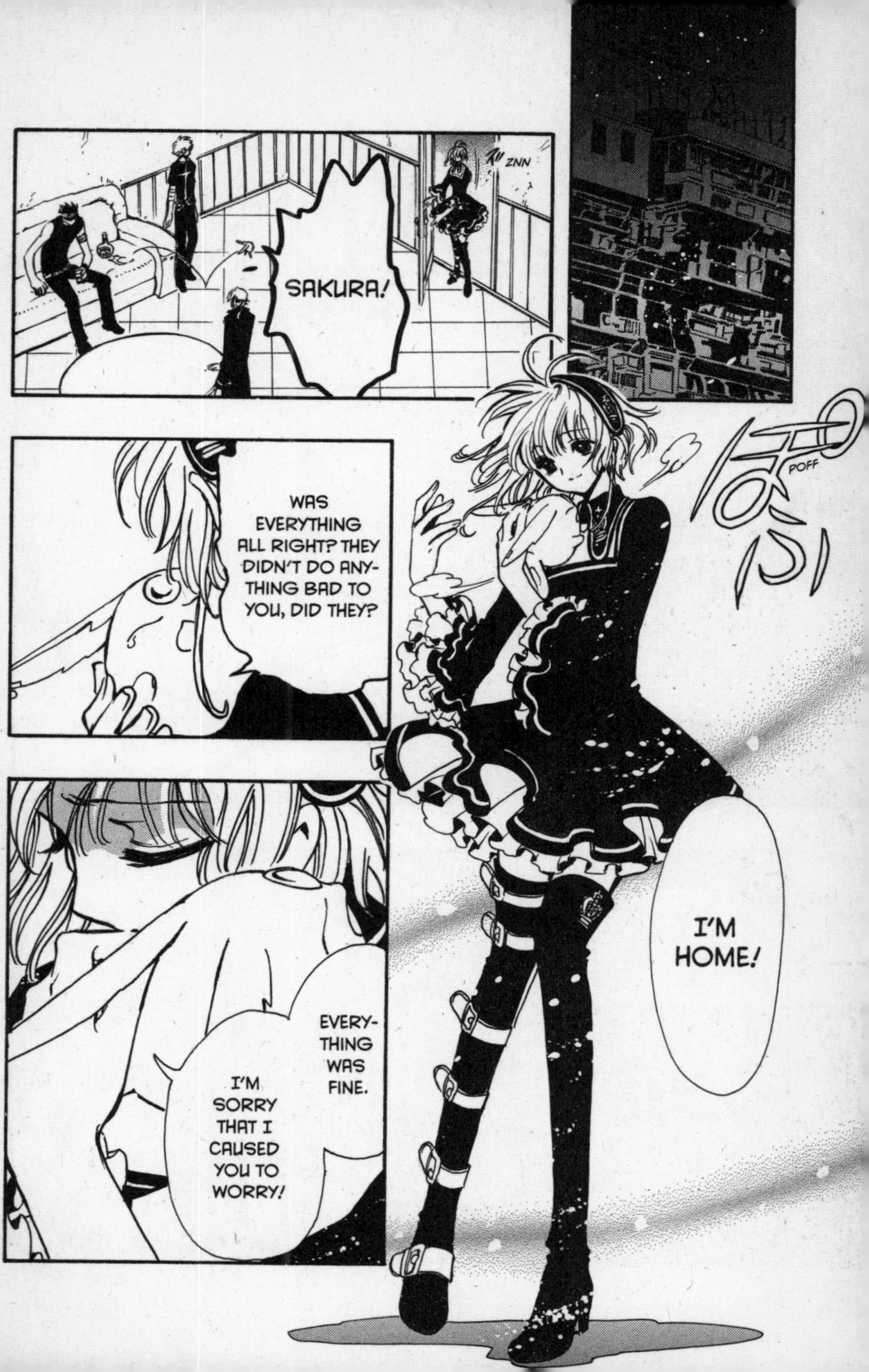
ぽふ
POFF
I'M HOME!
ZNN
SAKURA!
WAS EVERYTHING ALL RIGHT? THEY DIDN'T DO ANYTHING BAD TO YOU, DID THEY?
EVERYTHING WAS FINE.
I'M SORRY THAT I CAUSED YOU TO WORRY!

WELCOME BACK, SAKURA-CHAN.

THANK YOU. I'M BACK.

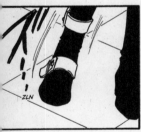

ZLN

SST

I THINK I'M A LITTLE TIRED.

I'M GOING STRAIGHT TO BED.

FORGIVE ME.

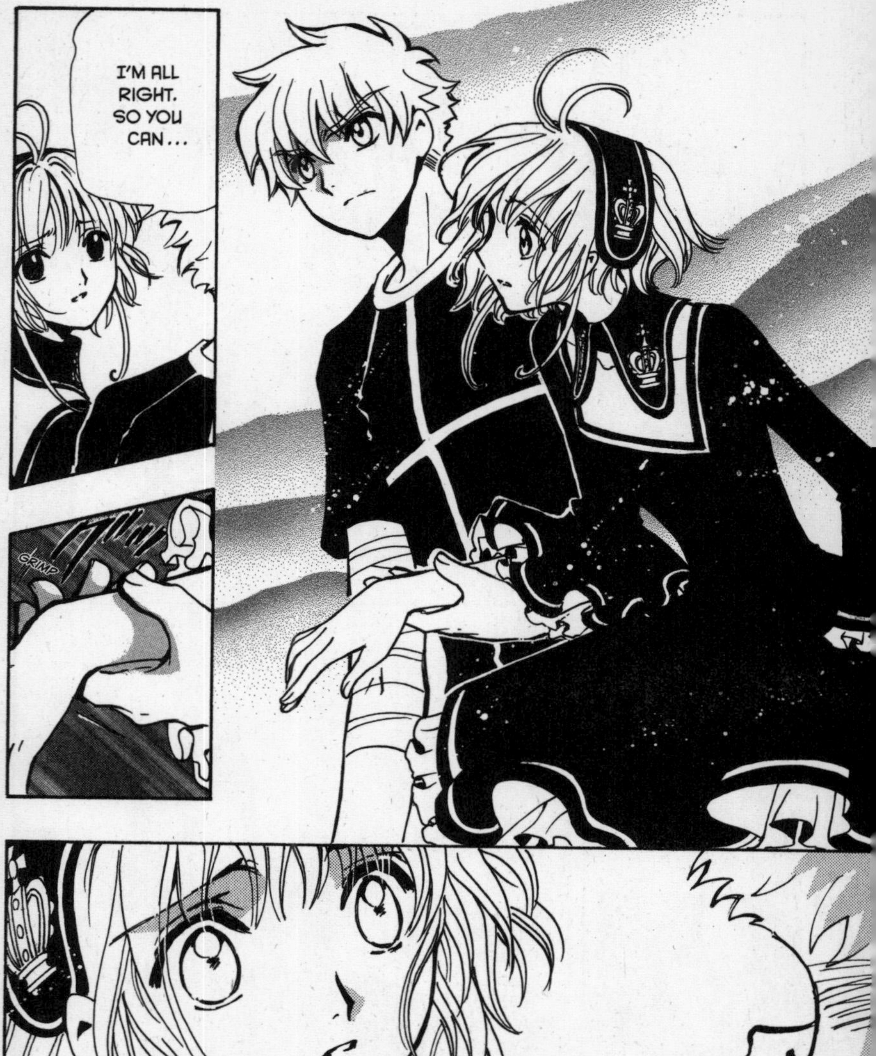
I'M ALL RIGHT. SO YOU CAN...
GRIMP

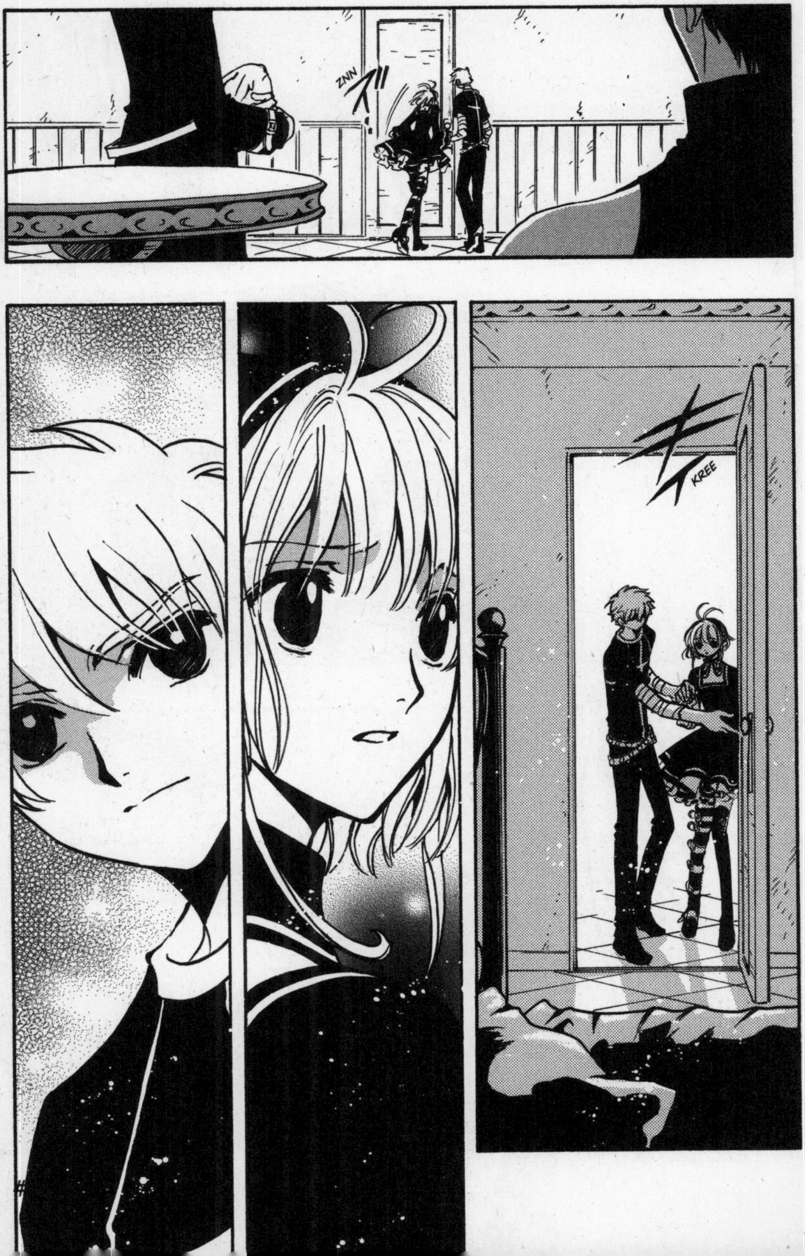
ZNN
KREE

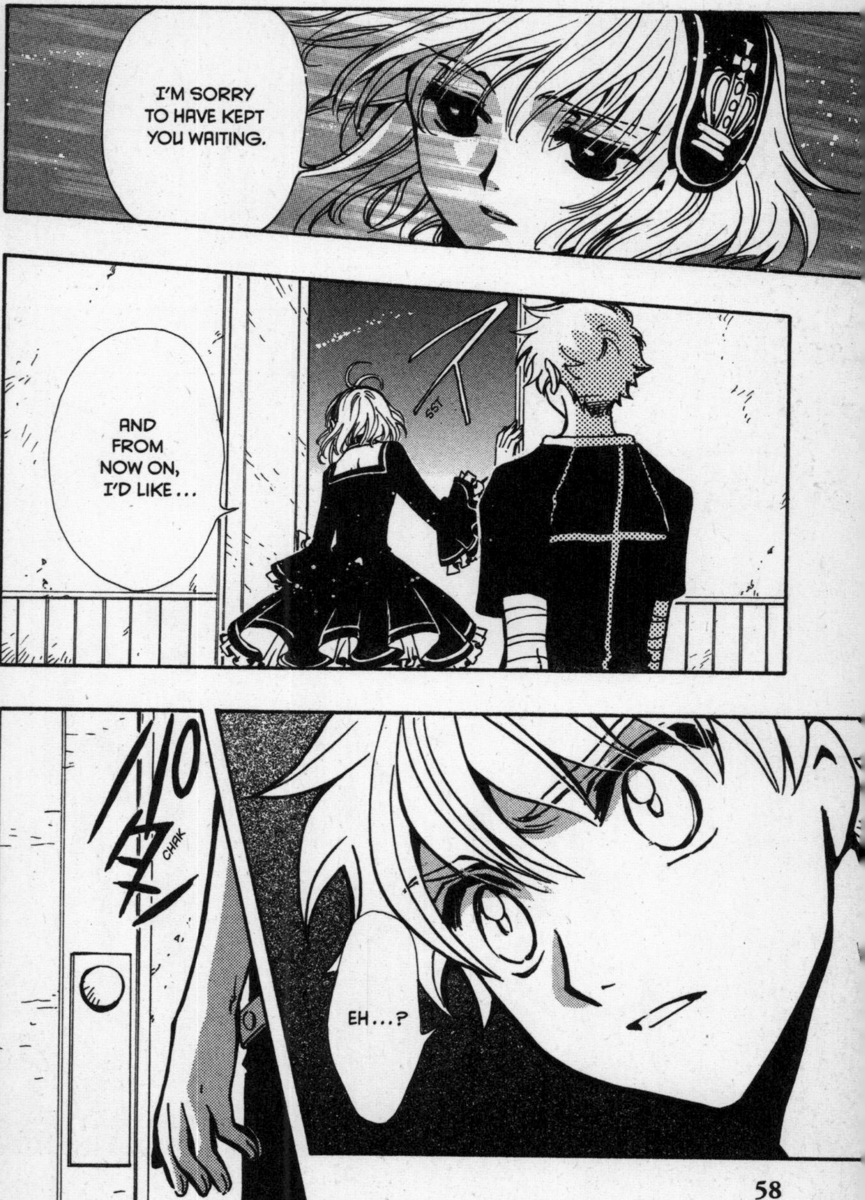
I'M SORRY TO HAVE KEPT YOU WAITING.
SST
AND FROM NOW ON, I'D LIKE...
EH...?
CHAK

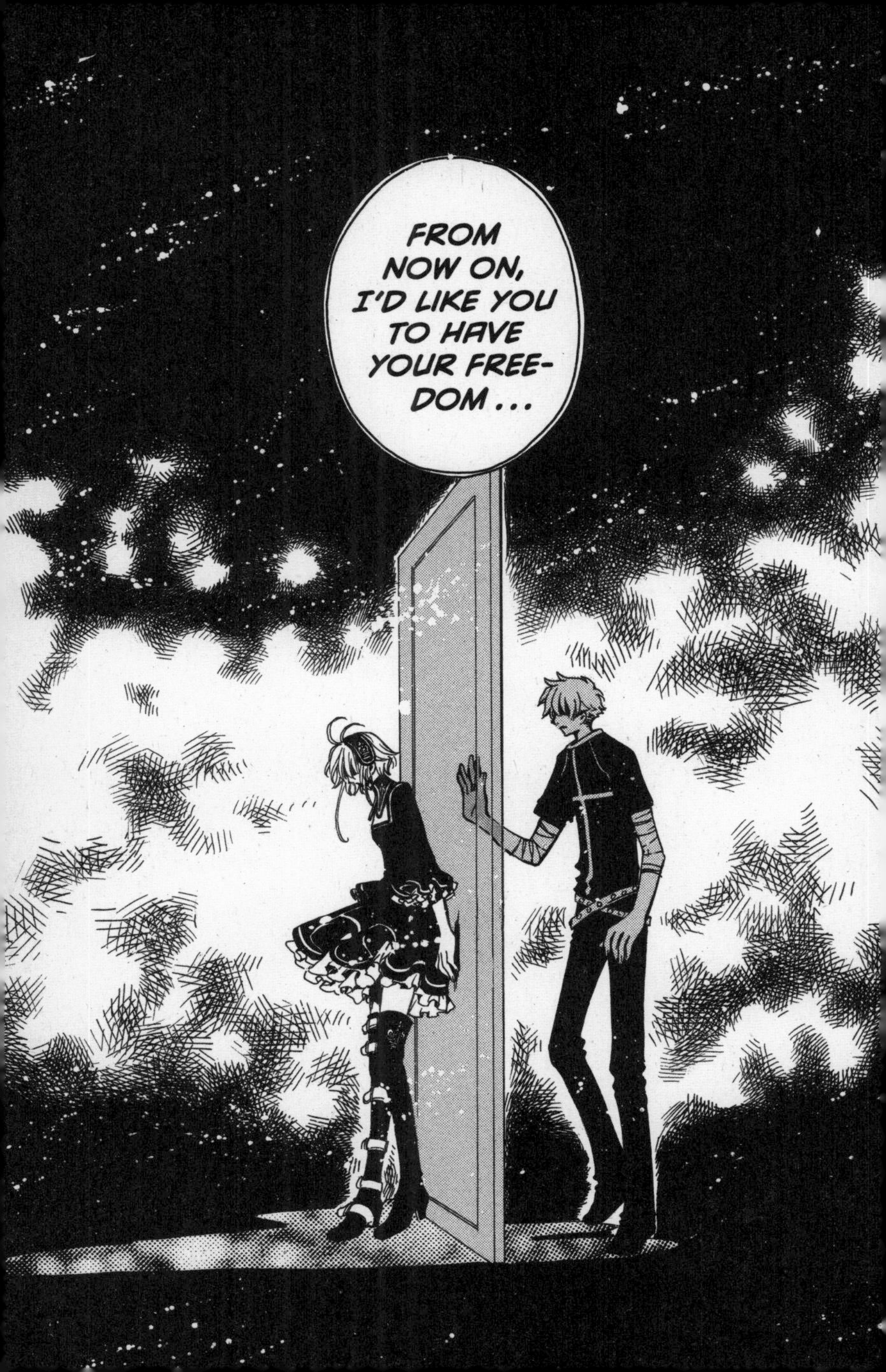
FROM NOW ON, I'D LIKE YOU TO HAVE YOUR FREE-DOM . . .

ツバサ

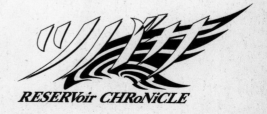

RESERVoir CHRoNiCLE

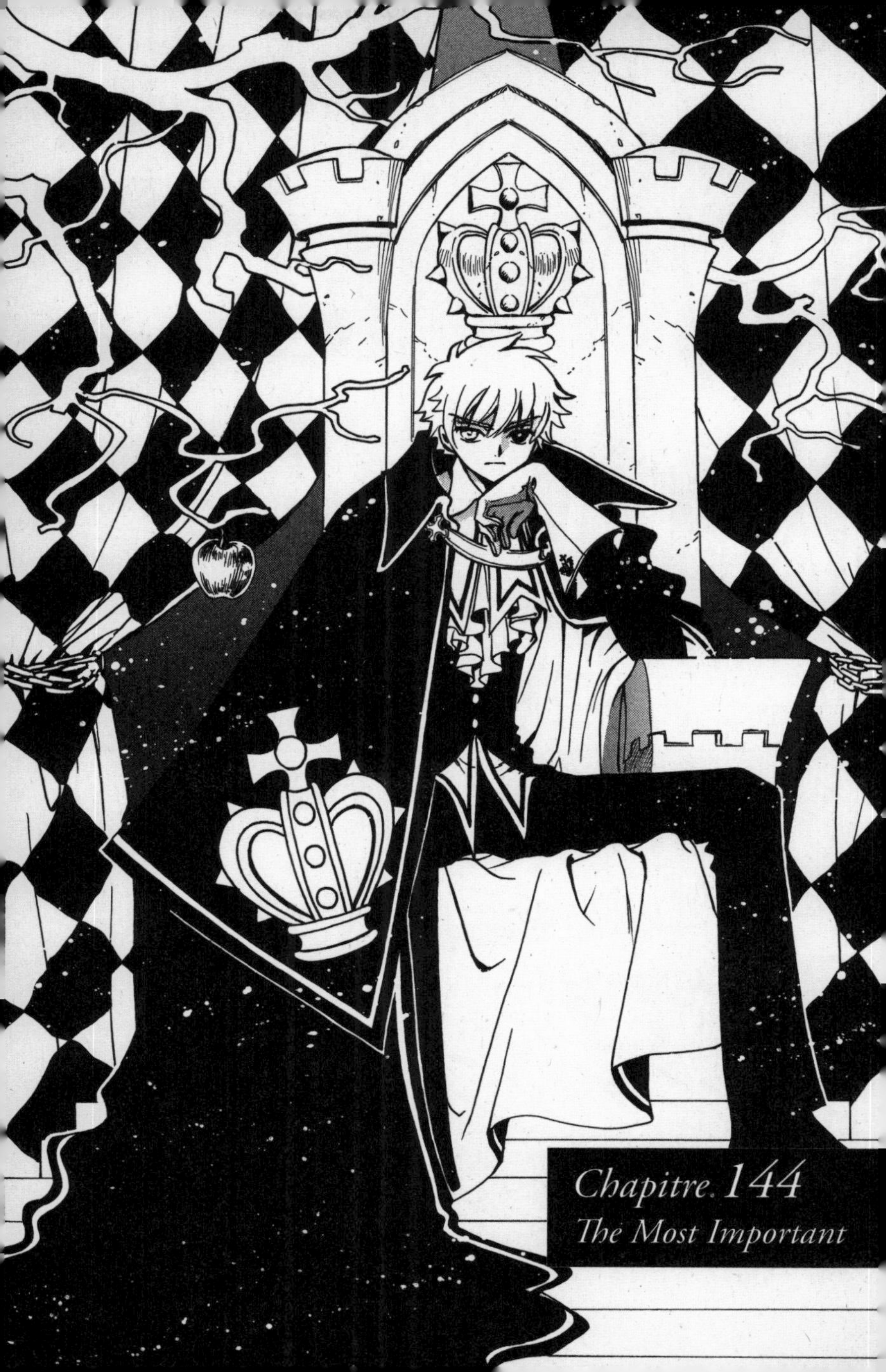
Chapitre. 144
The Most Important

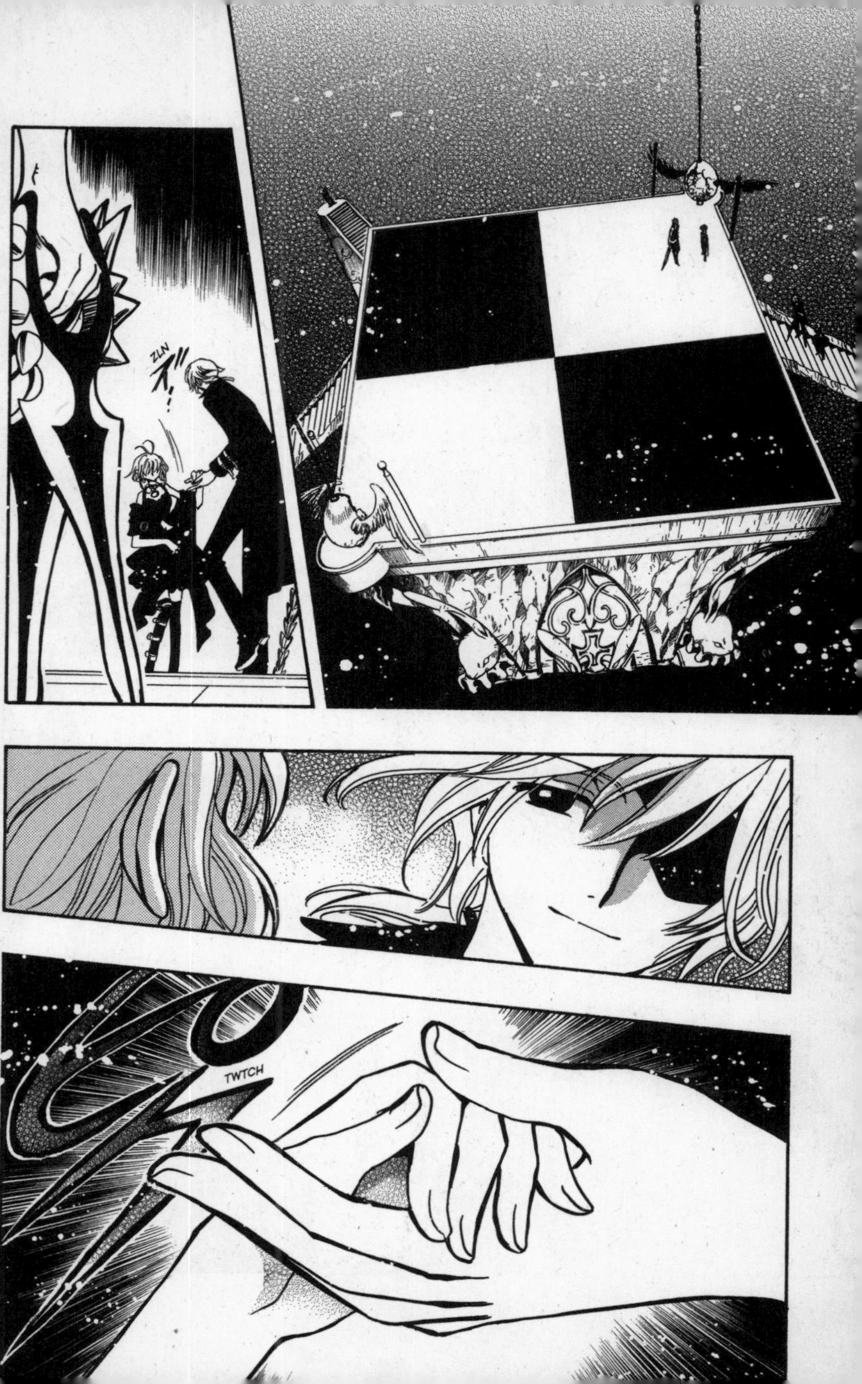
ZLN
TWTCH

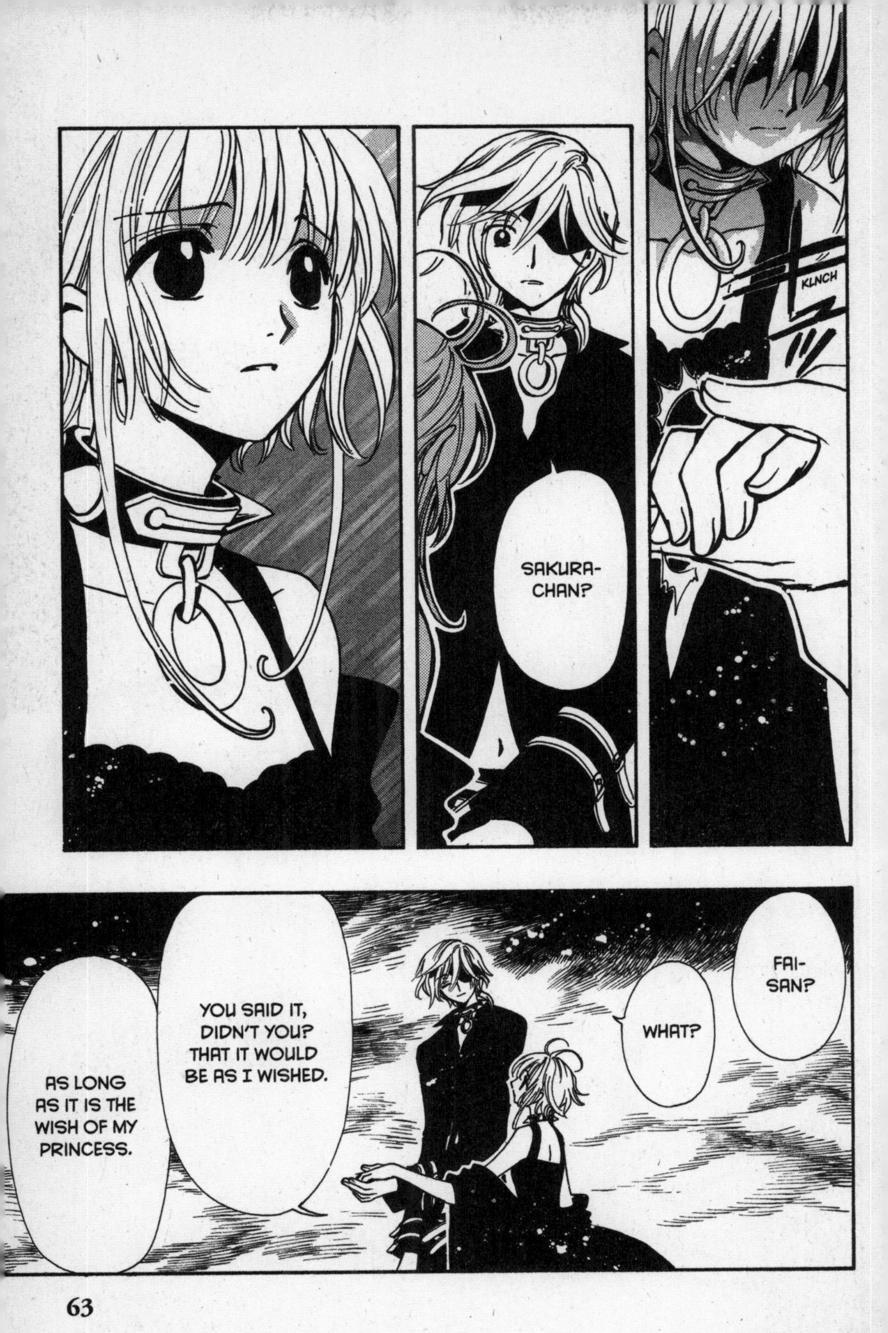
KLNCH
SAKURA-CHAN?
FAI-SAN?
WHAT?
YOU SAID IT, DIDN'T YOU? THAT IT WOULD BE AS I WISHED.
AS LONG AS IT IS THE WISH OF MY PRINCESS.

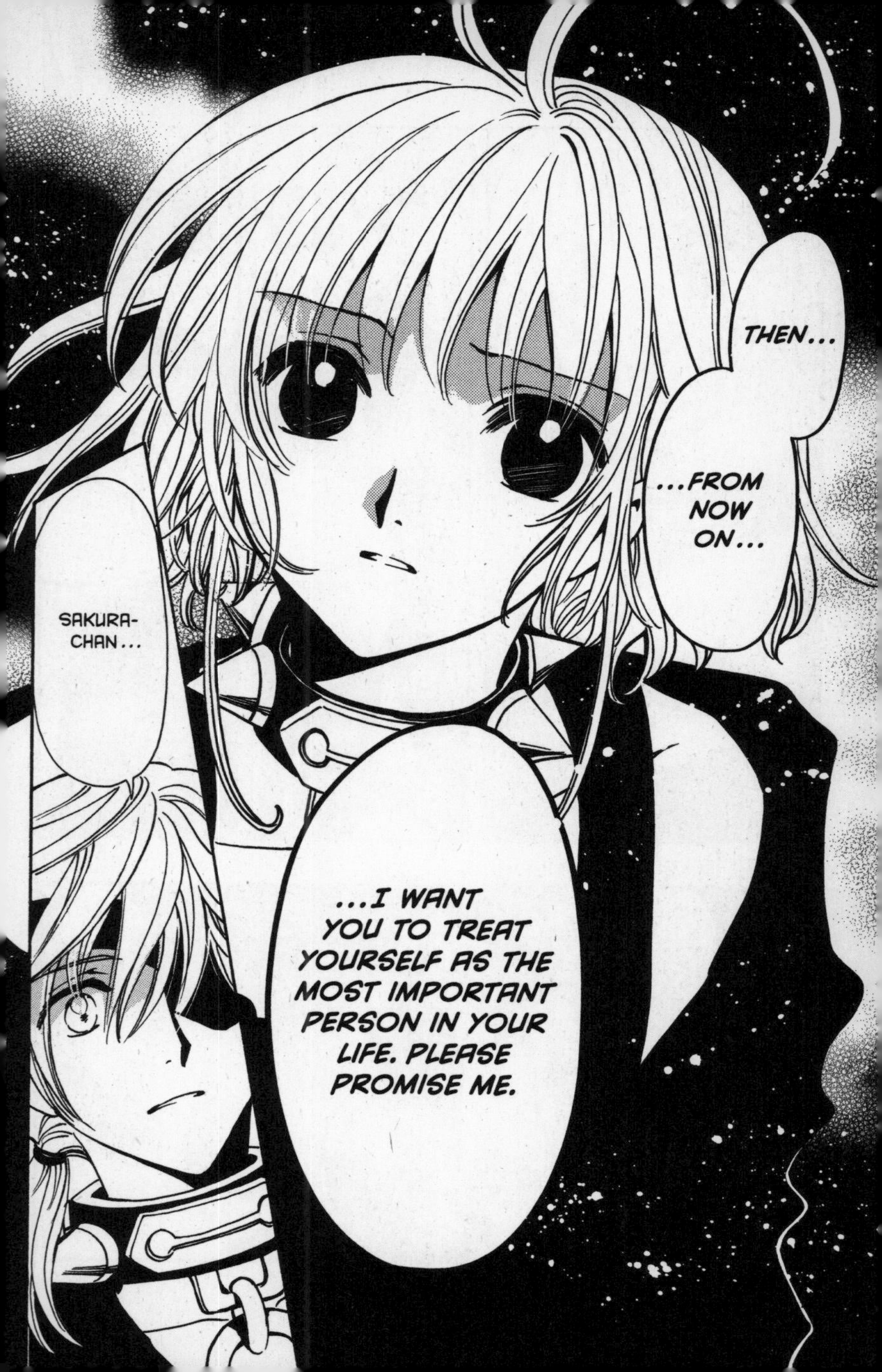
THEN...
...FROM NOW ON...
...I WANT YOU TO TREAT YOURSELF AS THE MOST IMPORTANT PERSON IN YOUR LIFE. PLEASE PROMISE ME.
SAKURA-CHAN...

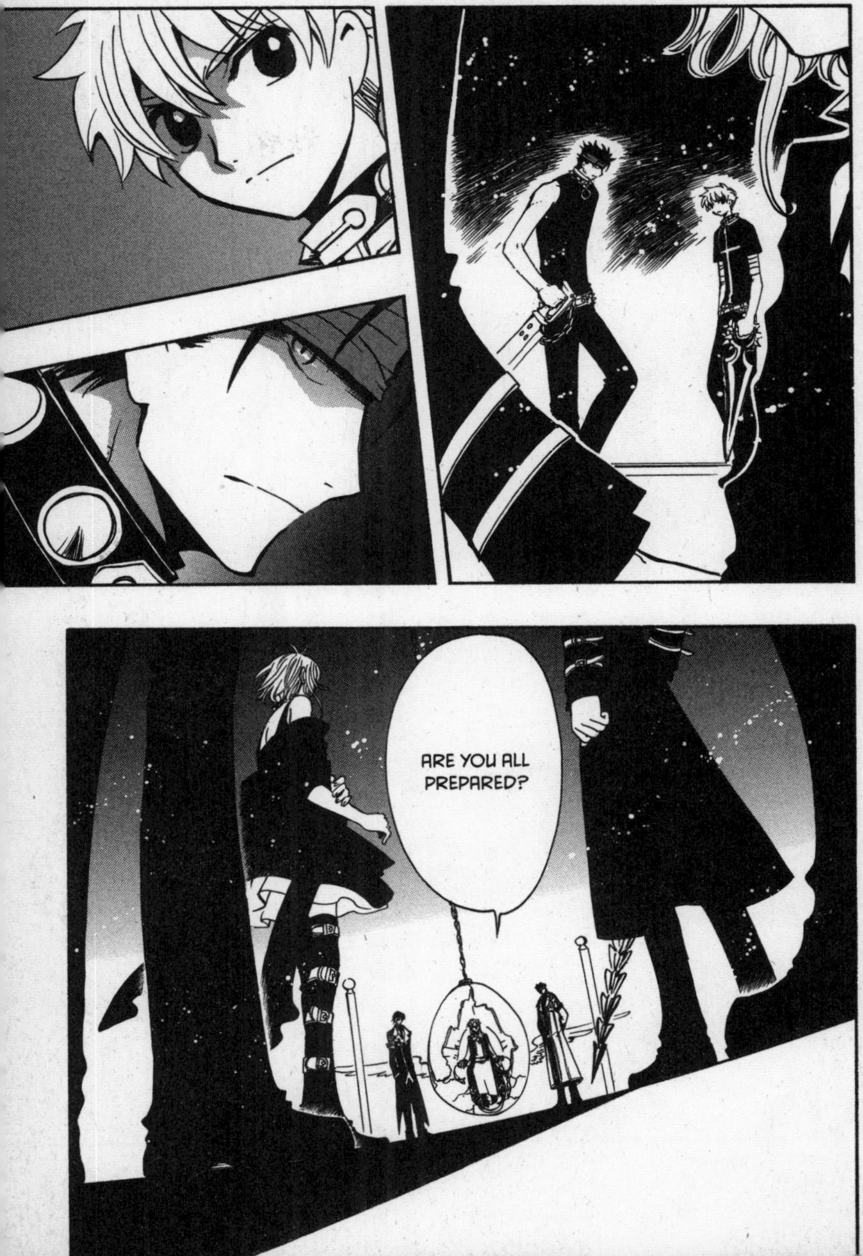
ARE YOU ALL
PREPARED?

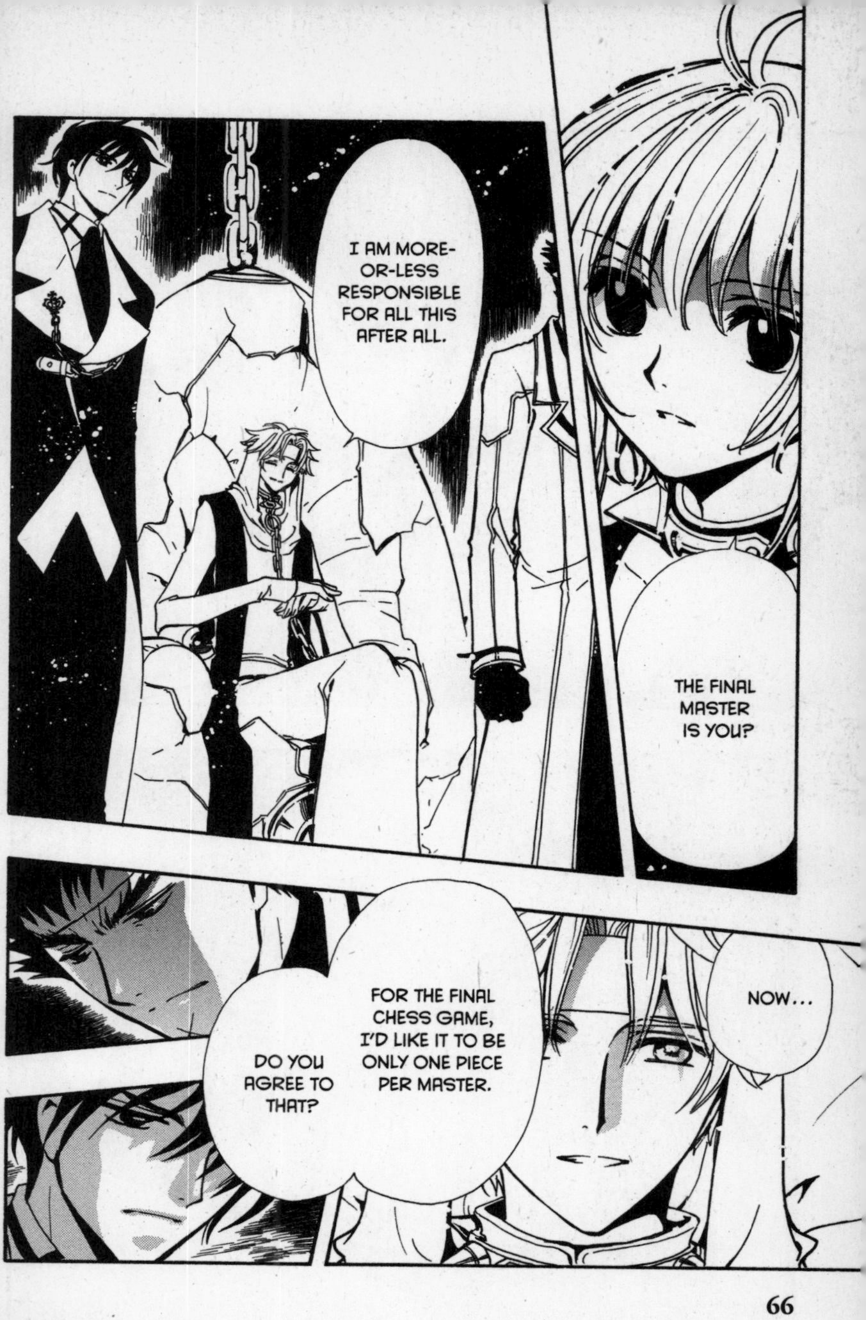
THE FINAL MASTER IS YOU?
I AM MORE-OR-LESS RESPONSIBLE FOR ALL THIS AFTER ALL.
NOW...
FOR THE FINAL CHESS GAME, I'D LIKE IT TO BE ONLY ONE PIECE PER MASTER.
DO YOU AGREE TO THAT?

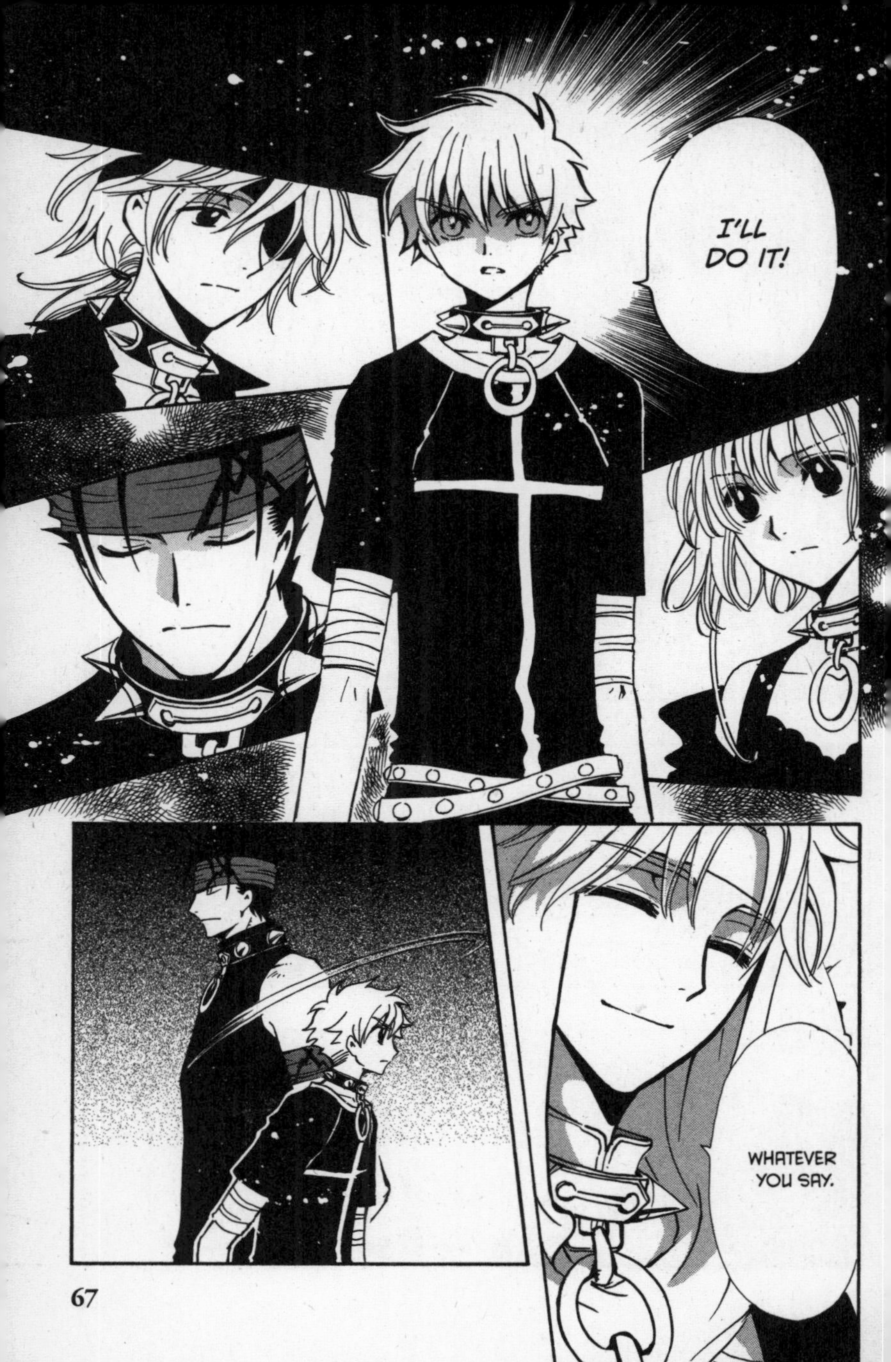
I'LL DO IT!
WHATEVER YOU SAY.

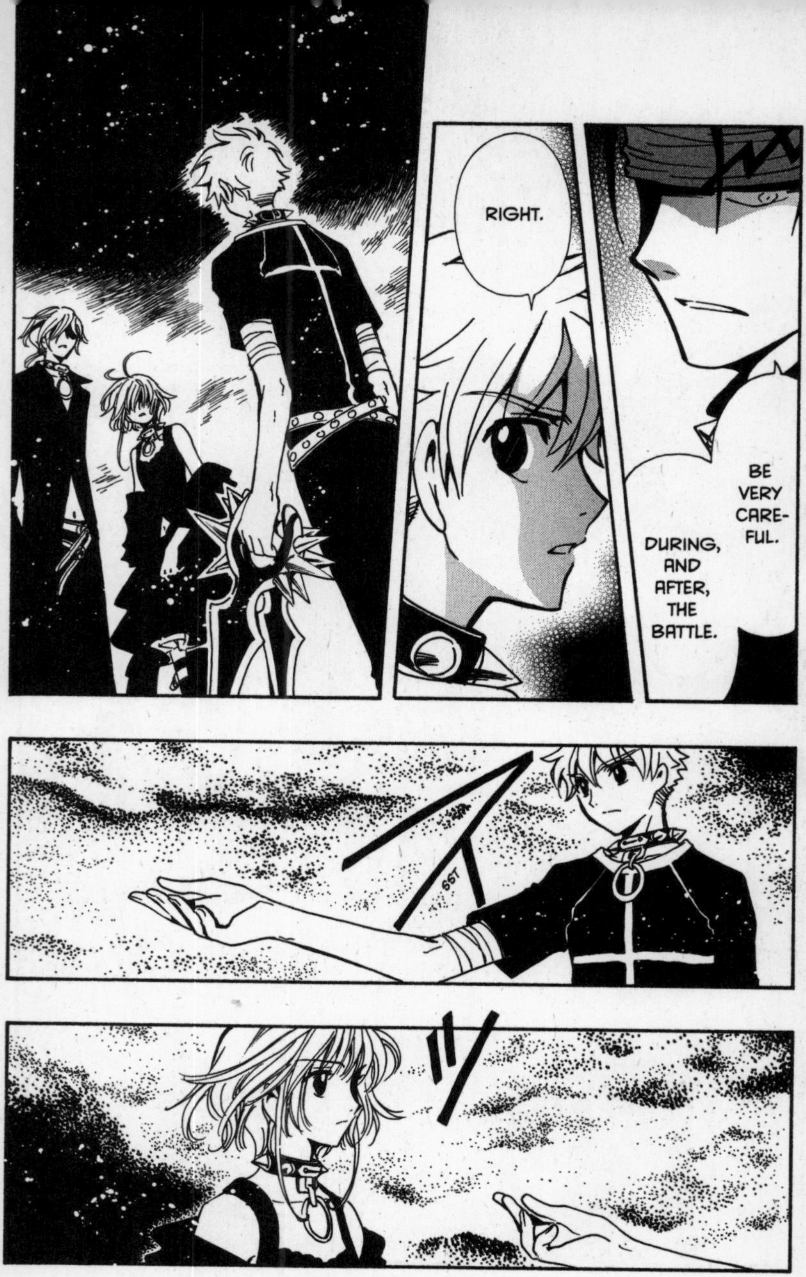
BE VERY CARE-FUL.
DURING, AND AFTER, THE BATTLE.
RIGHT.
SST

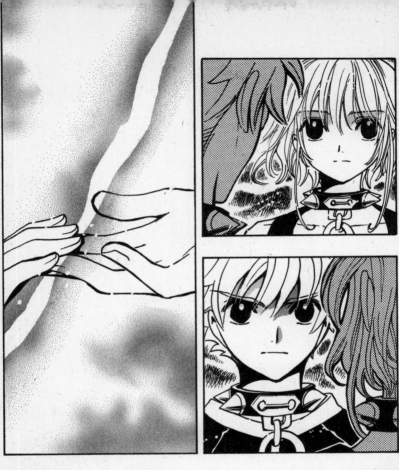

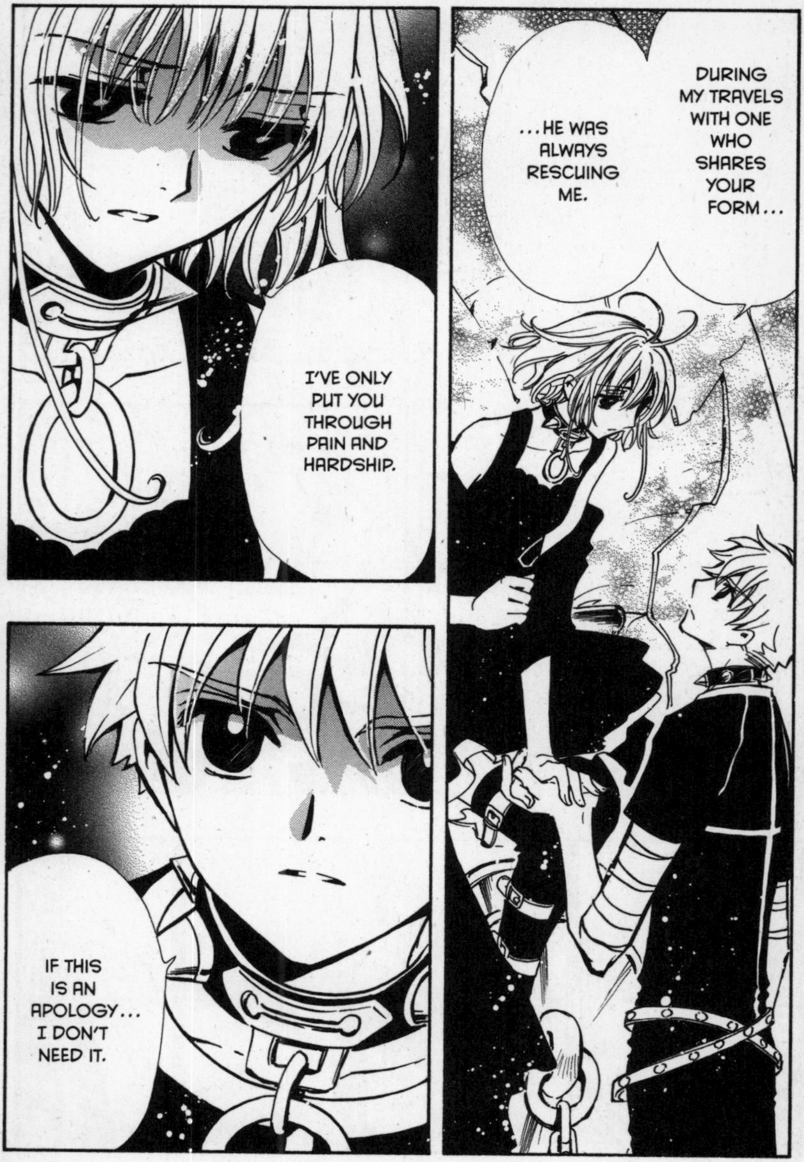
DURING MY TRAVELS WITH ONE WHO SHARES YOUR FORM...
...HE WAS ALWAYS RESCUING ME.
I'VE ONLY PUT YOU THROUGH PAIN AND HARDSHIP.
IF THIS IS AN APOLOGY... I DON'T NEED IT.

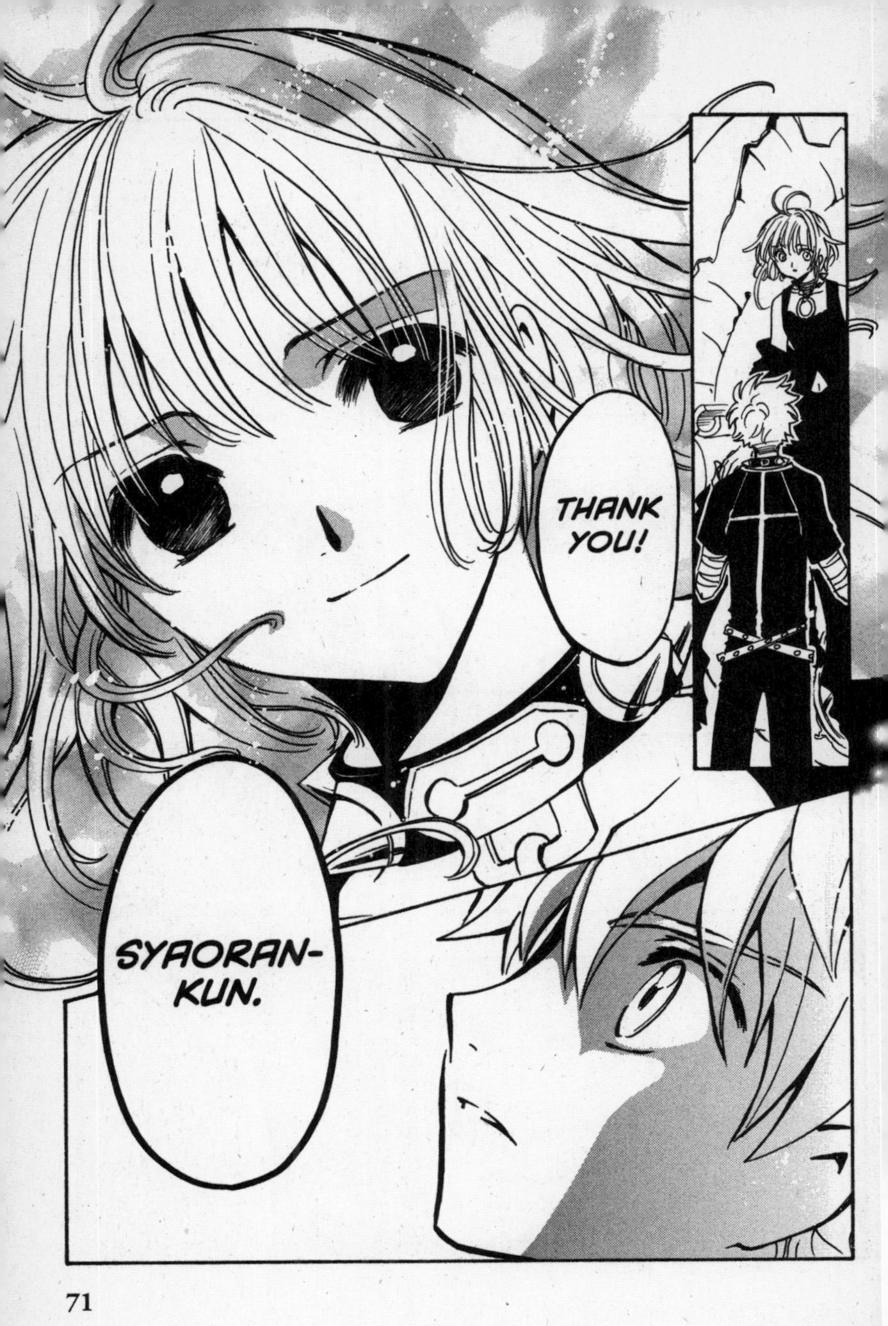
THANK YOU!
SYAORAN-KUN.

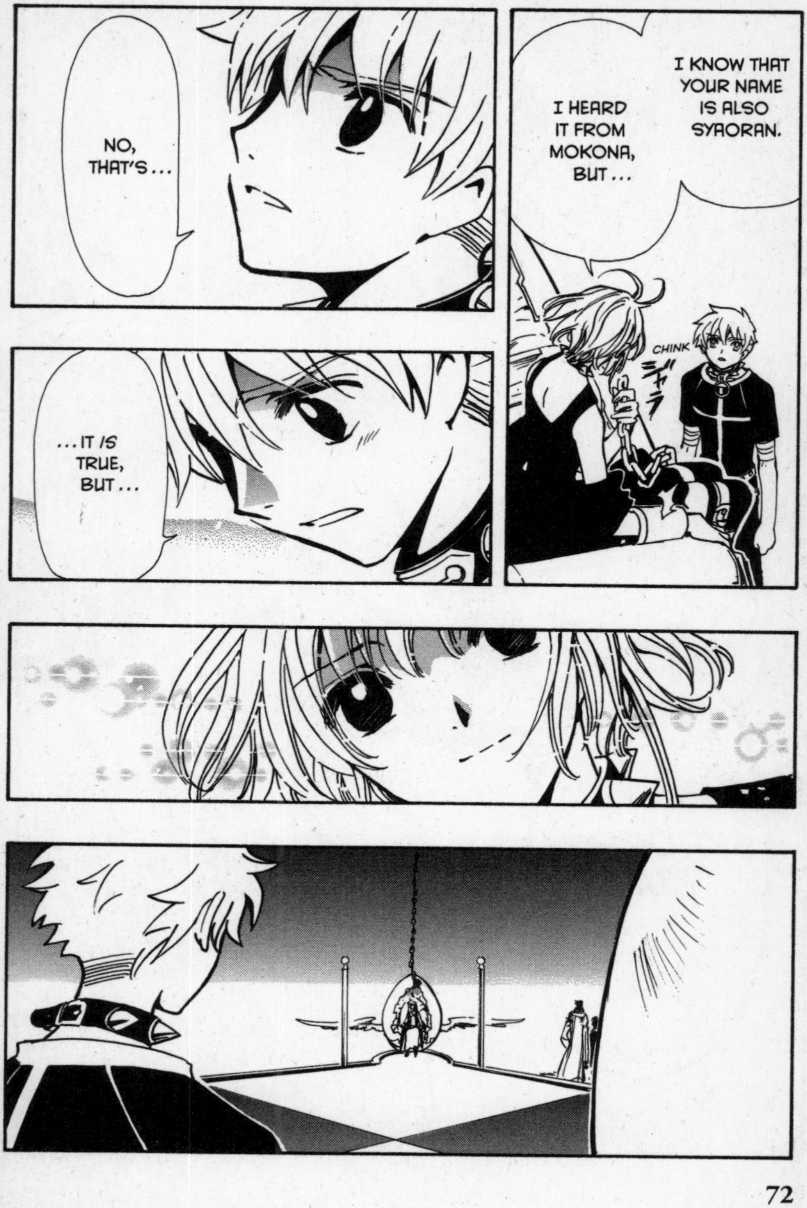
I KNOW THAT YOUR NAME IS ALSO SYAORAN.
I HEARD IT FROM MOKONA, BUT...
CHINK
NO, THAT'S...
...IT IS TRUE, BUT...

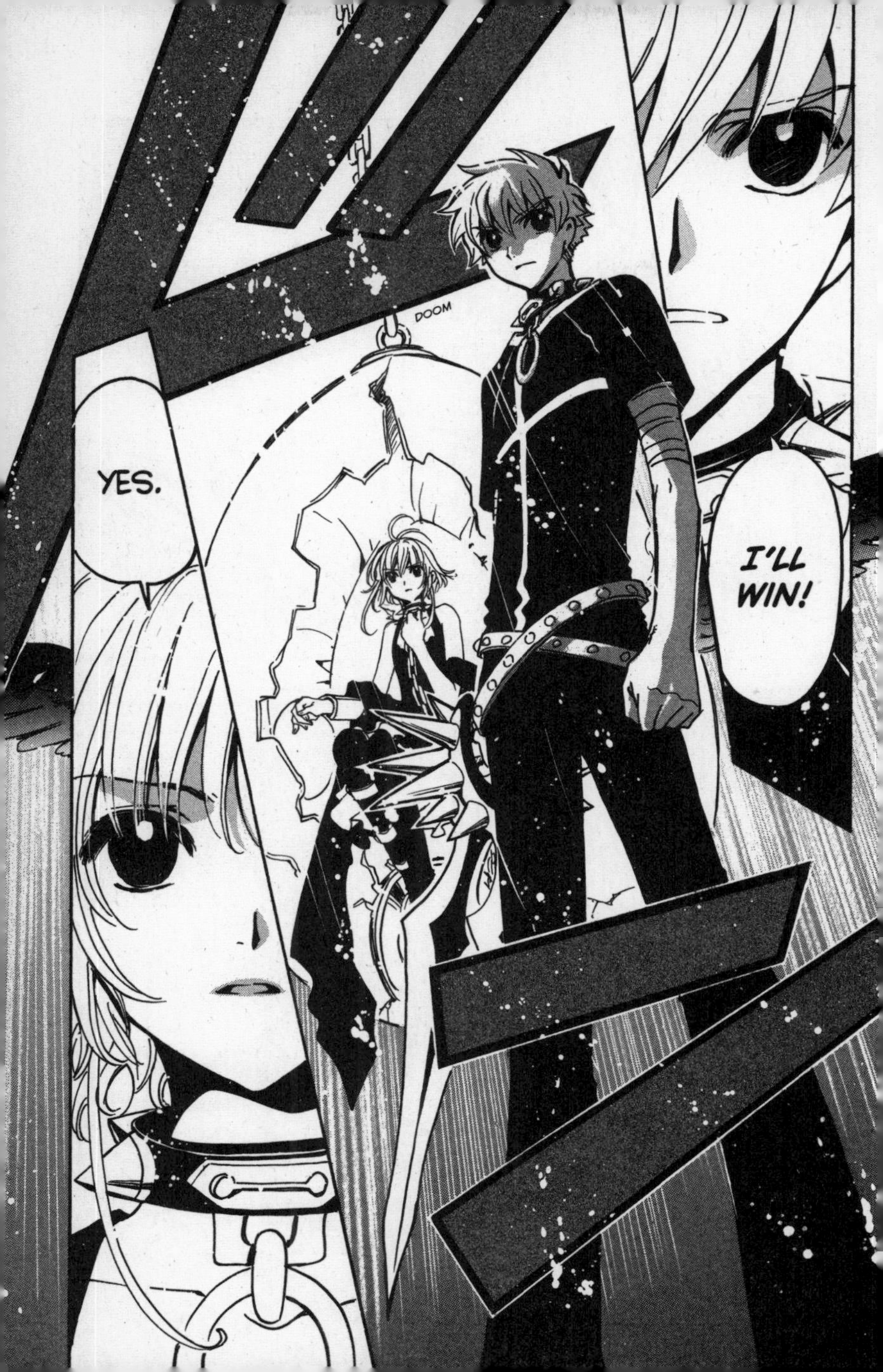
I'LL WIN!
DOOM
YES.

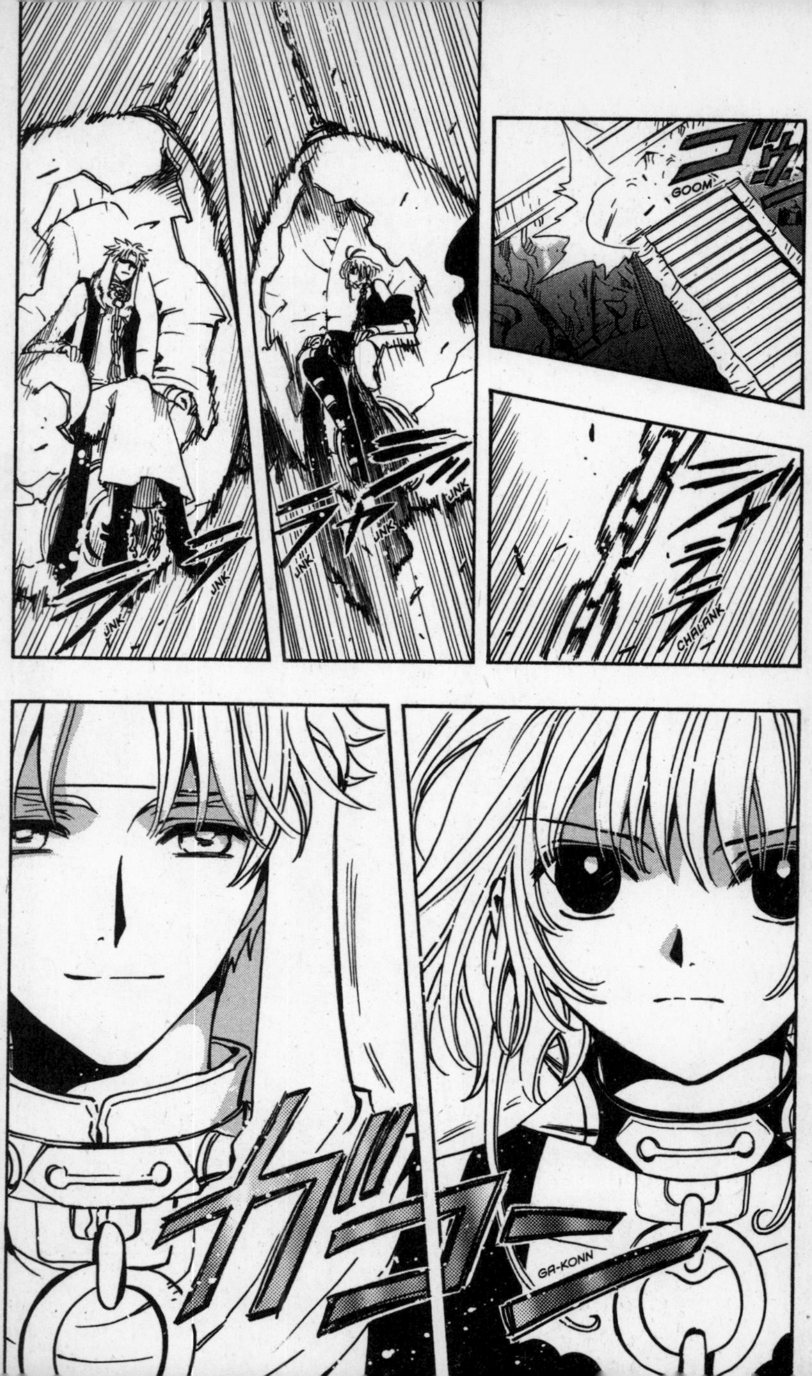
GOOM
CHALANK
JNK
JNK
JNK
JNK
JNK
GA-KONN

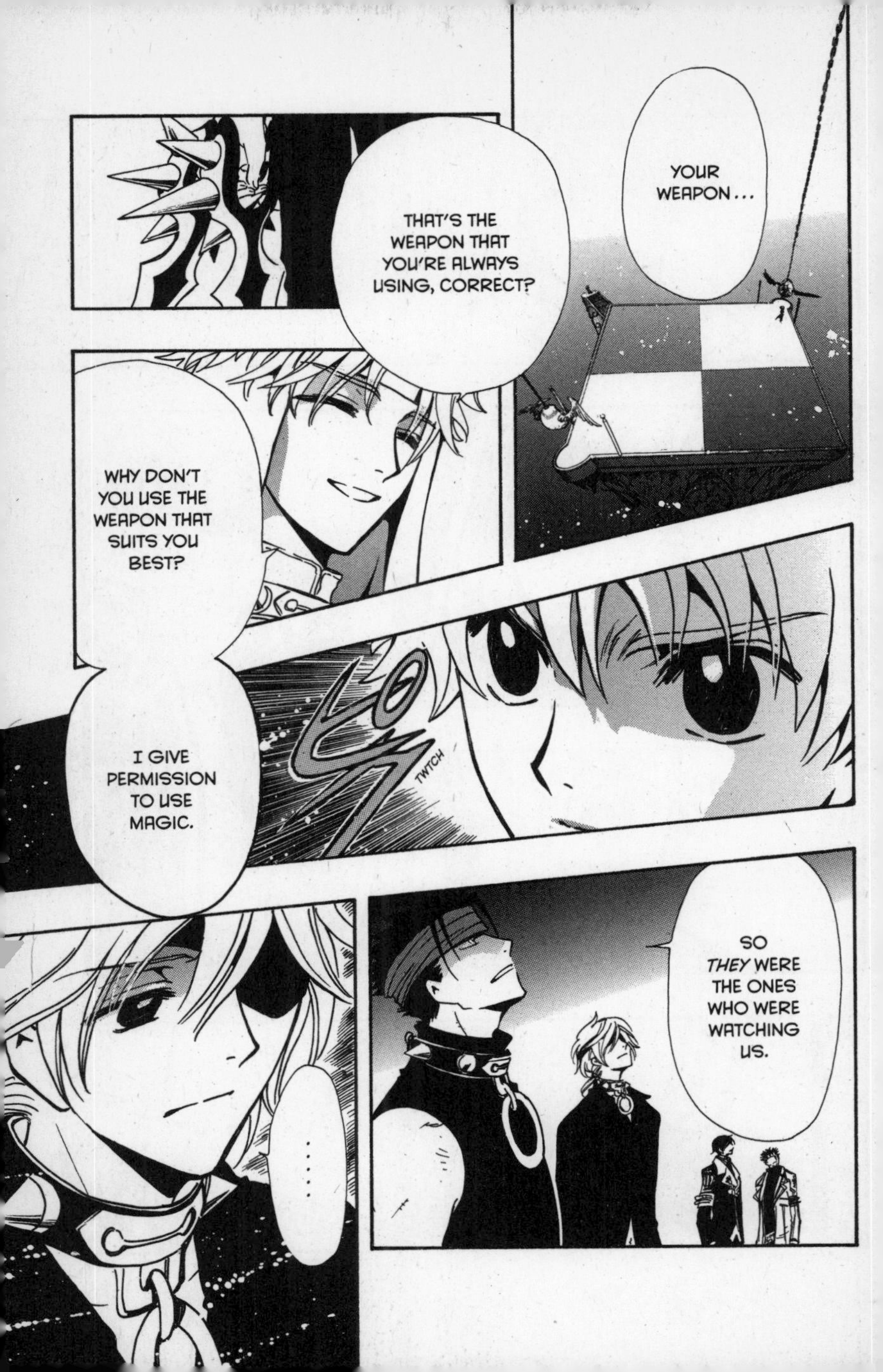

YOUR WEAPON...
THAT'S THE WEAPON THAT YOU'RE ALWAYS USING, CORRECT?
WHY DON'T YOU USE THE WEAPON THAT SUITS YOU BEST?
TWTCH
I GIVE PERMISSION TO USE MAGIC.
SO *THEY* WERE THE ONES WHO WERE WATCHING US.
.....

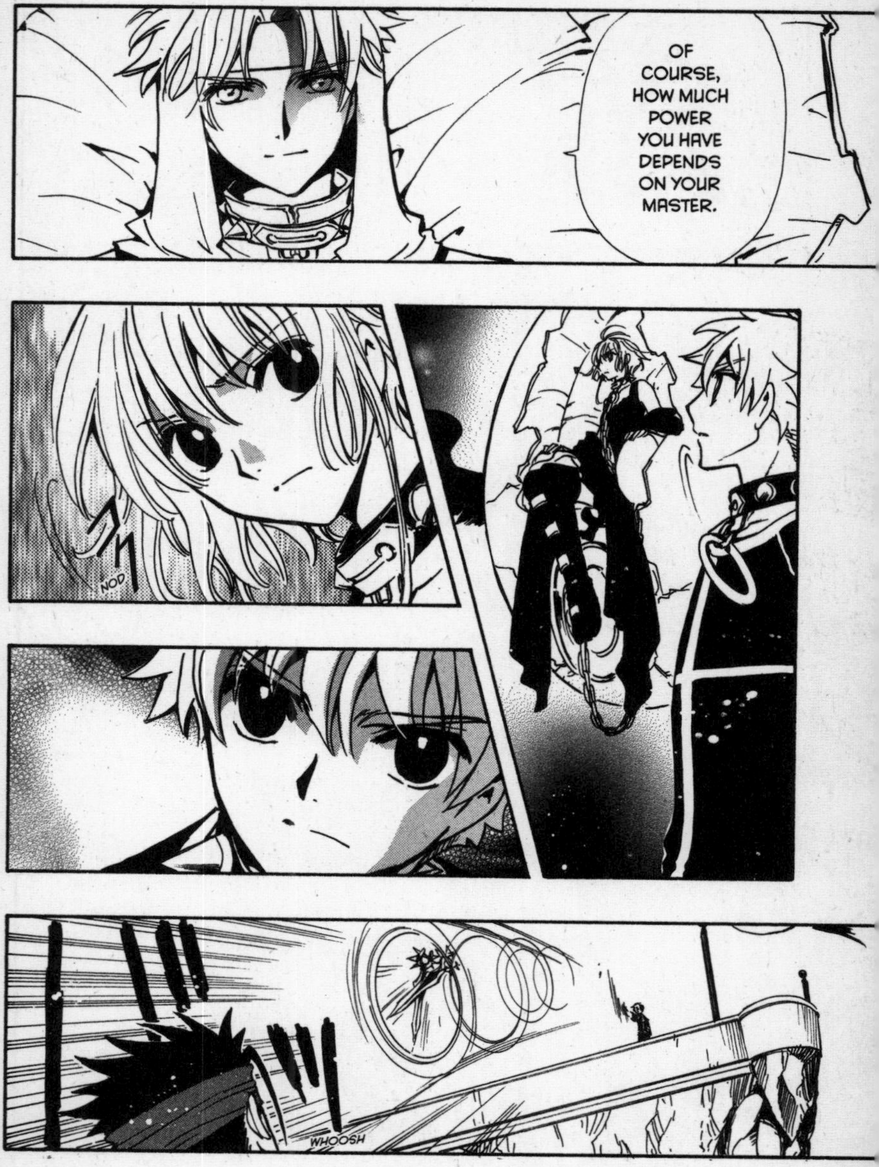
OF COURSE, HOW MUCH POWER YOU HAVE DEPENDS ON YOUR MASTER.
NOD
WHOOSH

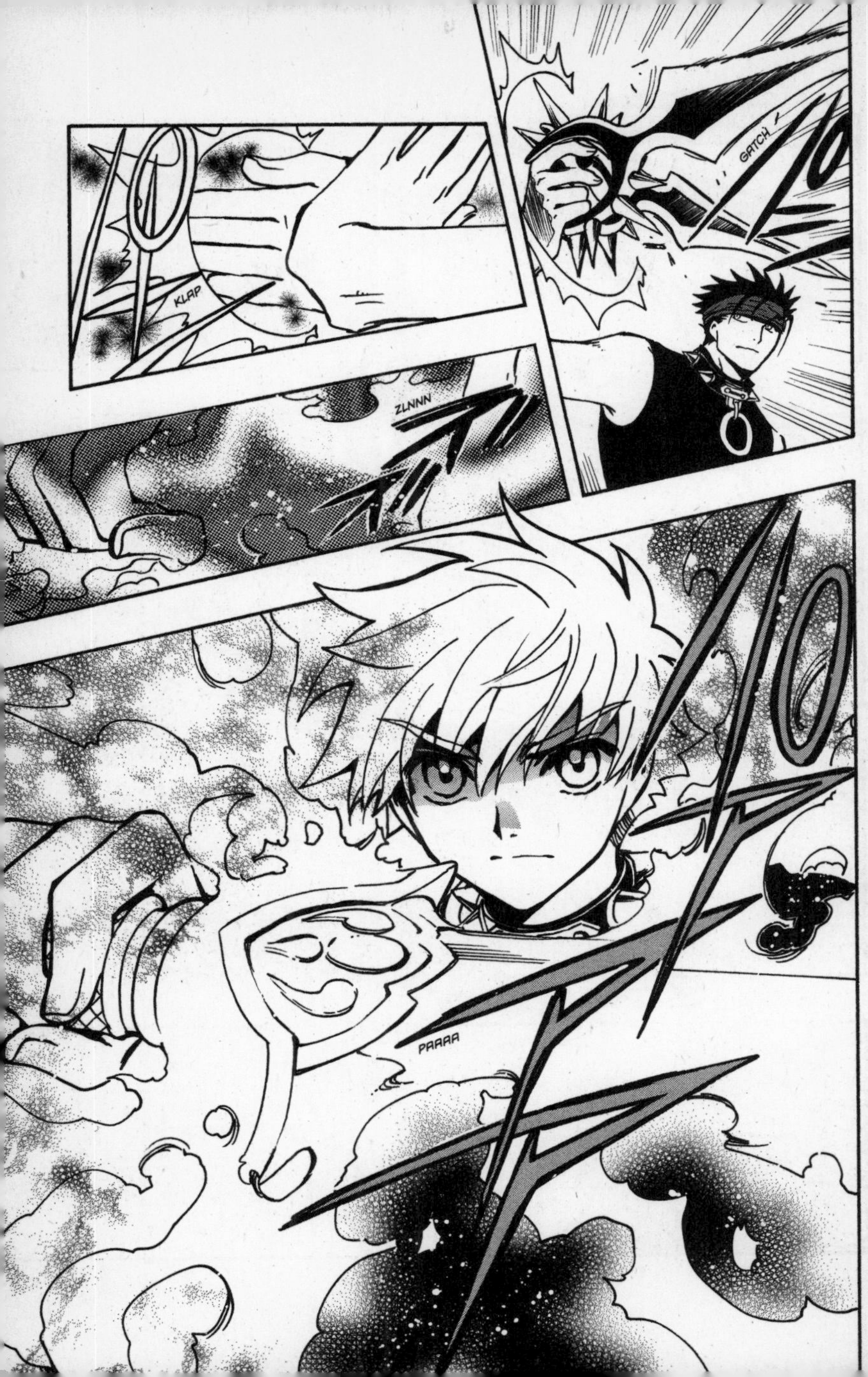
GATCH
KLAP
ZLNNN
PARRA

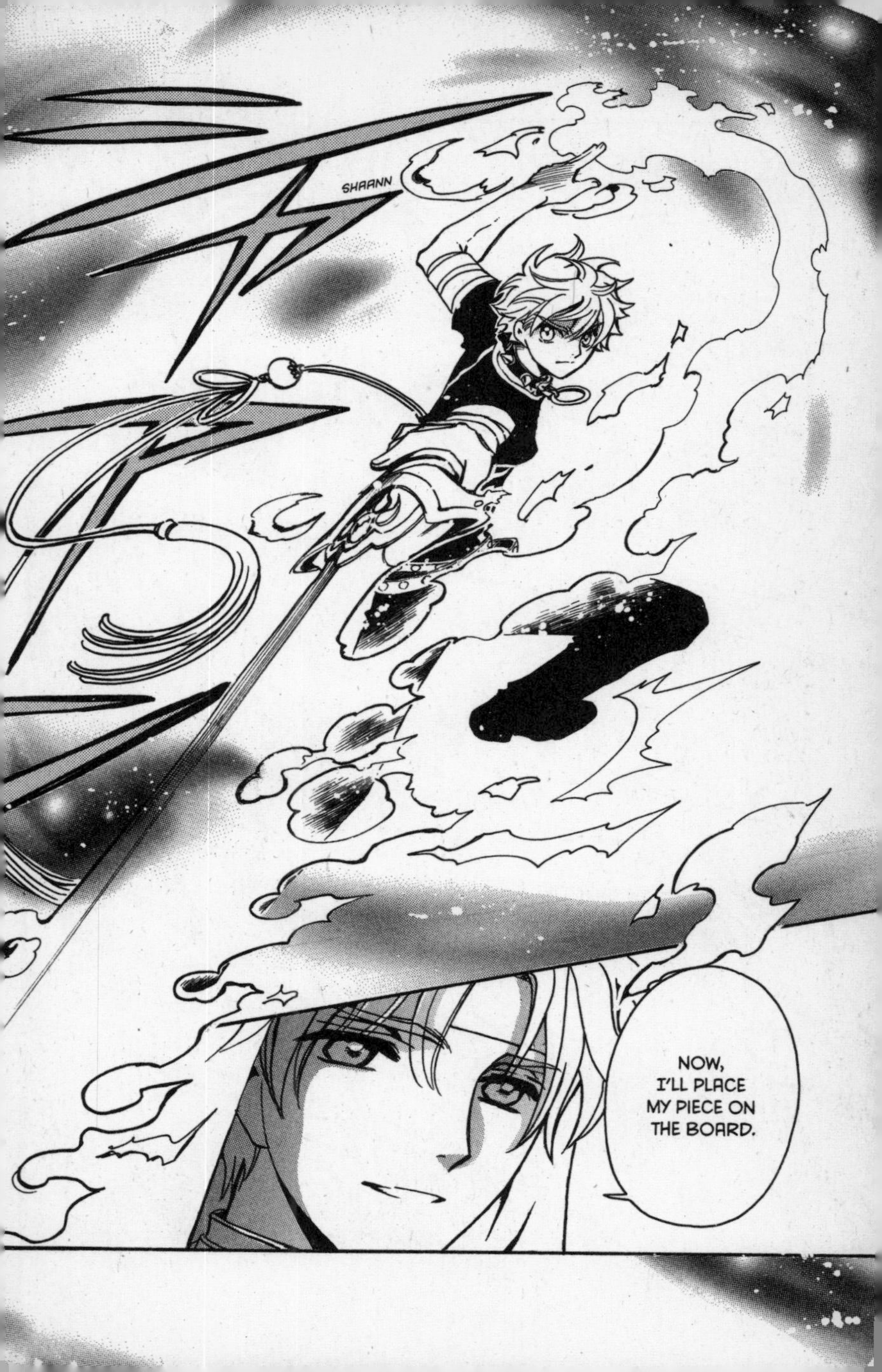
SHAANN
NOW, I'LL PLACE MY PIECE ON THE BOARD.

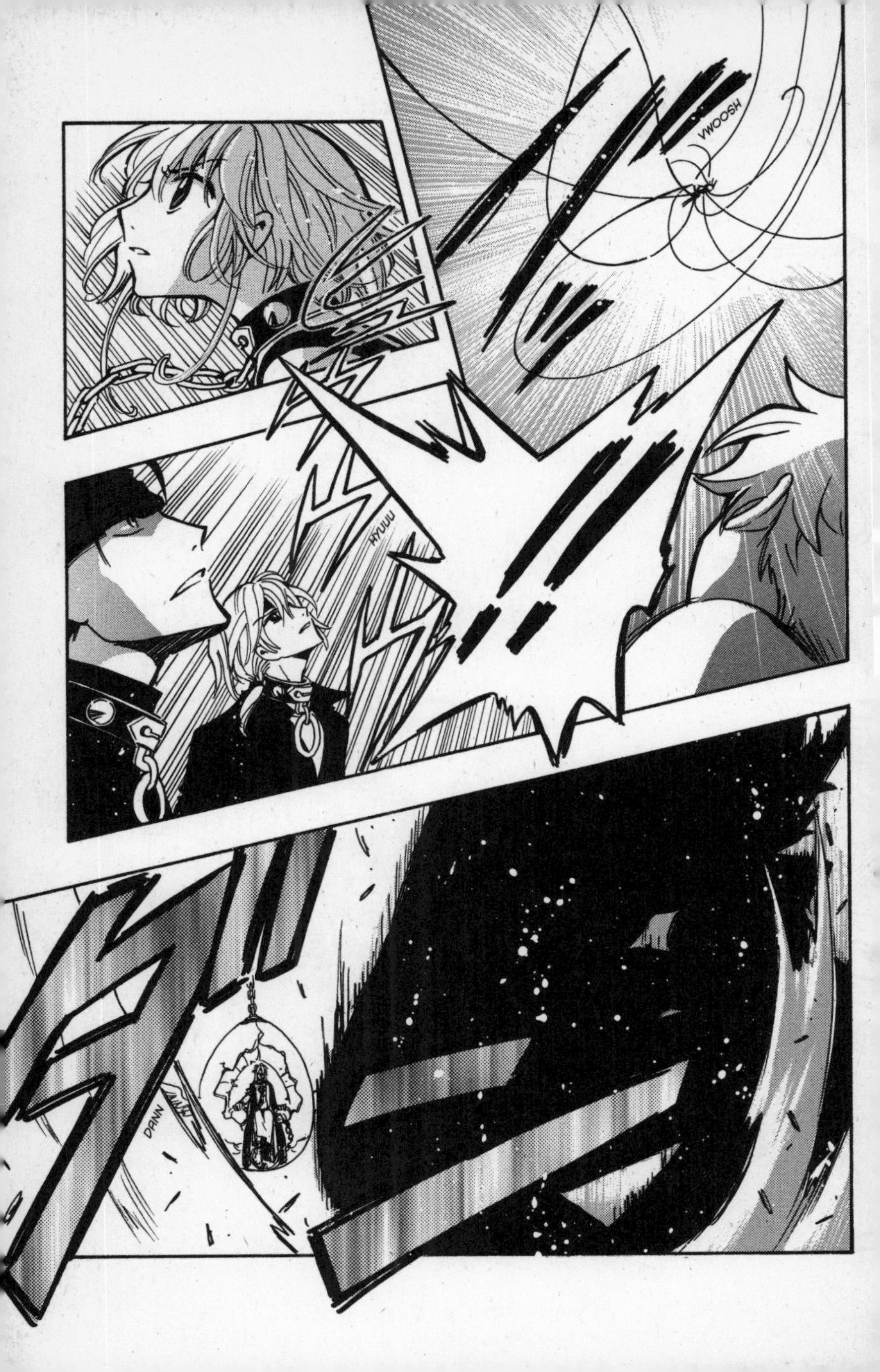
VWOOSH
HYUUU
DANN

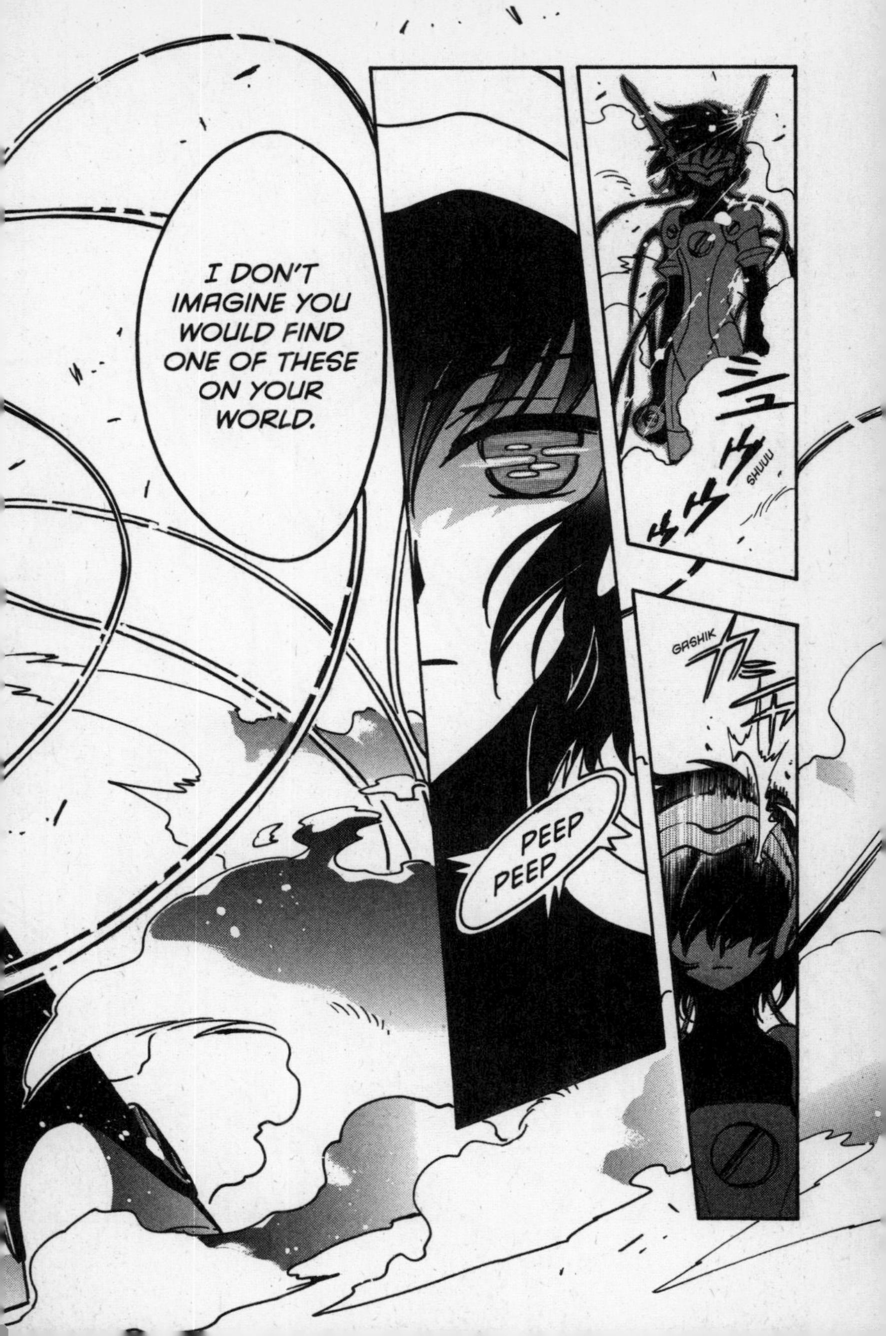
SHUUU
GASHIK
PEEP PEEP
I DON'T IMAGINE YOU WOULD FIND ONE OF THESE ON YOUR WORLD.

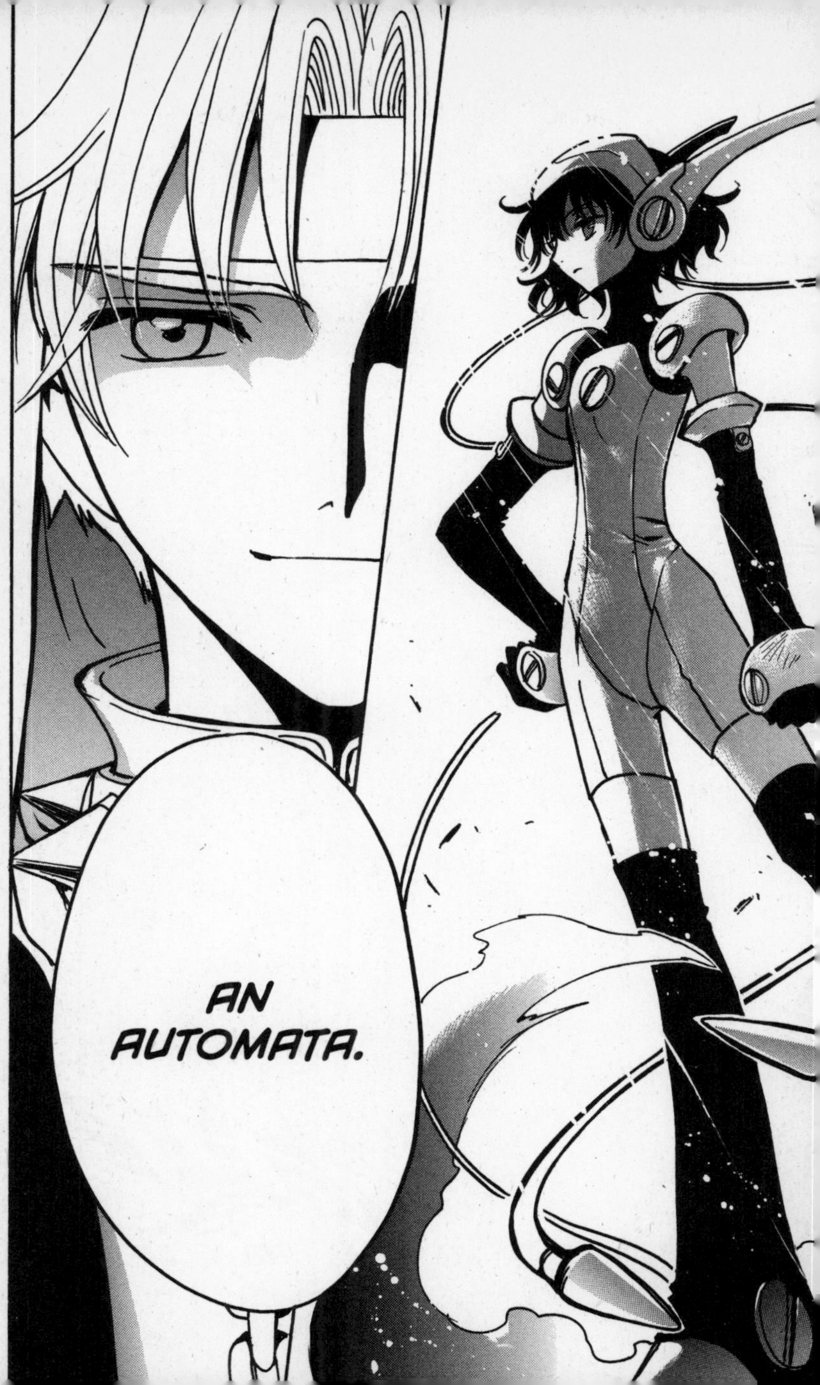
AN AUTOMATA.

ツバサ
RESERVoir CHRoNiCLE

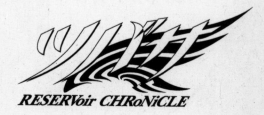

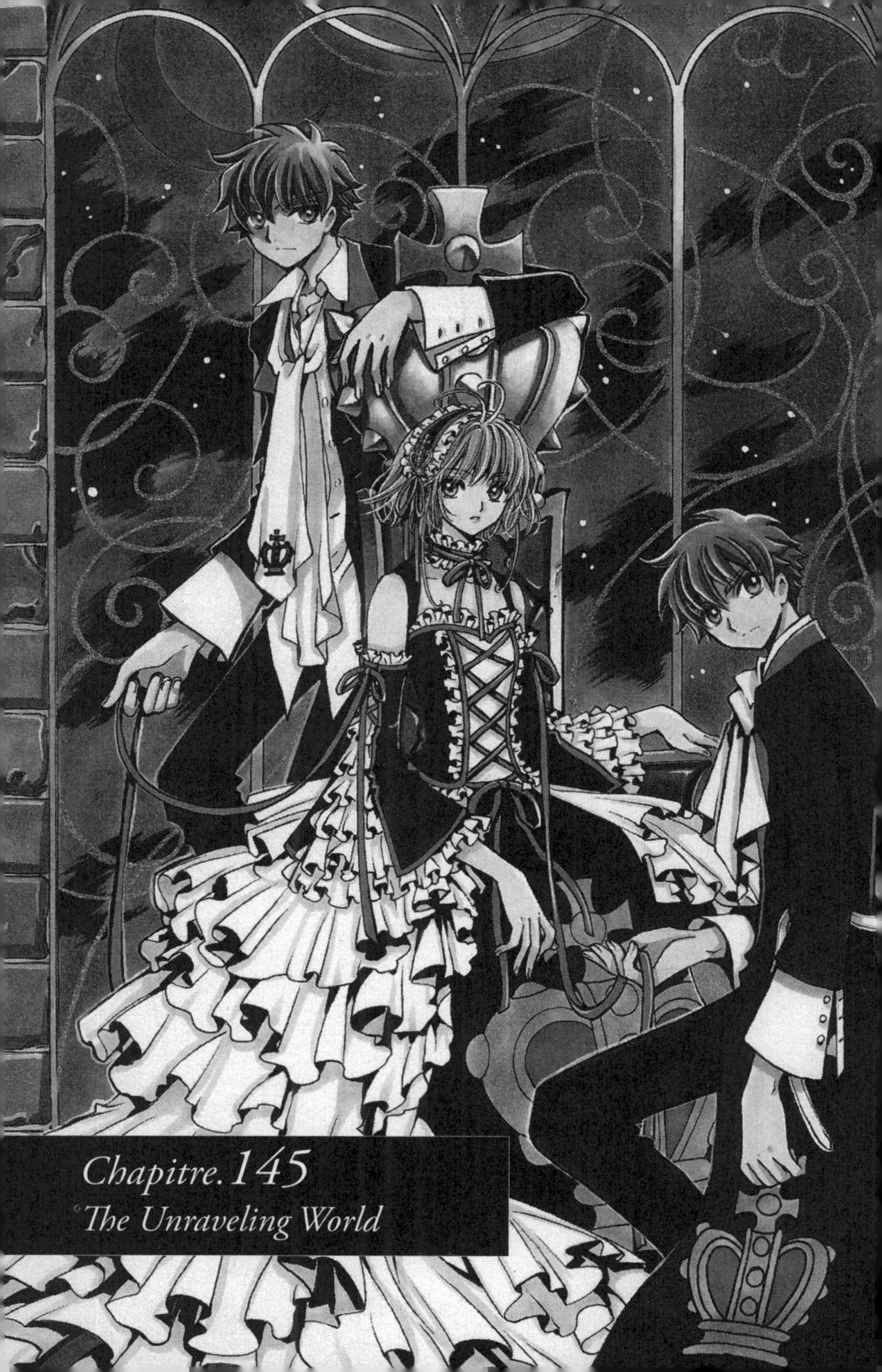

Chapitre. 145

The Unraveling World

ツバサ

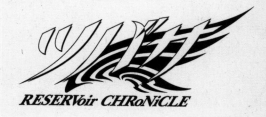

RESERVoir CHRoNiCLE

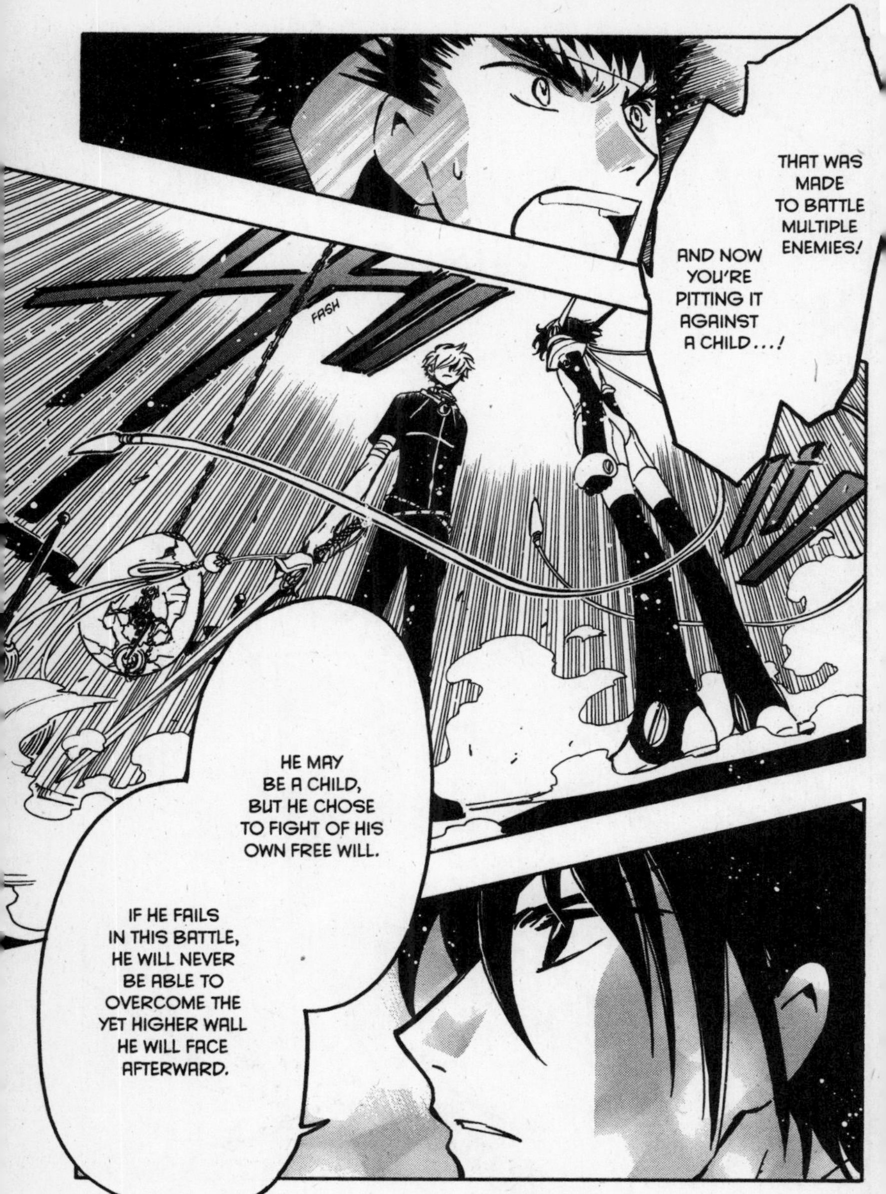
THAT WAS MADE TO BATTLE MULTIPLE ENEMIES!
AND NOW YOU'RE PITTING IT AGAINST A CHILD...!
FASH
HE MAY BE A CHILD, BUT HE CHOSE TO FIGHT OF HIS OWN FREE WILL.
IF HE FAILS IN THIS BATTLE, HE WILL NEVER BE ABLE TO OVERCOME THE YET HIGHER WALL HE WILL FACE AFTERWARD.

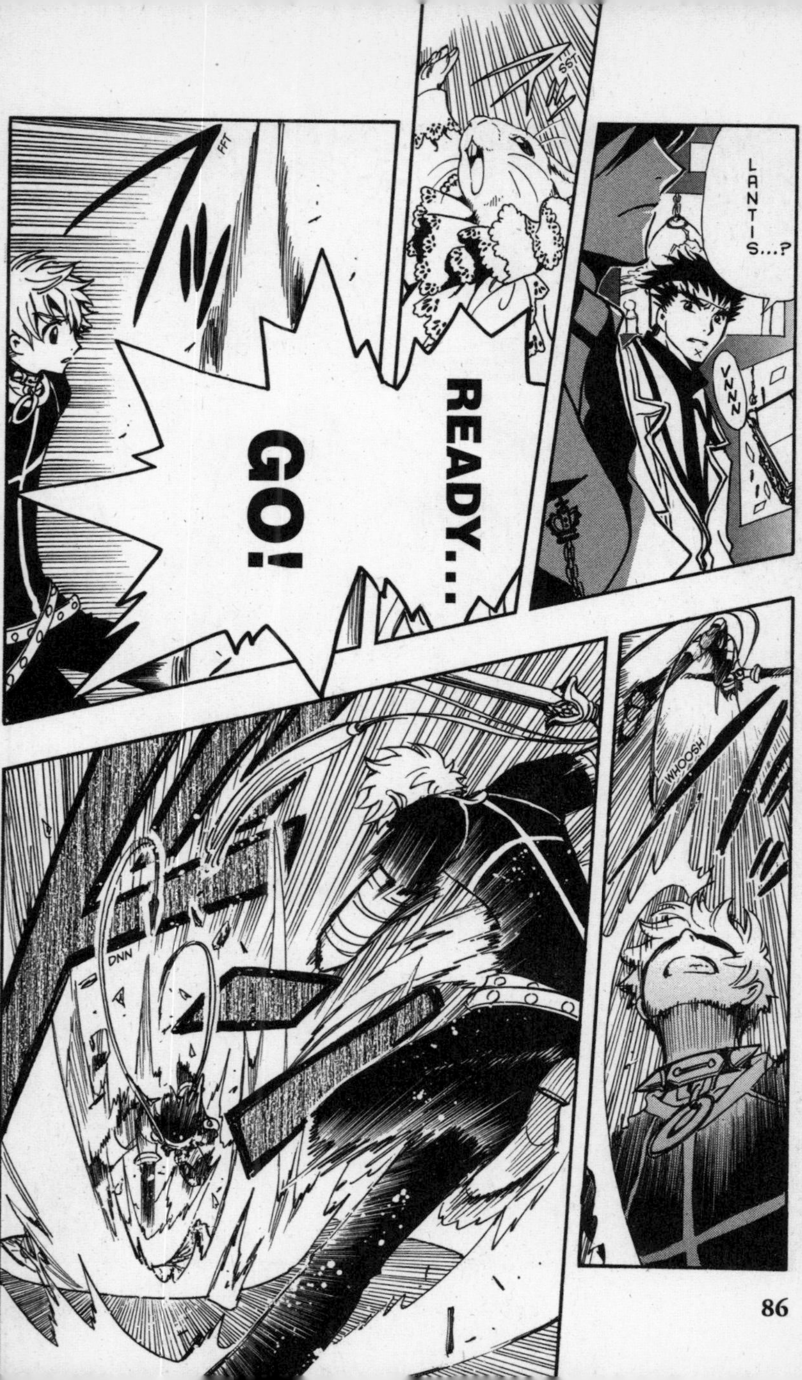
LANTIS...?
VNNN
SST
FFT
READY...
GO!
WHOOSH
DNN

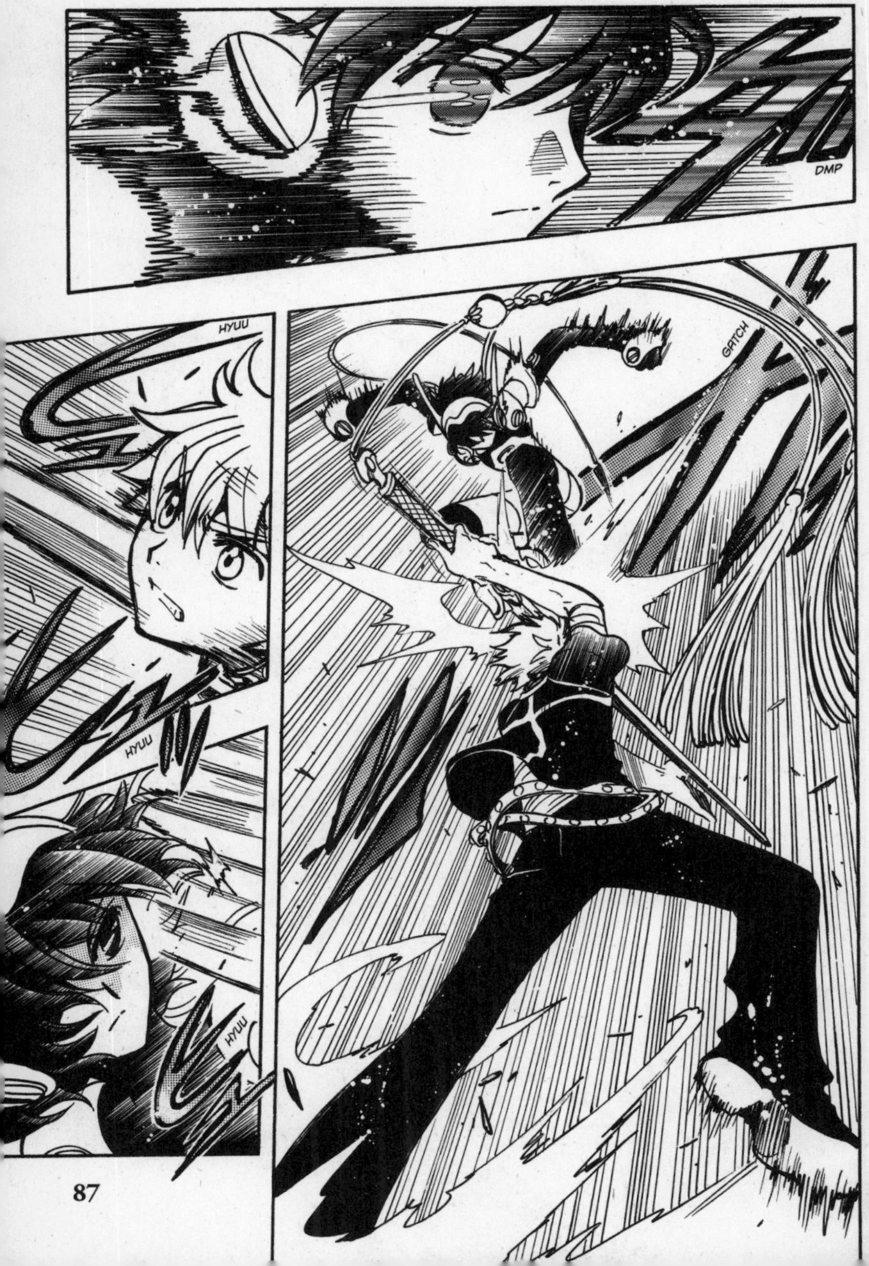
DMP
GATCH
HYUU
HYUU
HYUU

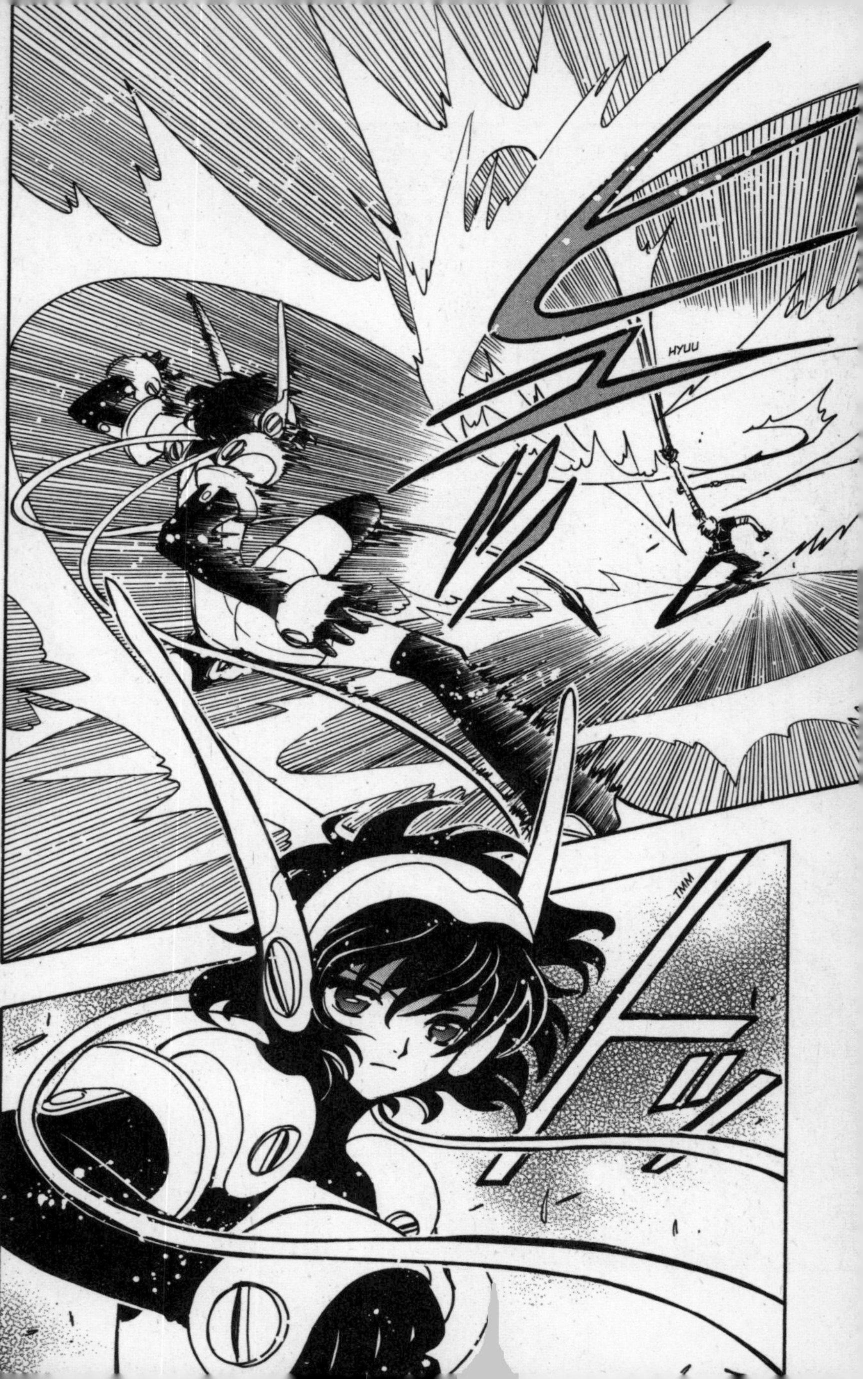
HYUU
TMM

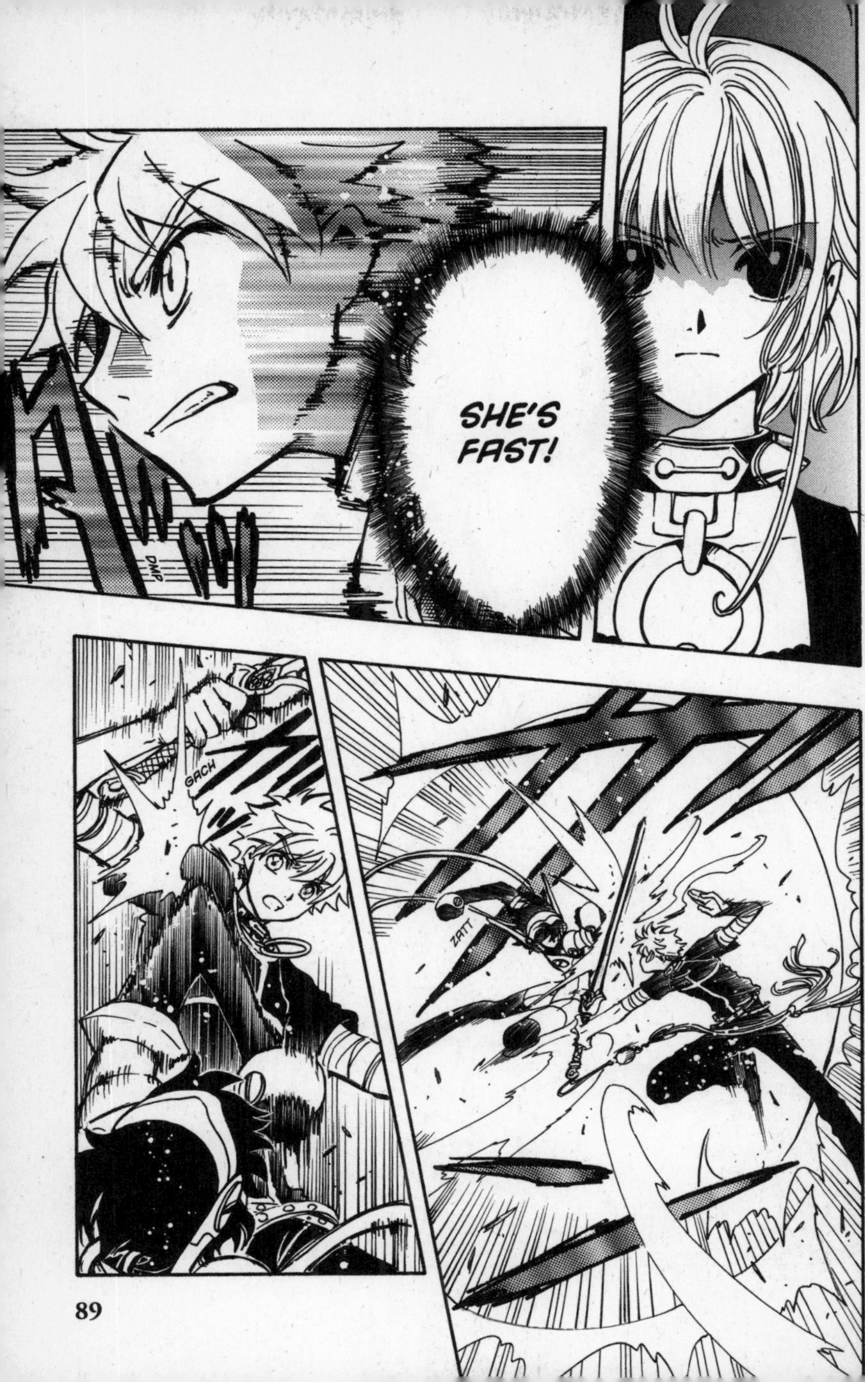
SHE'S FAST!
DMP
ZATT
GACH

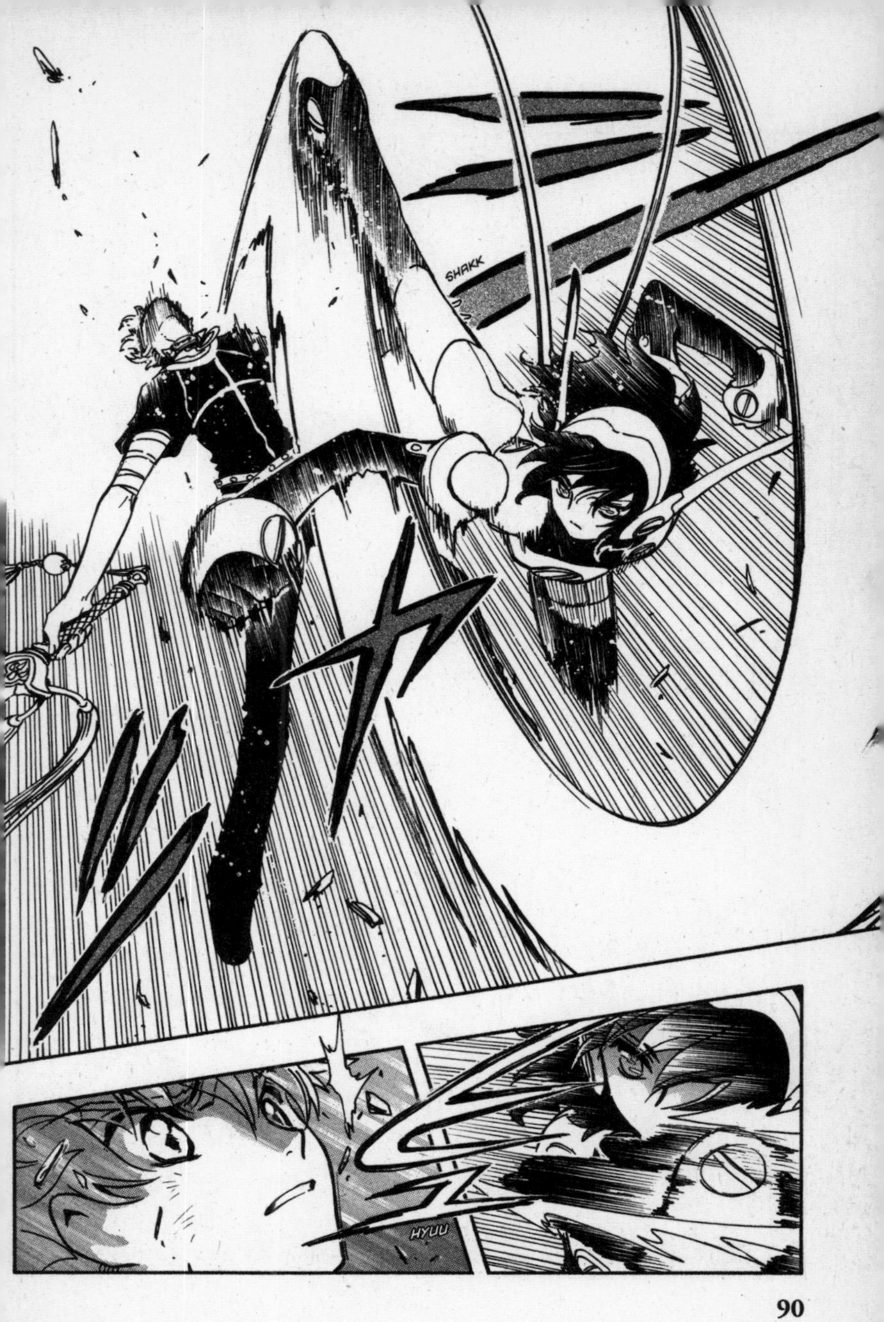
SHAKK
HYUU

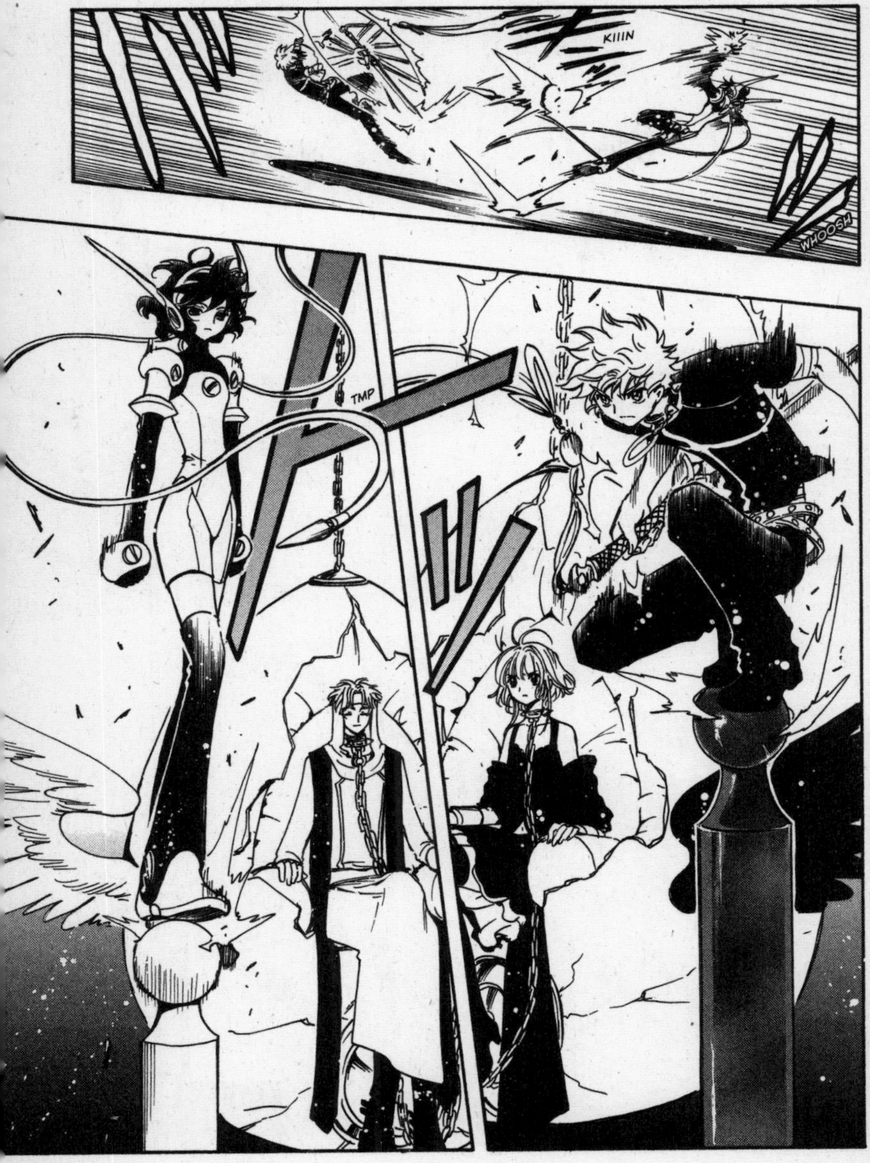
KIIIN
WHOOSH
TMP

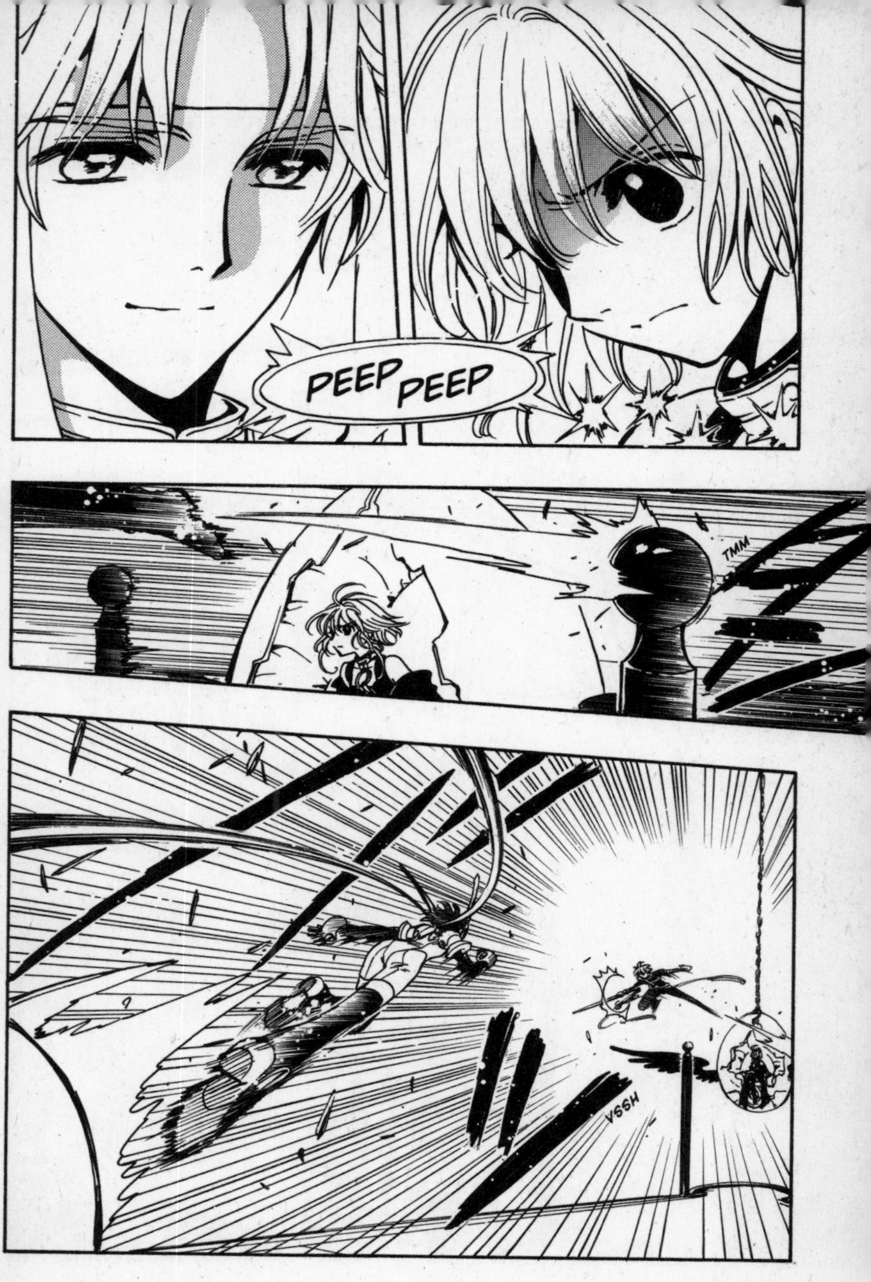
PEEP PEEP
TMM
VSSH

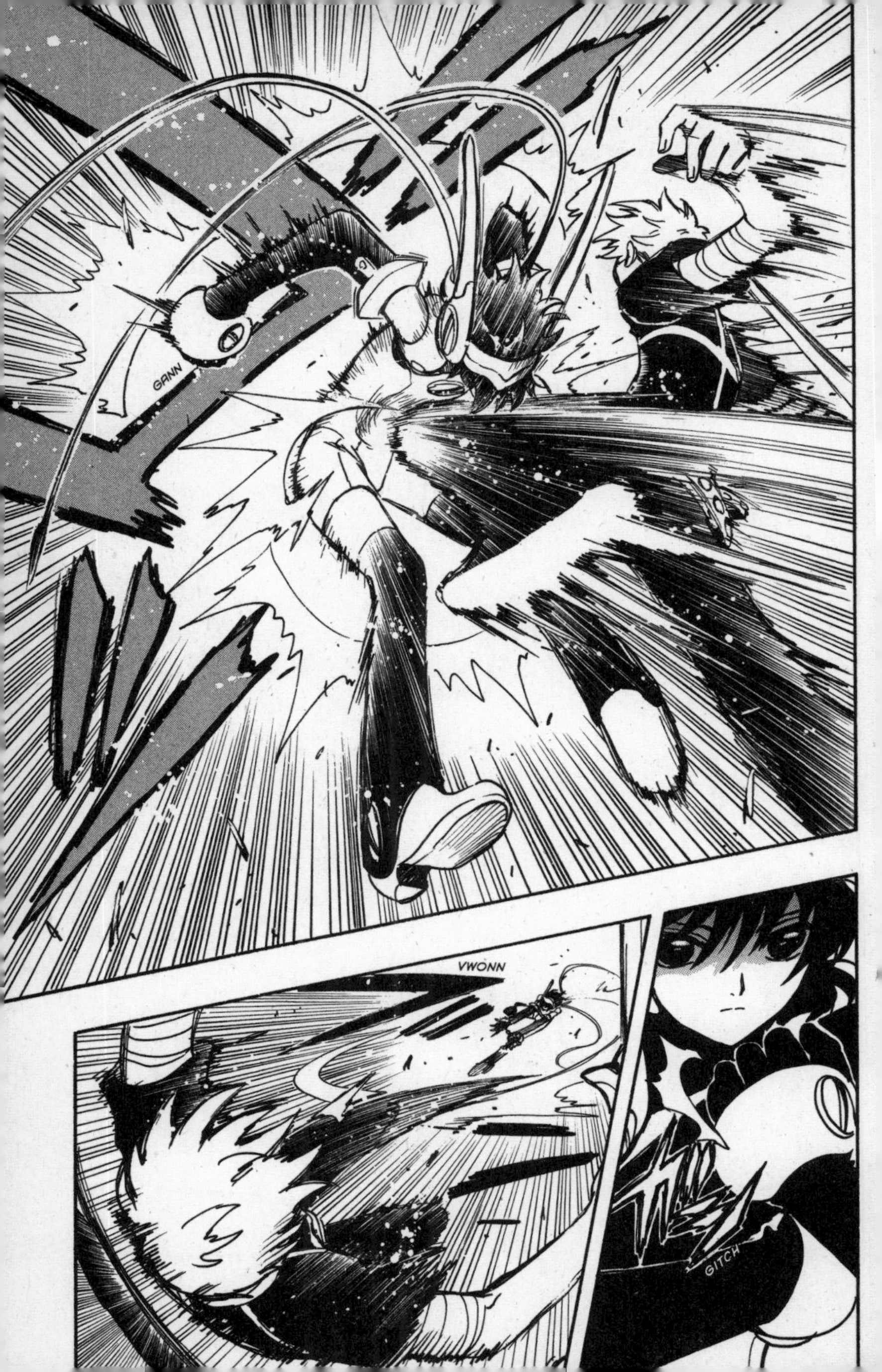
GANN
GITCH
VWONN

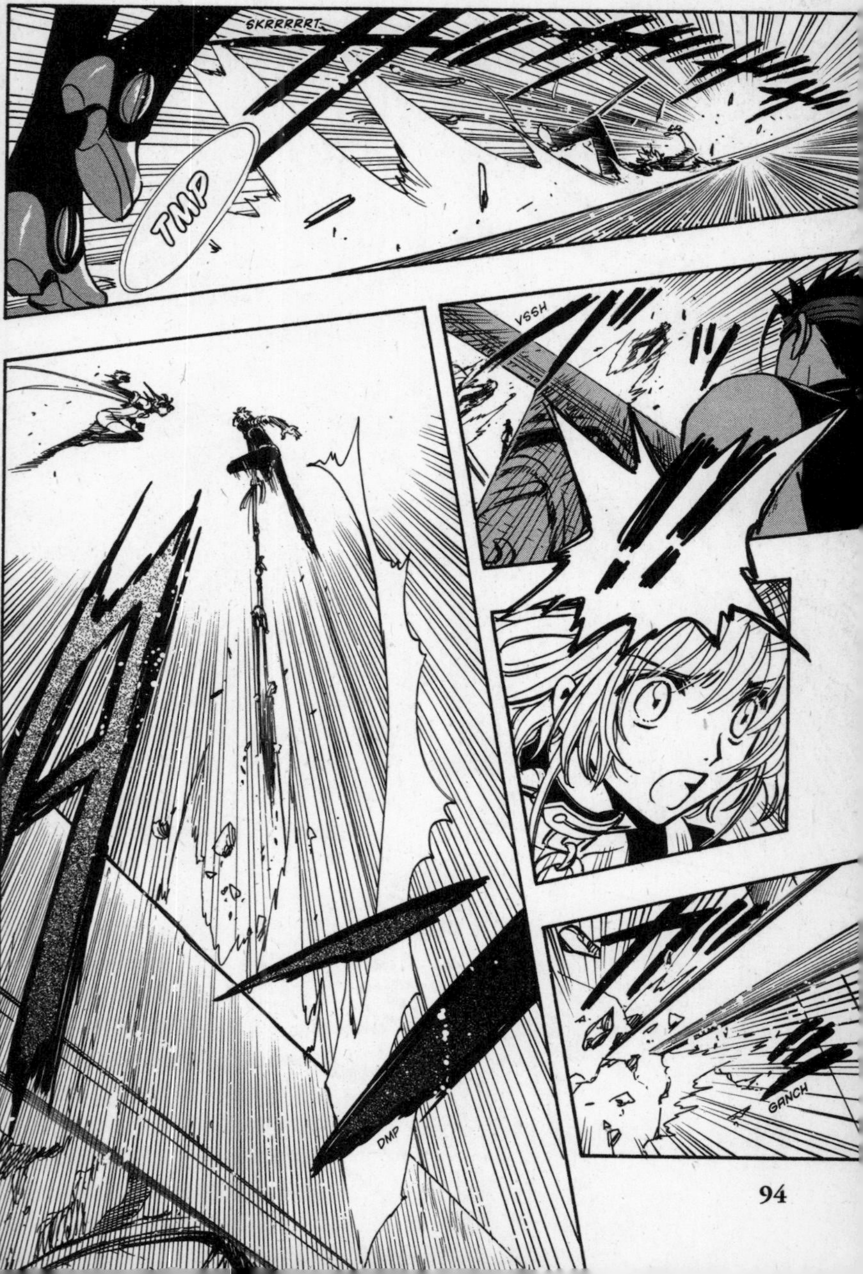
SKRRRRRT
TMP
VSSH
GANCH
DMP

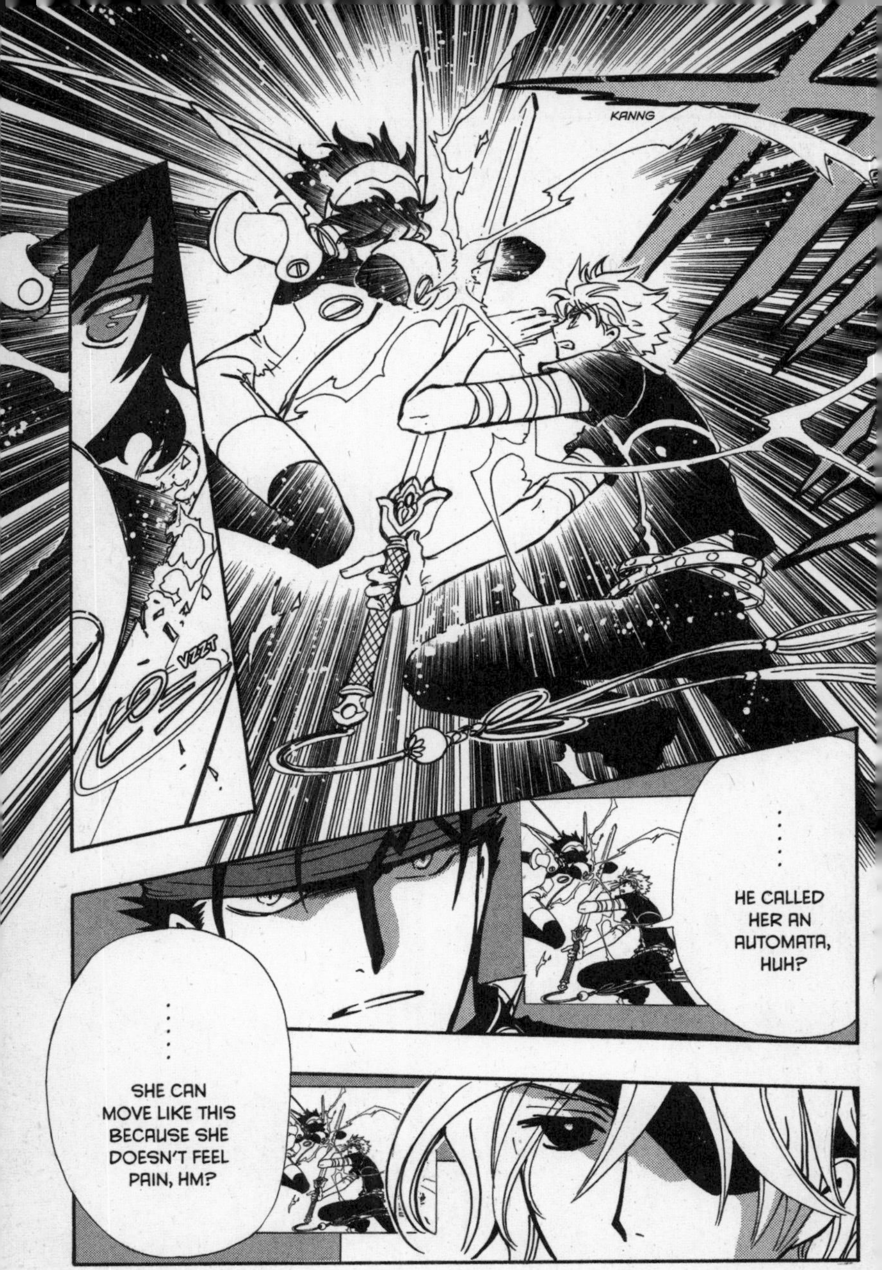
KANNG
VZZT
. . . .
HE CALLED HER AN AUTOMATA, HUH?
. . . .
SHE CAN MOVE LIKE THIS BECAUSE SHE DOESN'T FEEL PAIN, HM?

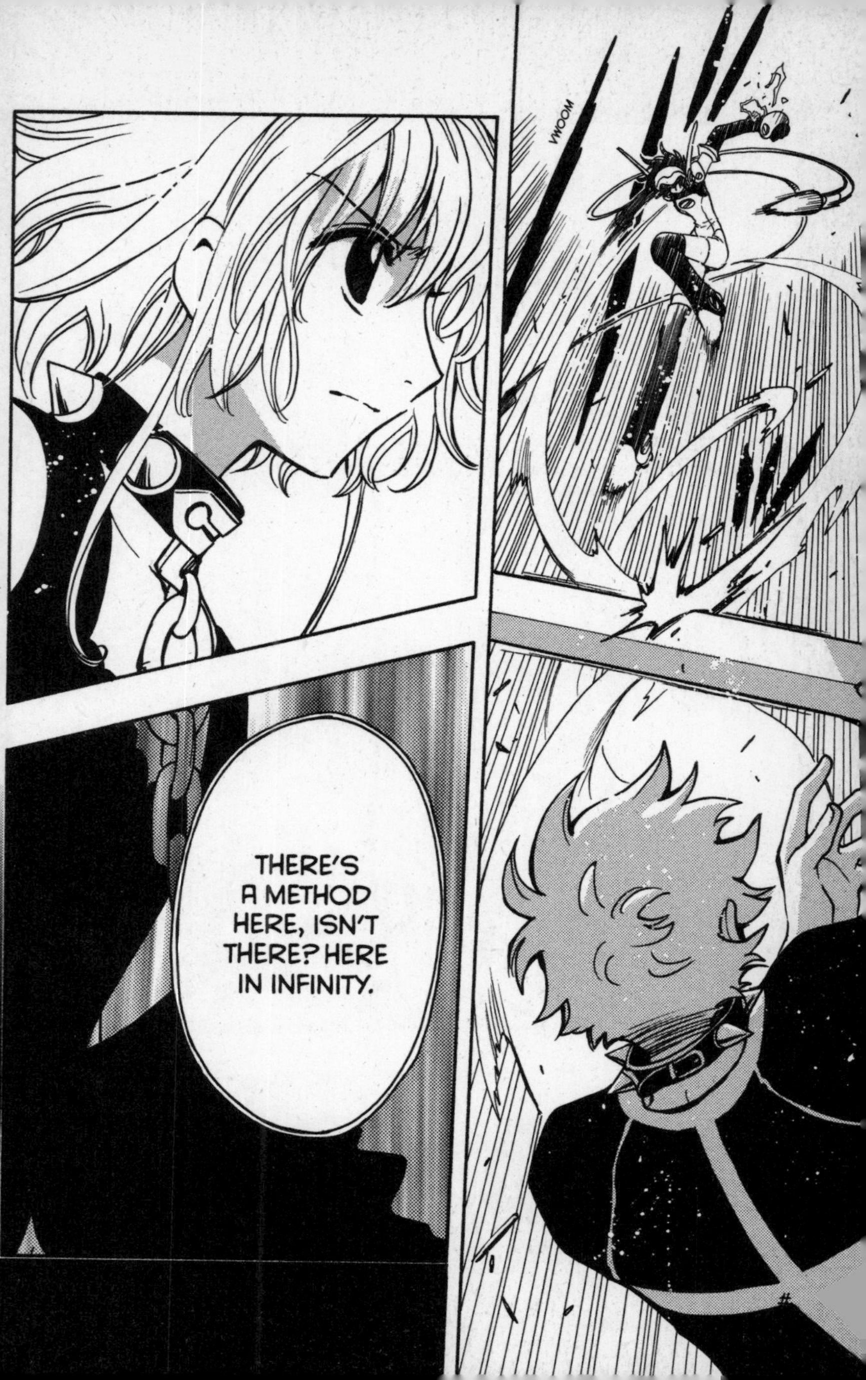
VWOOM
THERE'S A METHOD HERE, ISN'T THERE? HERE IN INFINITY.

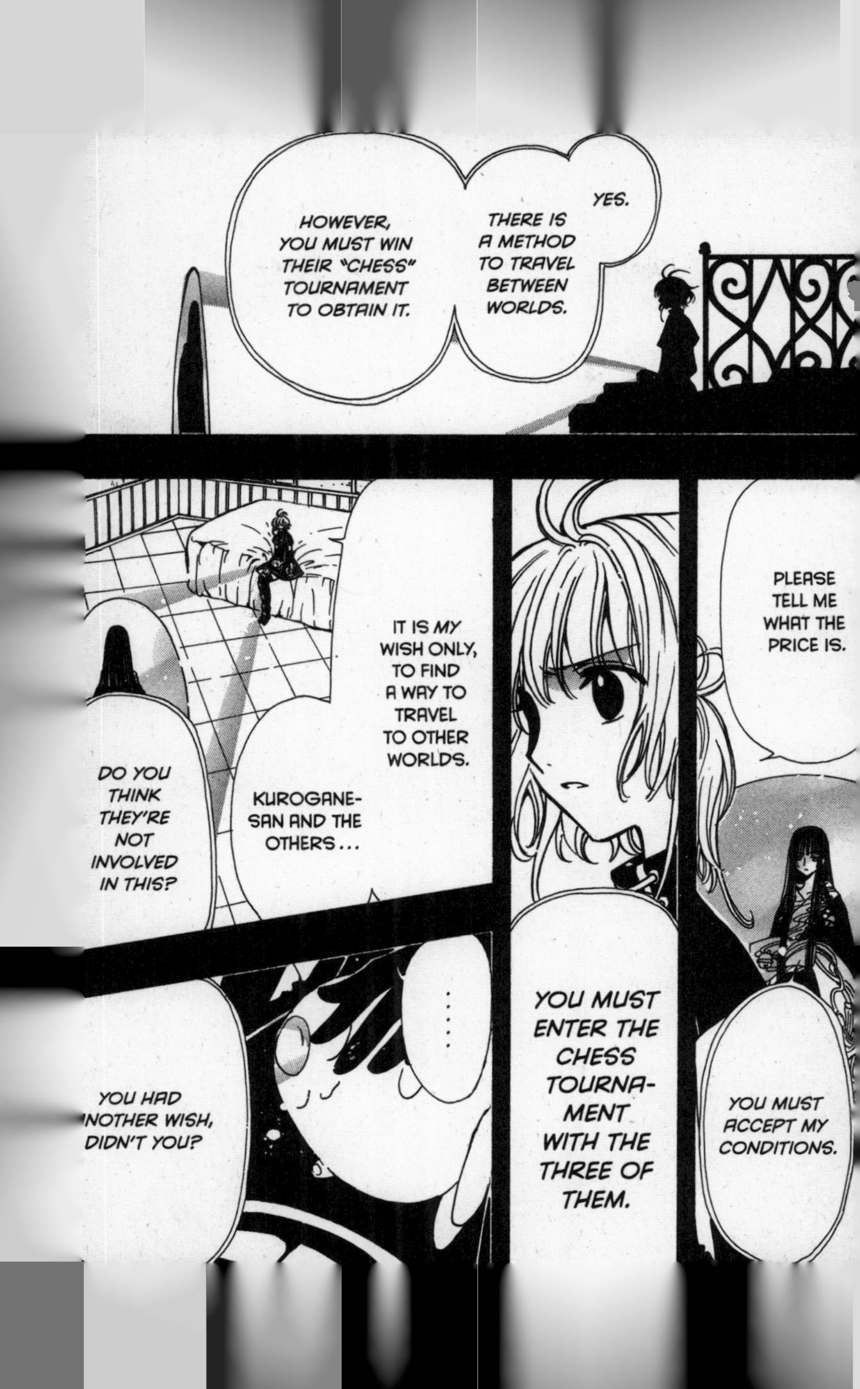
YES.
THERE IS A METHOD TO TRAVEL BETWEEN WORLDS.
HOWEVER, YOU MUST WIN THEIR "CHESS" TOURNAMENT TO OBTAIN IT.
PLEASE TELL ME WHAT THE PRICE IS.
YOU MUST ACCEPT MY CONDITIONS.
YOU MUST ENTER THE CHESS TOURNA-MENT WITH THE THREE OF THEM.
IT IS MY WISH ONLY, TO FIND A WAY TO TRAVEL TO OTHER WORLDS.
KUROGANE-SAN AND THE OTHERS...
DO YOU THINK THEY'RE NOT INVOLVED IN THIS?
.....
YOU HAD NOTHER WISH, DIDN'T YOU?

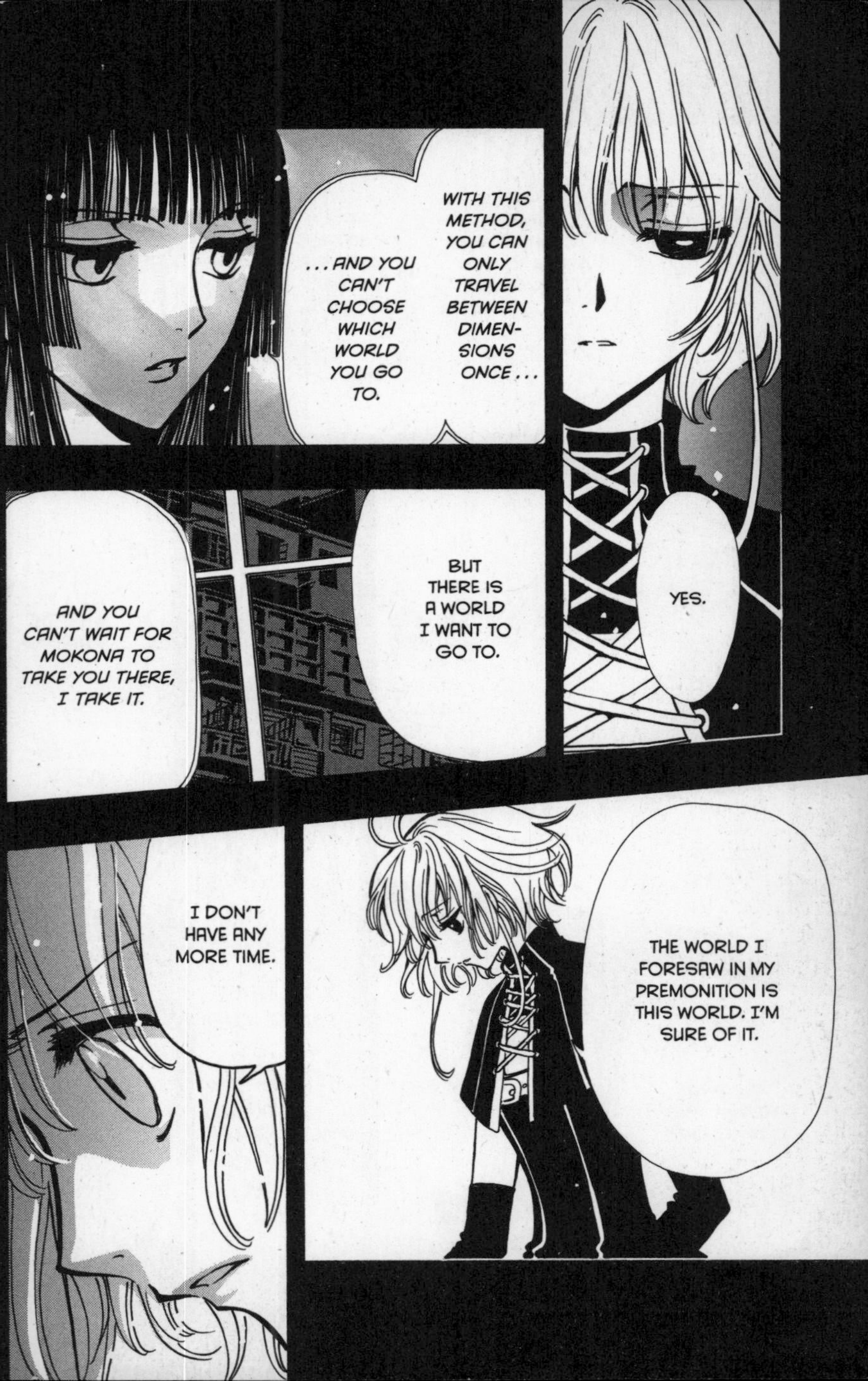
YES.
WITH THIS METHOD, YOU CAN ONLY TRAVEL BETWEEN DIMENSIONS ONCE . . .
. . . AND YOU CAN'T CHOOSE WHICH WORLD YOU GO TO.
BUT THERE IS A WORLD I WANT TO GO TO.
AND YOU CAN'T WAIT FOR MOKONA TO TAKE YOU THERE, I TAKE IT.
THE WORLD I FORESAW IN MY PREMONITION IS THIS WORLD. I'M SURE OF IT.
I DON'T HAVE ANY MORE TIME.

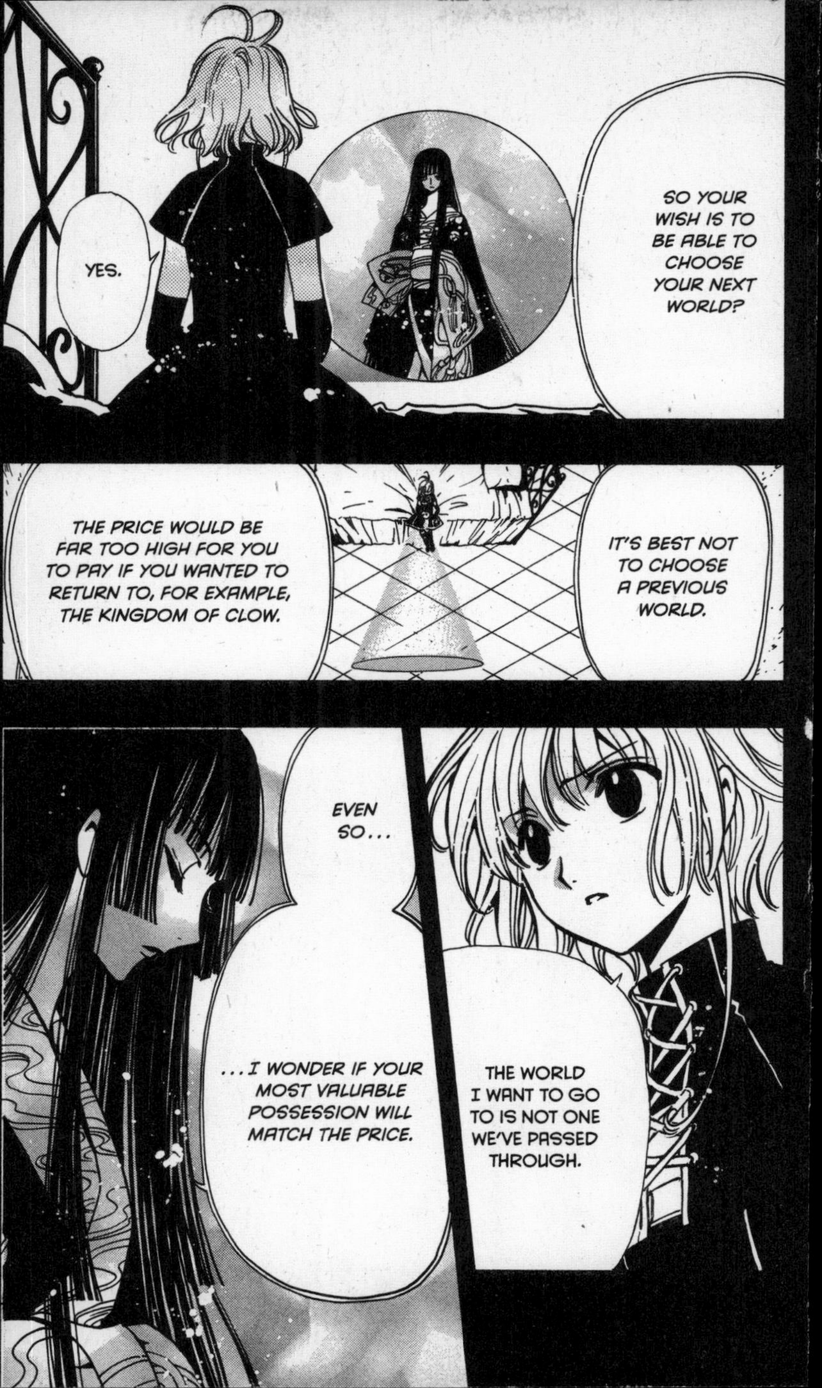
SO YOUR WISH IS TO BE ABLE TO CHOOSE YOUR NEXT WORLD?
YES.
IT'S BEST NOT TO CHOOSE A PREVIOUS WORLD.
THE PRICE WOULD BE FAR TOO HIGH FOR YOU TO PAY IF YOU WANTED TO RETURN TO, FOR EXAMPLE, THE KINGDOM OF CLOW.
THE WORLD I WANT TO GO TO IS NOT ONE WE'VE PASSED THROUGH.
EVEN SO...
...I WONDER IF YOUR MOST VALUABLE POSSESSION WILL MATCH THE PRICE.

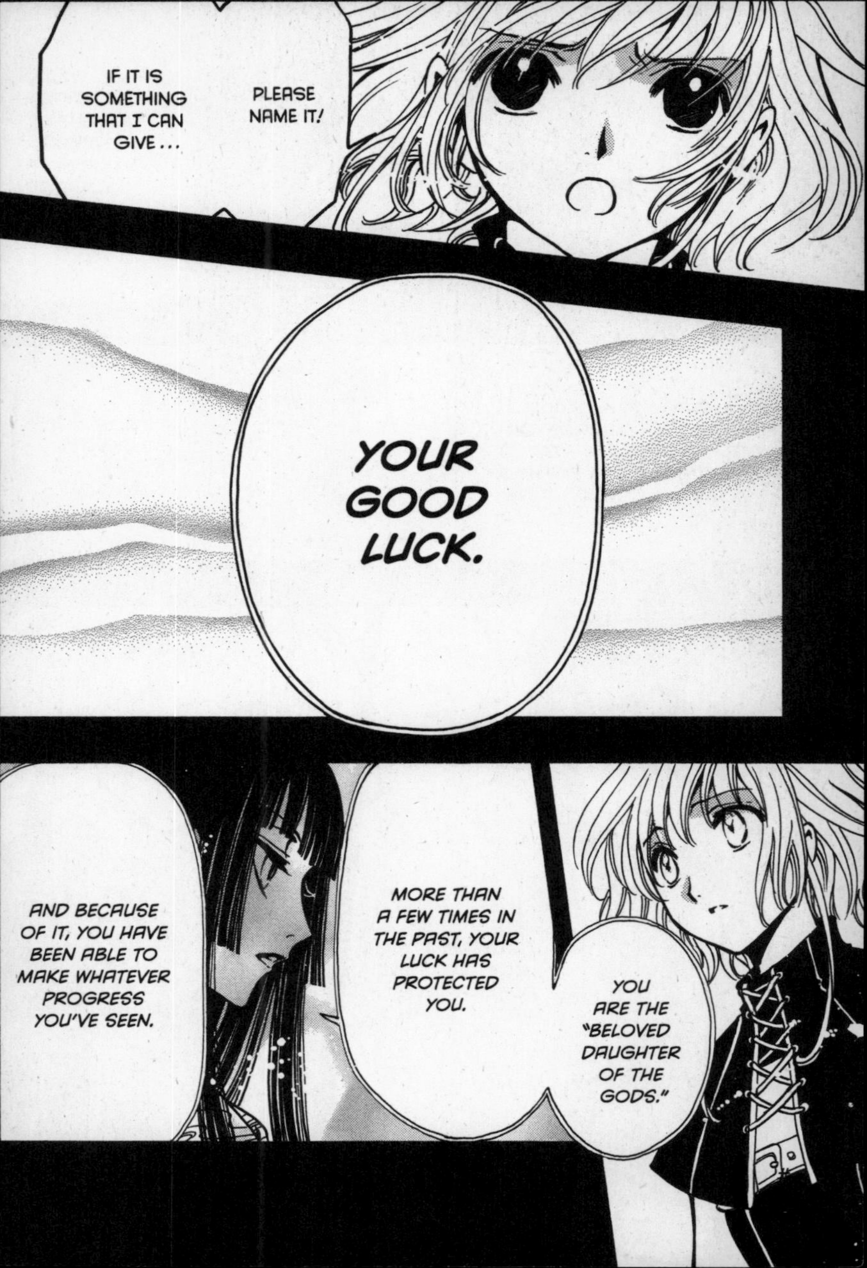
IF IT IS SOMETHING THAT I CAN GIVE...
PLEASE NAME IT!
YOUR GOOD LUCK.
YOU ARE THE "BELOVED DAUGHTER OF THE GODS."
MORE THAN A FEW TIMES IN THE PAST, YOUR LUCK HAS PROTECTED YOU.
AND BECAUSE OF IT, YOU HAVE BEEN ABLE TO MAKE WHATEVER PROGRESS YOU'VE SEEN.

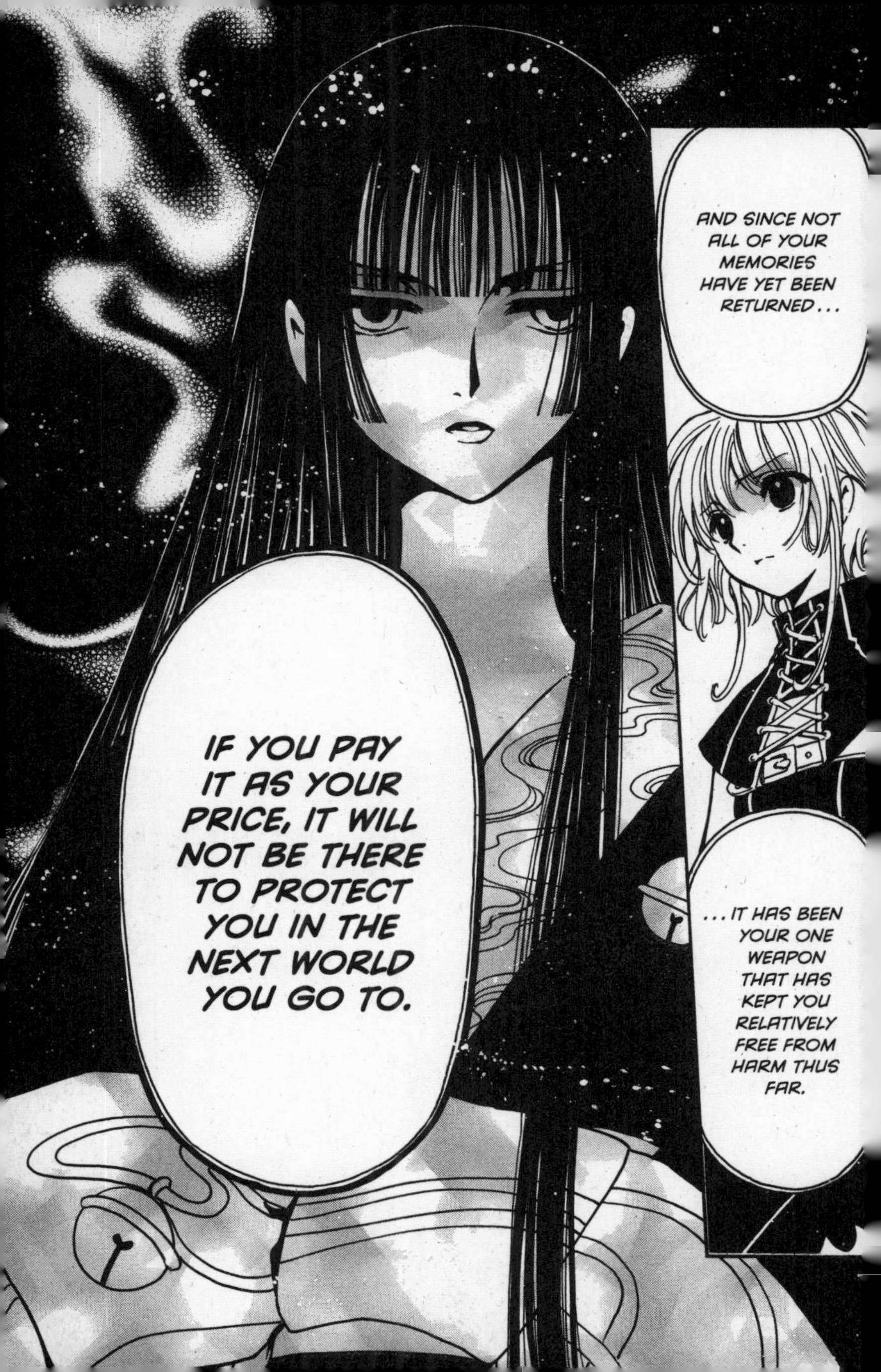
AND SINCE NOT ALL OF YOUR MEMORIES HAVE YET BEEN RETURNED...
...IT HAS BEEN YOUR ONE WEAPON THAT HAS KEPT YOU RELATIVELY FREE FROM HARM THUS FAR.
IF YOU PAY IT AS YOUR PRICE, IT WILL NOT BE THERE TO PROTECT YOU IN THE NEXT WORLD YOU GO TO.

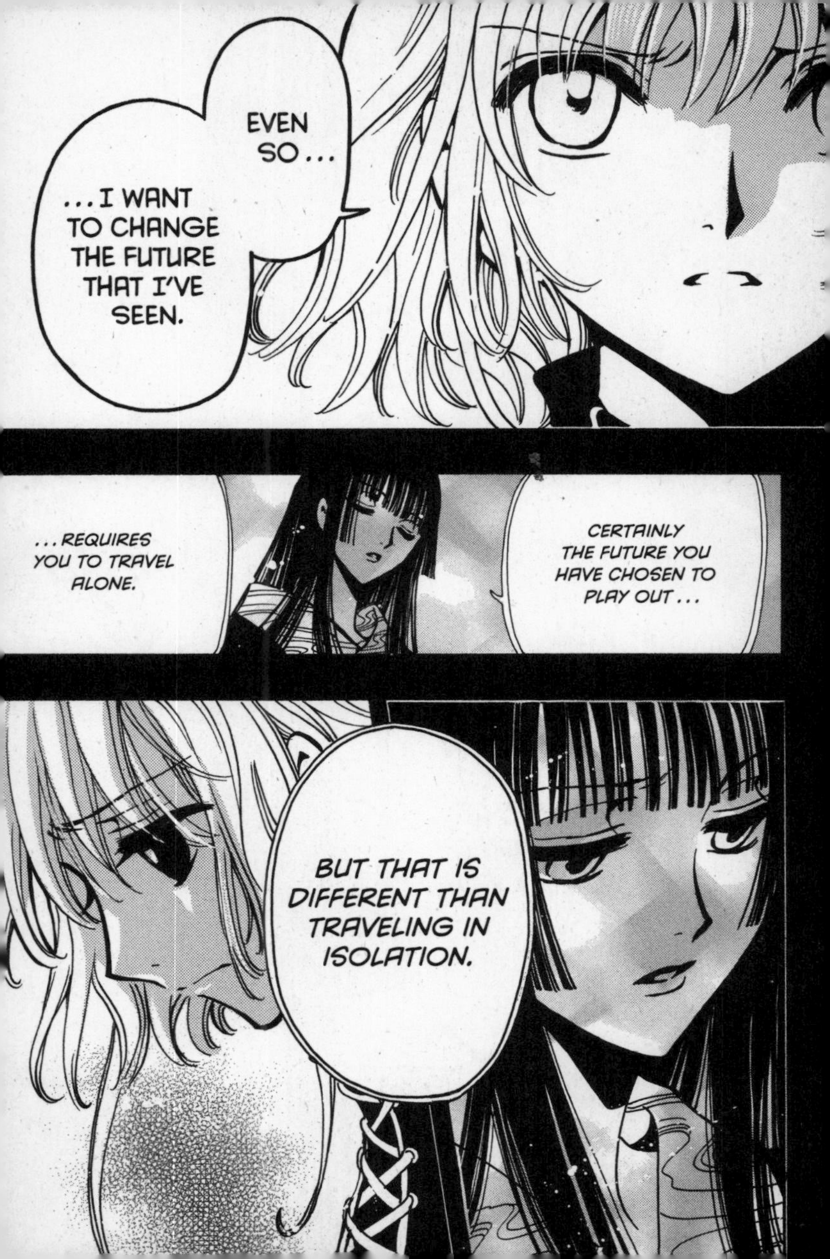
EVEN SO...
...I WANT TO CHANGE THE FUTURE THAT I'VE SEEN.
CERTAINLY THE FUTURE YOU HAVE CHOSEN TO PLAY OUT...
...REQUIRES YOU TO TRAVEL ALONE.
BUT THAT IS DIFFERENT THAN TRAVELING IN ISOLATION.

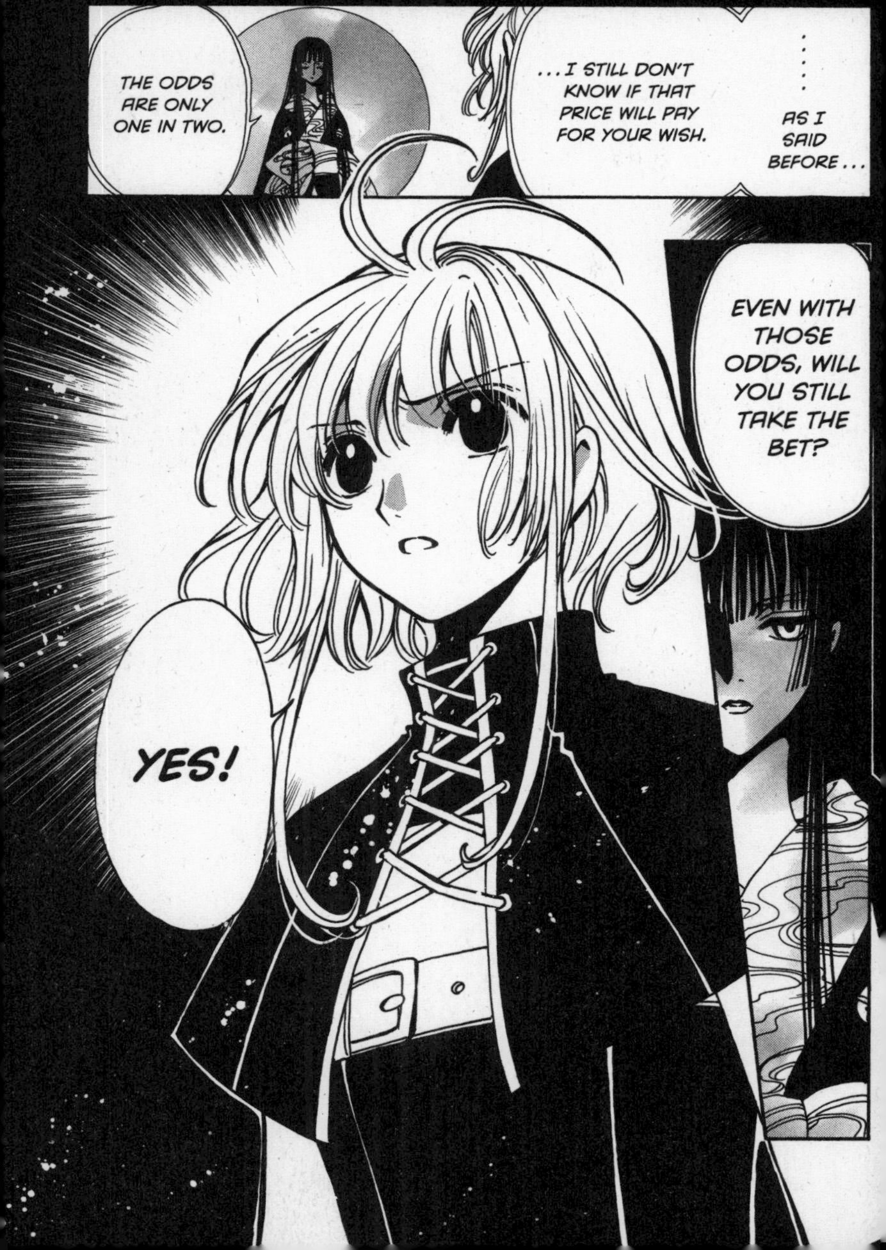
.....
AS I SAID BEFORE...
...I STILL DON'T KNOW IF THAT PRICE WILL PAY FOR YOUR WISH.
THE ODDS ARE ONLY ONE IN TWO.
EVEN WITH THOSE ODDS, WILL YOU STILL TAKE THE BET?
YES!

ツバサ
RESERVoir CHRoNiCLE

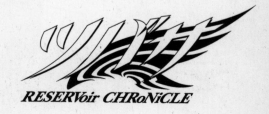

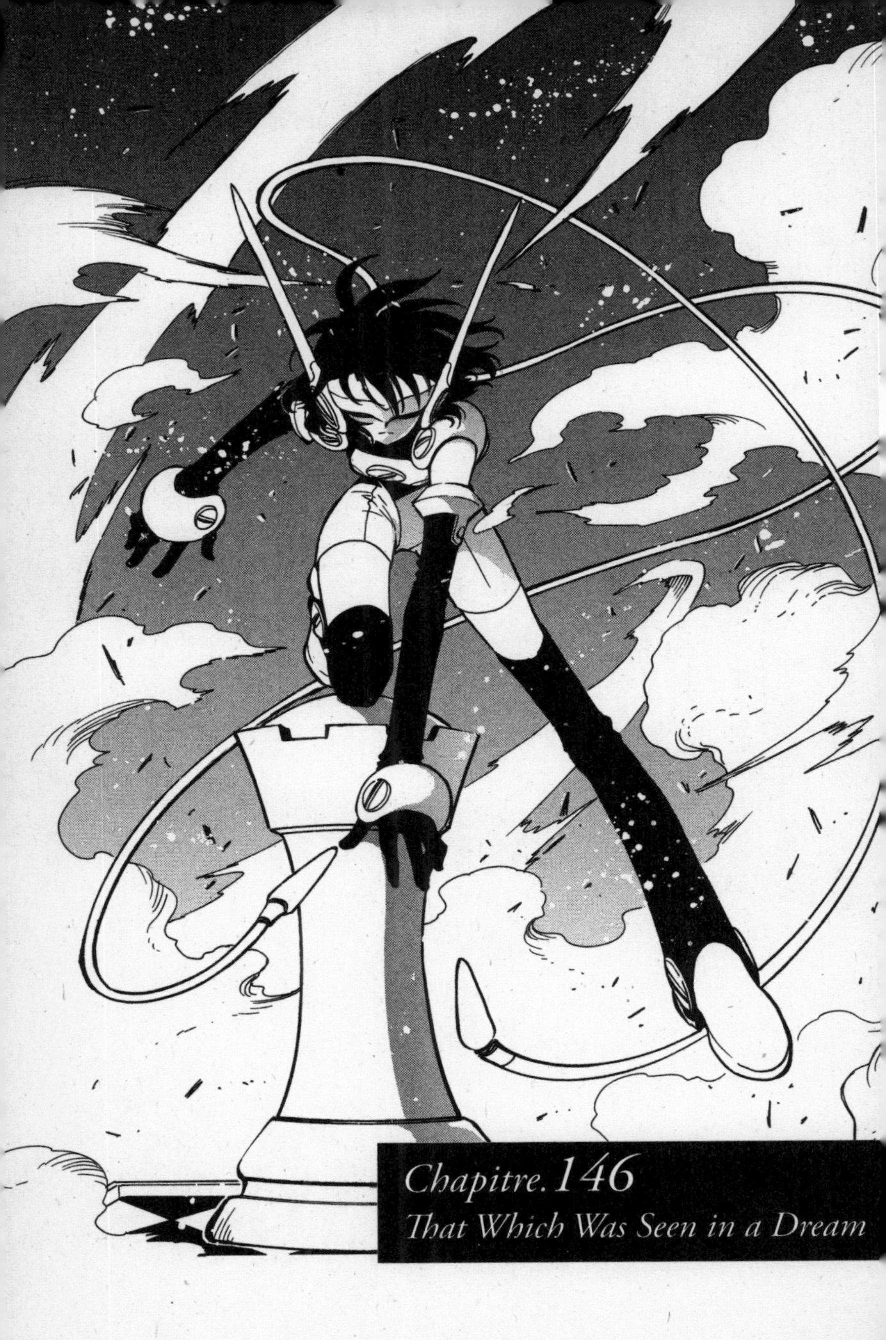

Chapitre. 146
That Which Was Seen in a Dream

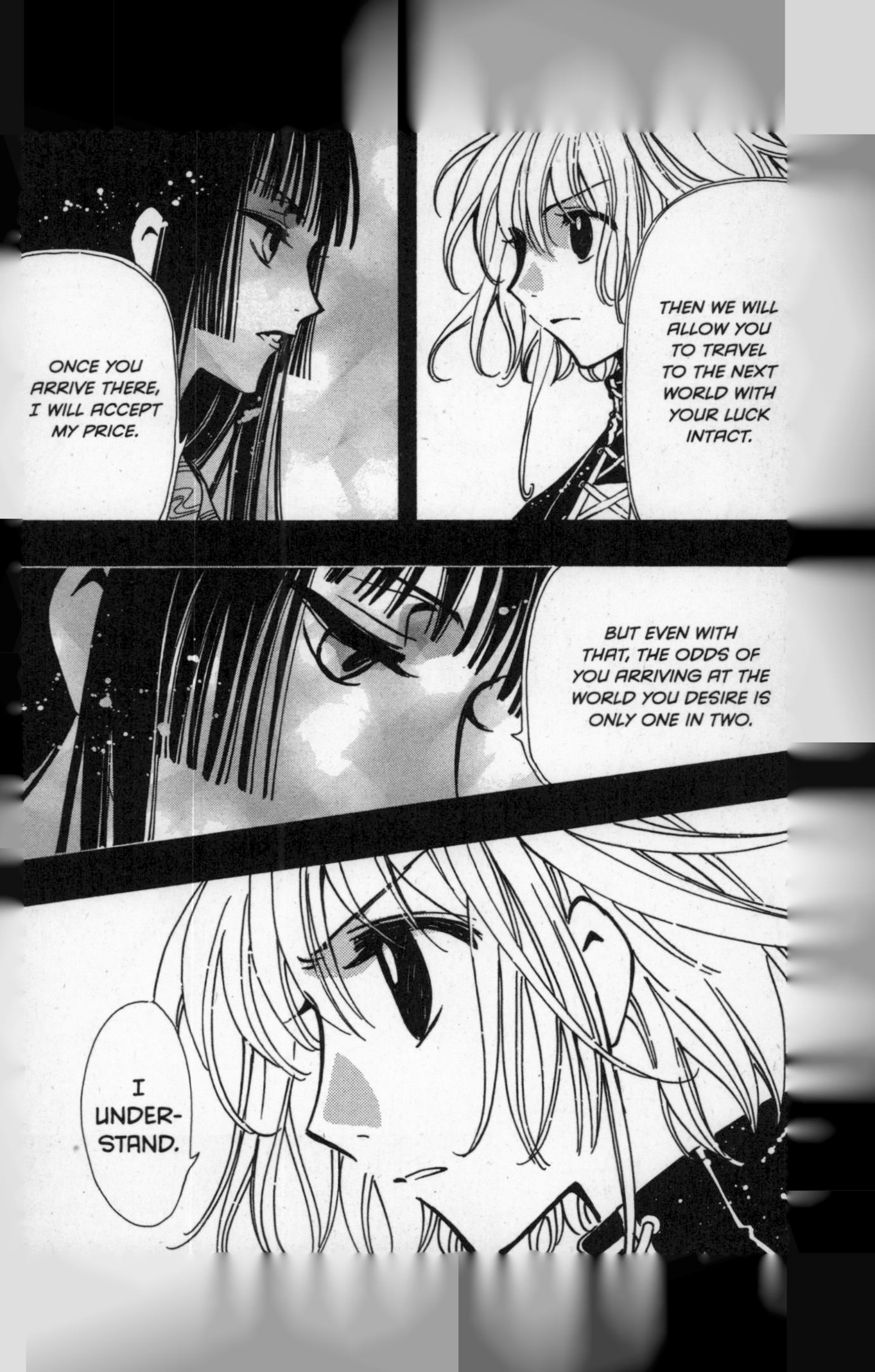
THEN WE WILL ALLOW YOU TO TRAVEL TO THE NEXT WORLD WITH YOUR LUCK INTACT.
ONCE YOU ARRIVE THERE, I WILL ACCEPT MY PRICE.
BUT EVEN WITH THAT, THE ODDS OF YOU ARRIVING AT THE WORLD YOU DESIRE IS ONLY ONE IN TWO.
I UNDER-STAND.

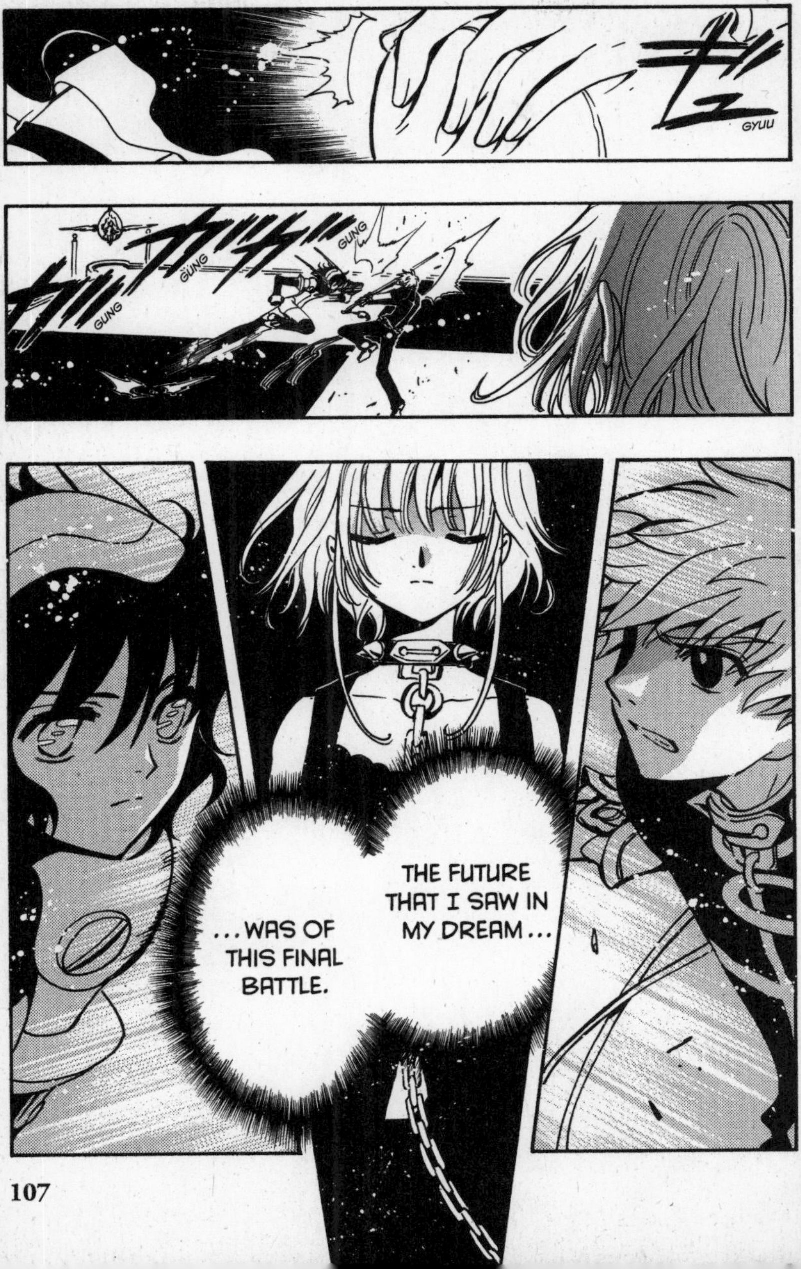
GYUU
GUNG
GUNG
GUNG
THE FUTURE THAT I SAW IN MY DREAM...
...WAS OF THIS FINAL BATTLE.

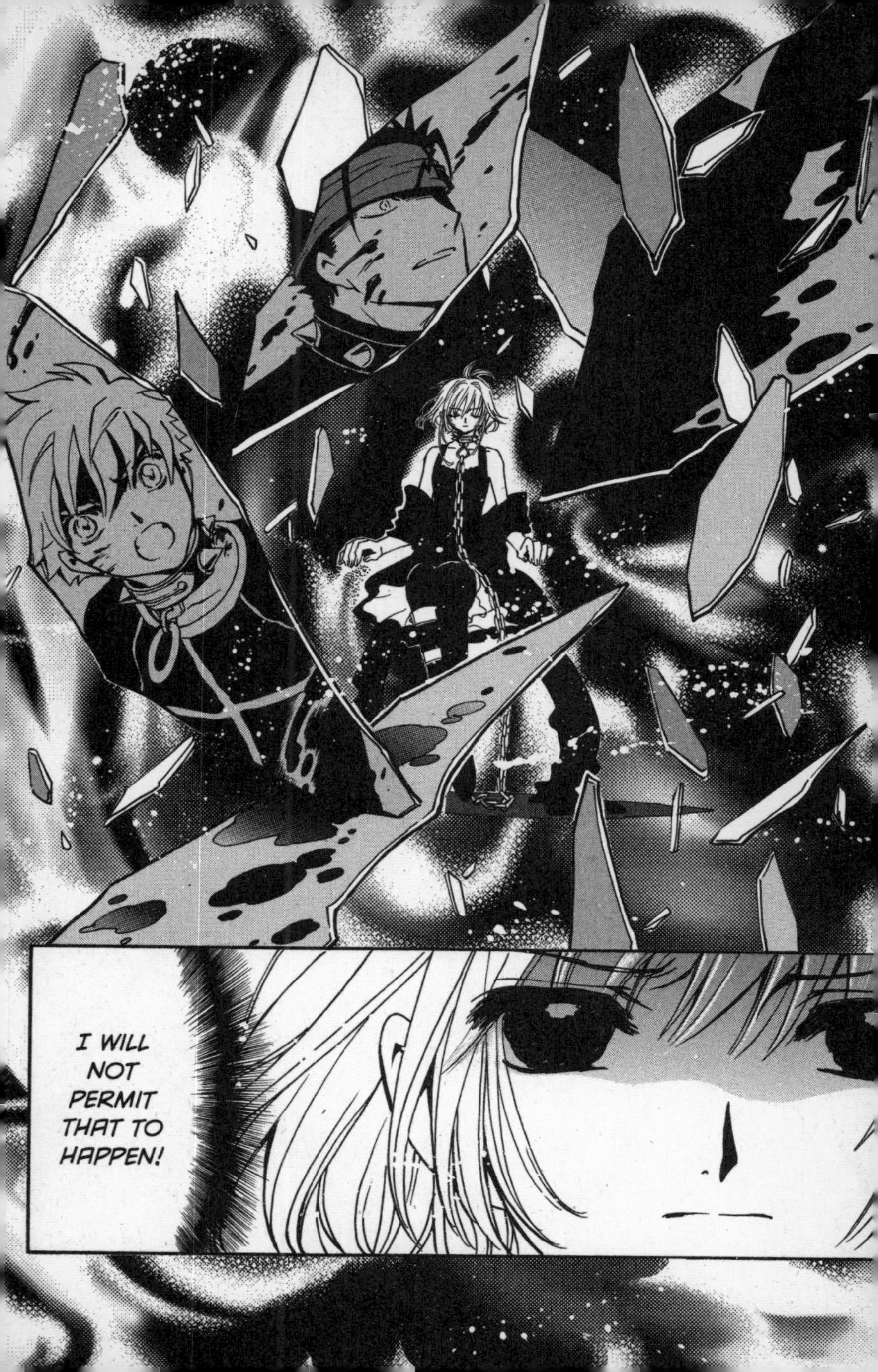
I WILL NOT PERMIT THAT TO HAPPEN!

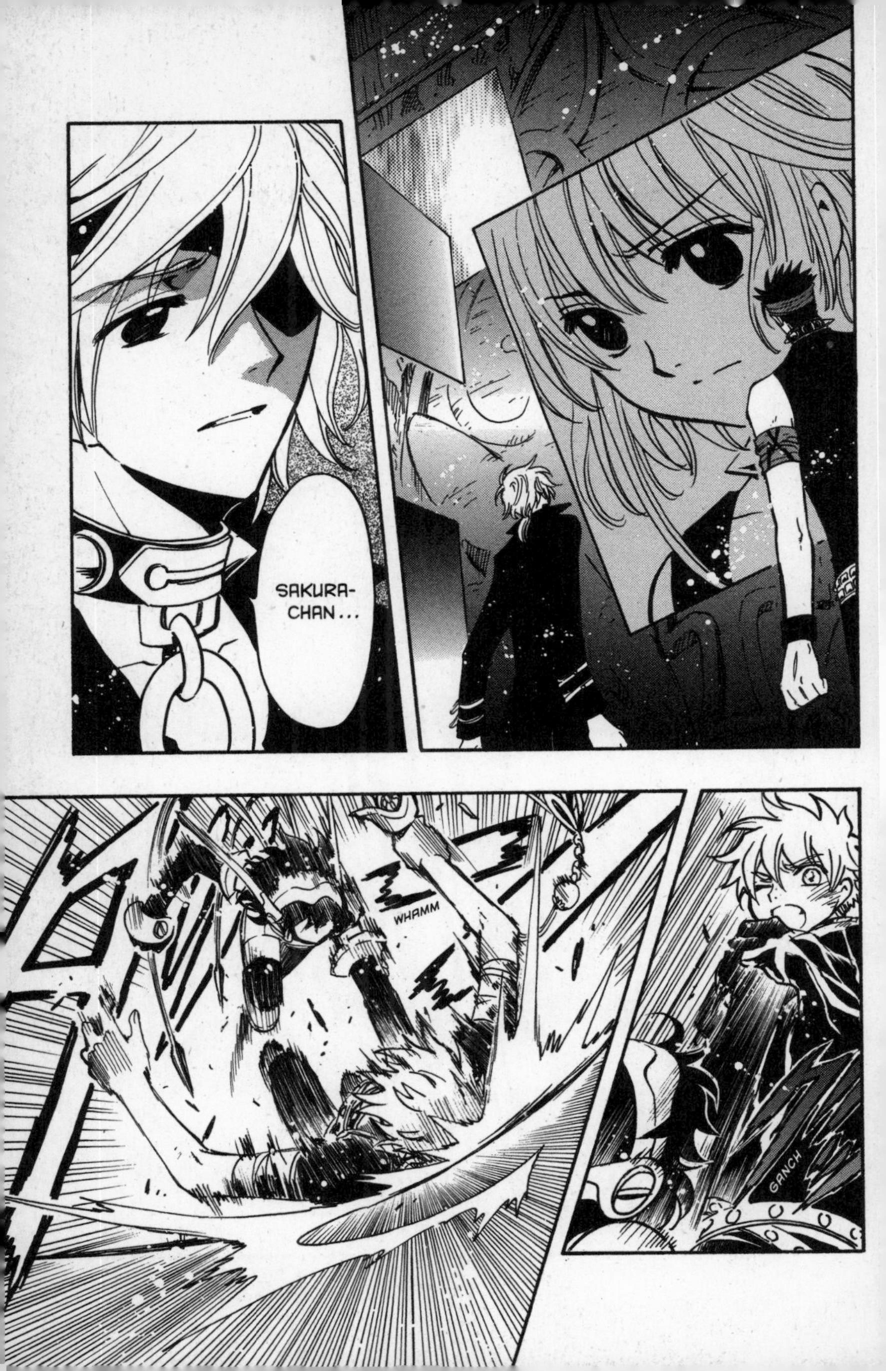
SAKURA-CHAN...
GANCH
WHAMM

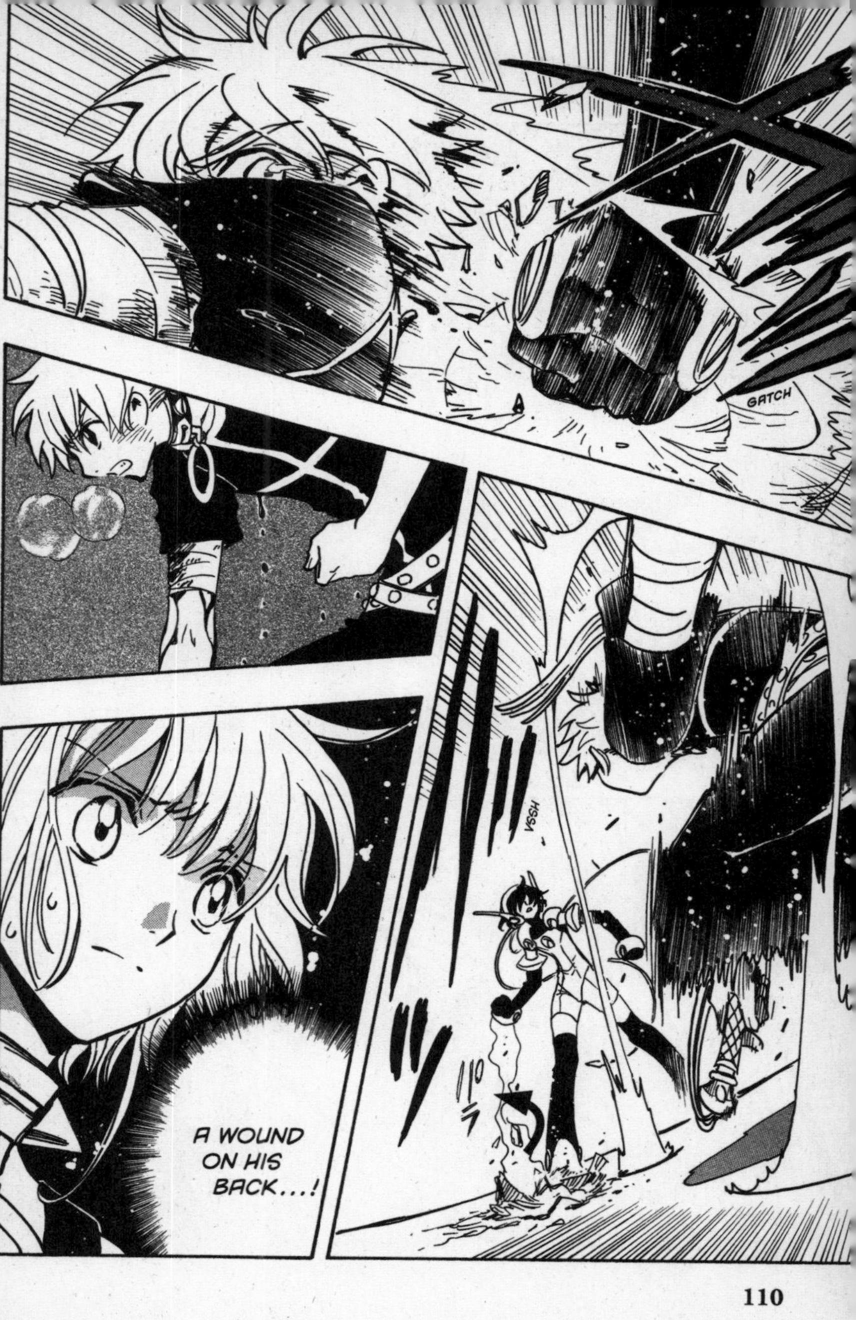
GATCH
VSSH
A WOUND ON HIS BACK...!

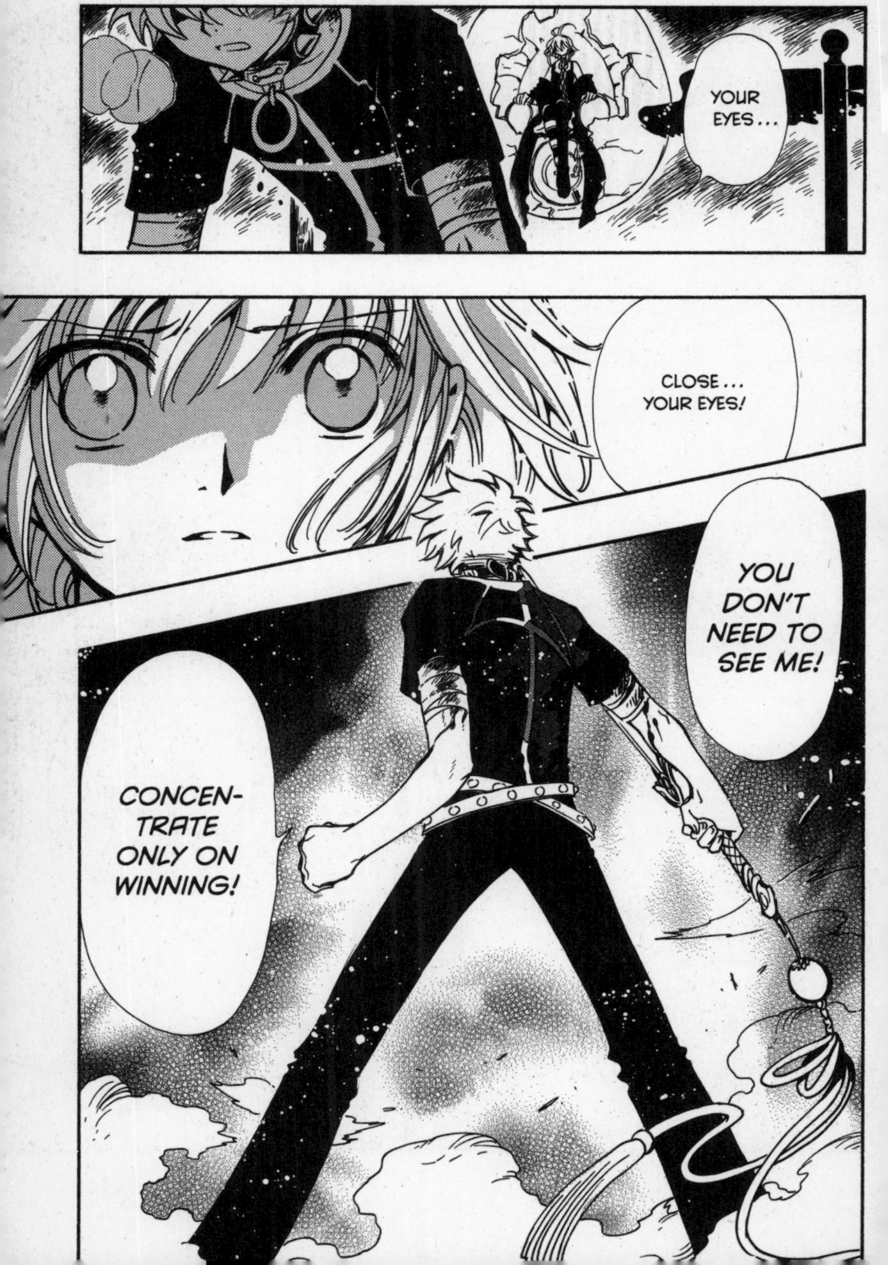
YOUR EYES...
CLOSE... YOUR EYES!
YOU DON'T NEED TO SEE ME!
CONCEN-TRATE ONLY ON WINNING!

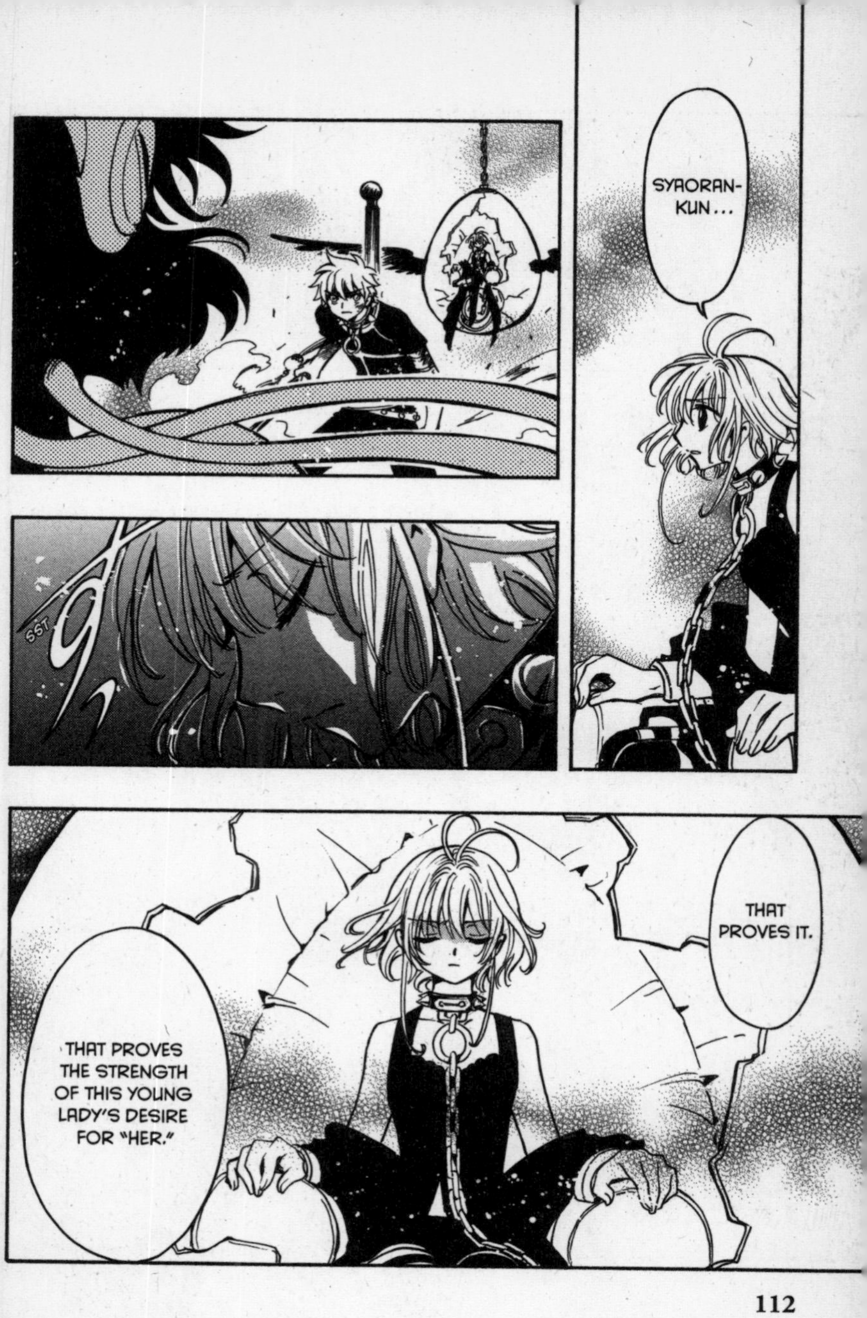
SYAORAN-KUN...
SST
THAT PROVES IT.
THAT PROVES THE STRENGTH OF THIS YOUNG LADY'S DESIRE FOR "HER."

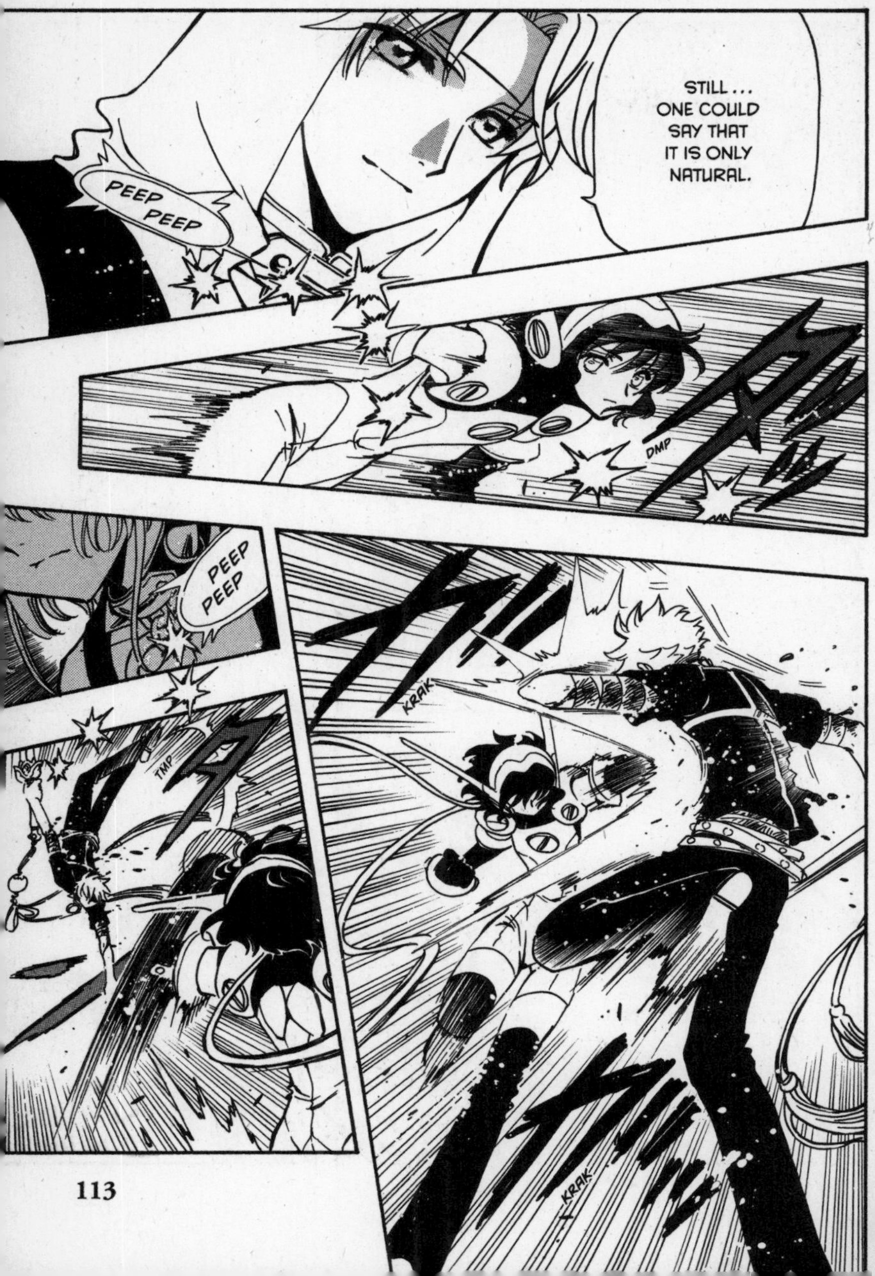
STILL . . . ONE COULD SAY THAT IT IS ONLY NATURAL.
PEEP PEEP
DMP
KRAK
KRAK
PEEP PEEP
TMP

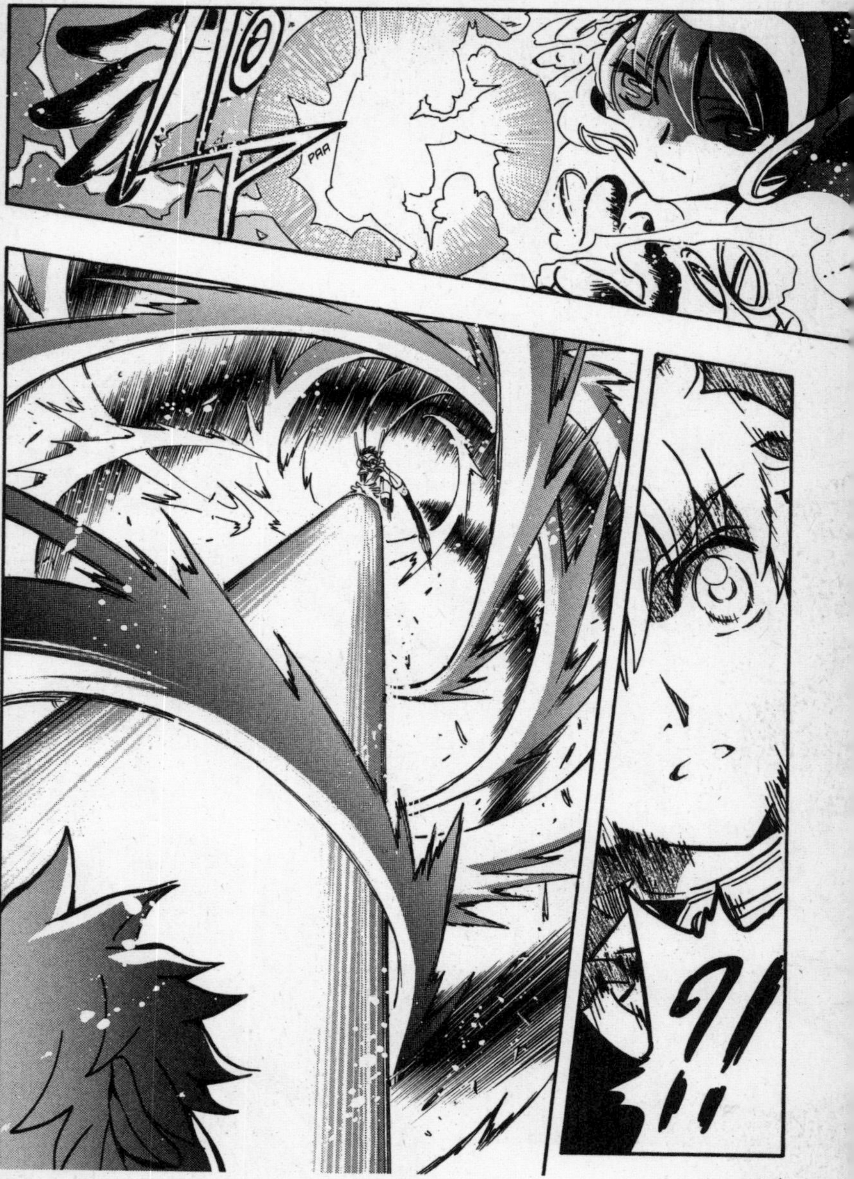
PAA
?!

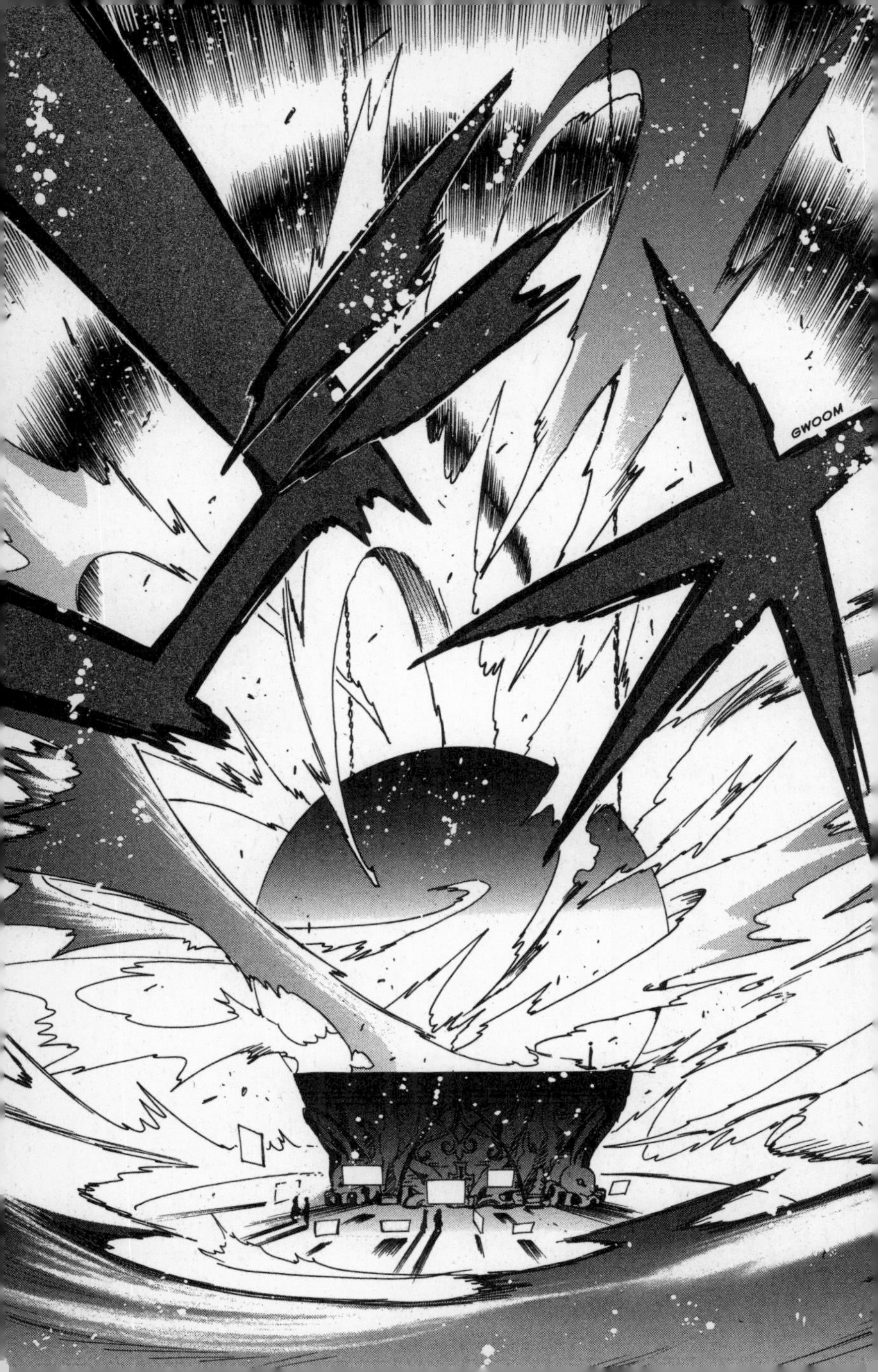
GWOOM

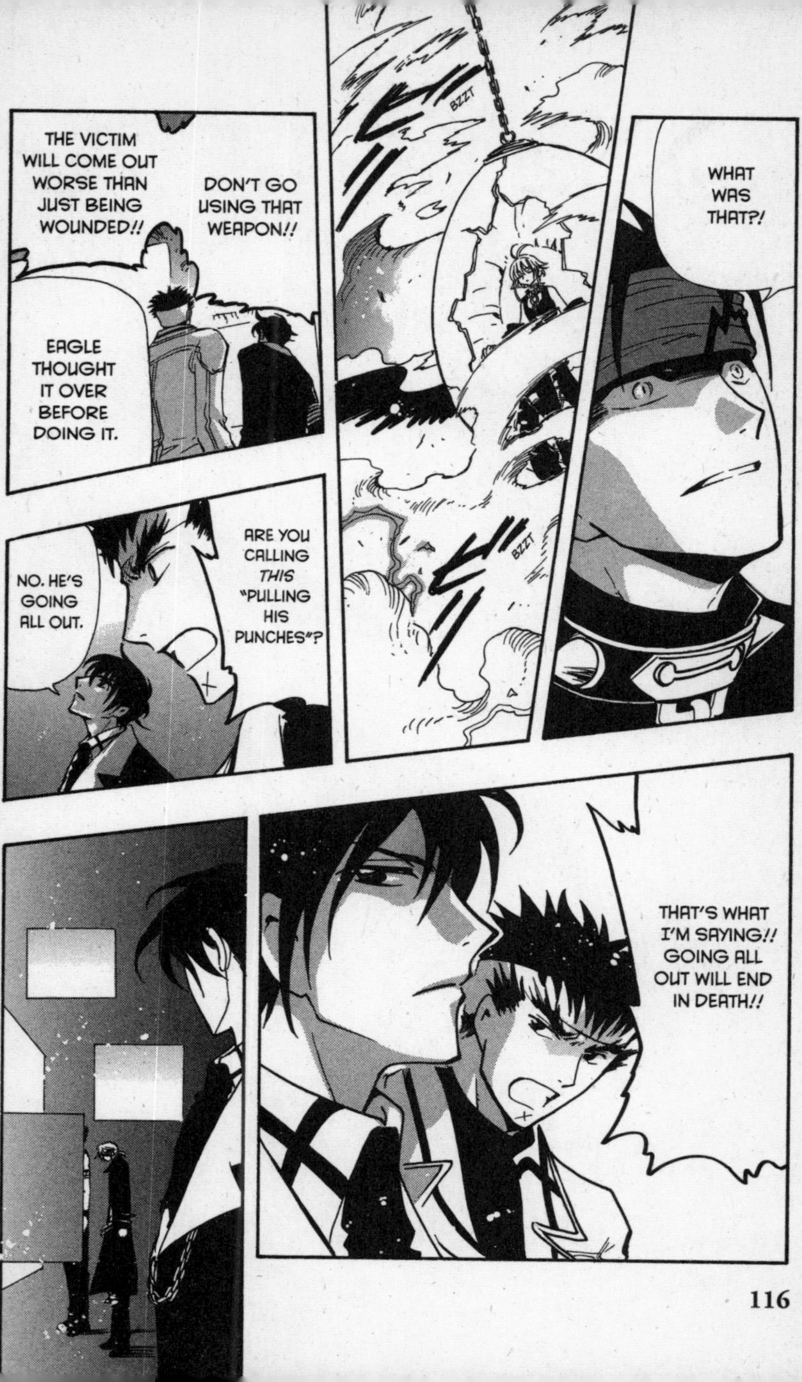
WHAT WAS THAT?!
BZZT
BZZT
DON'T GO USING THAT WEAPON!!
THE VICTIM WILL COME OUT WORSE THAN JUST BEING WOUNDED!!
EAGLE THOUGHT IT OVER BEFORE DOING IT.
ARE YOU CALLING *THIS* "PULLING HIS PUNCHES"?
NO. HE'S GOING ALL OUT.
THAT'S WHAT I'M SAYING!! GOING ALL OUT WILL END IN DEATH!!

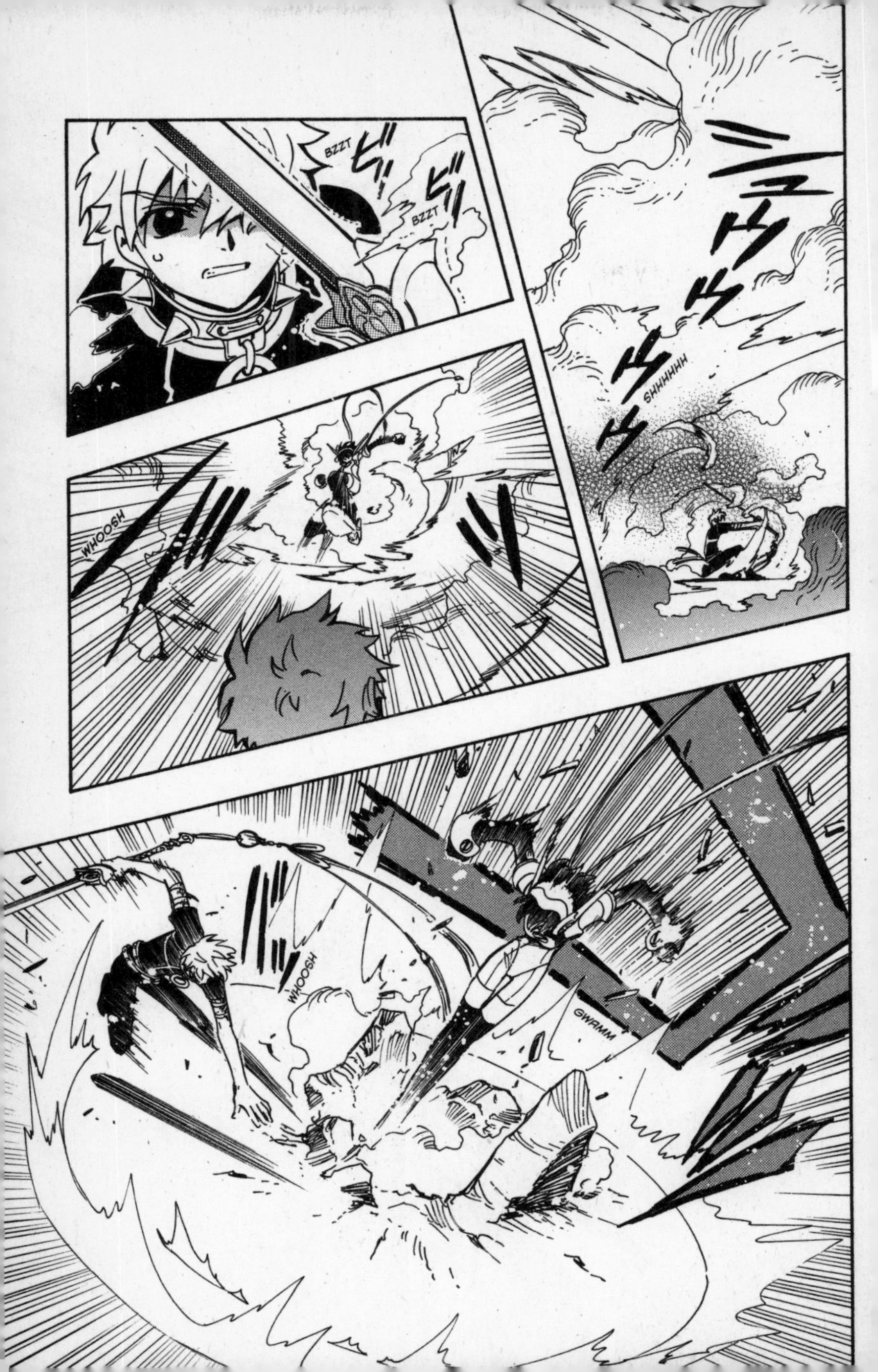
SHHHHHH
BZZT
BZZT
WHOOSH
GWAMM
WHOOSH

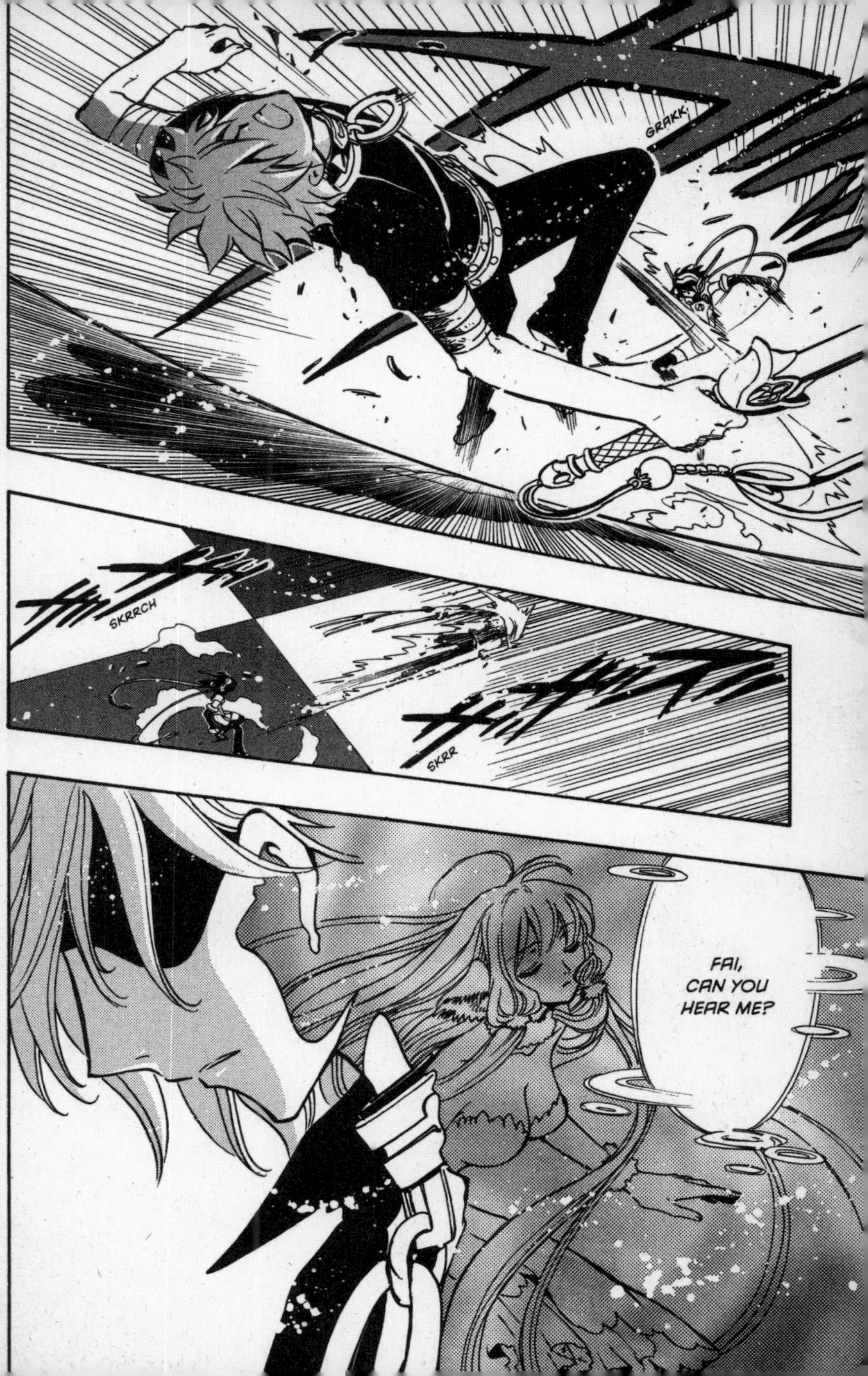
GRAKK
SKRR
SKRRCH
FAI, CAN YOU HEAR ME?

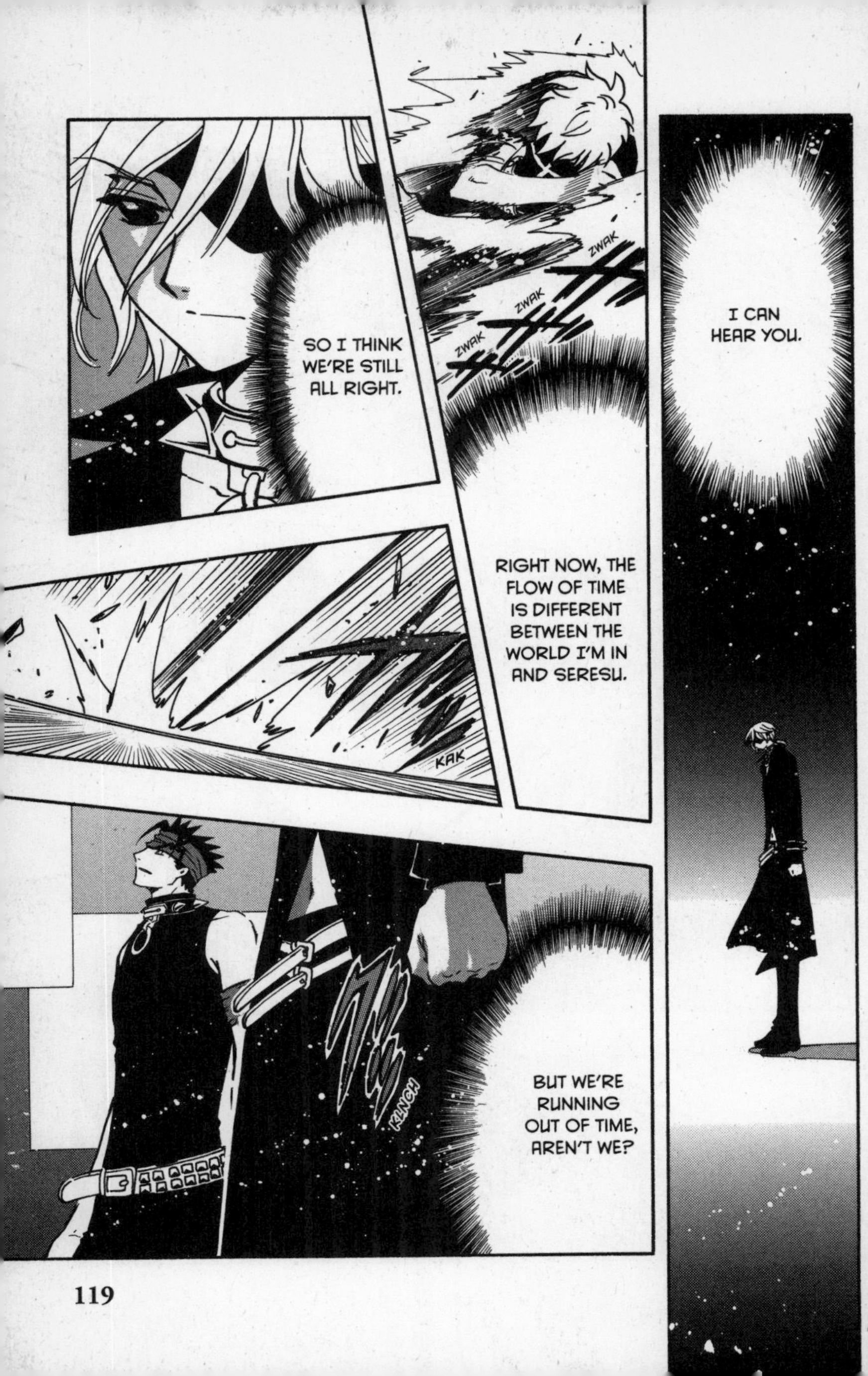
I CAN HEAR YOU.
ZWAK
ZWAK
ZWAK
SO I THINK WE'RE STILL ALL RIGHT.
RIGHT NOW, THE FLOW OF TIME IS DIFFERENT BETWEEN THE WORLD I'M IN AND SERESU.
KAK
BUT WE'RE RUNNING OUT OF TIME, AREN'T WE?
KLNCH

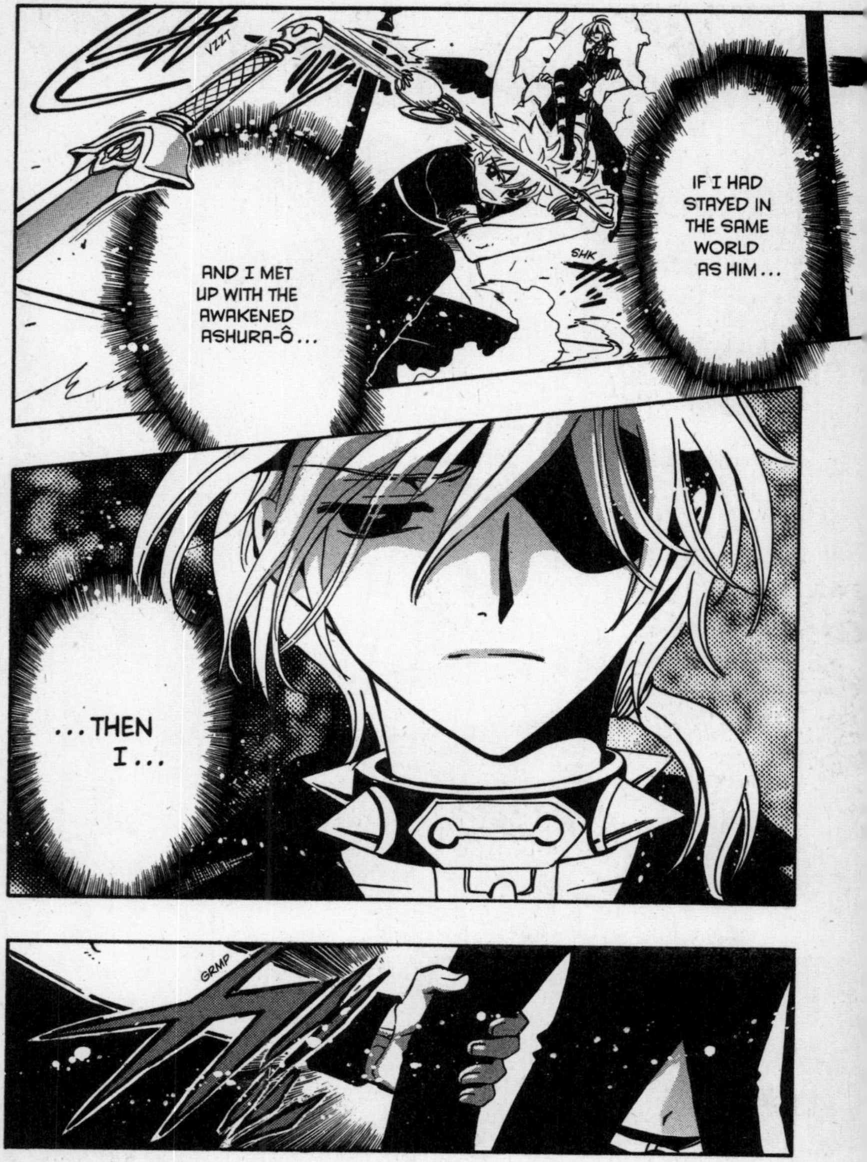
IF I HAD STAYED IN THE SAME WORLD AS HIM...
VZZT
SHK
AND I MET UP WITH THE AWAKENED ASHURA-Ô...
...THEN I...
GRMP

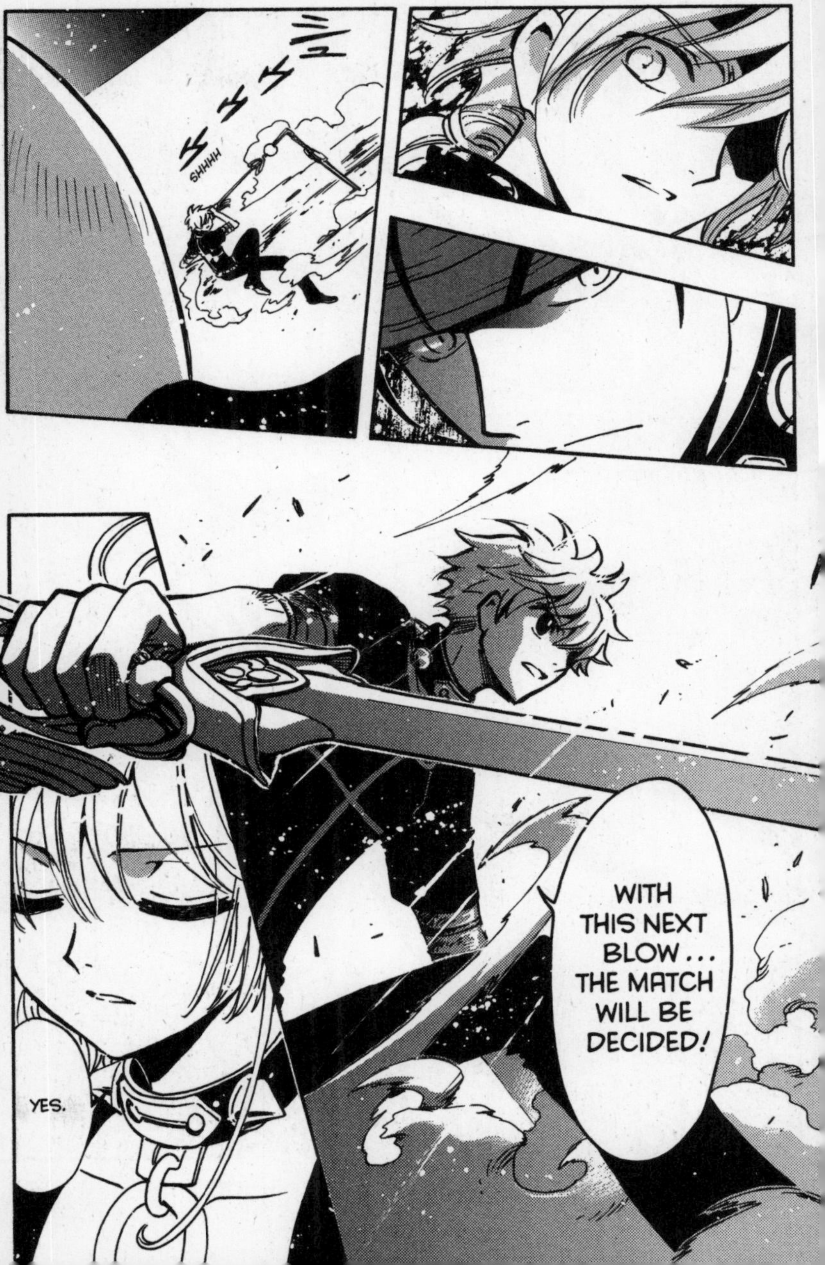
SHHHH
WITH THIS NEXT BLOW... THE MATCH WILL BE DECIDED!
YES.

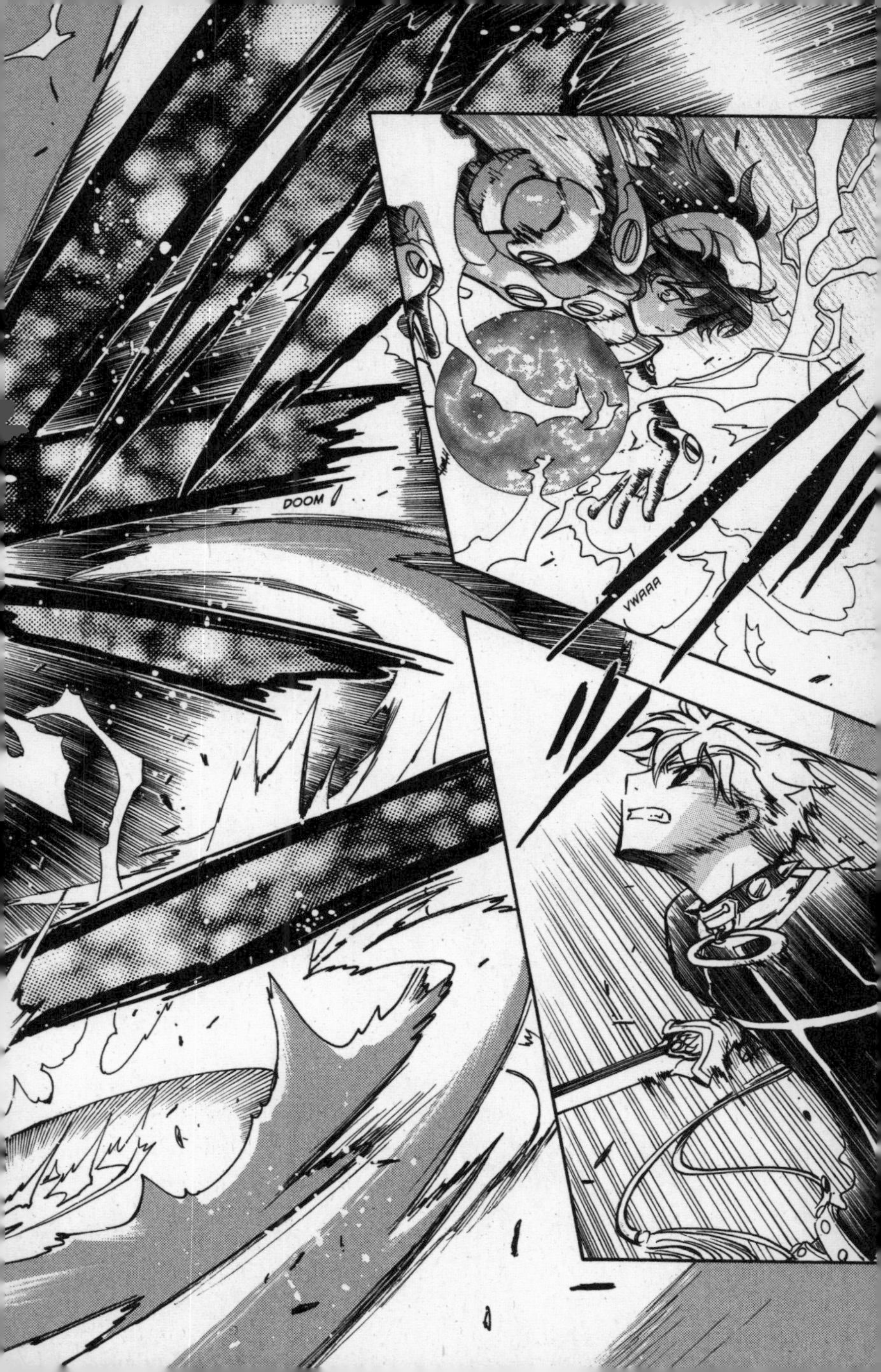
DOOM
VWAAA

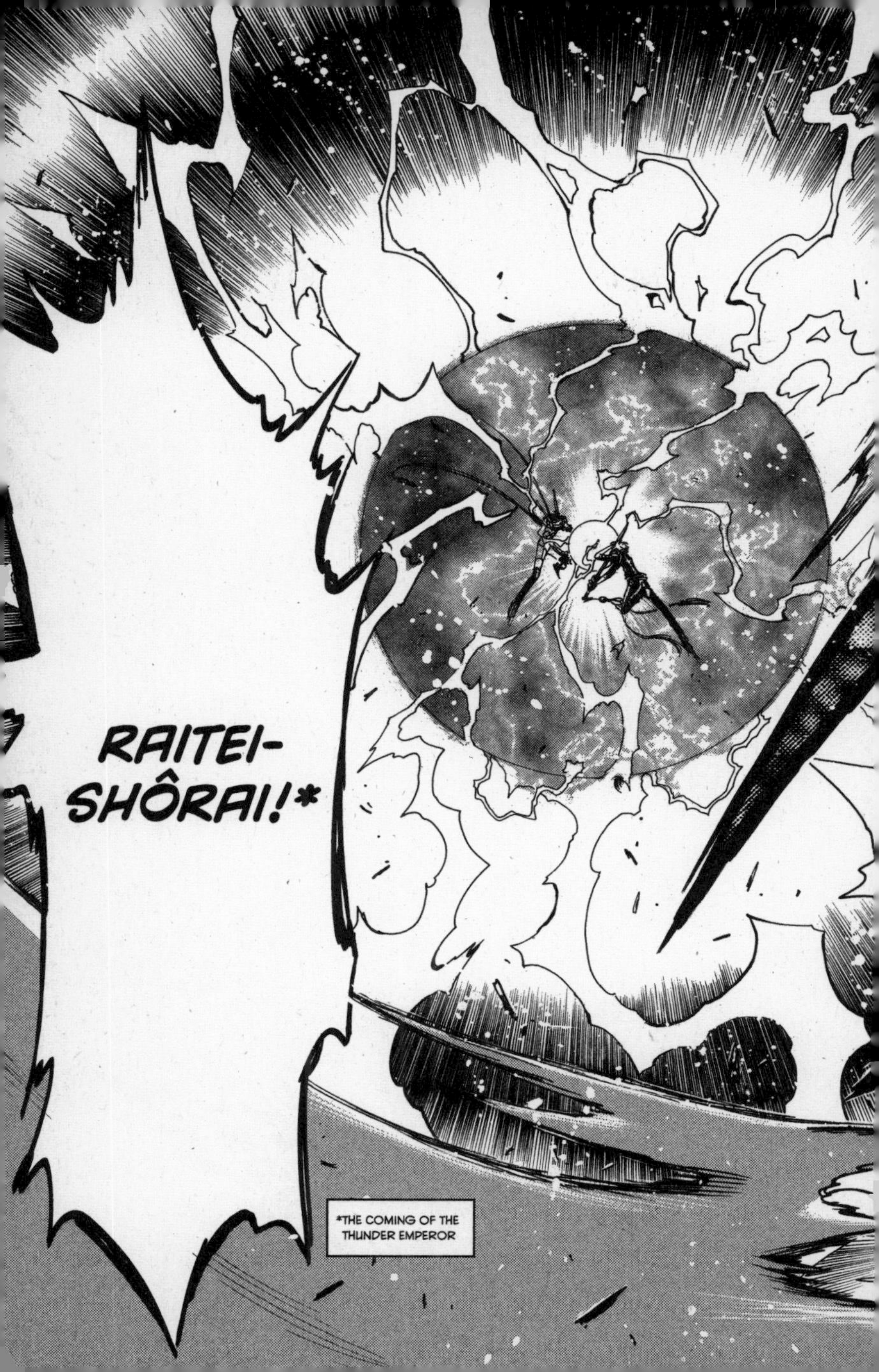
RAITEI-SHÔRAI!*
*THE COMING OF THE THUNDER EMPEROR

ツバサ

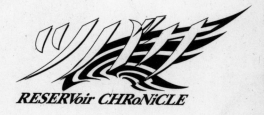

RESERVoir CHRoNiCLE

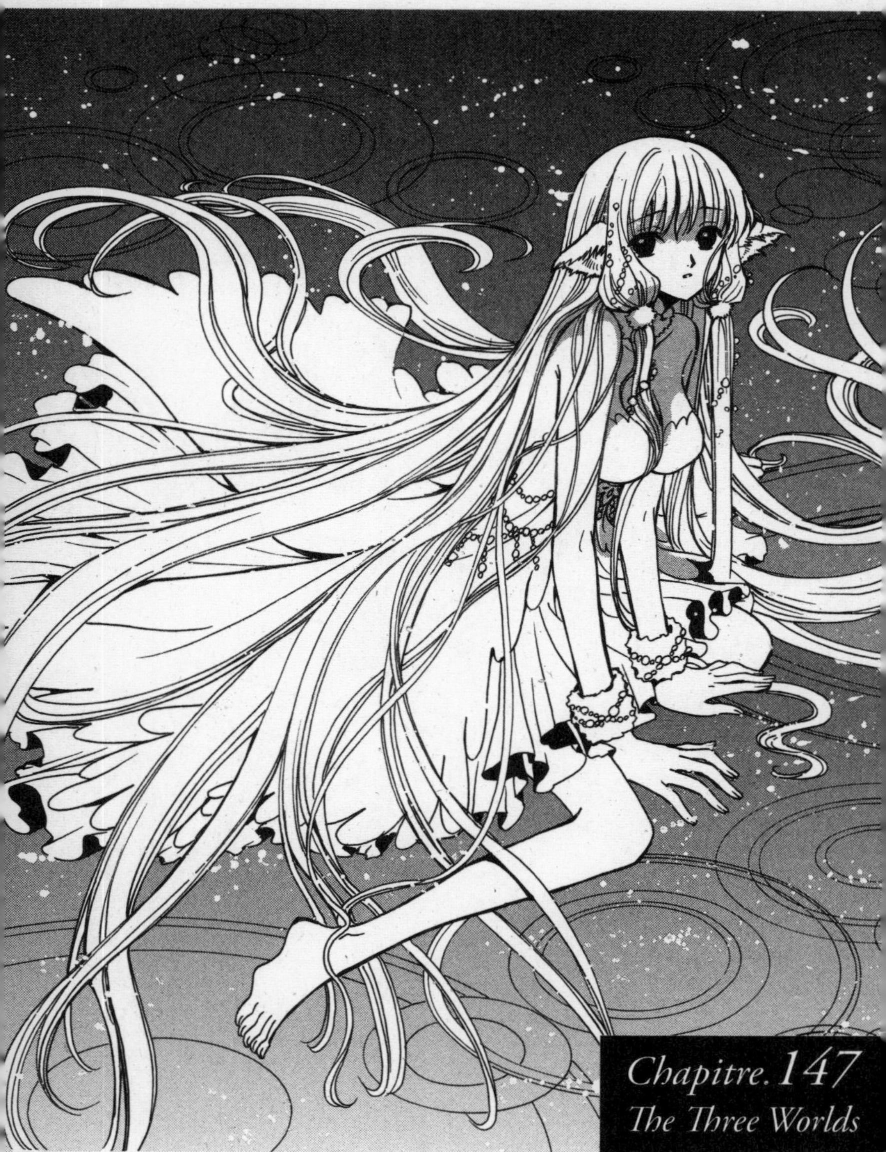
Chapitre. 147
The Three Worlds

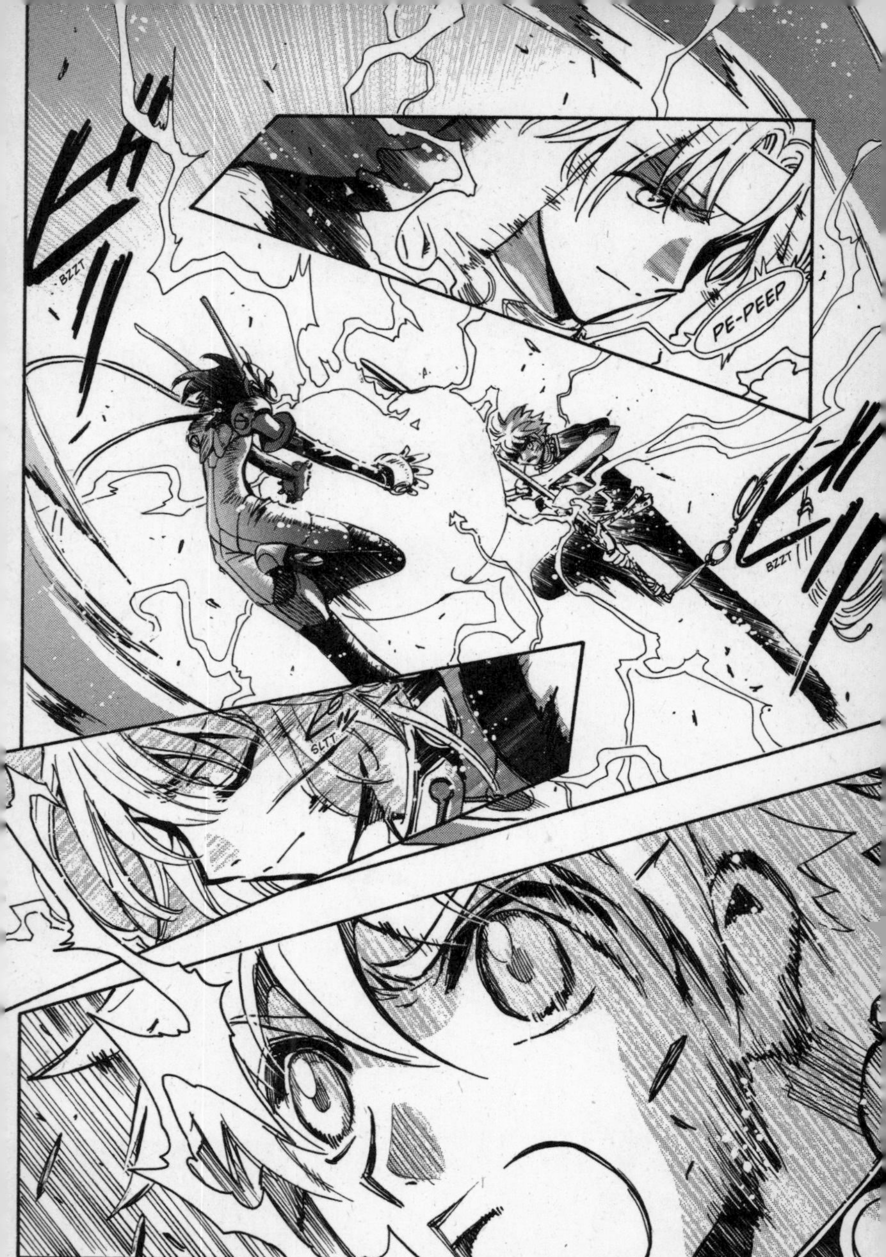
PE-PEEP
BZZT
BZZT
SLTT

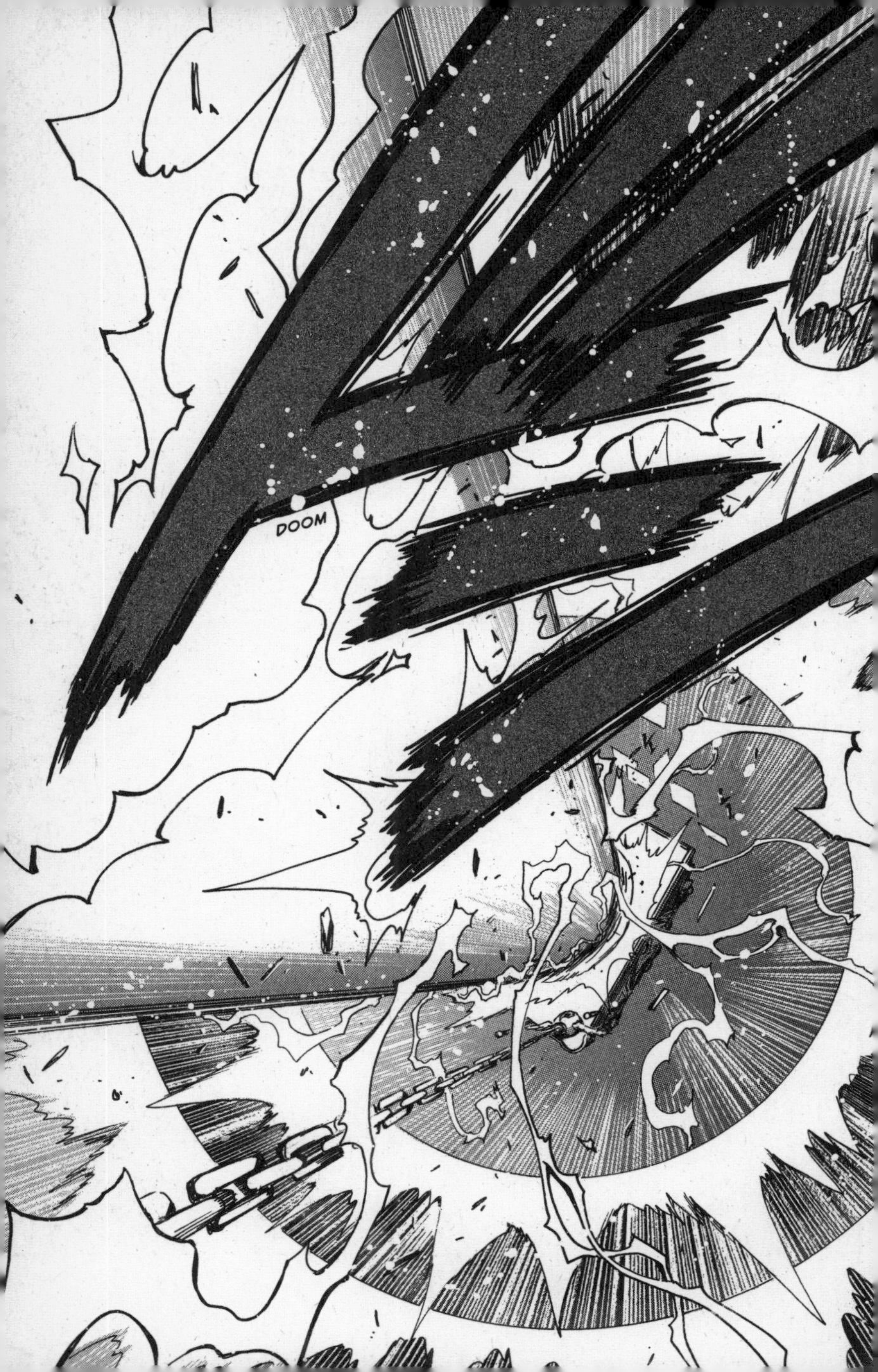
DOOM

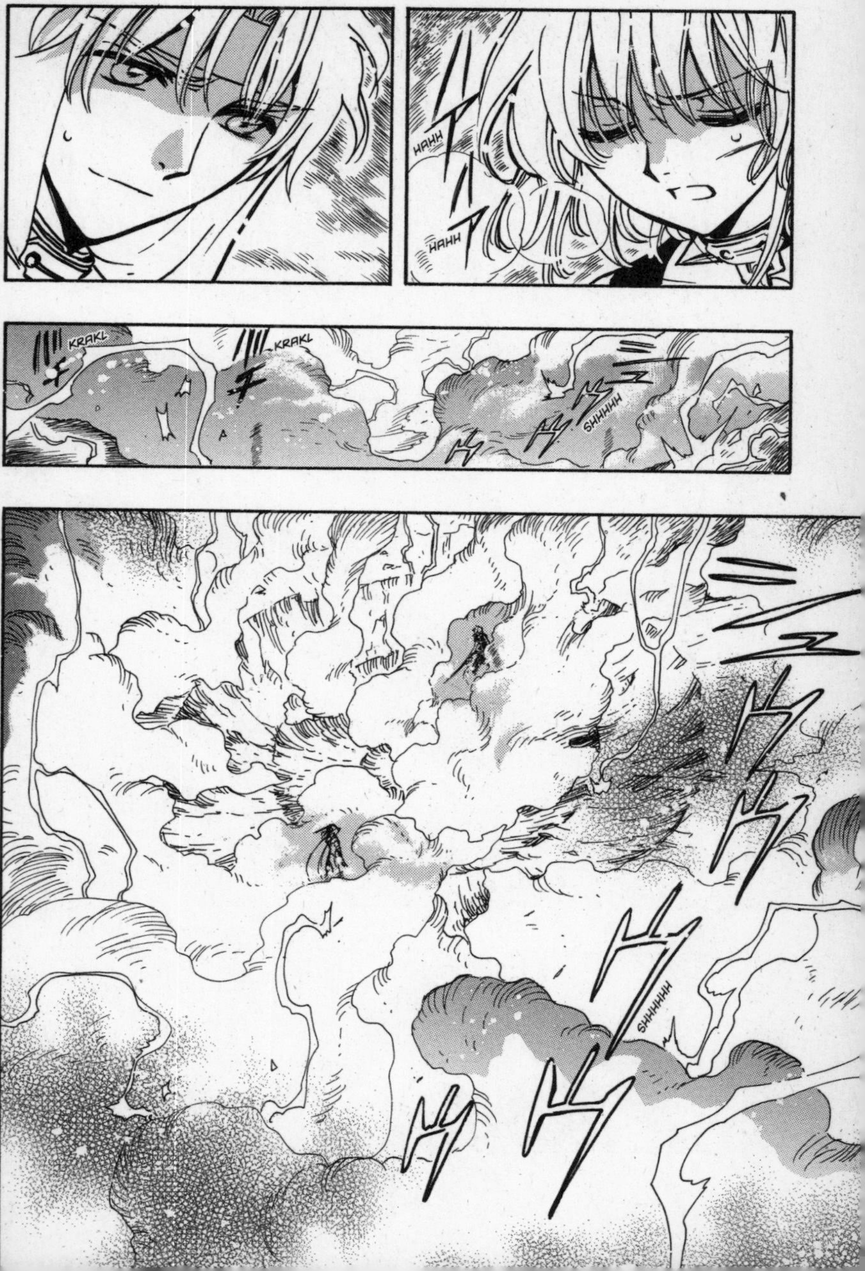
HAHH
HAHH
KRAKL
KRAKL
SHHHHH
SHHHHH

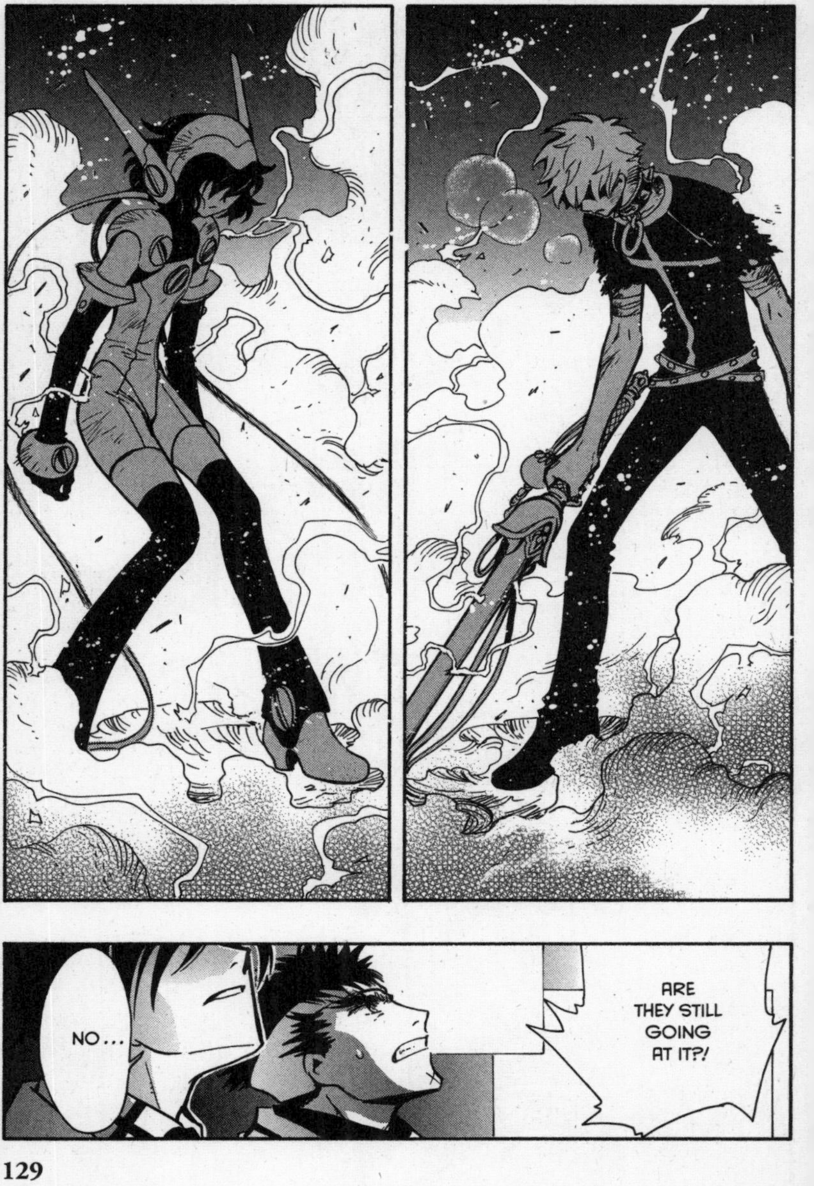
ARE THEY STILL GOING AT IT?!
NO…

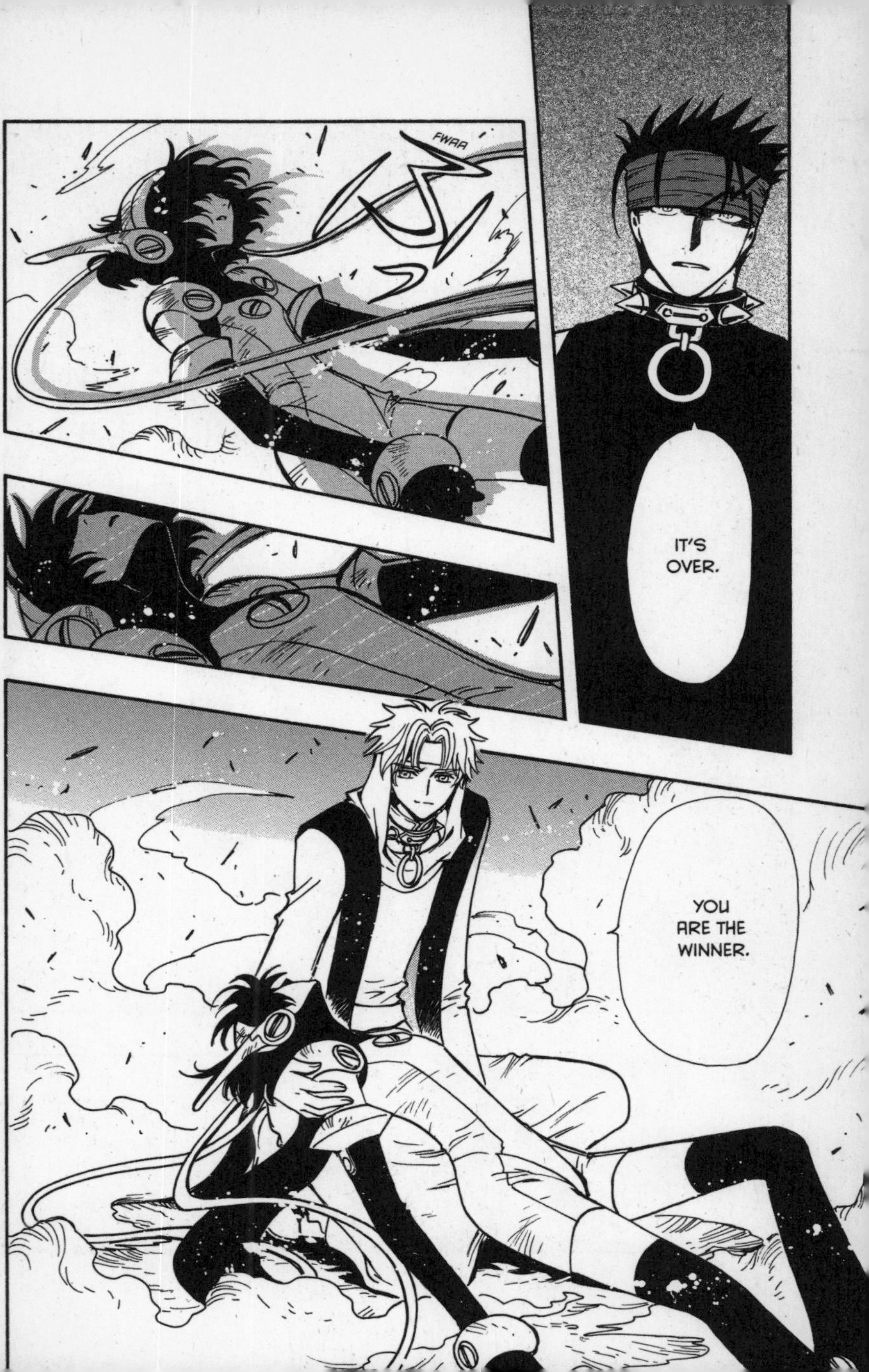
IT'S OVER.
FWAA
YOU ARE THE WINNER.

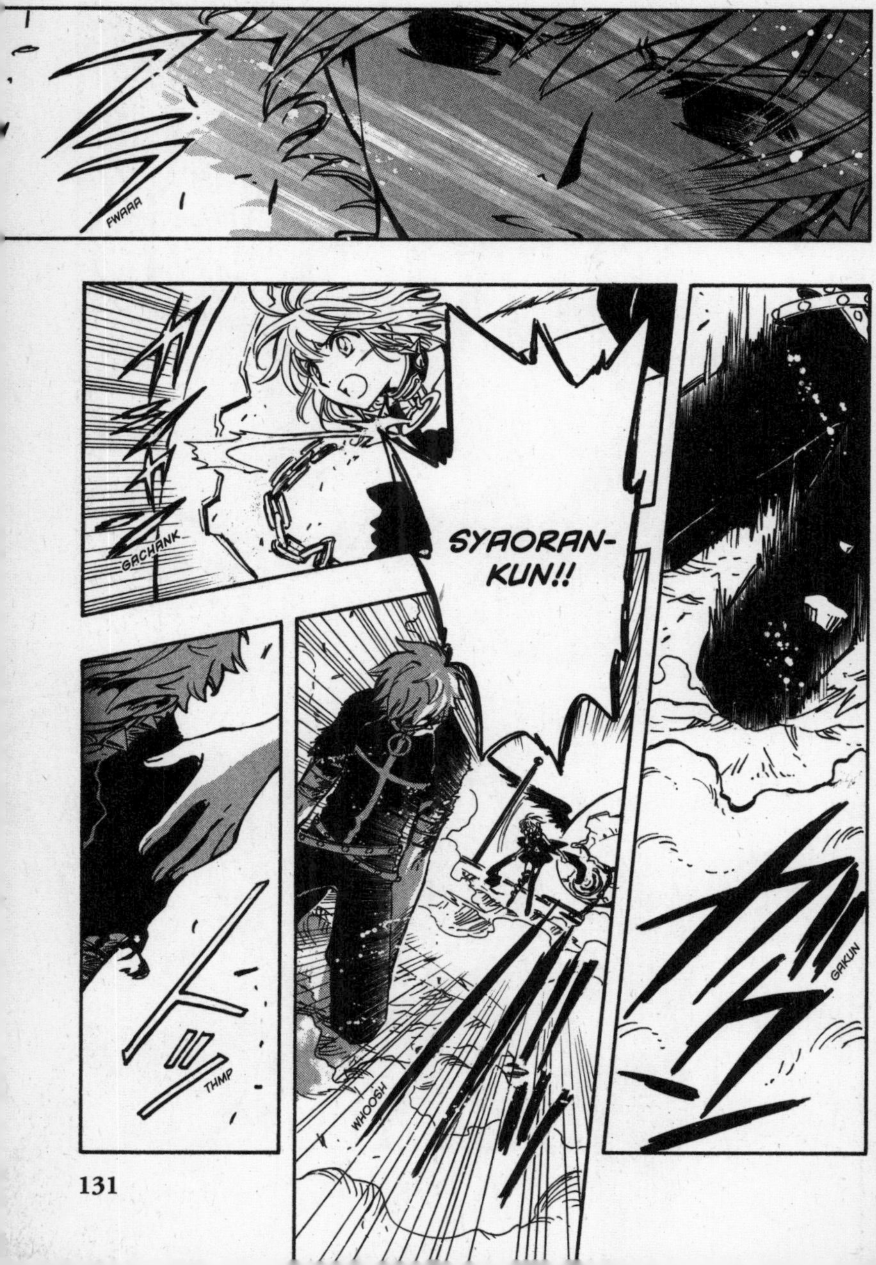
FWAAA
GAKUN
GACHANK
SYAORAN-KUN!!
WHOOSH
THMP

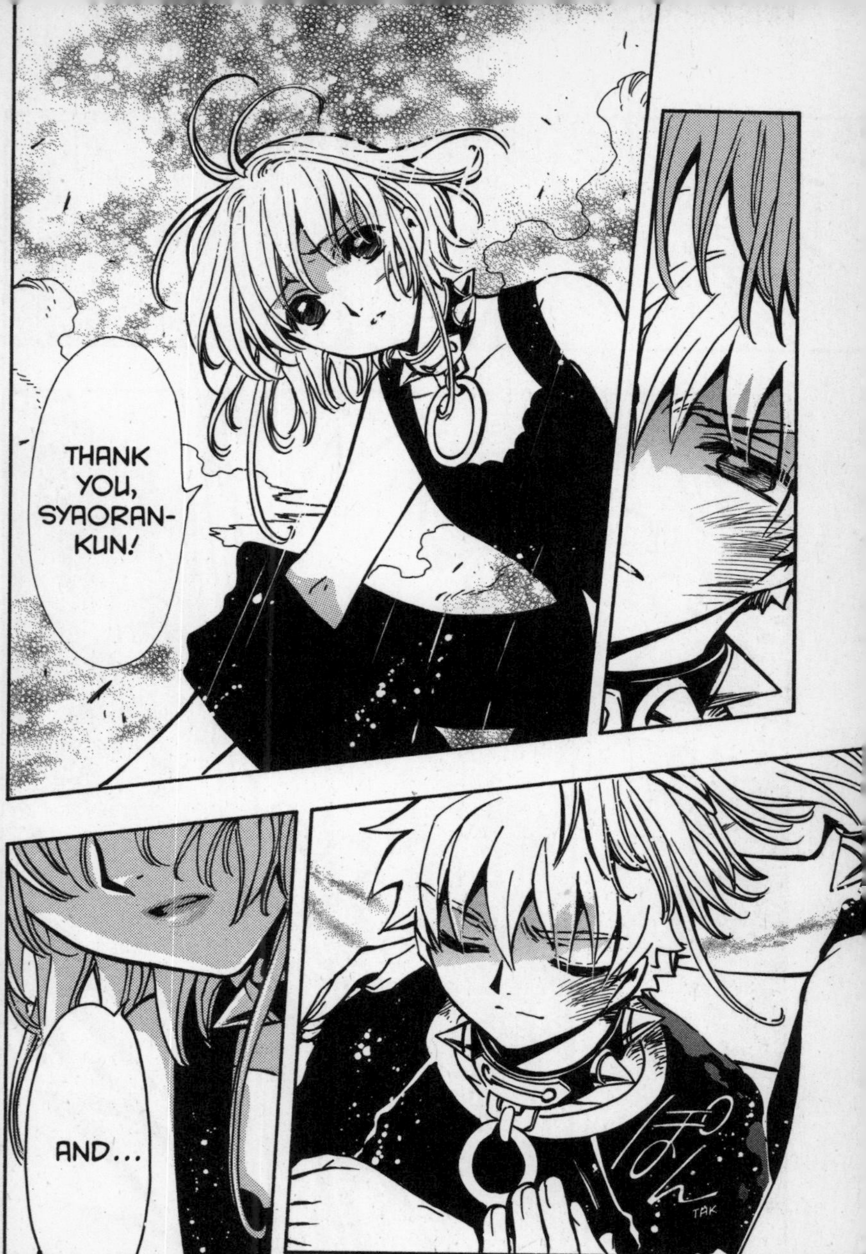
THANK YOU, SYAORAN-KUN!
TAK
AND...

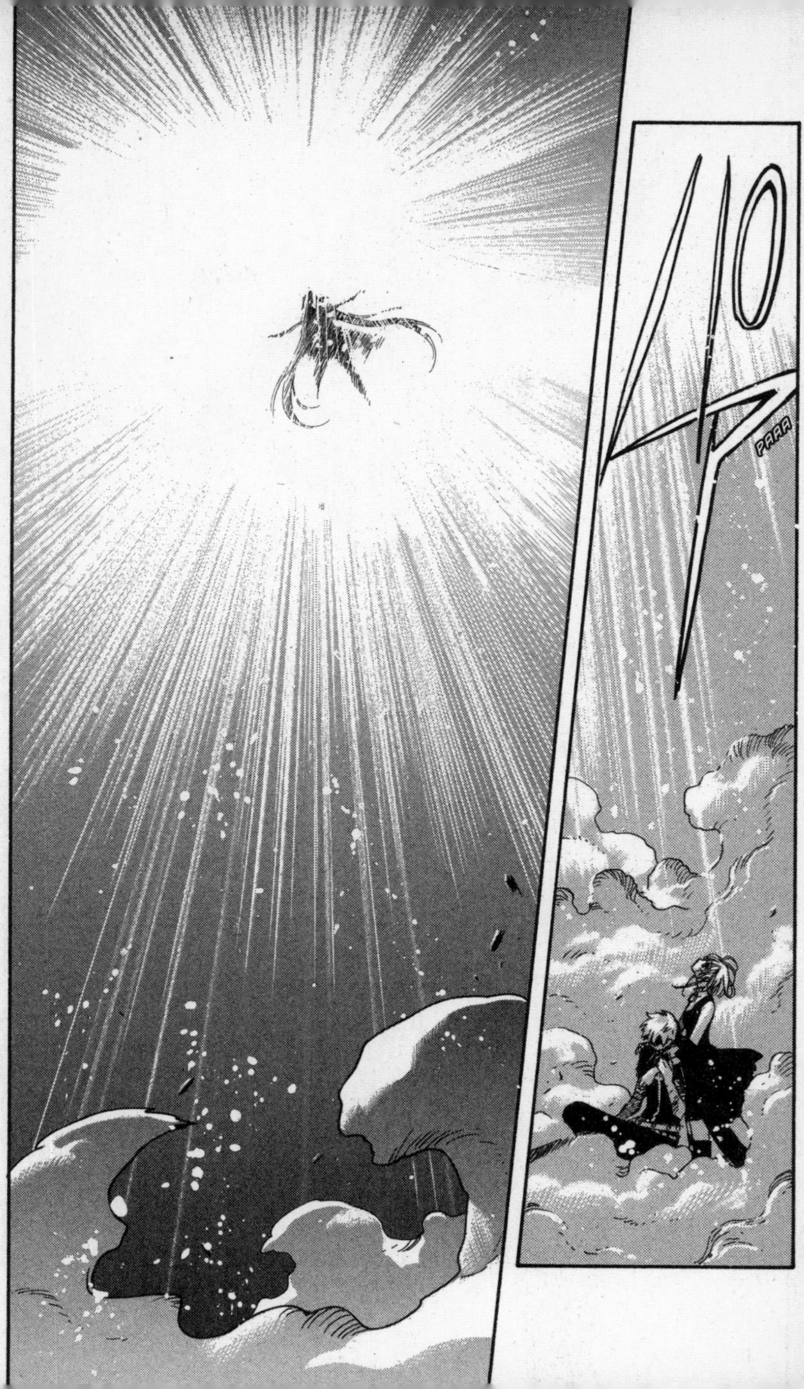
PAAA

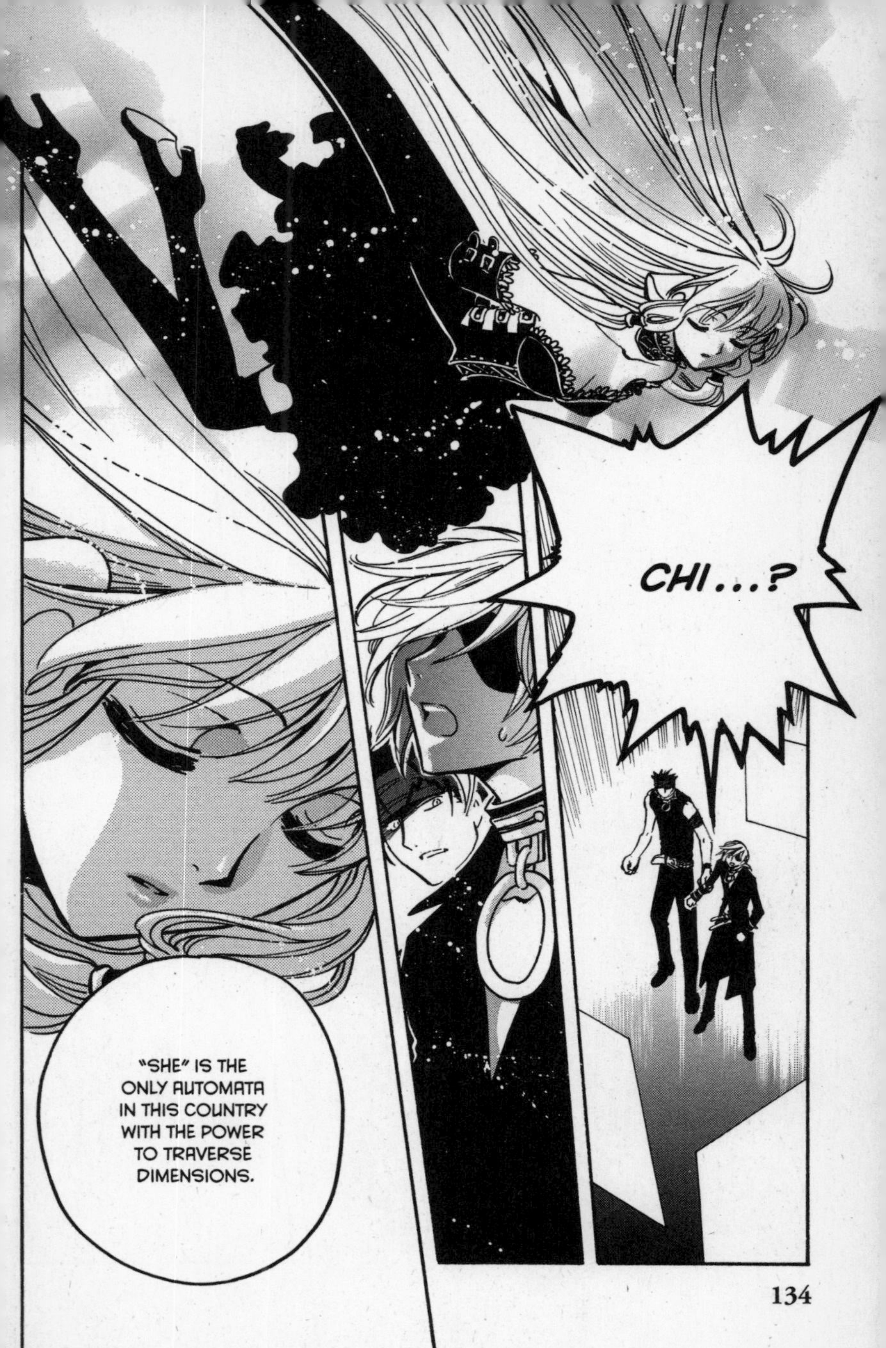
CHI...?
"SHE" IS THE ONLY AUTOMATA IN THIS COUNTRY WITH THE POWER TO TRAVERSE DIMENSIONS.

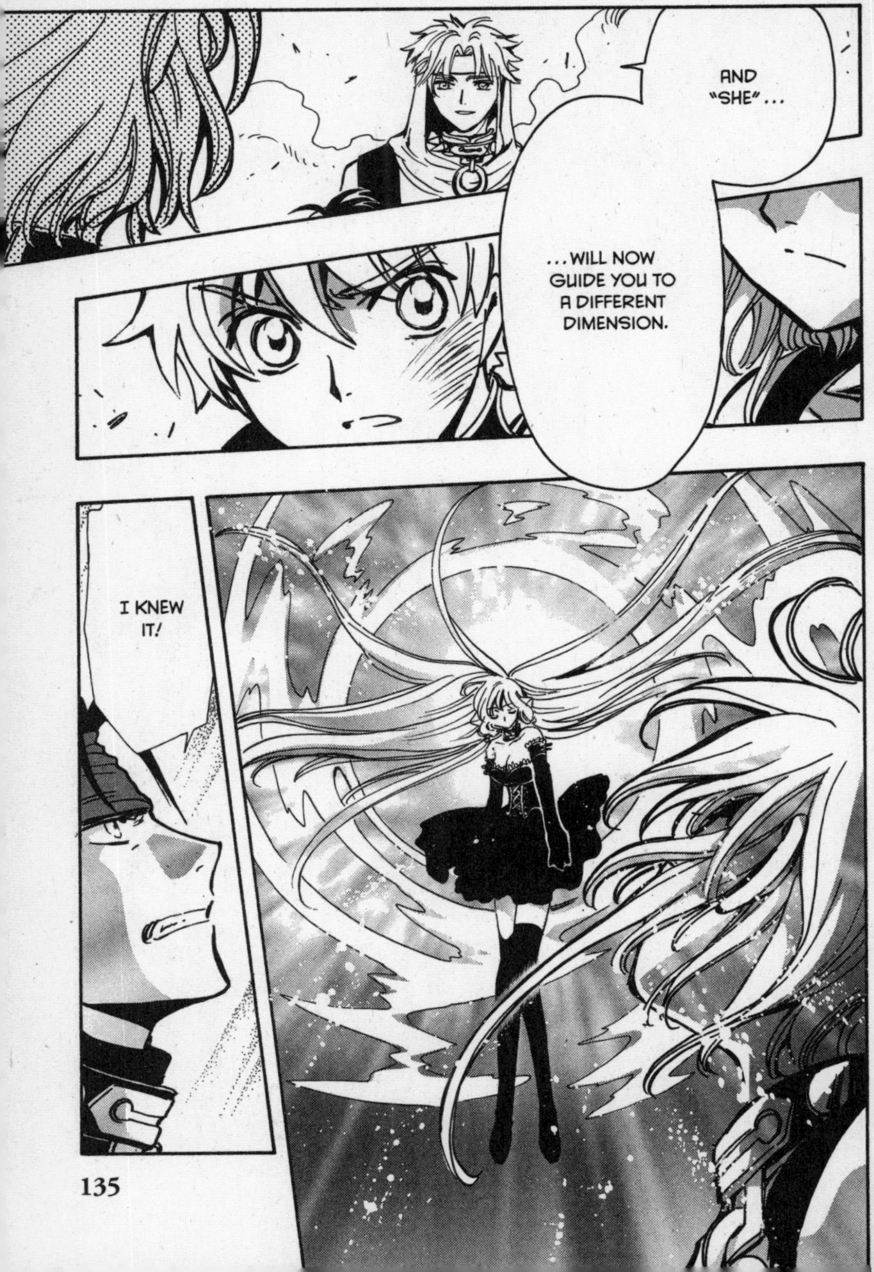
AND "SHE"...
...WILL NOW GUIDE YOU TO A DIFFERENT DIMENSION.
I KNEW IT!

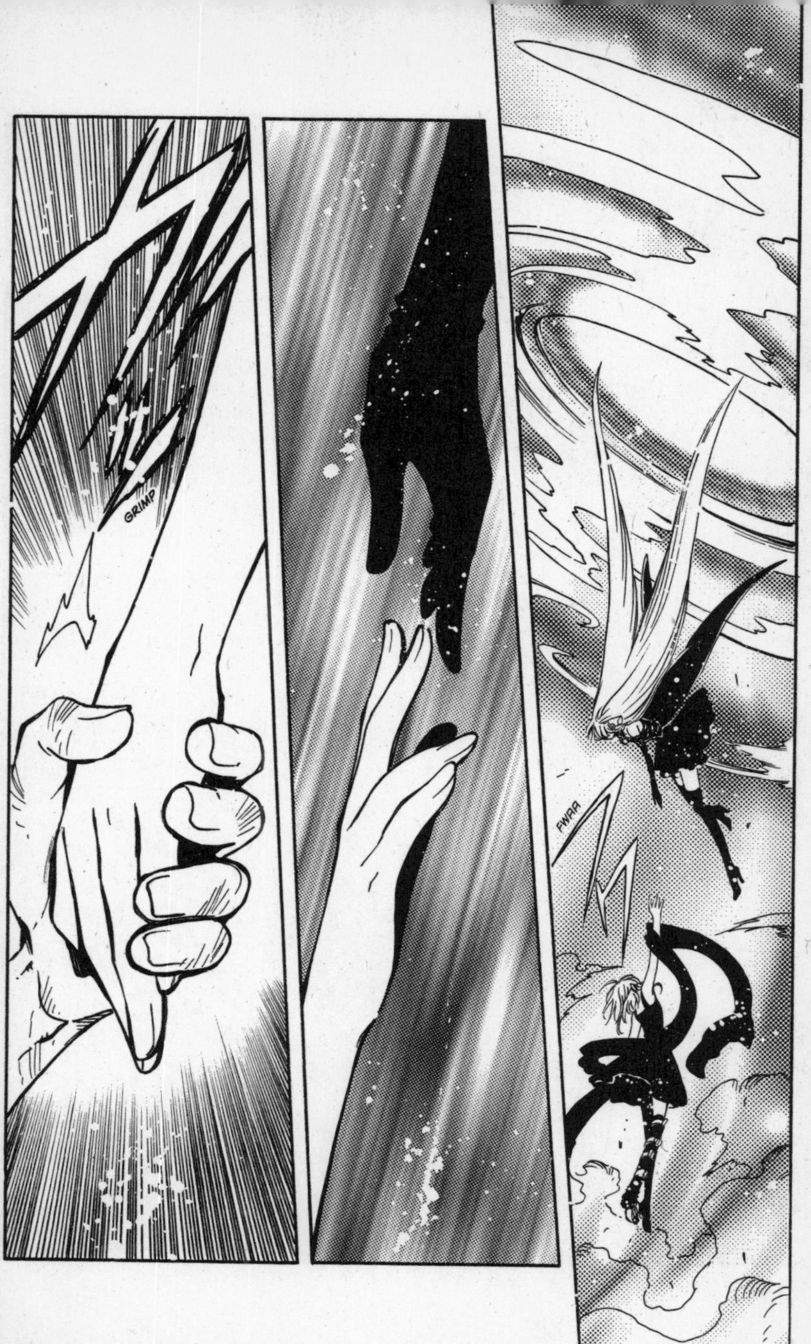
FWAA
GRIMP

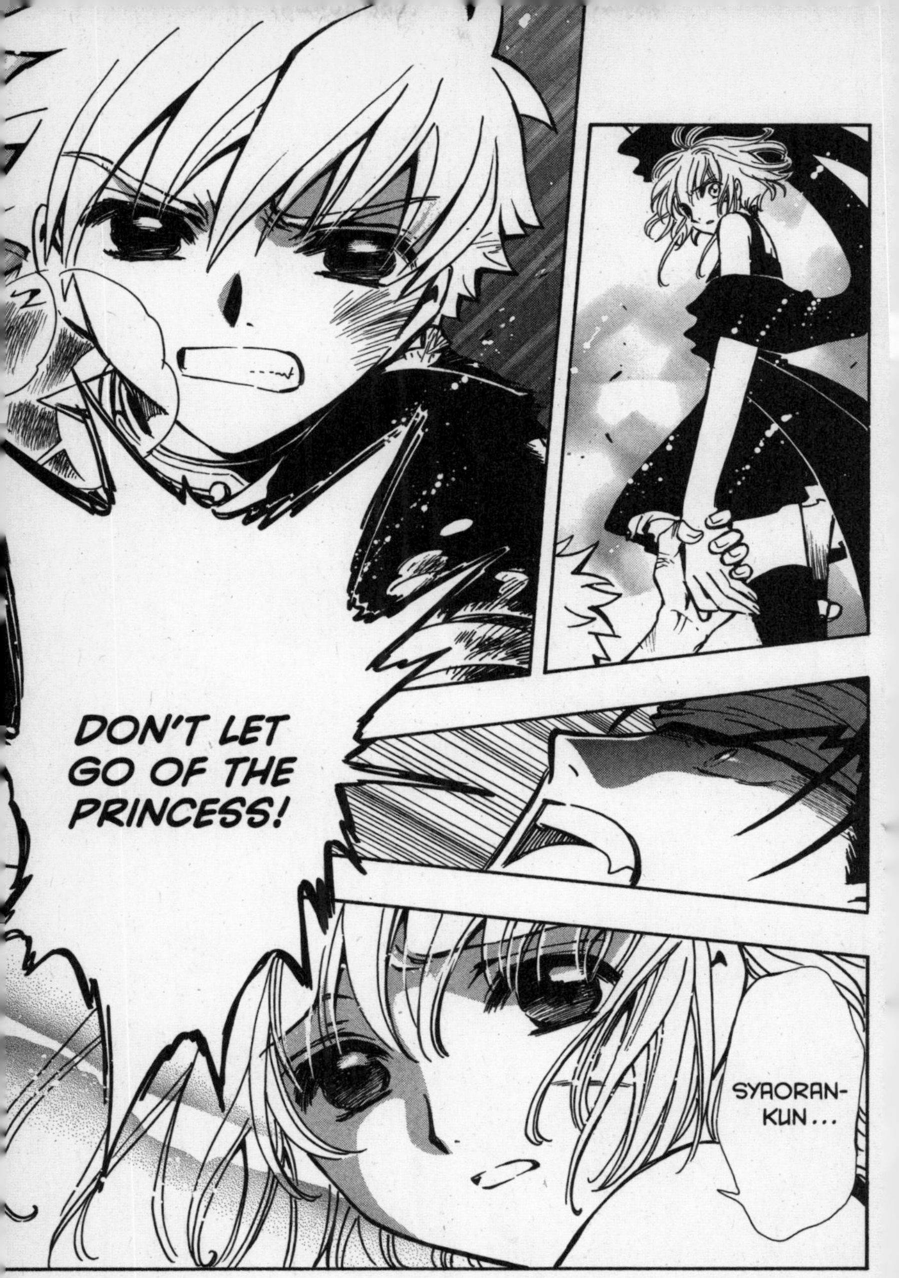
DON'T LET GO OF THE PRINCESS!
SYAORAN-KUN...

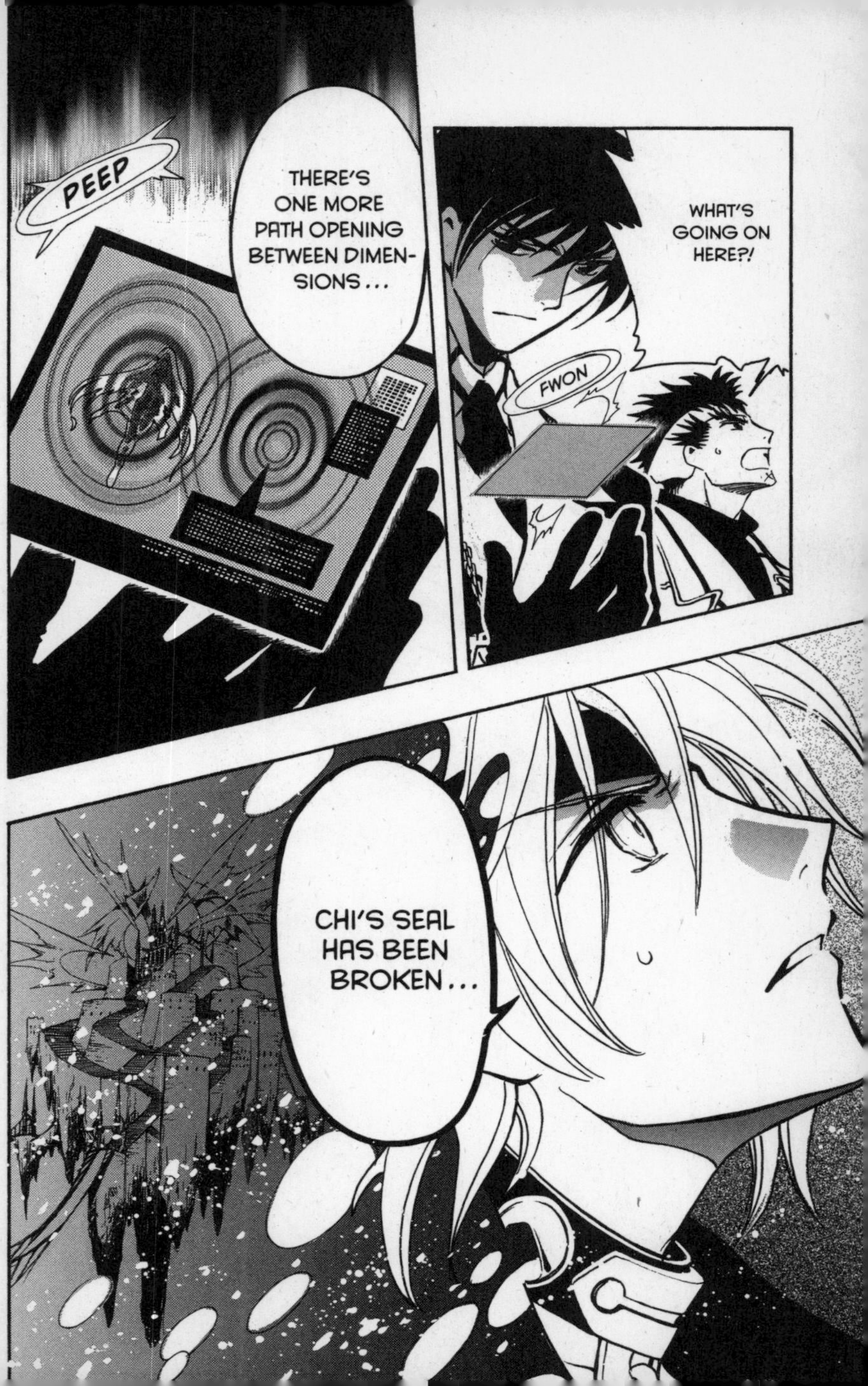
WHAT'S GOING ON HERE?!
FWON
THERE'S ONE MORE PATH OPENING BETWEEN DIMEN-SIONS...
PEEP
CHI'S SEAL HAS BEEN BROKEN...

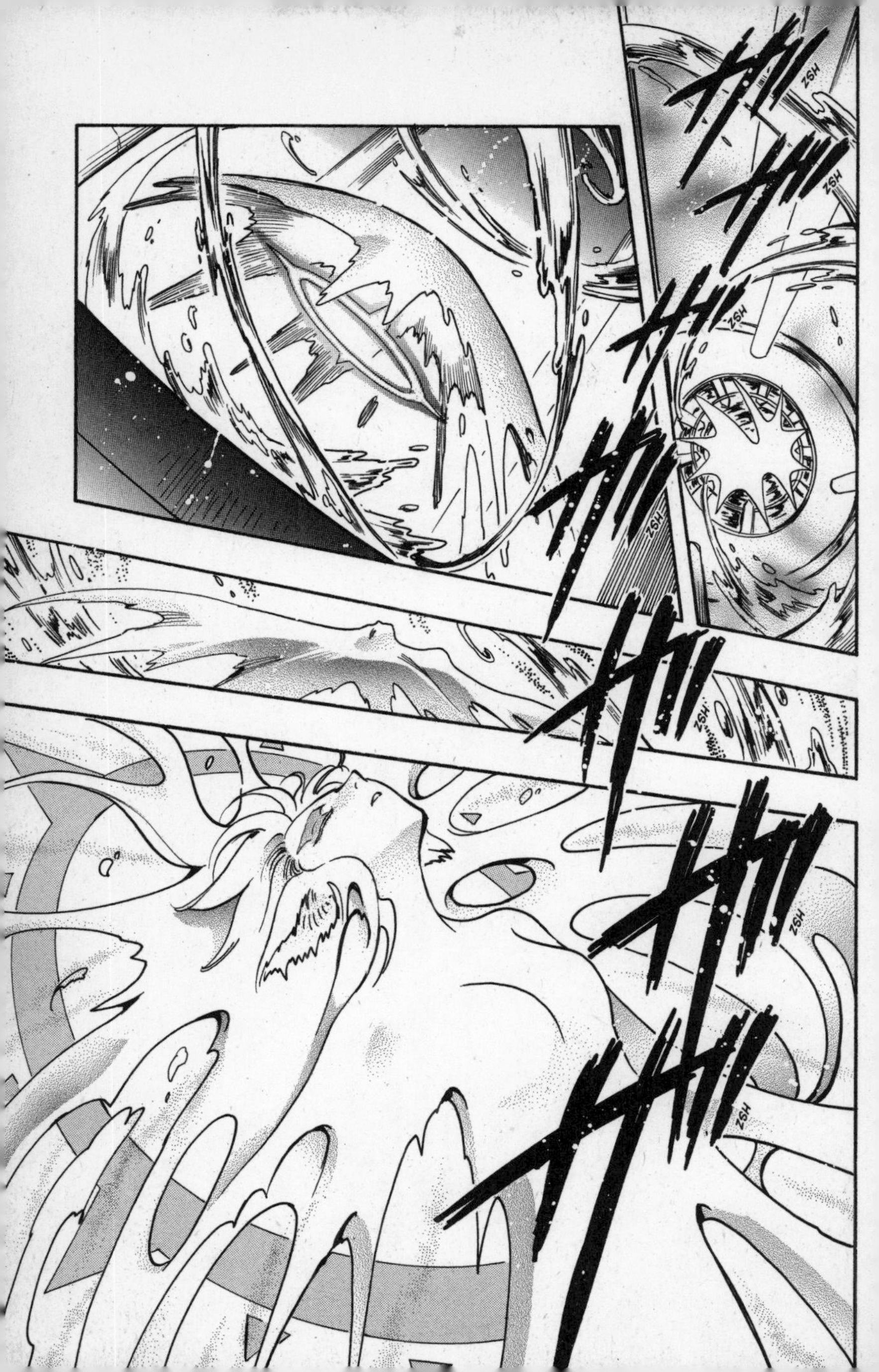
ZSH
ZSH
ZSH
ZSH
ZSH
ZSH
ZSH

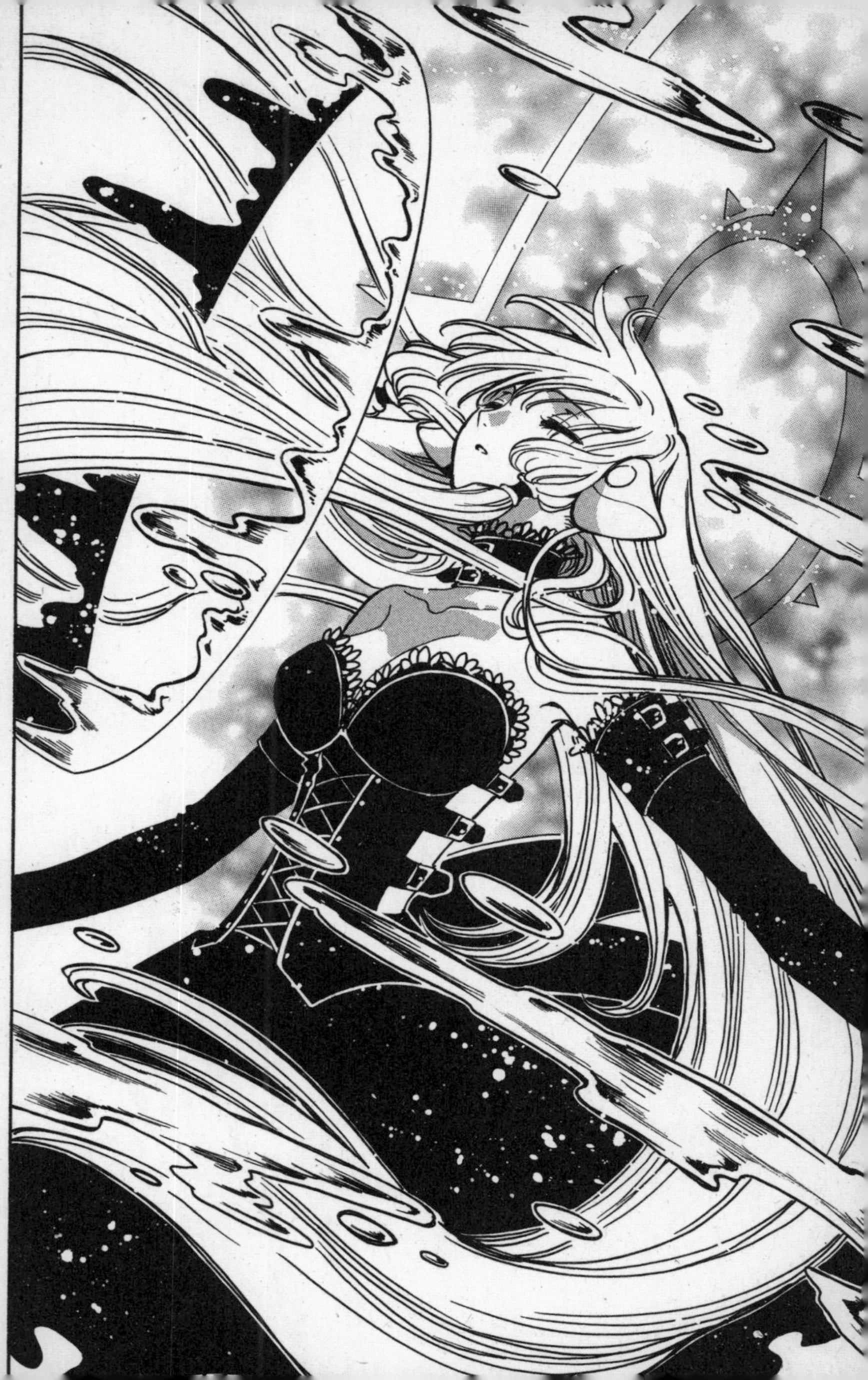

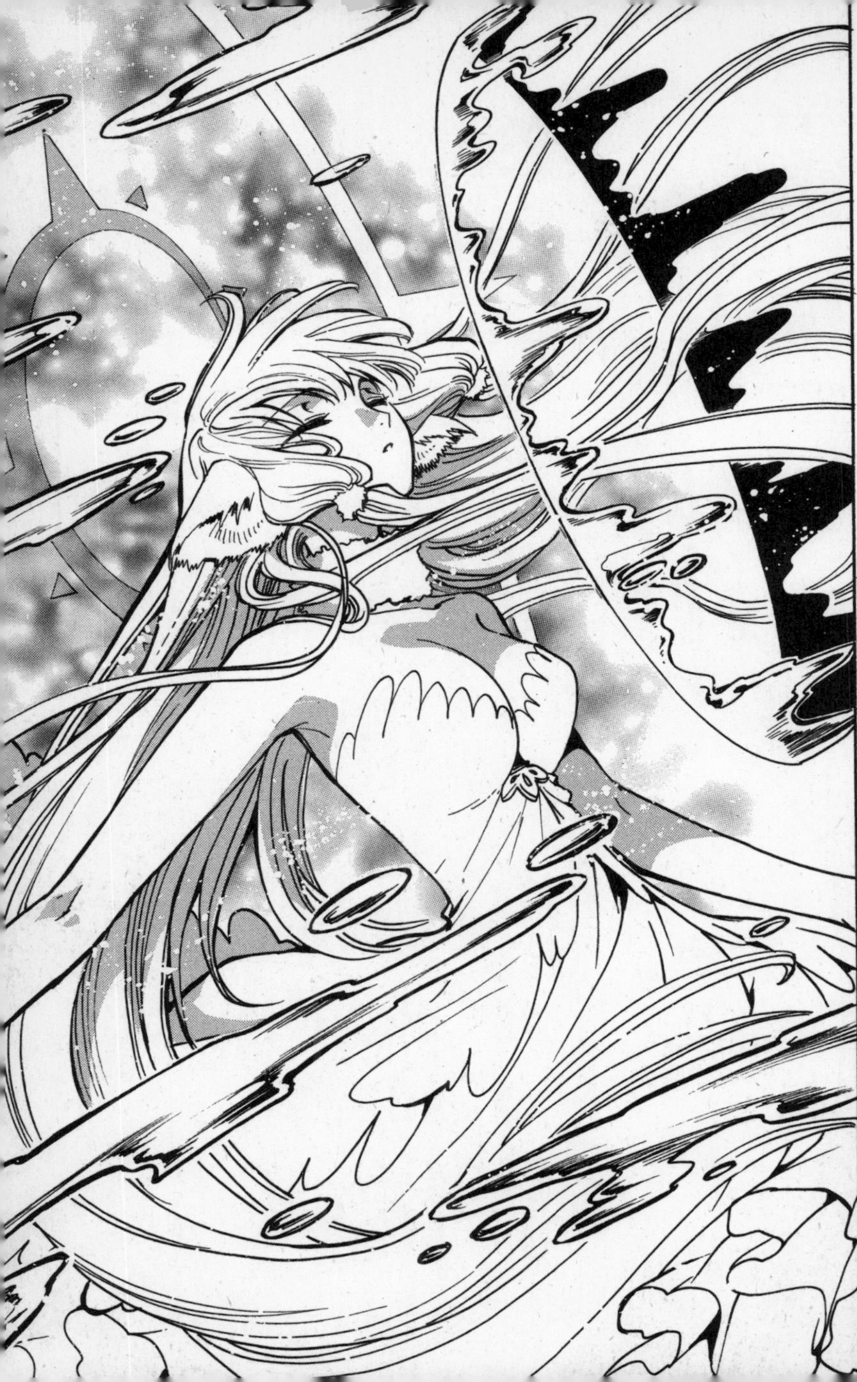

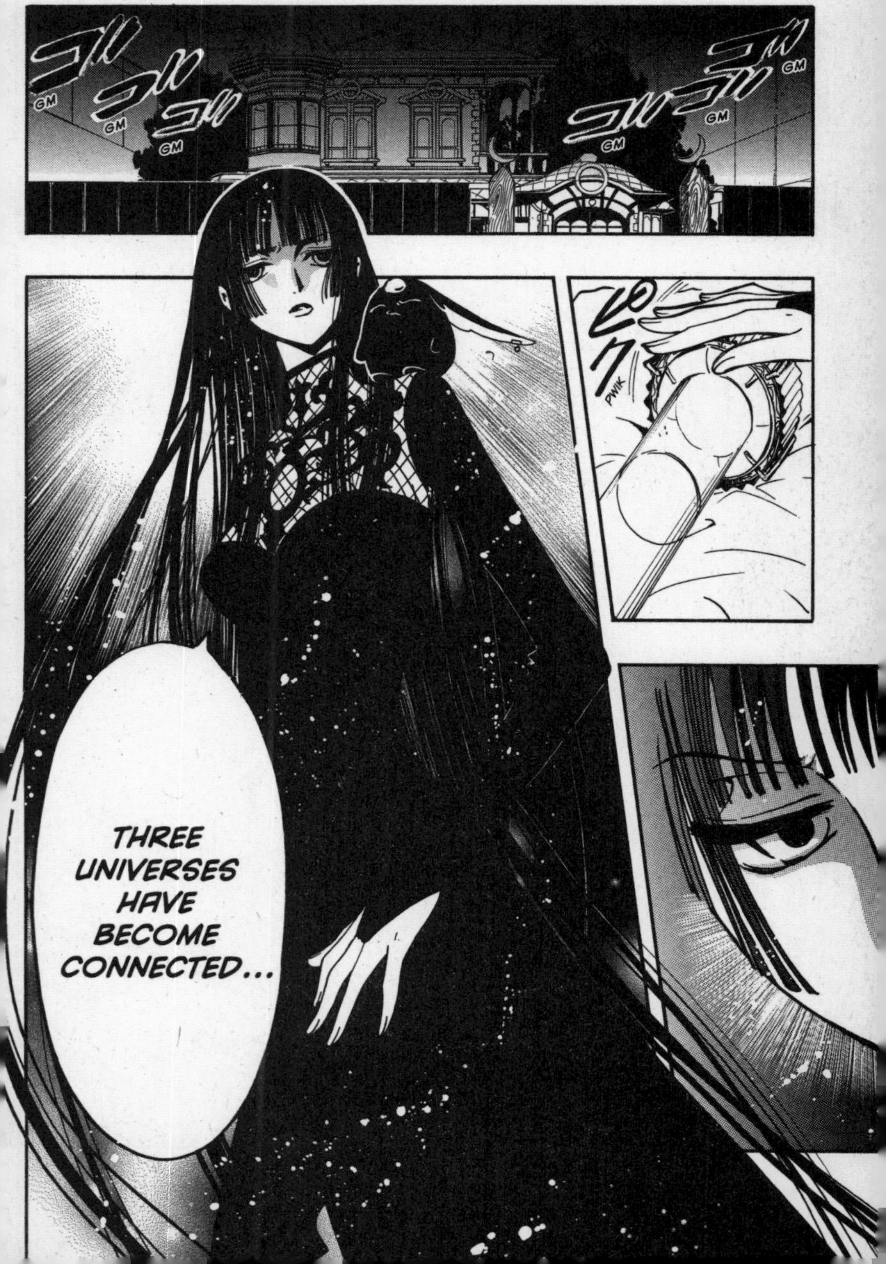
GM
GM
GM
GM
GM
GM
PWIK
THREE UNIVERSES HAVE BECOME CONNECTED...

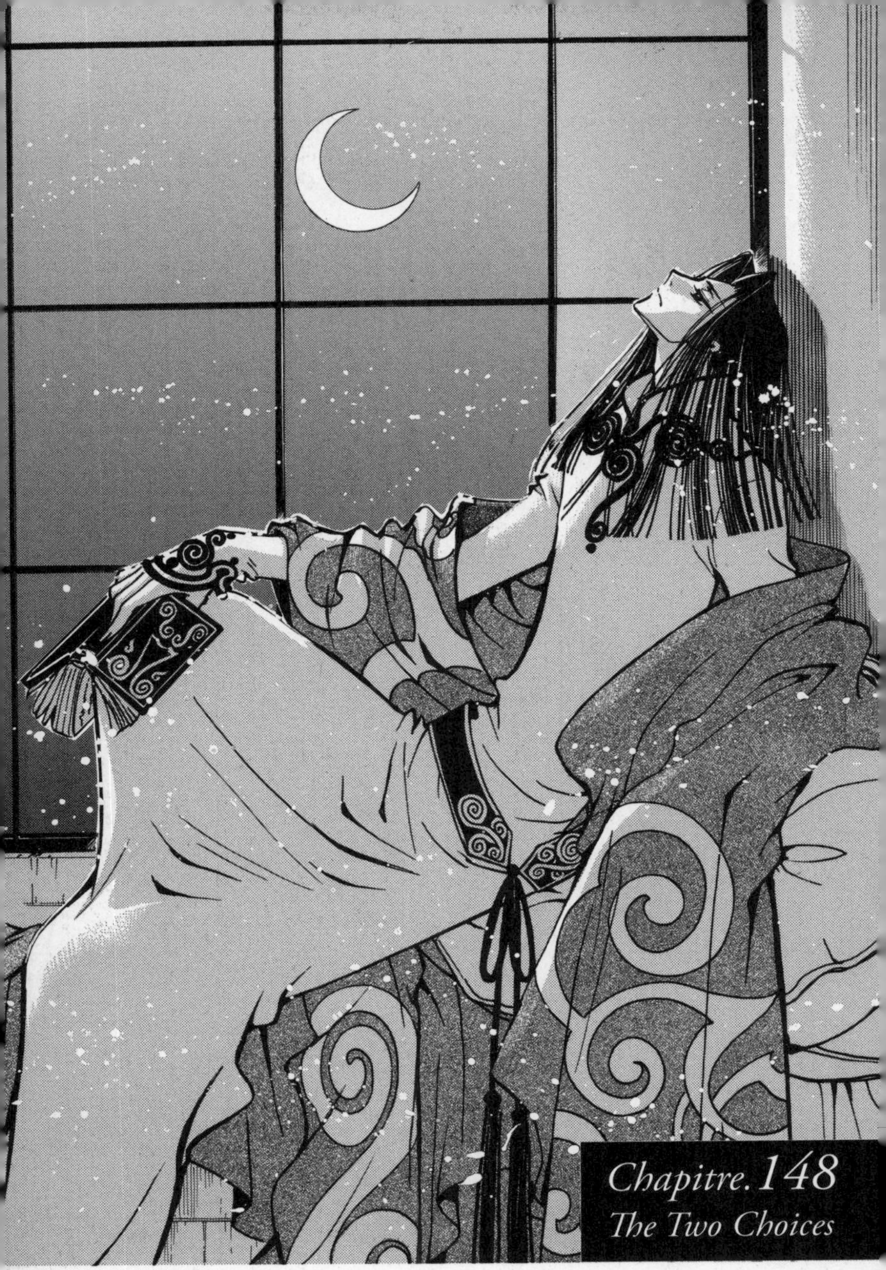

Chapitre. 148
The Two Choices

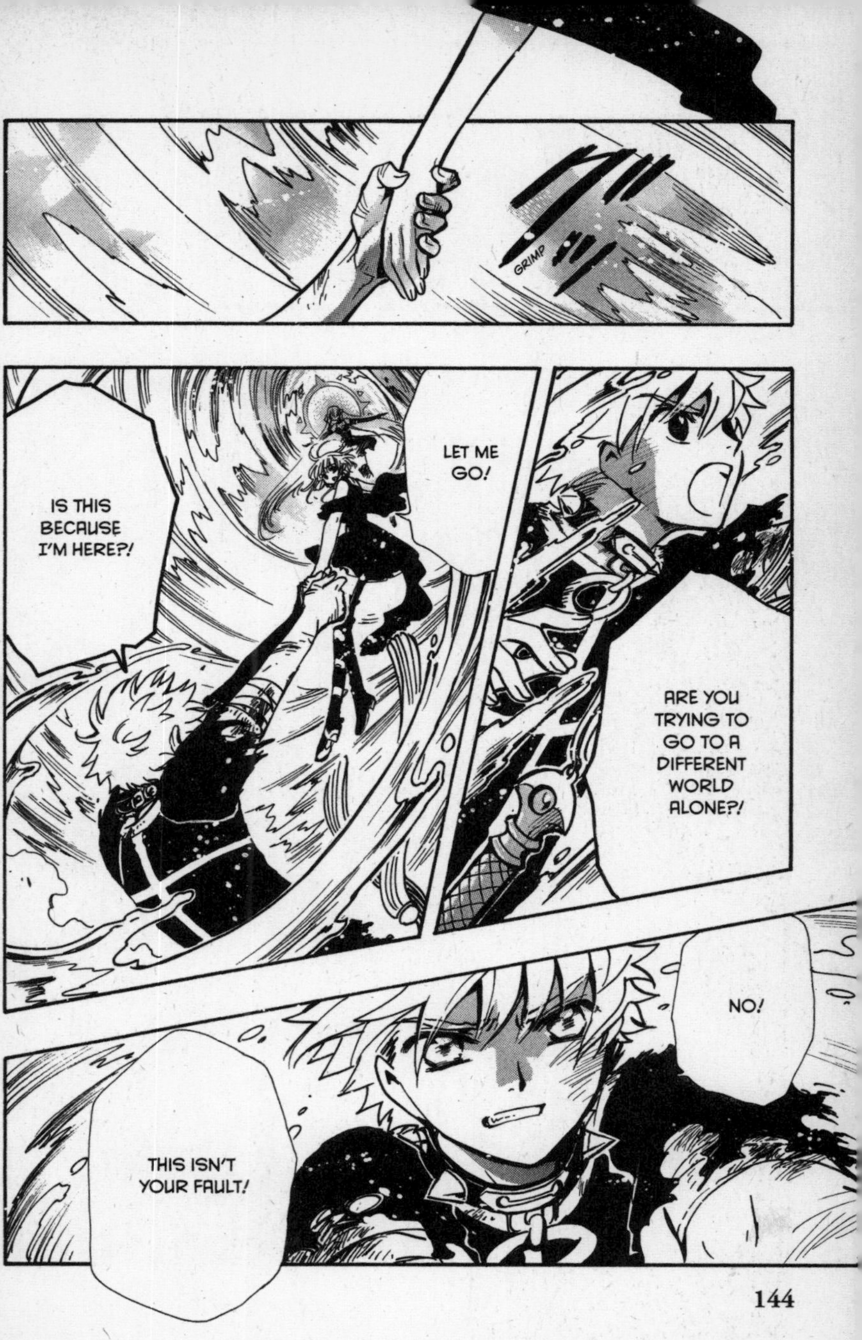
GRIMP
LET ME GO!
ARE YOU TRYING TO GO TO A DIFFERENT WORLD ALONE?!
IS THIS BECAUSE I'M HERE?!
NO!
THIS ISN'T YOUR FAULT!

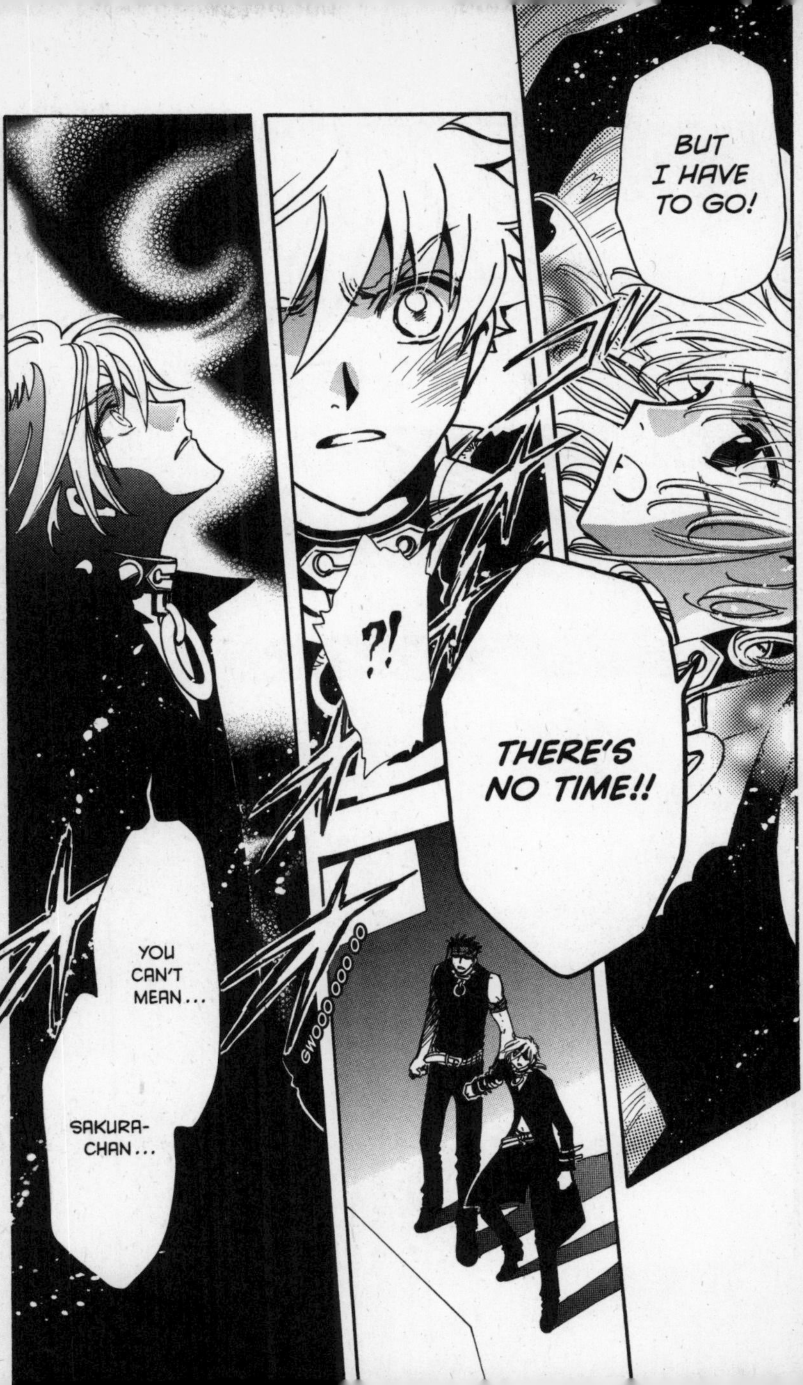
BUT I HAVE TO GO!
THERE'S NO TIME!!
?!
GWOOO OOO OO
YOU CAN'T MEAN...
SAKURA-CHAN...

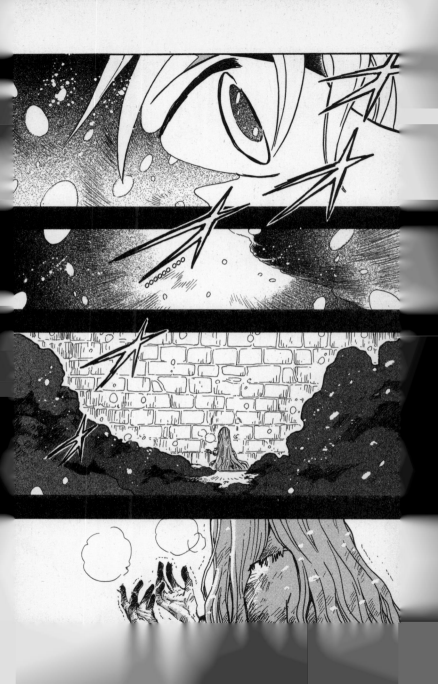

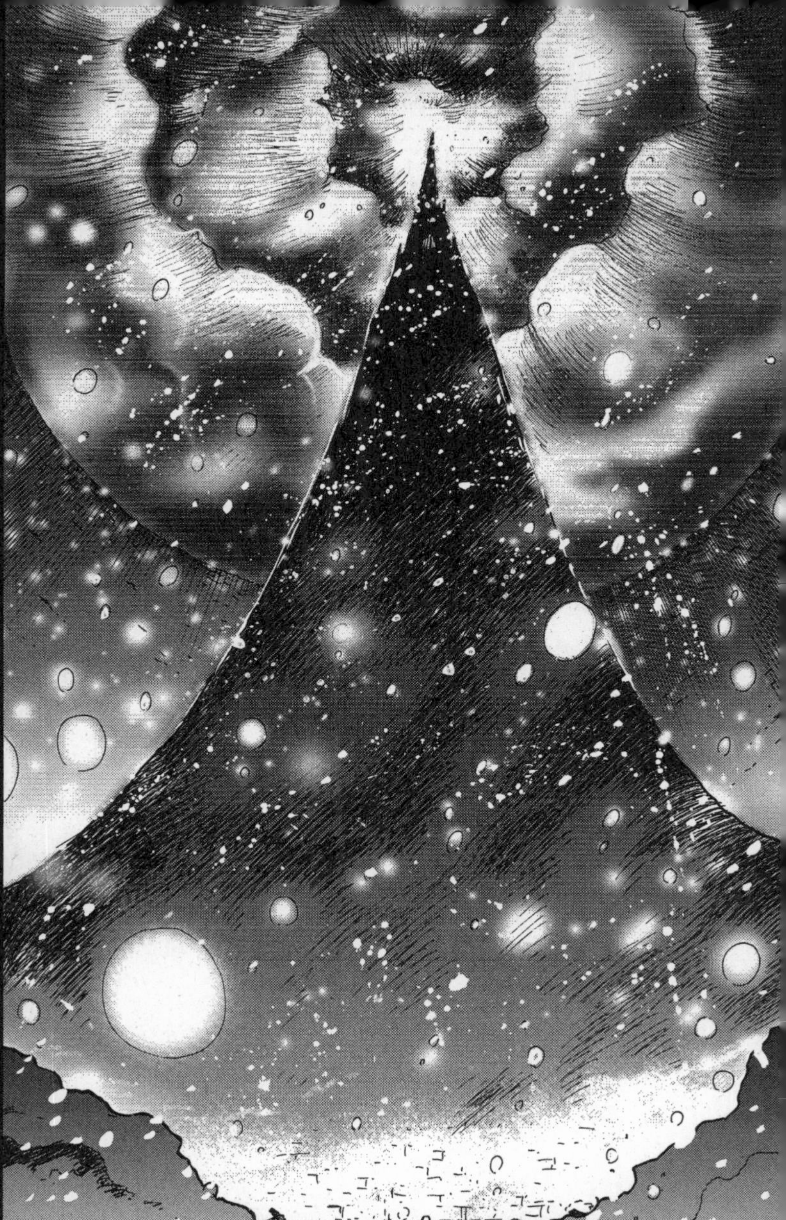

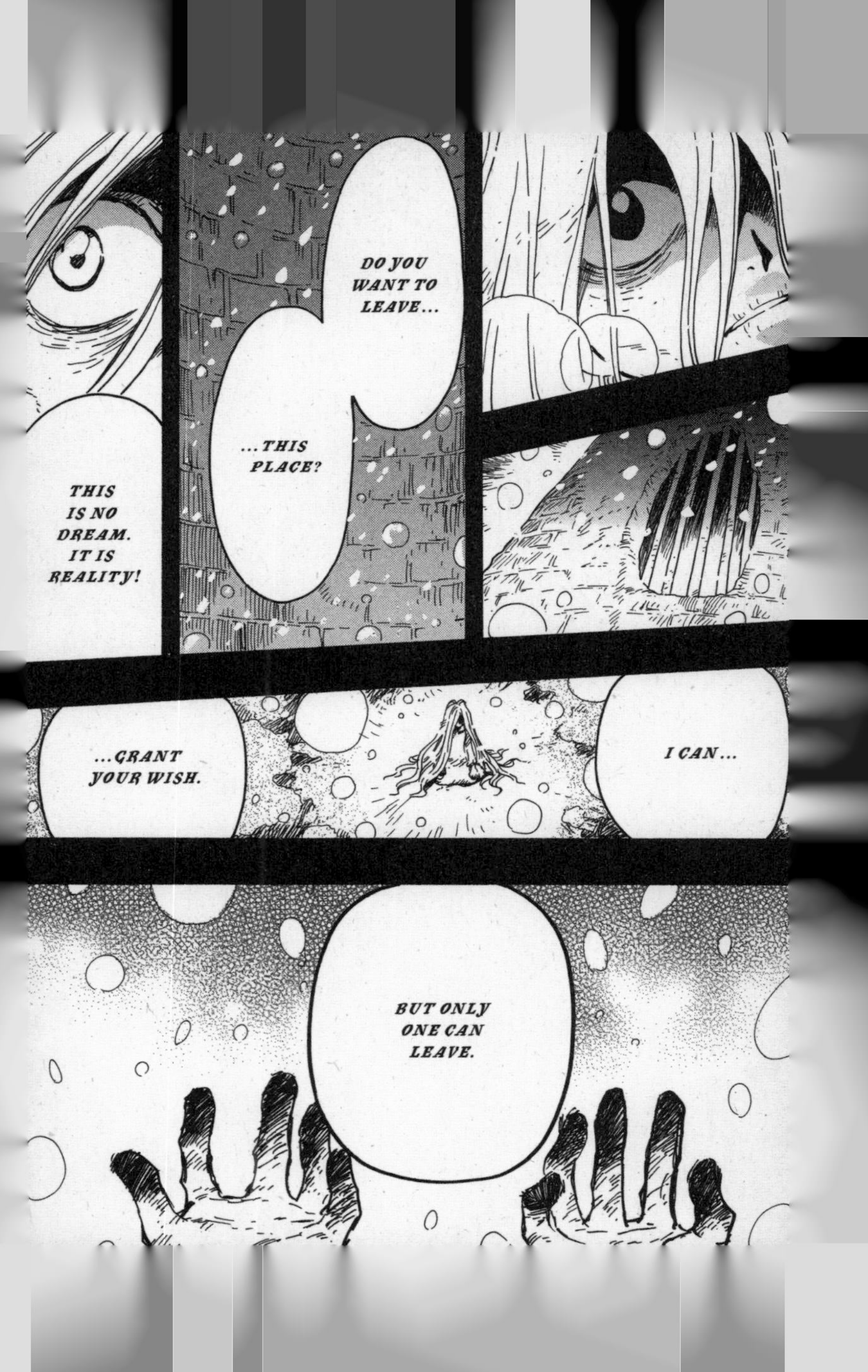
DO YOU WANT TO LEAVE...
...THIS PLACE?
THIS IS NO DREAM. IT IS REALITY!
I CAN...
...GRANT YOUR WISH.
BUT ONLY ONE CAN LEAVE.

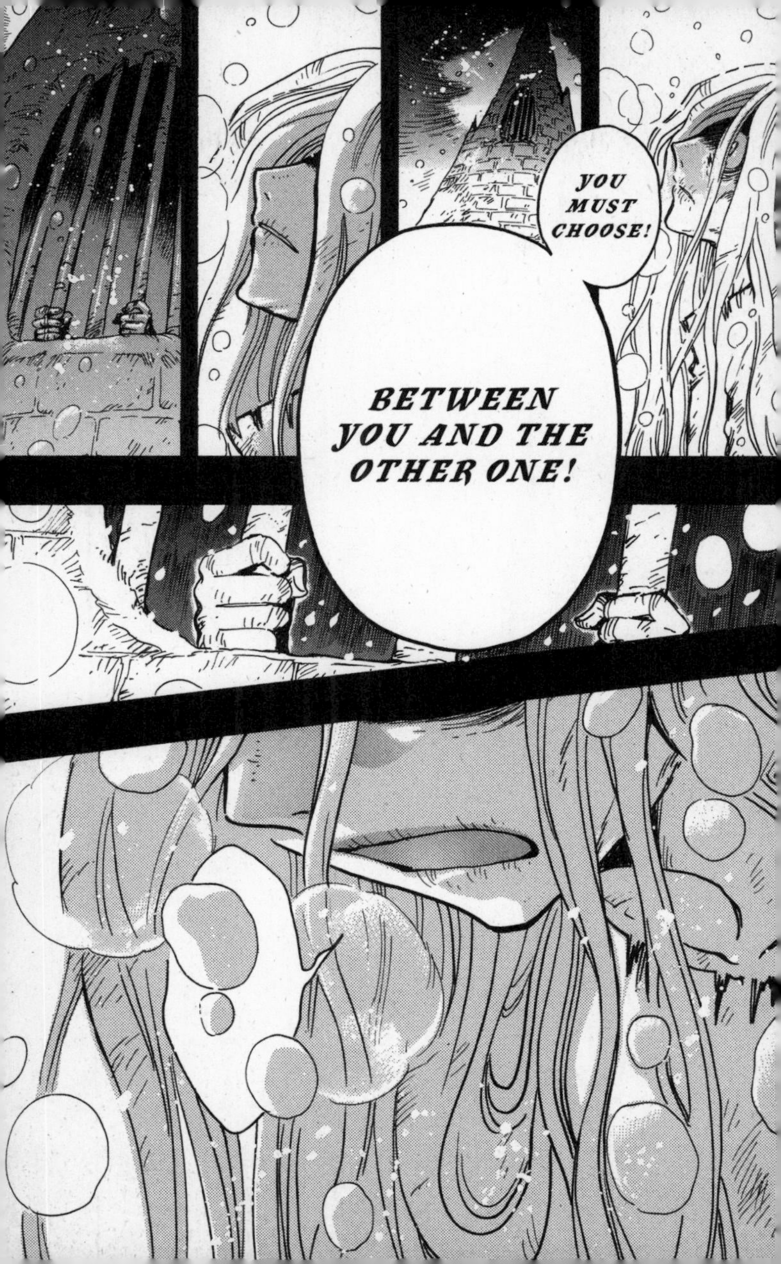
YOU MUST CHOOSE!
BETWEEN YOU AND THE OTHER ONE!

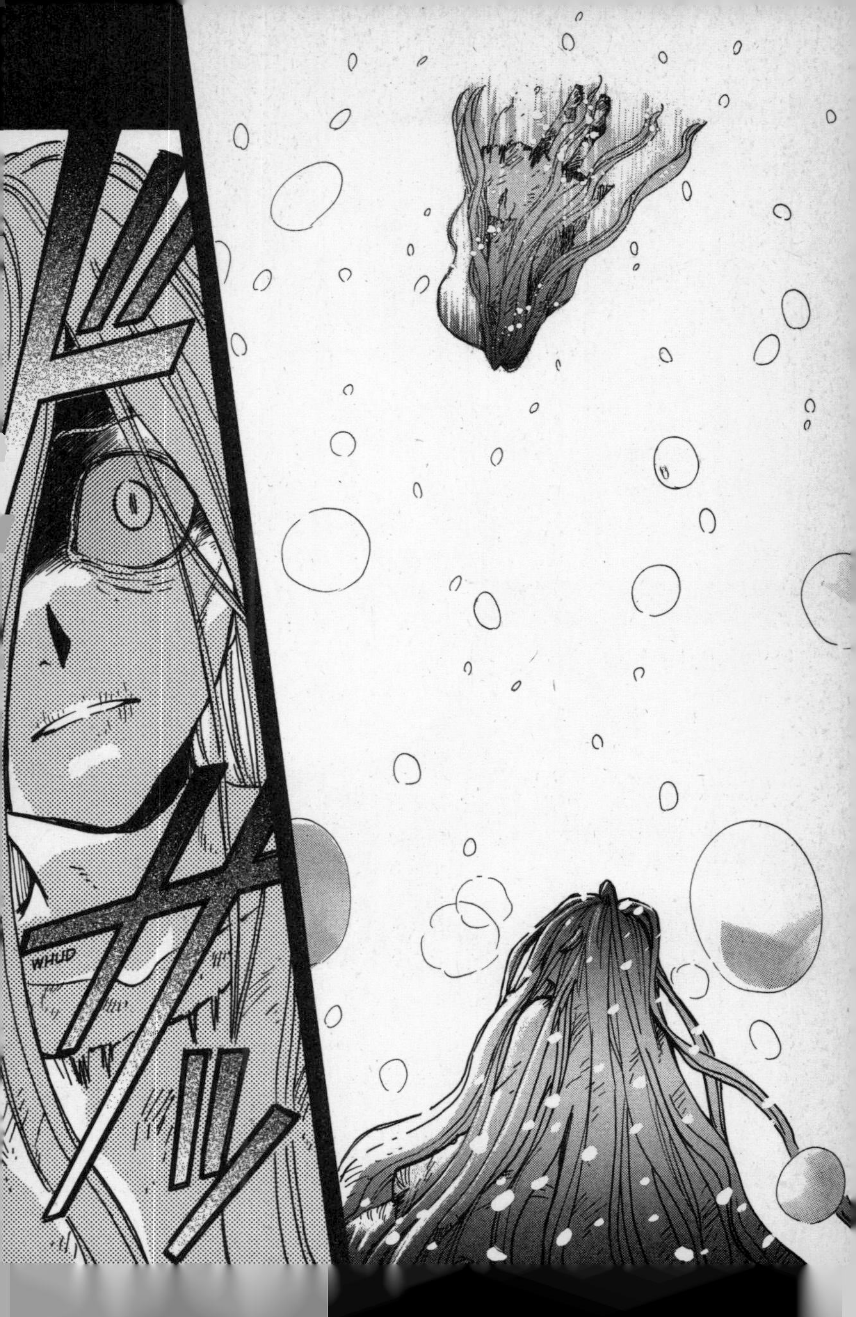
WHUD

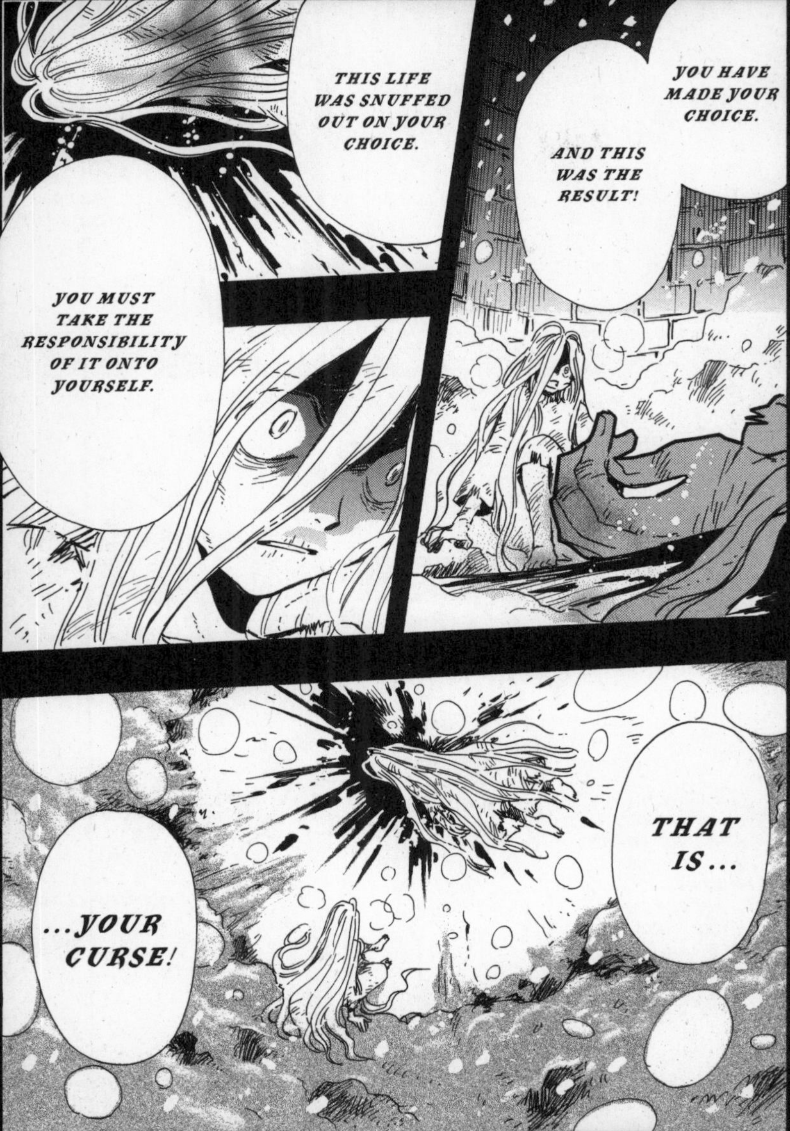
YOU HAVE MADE YOUR CHOICE.
AND THIS WAS THE RESULT!
THIS LIFE WAS SNUFFED OUT ON YOUR CHOICE.
YOU MUST TAKE THE RESPONSIBILITY OF IT ONTO YOURSELF.
THAT IS...
...YOUR CURSE!

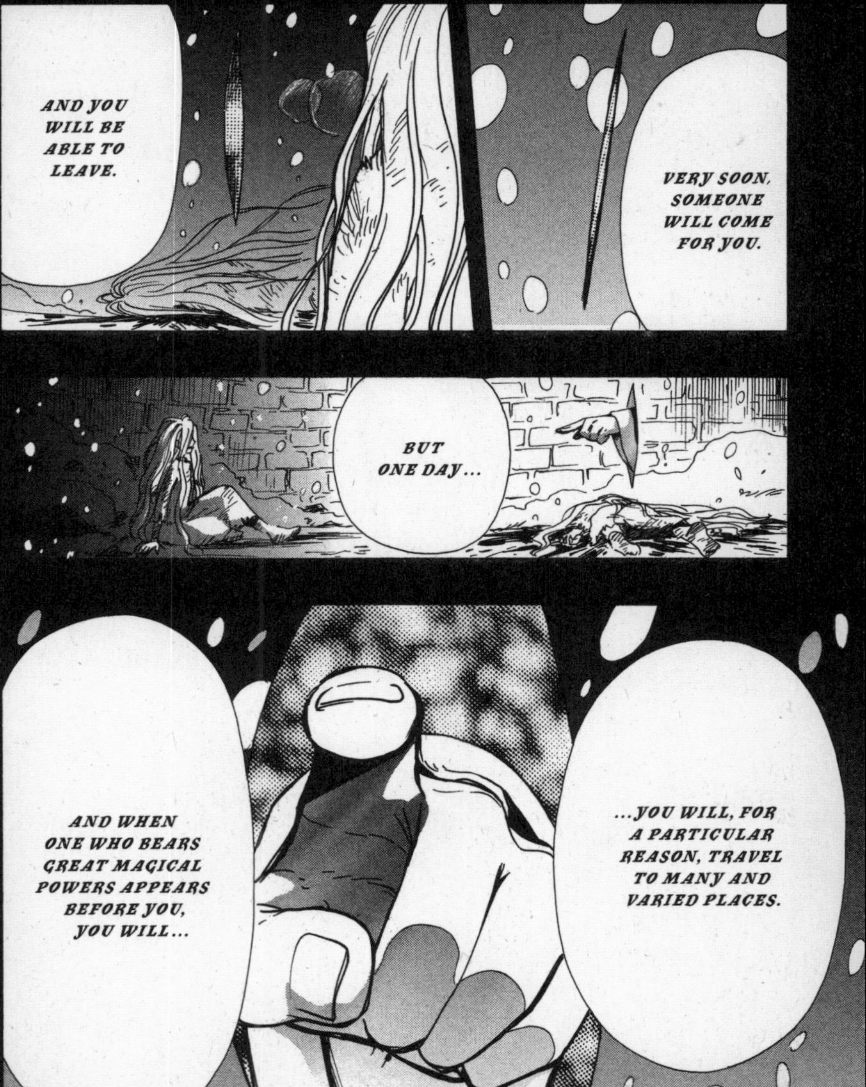
VERY SOON, SOMEONE WILL COME FOR YOU.
AND YOU WILL BE ABLE TO LEAVE.
BUT ONE DAY...
AND WHEN ONE WHO BEARS GREAT MAGICAL POWERS APPEARS BEFORE YOU, YOU WILL...
...YOU WILL, FOR A PARTICULAR REASON, TRAVEL TO MANY AND VARIED PLACES.

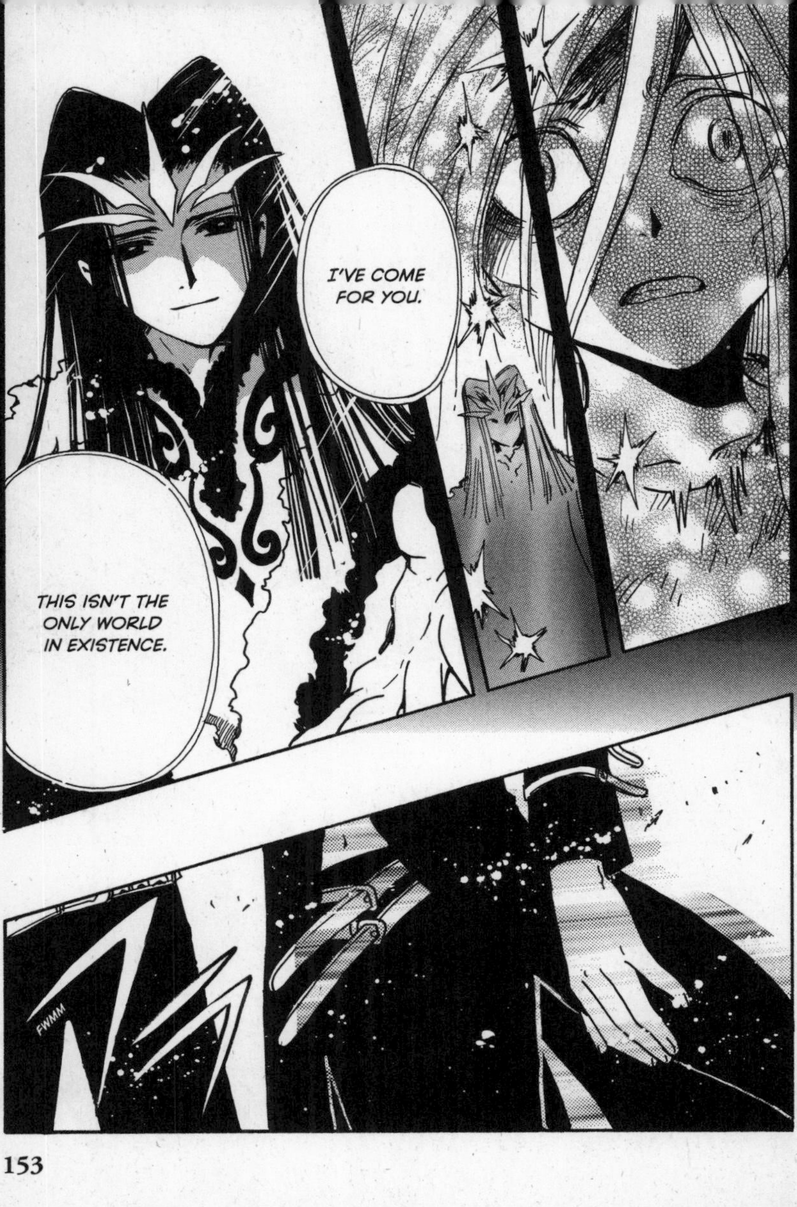
I'VE COME FOR YOU.
THIS ISN'T THE ONLY WORLD IN EXISTENCE.
FWMM

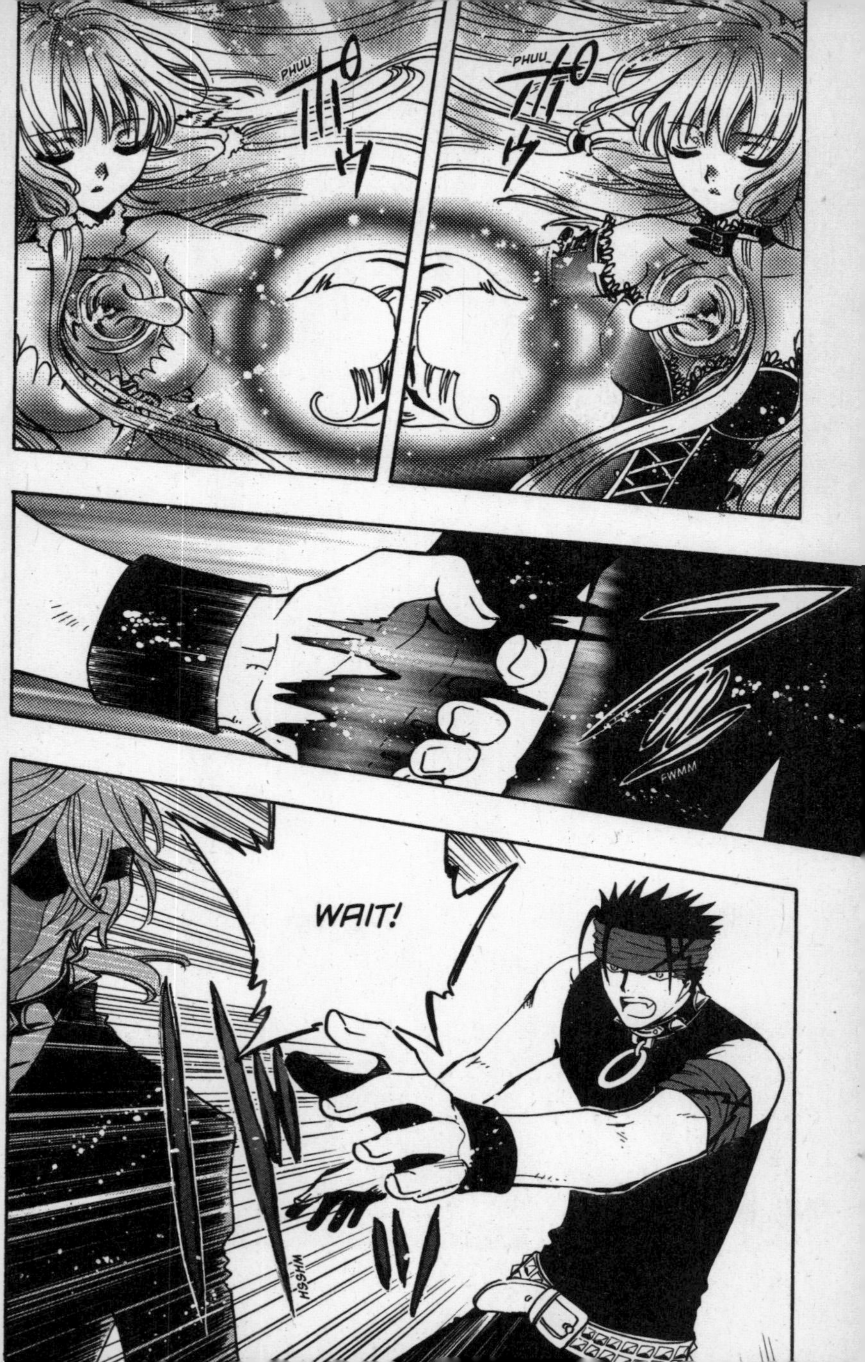
PHUU
PHUU
FWMM
WAIT!
WHSSH

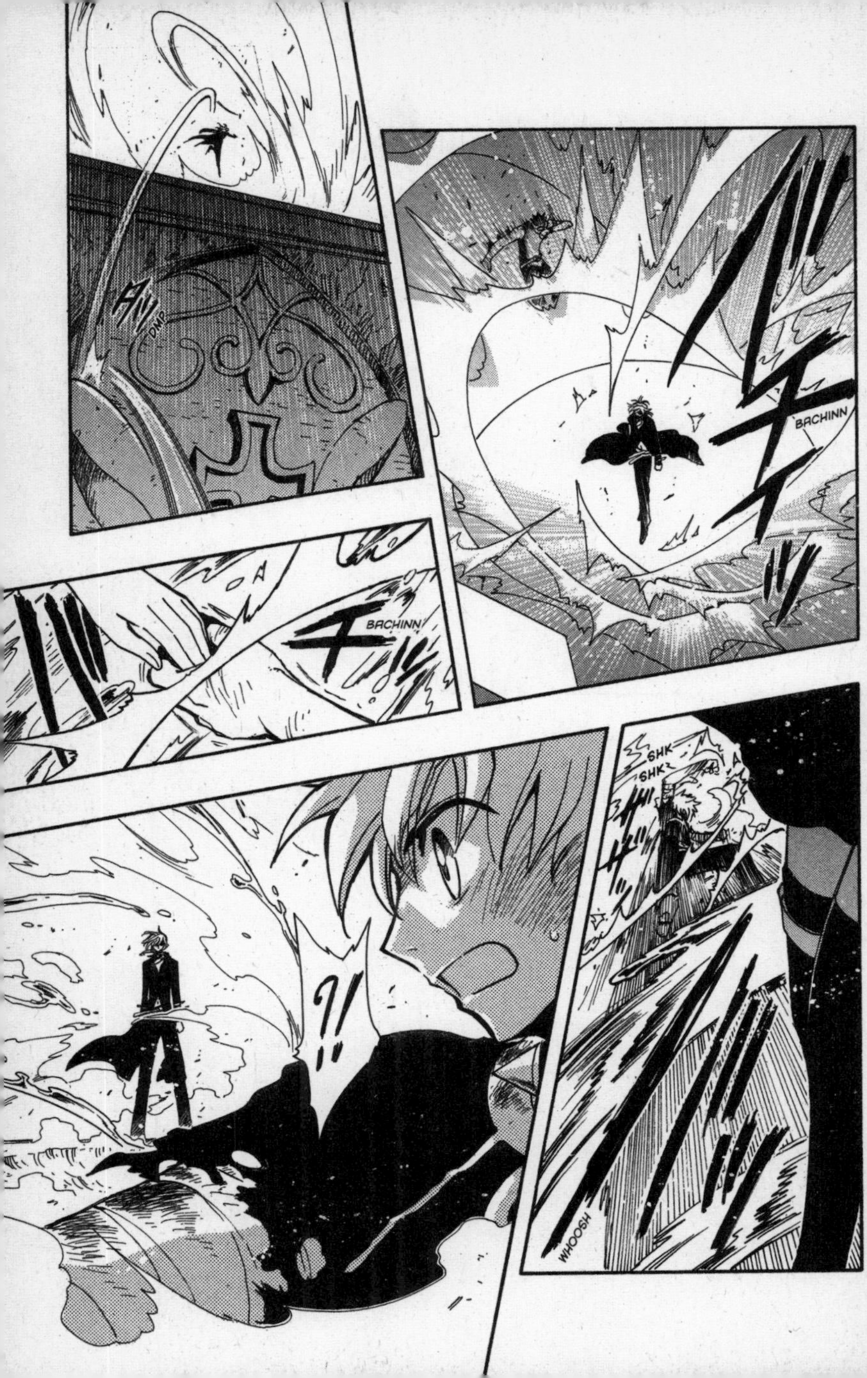
BACHINN
DMP
BACHINN
SHK
SHK
WHOOSH
?!!

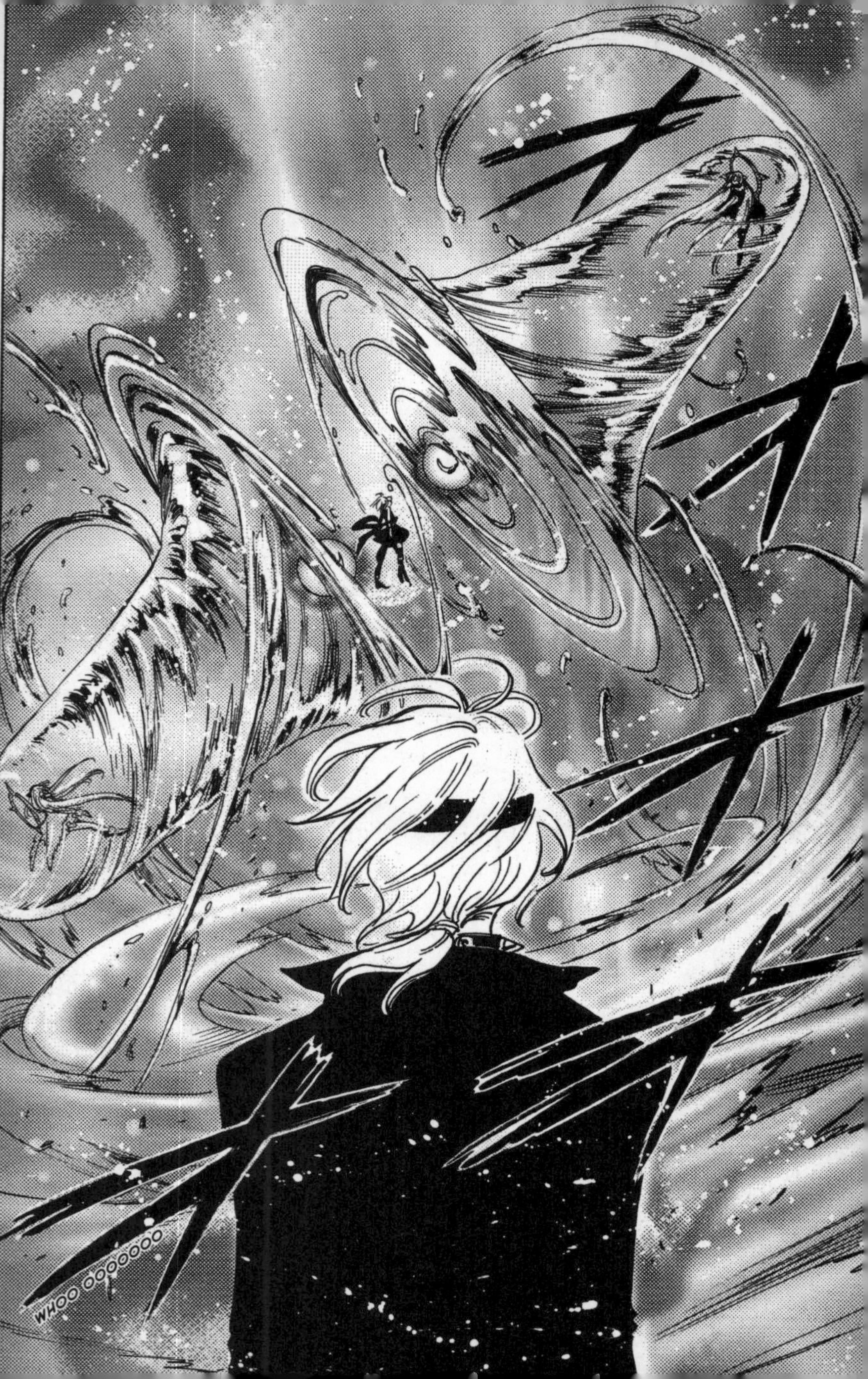
WHOO OOOOOOO

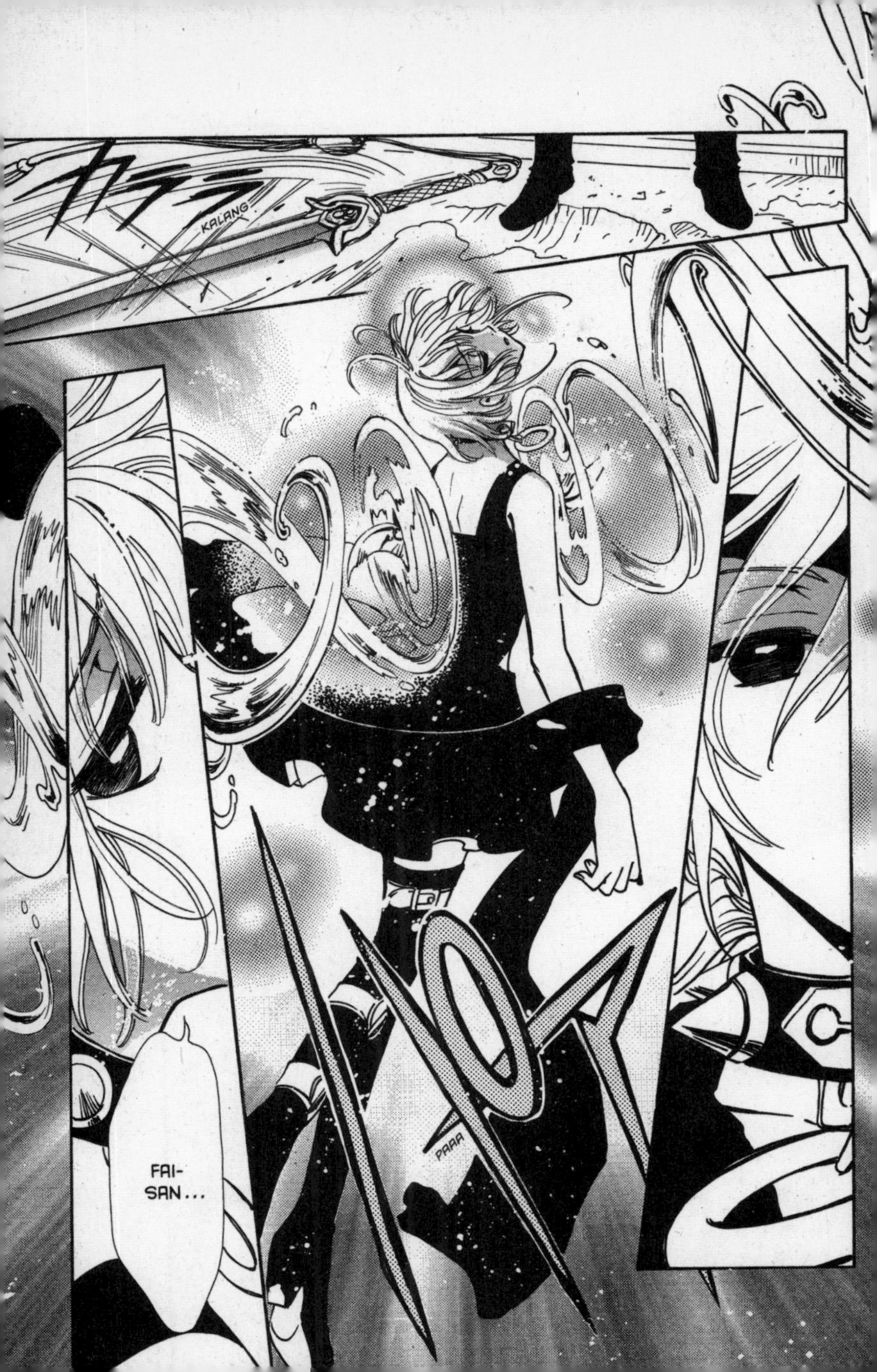
カララ
KALANG
PAAA
FAI-
SAN...

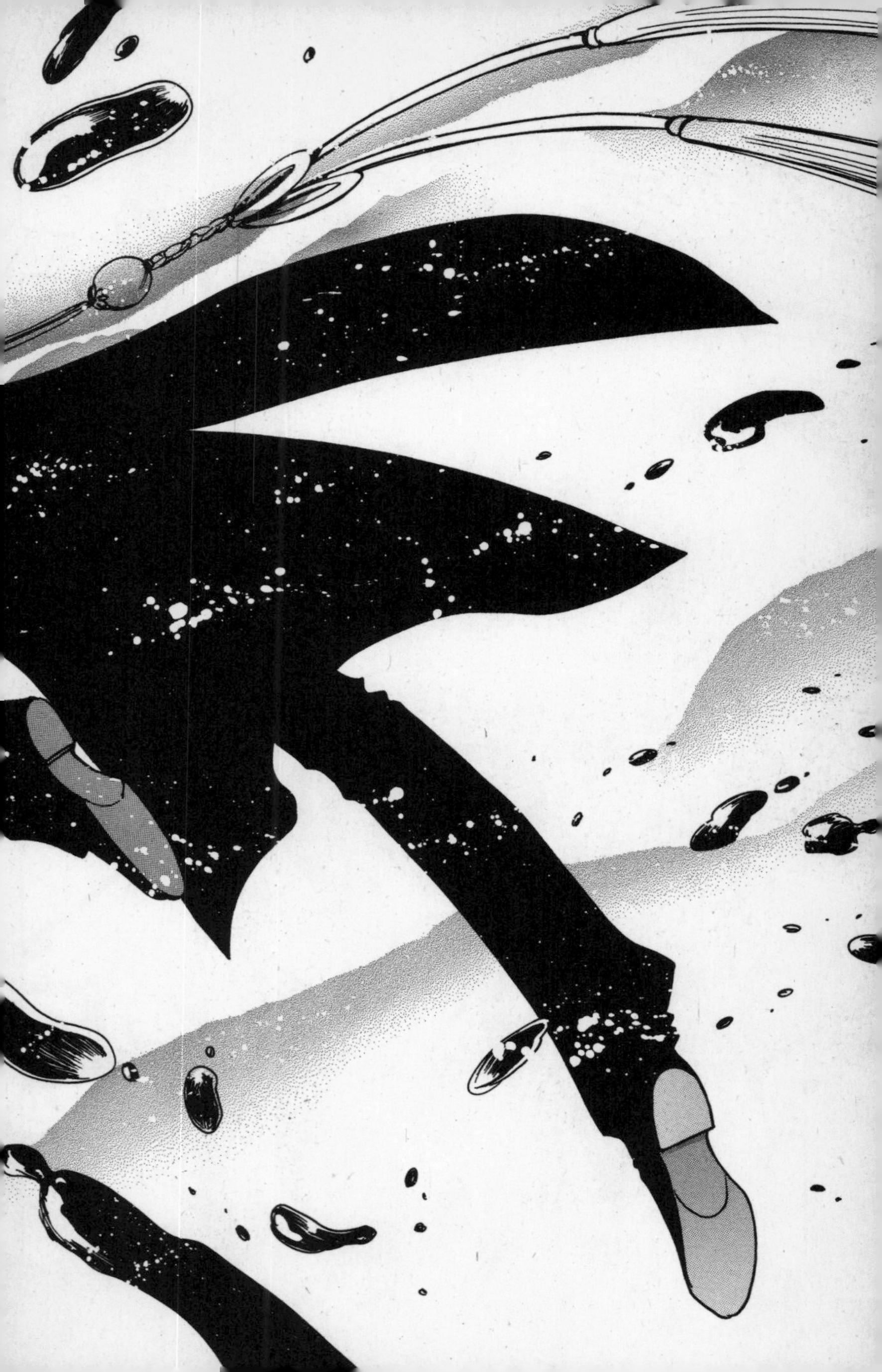

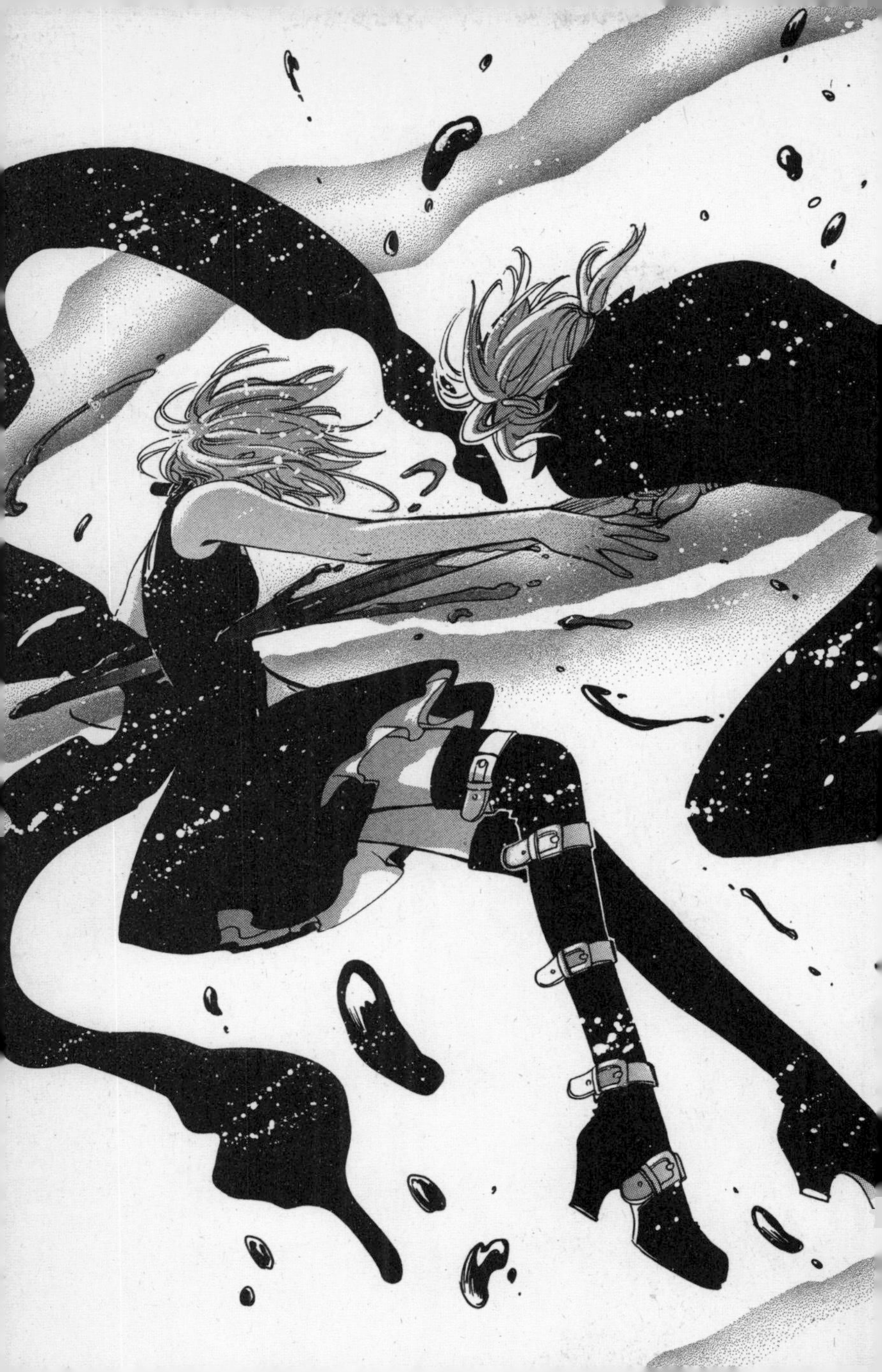

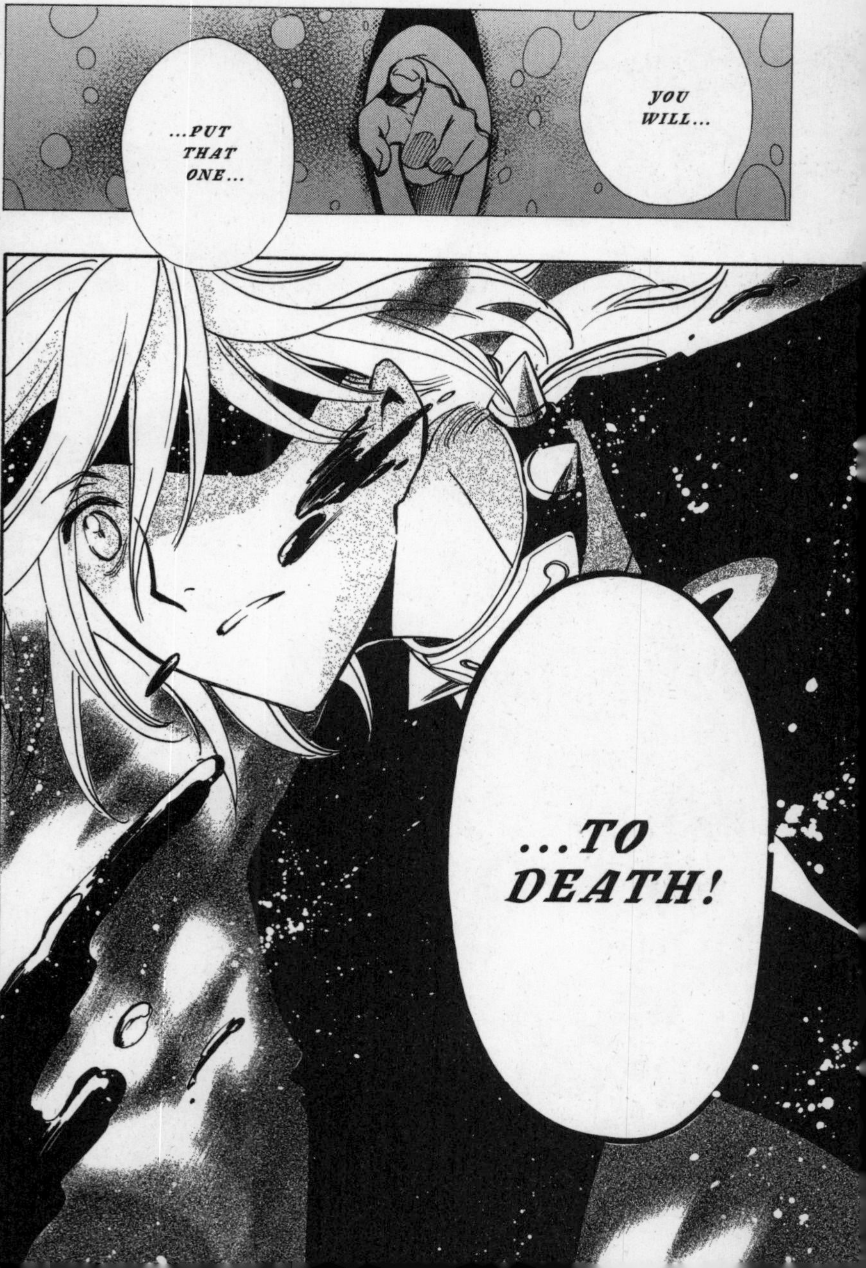
YOU WILL...
...PUT THAT ONE...
...TO DEATH!

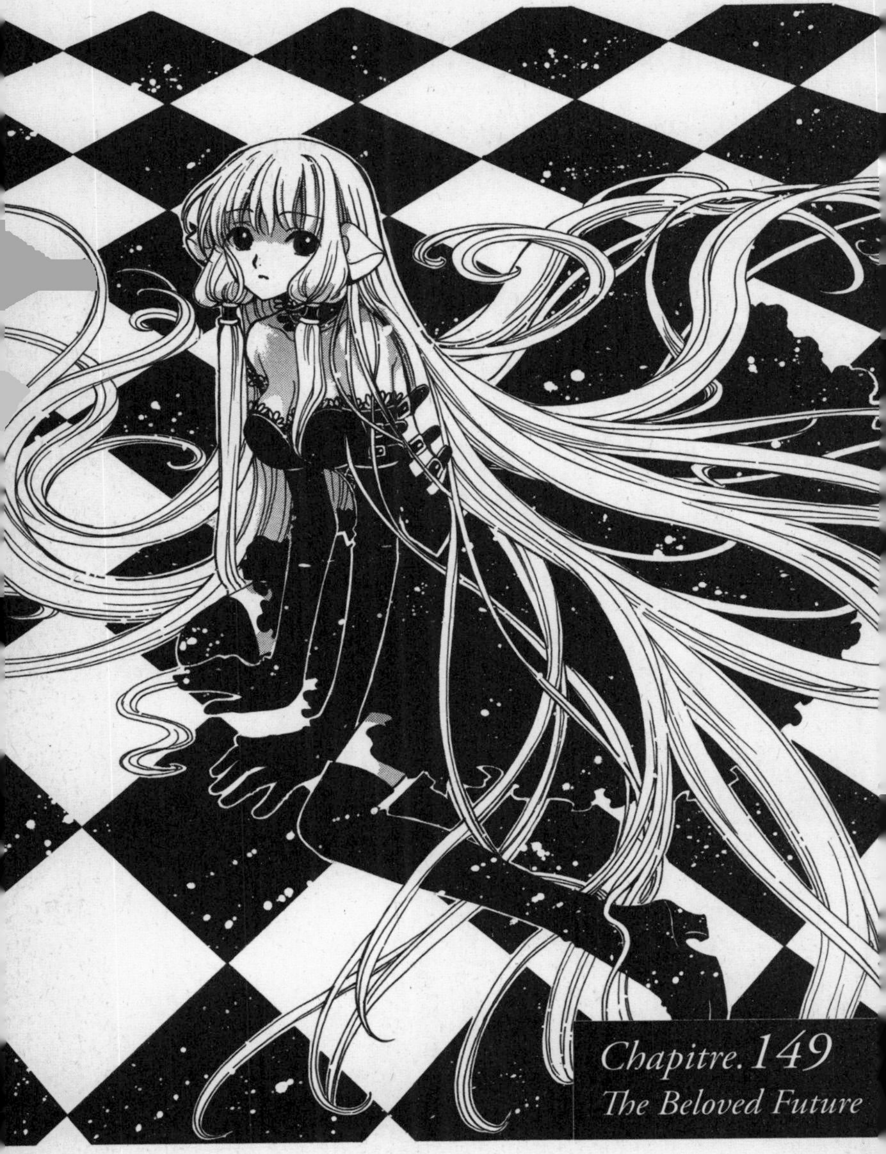

Chapitre. 149
The Beloved Future

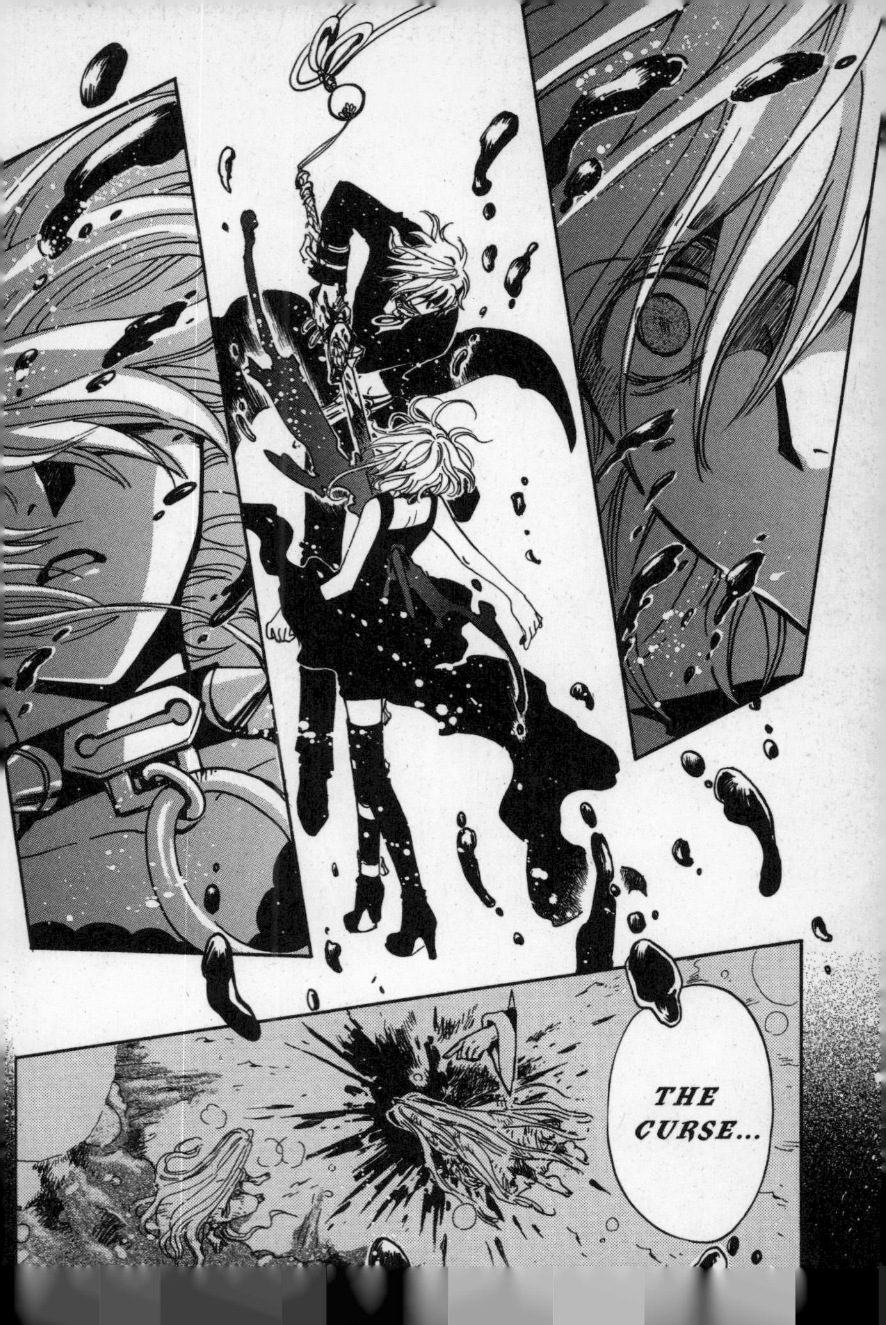
THE CURSE...

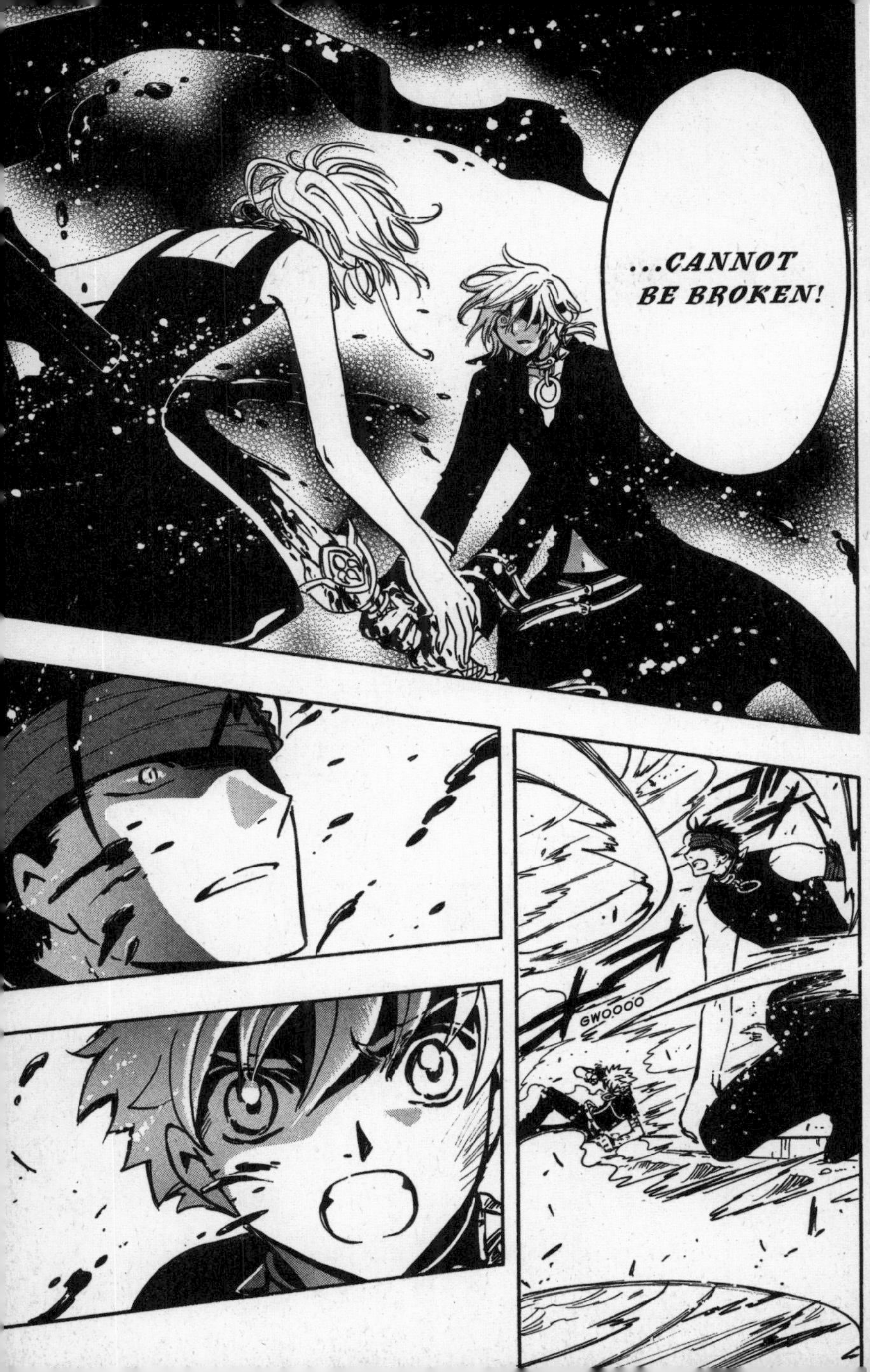
...CANNOT BE BROKEN!
GWOOOO

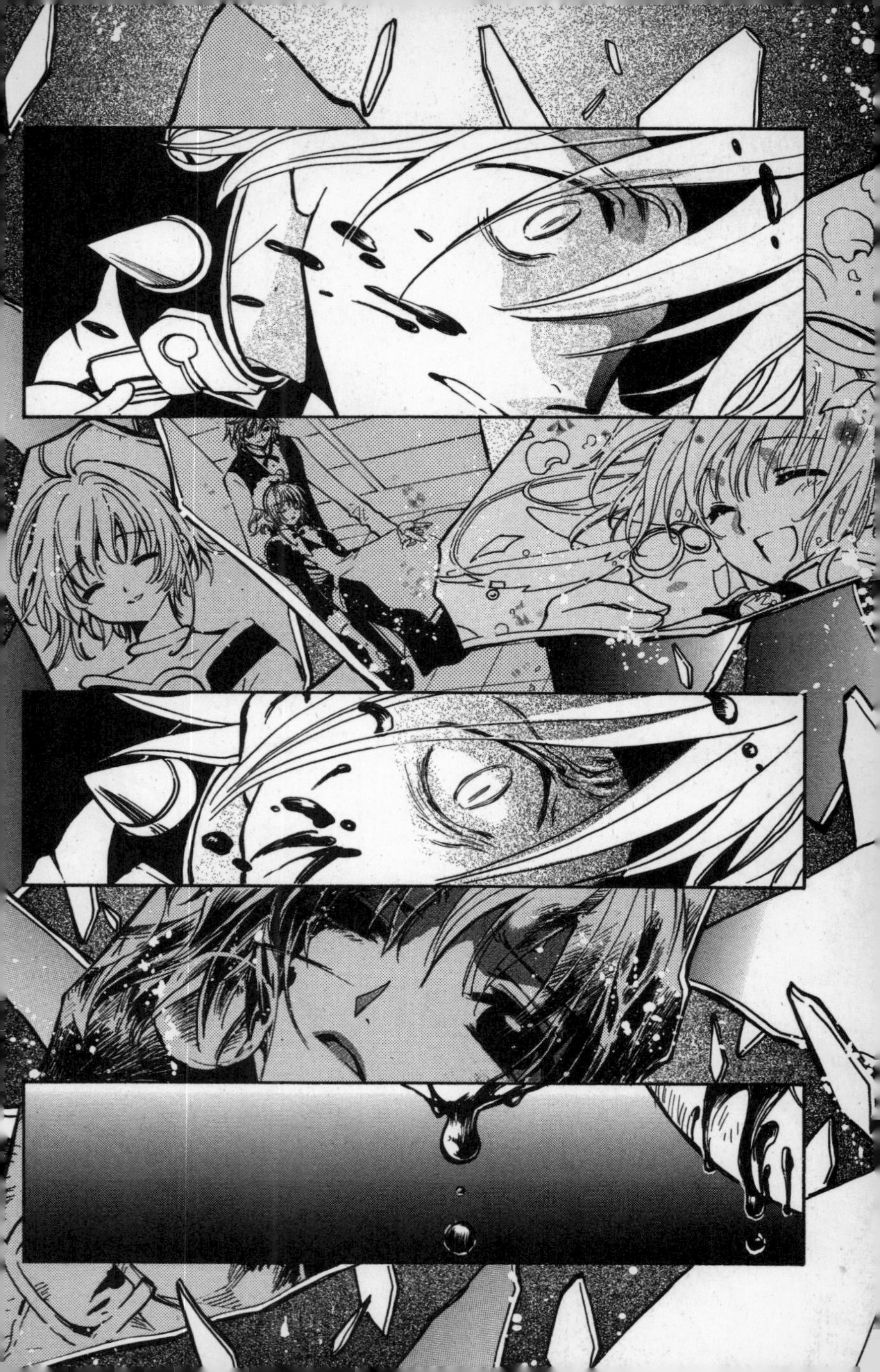

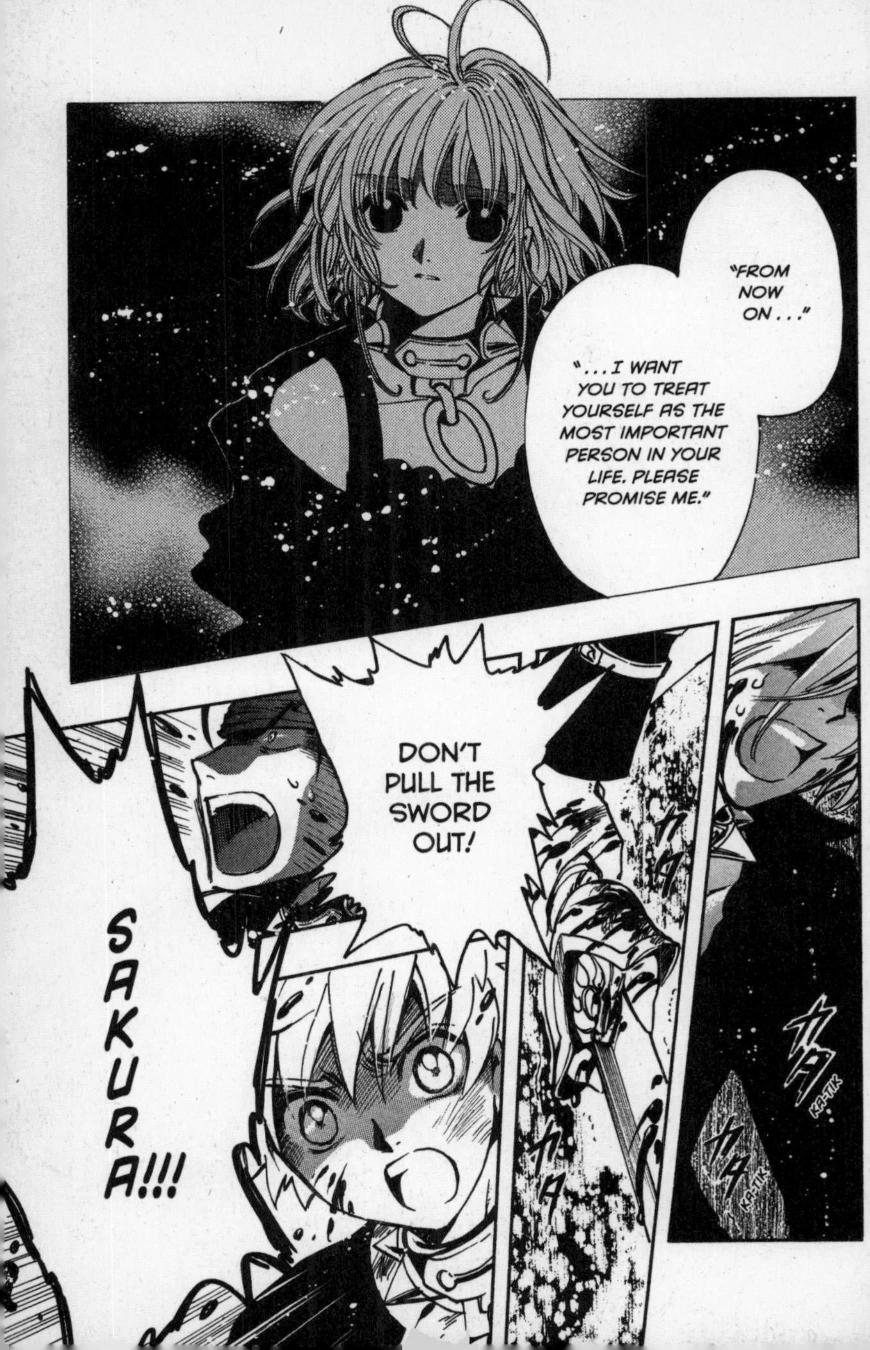
"FROM NOW ON . . ."
". . . I WANT YOU TO TREAT YOURSELF AS THE MOST IMPORTANT PERSON IN YOUR LIFE. PLEASE PROMISE ME."
KA-TIK
KA-TIK
DON'T PULL THE SWORD OUT!
SAKURA!!!

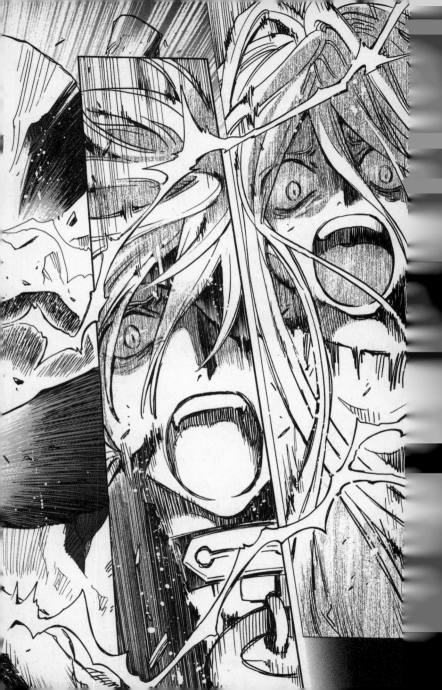

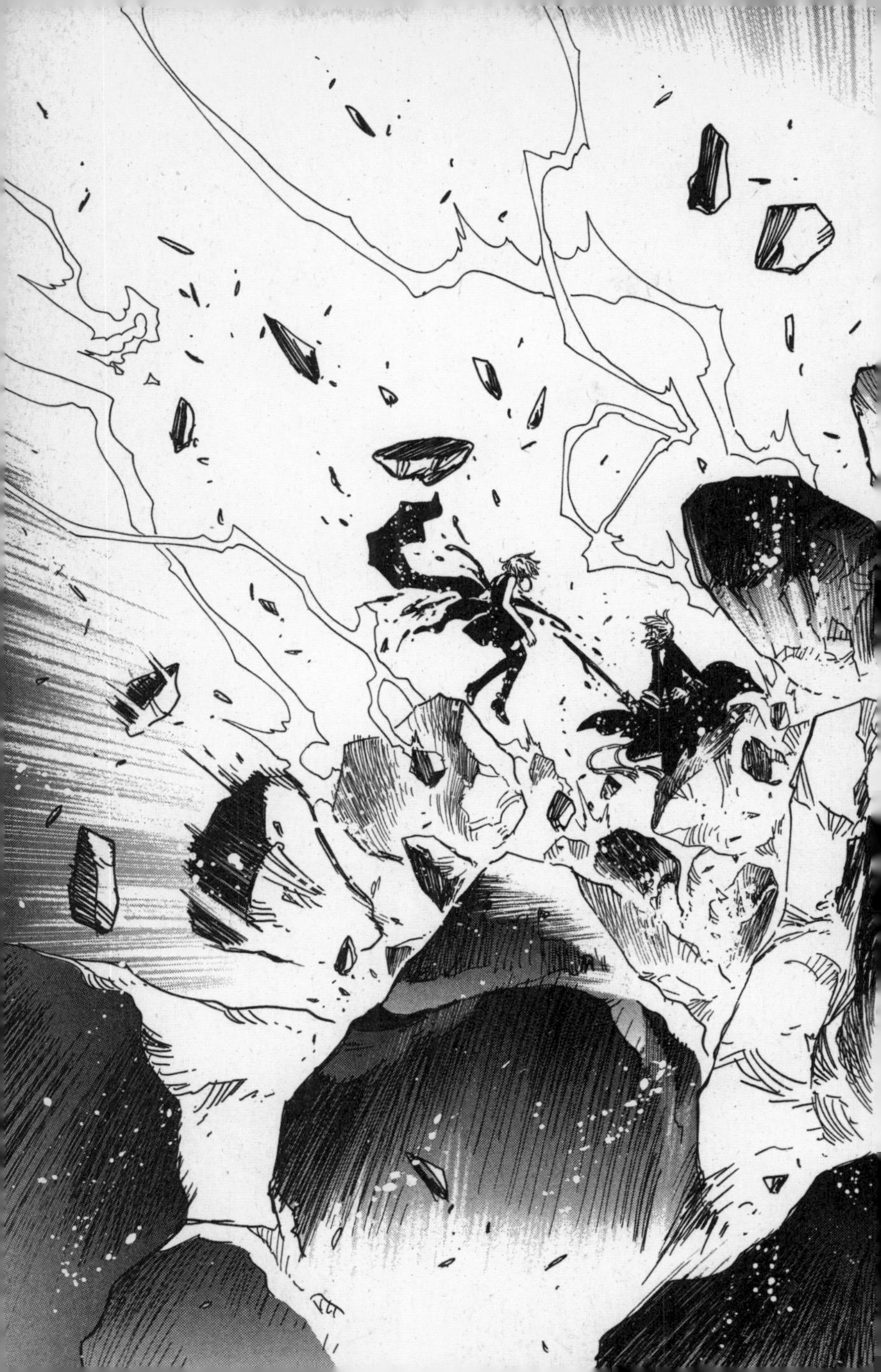

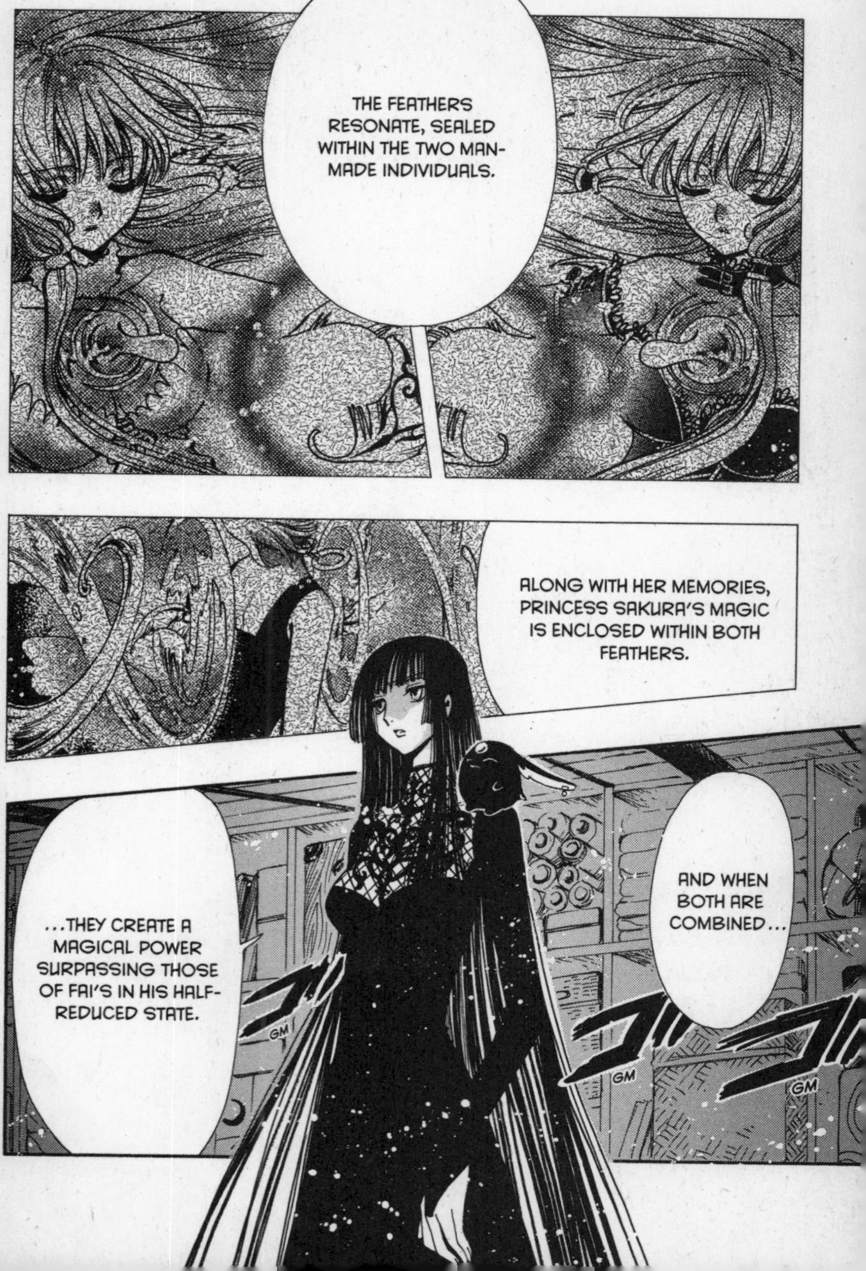
THE FEATHERS RESONATE, SEALED WITHIN THE TWO MAN-MADE INDIVIDUALS.
ALONG WITH HER MEMORIES, PRINCESS SAKURA'S MAGIC IS ENCLOSED WITHIN BOTH FEATHERS.
AND WHEN BOTH ARE COMBINED...
GM
GM
GM
...THEY CREATE A MAGICAL POWER SURPASSING THOSE OF FAI'S IN HIS HALF-REDUCED STATE.

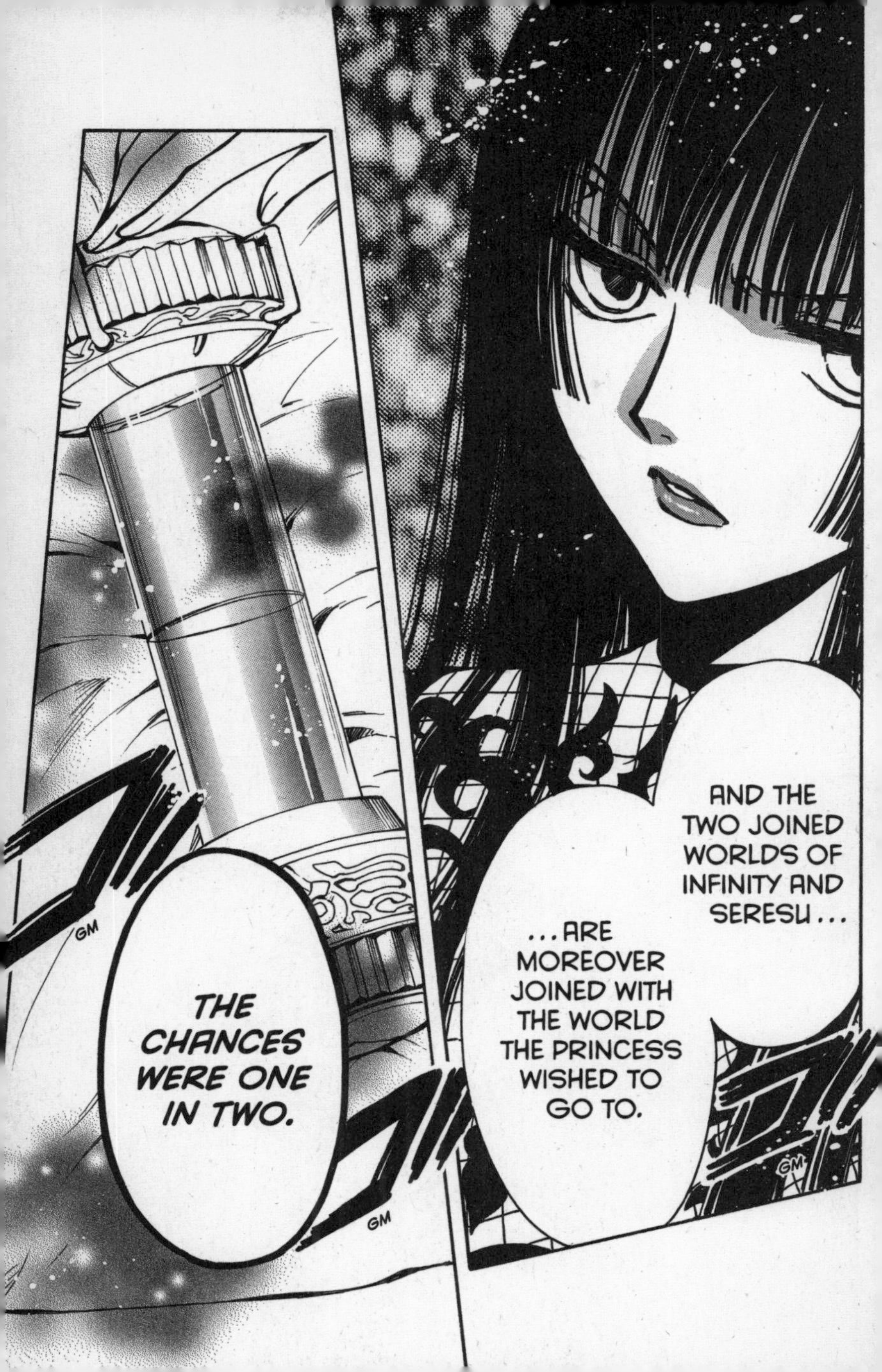
AND THE TWO JOINED WORLDS OF INFINITY AND SERESU...
...ARE MOREOVER JOINED WITH THE WORLD THE PRINCESS WISHED TO GO TO.
GM
THE CHANCES WERE ONE IN TWO.
GM
GM

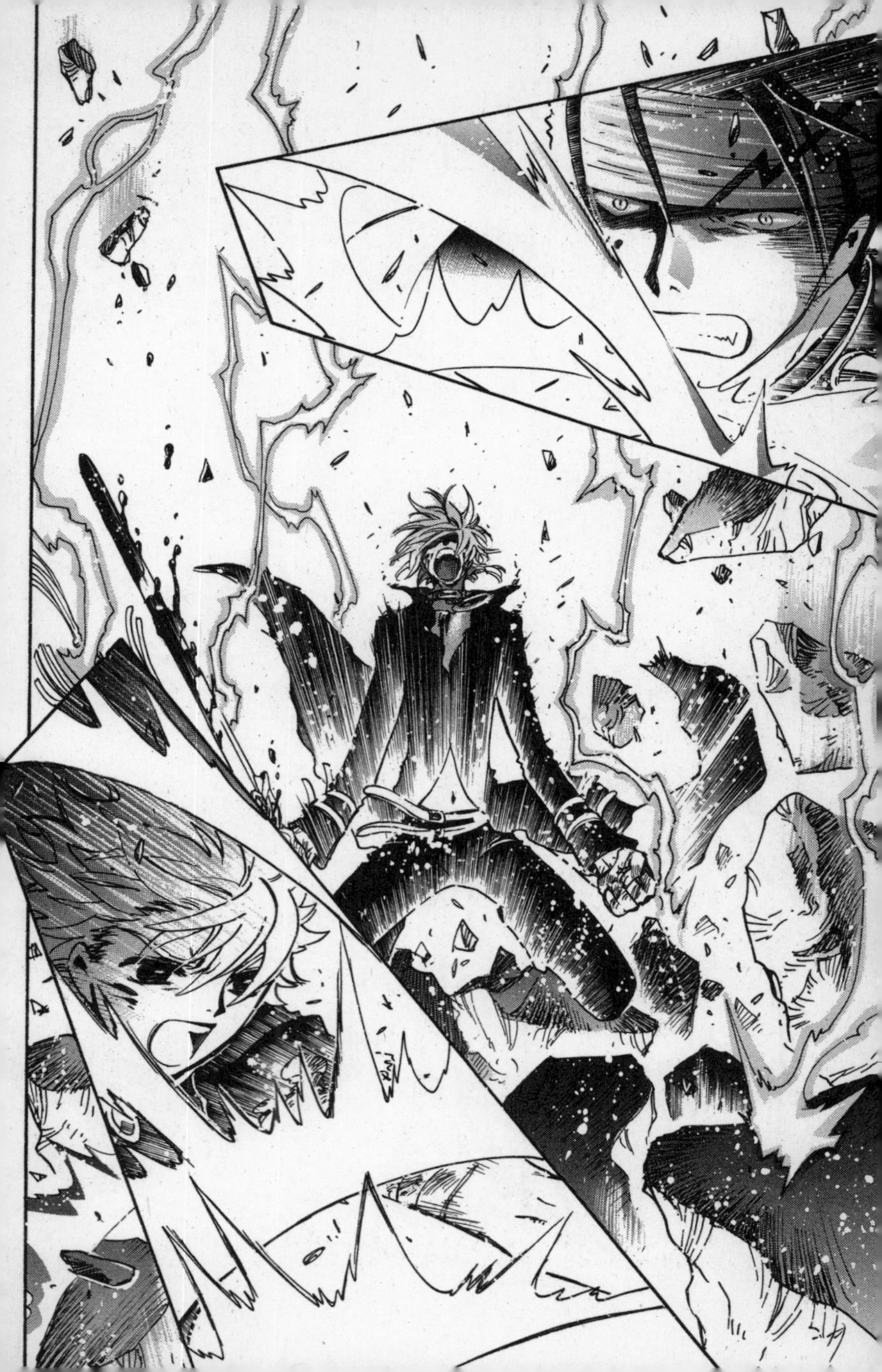

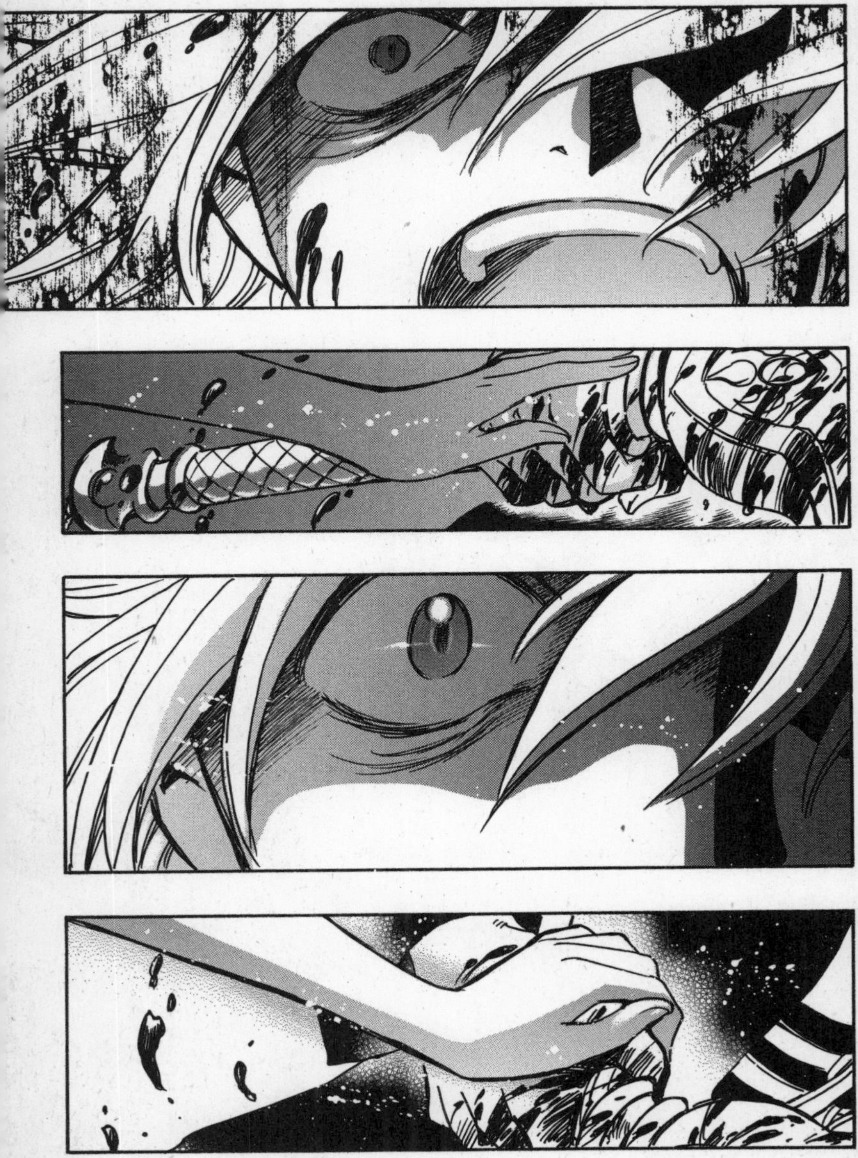

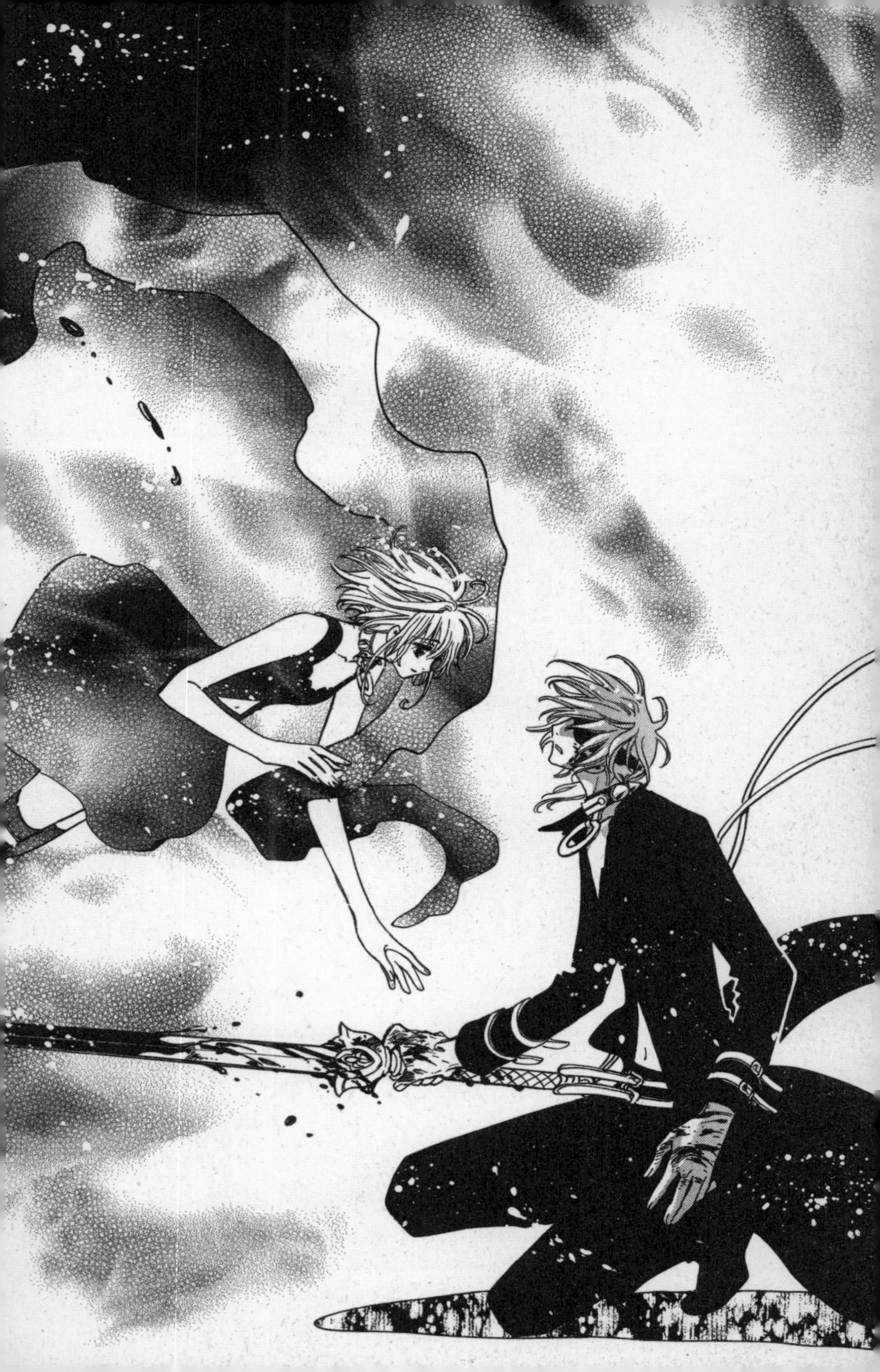

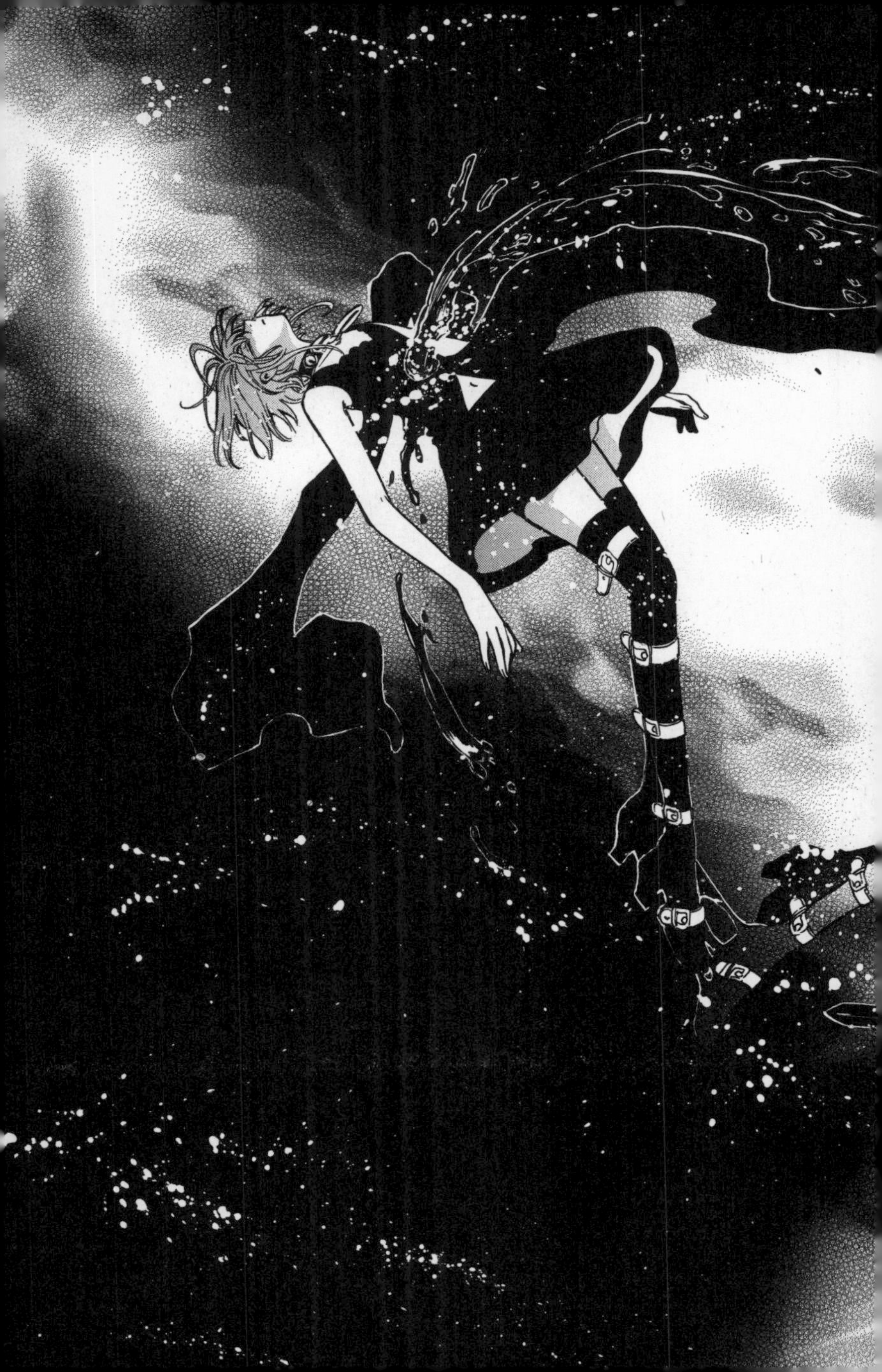

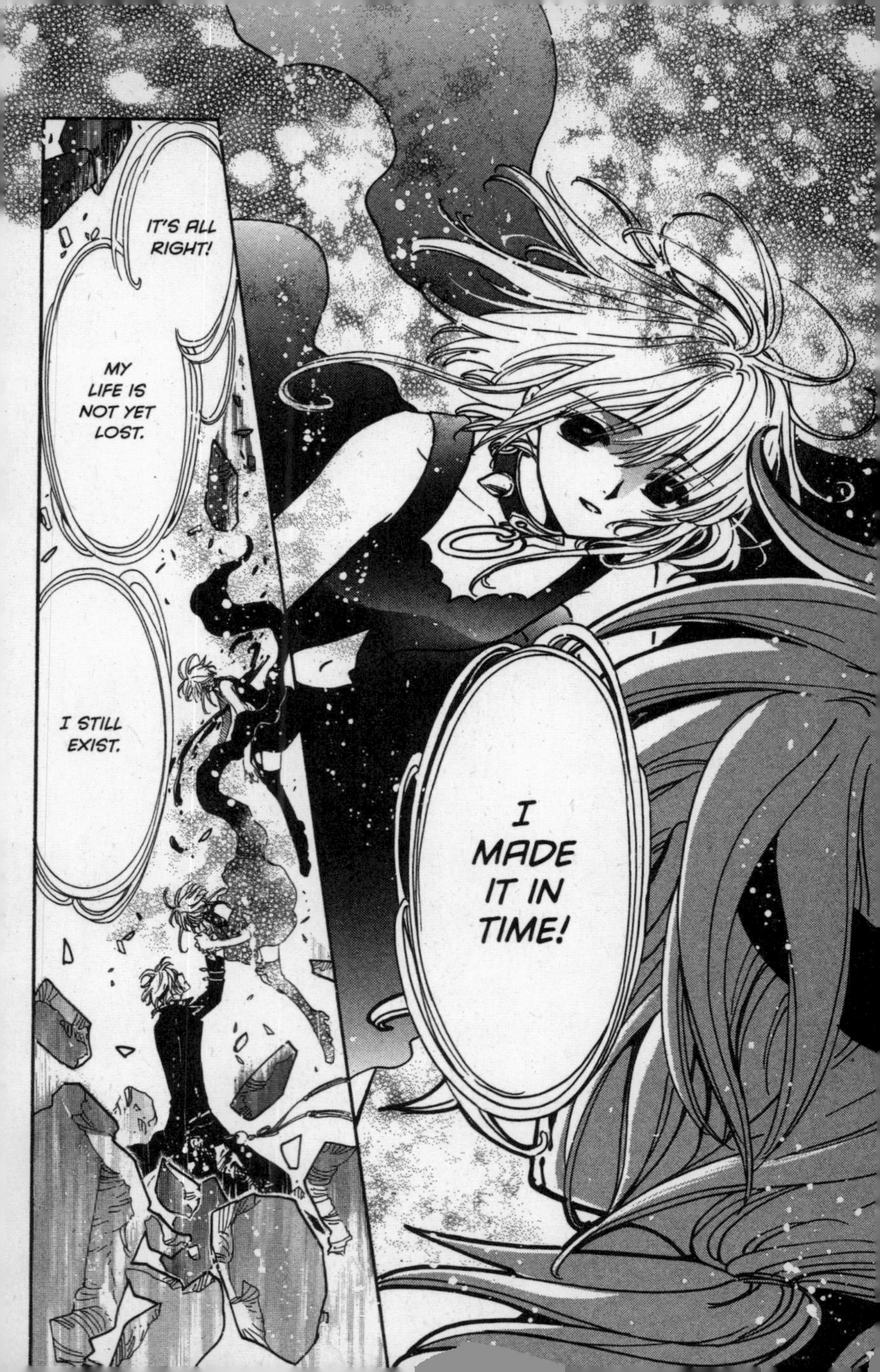
I MADE IT IN TIME!
IT'S ALL RIGHT!
MY LIFE IS NOT YET LOST.
I STILL EXIST.

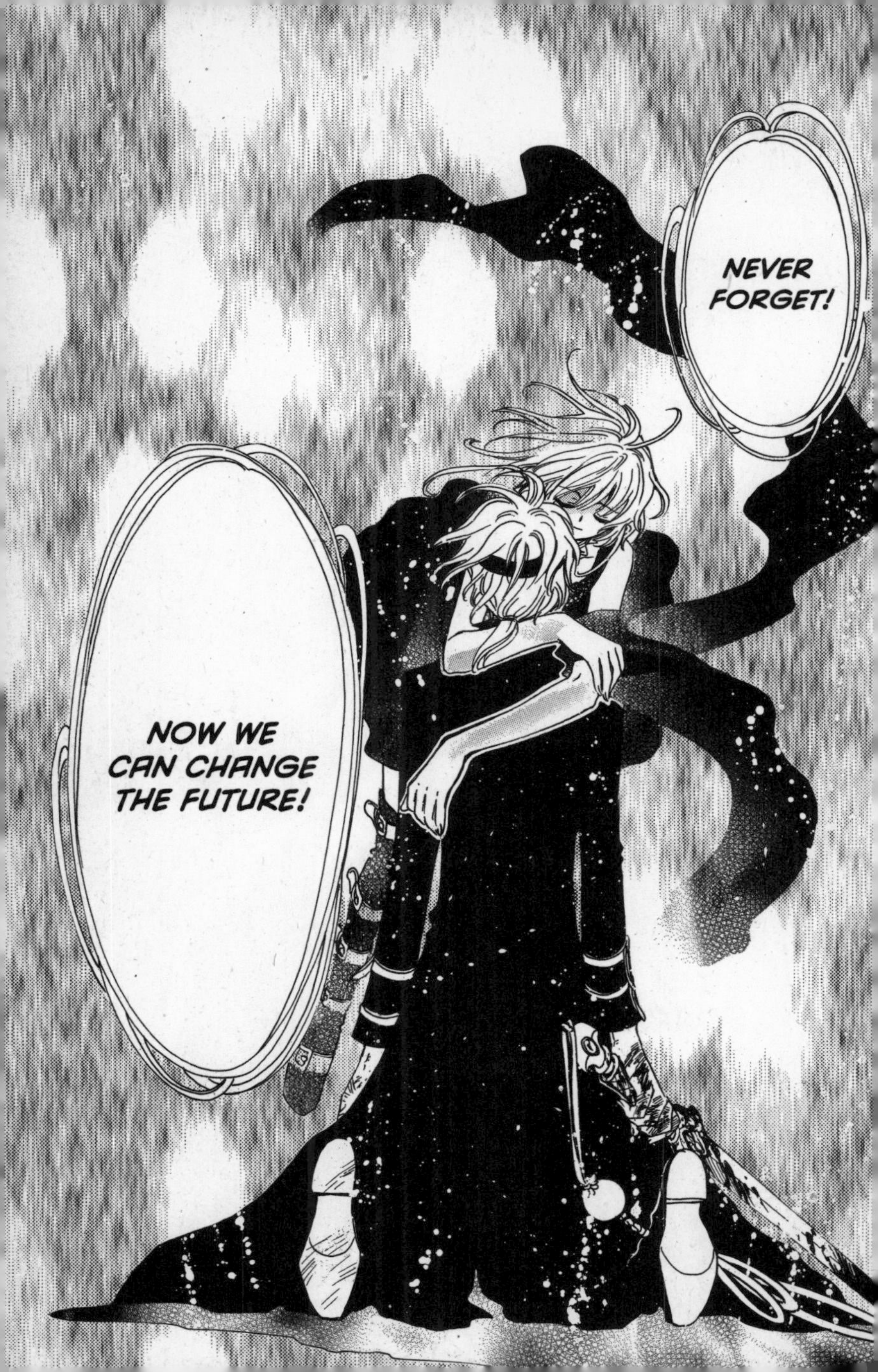
NEVER FORGET!
NOW WE CAN CHANGE THE FUTURE!

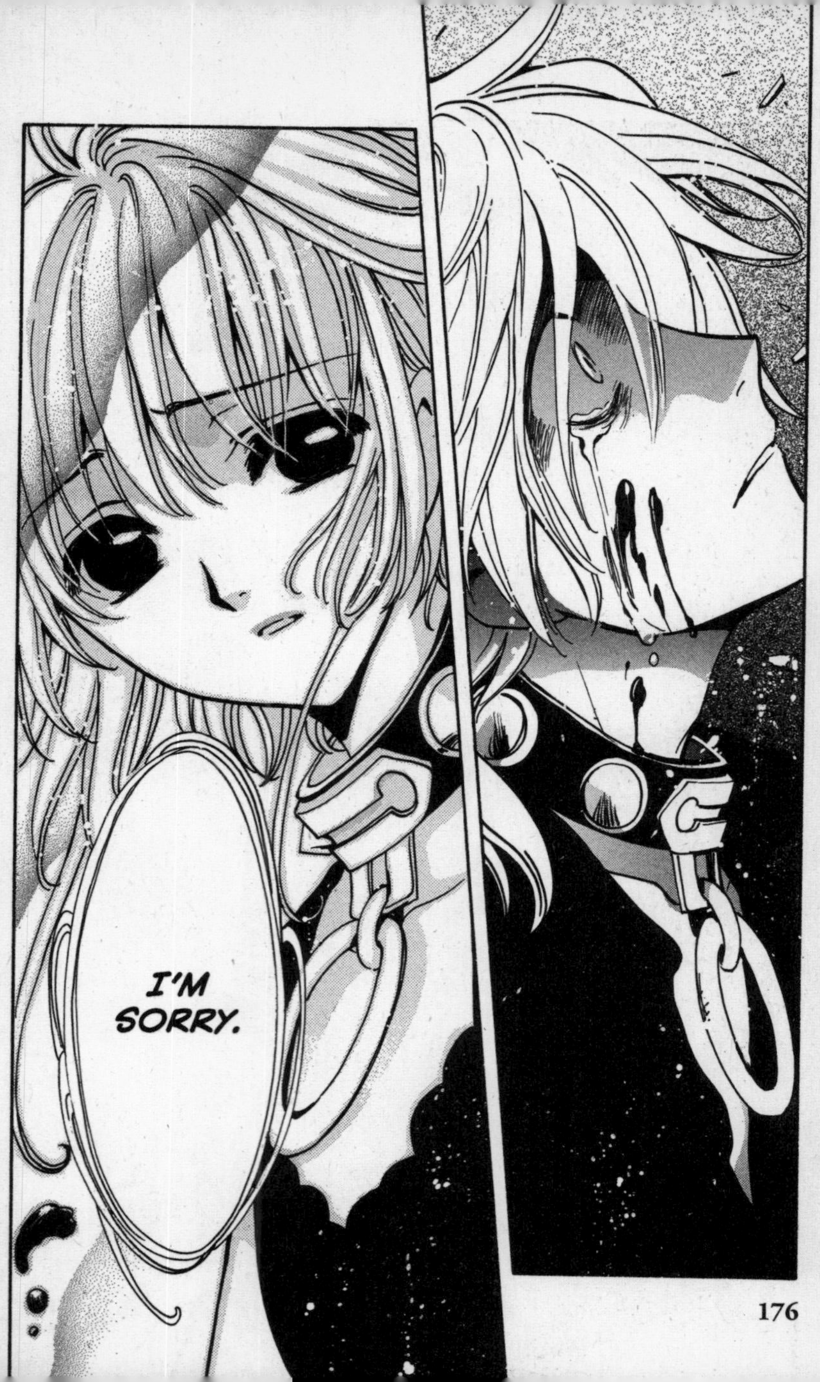
I'M SORRY.

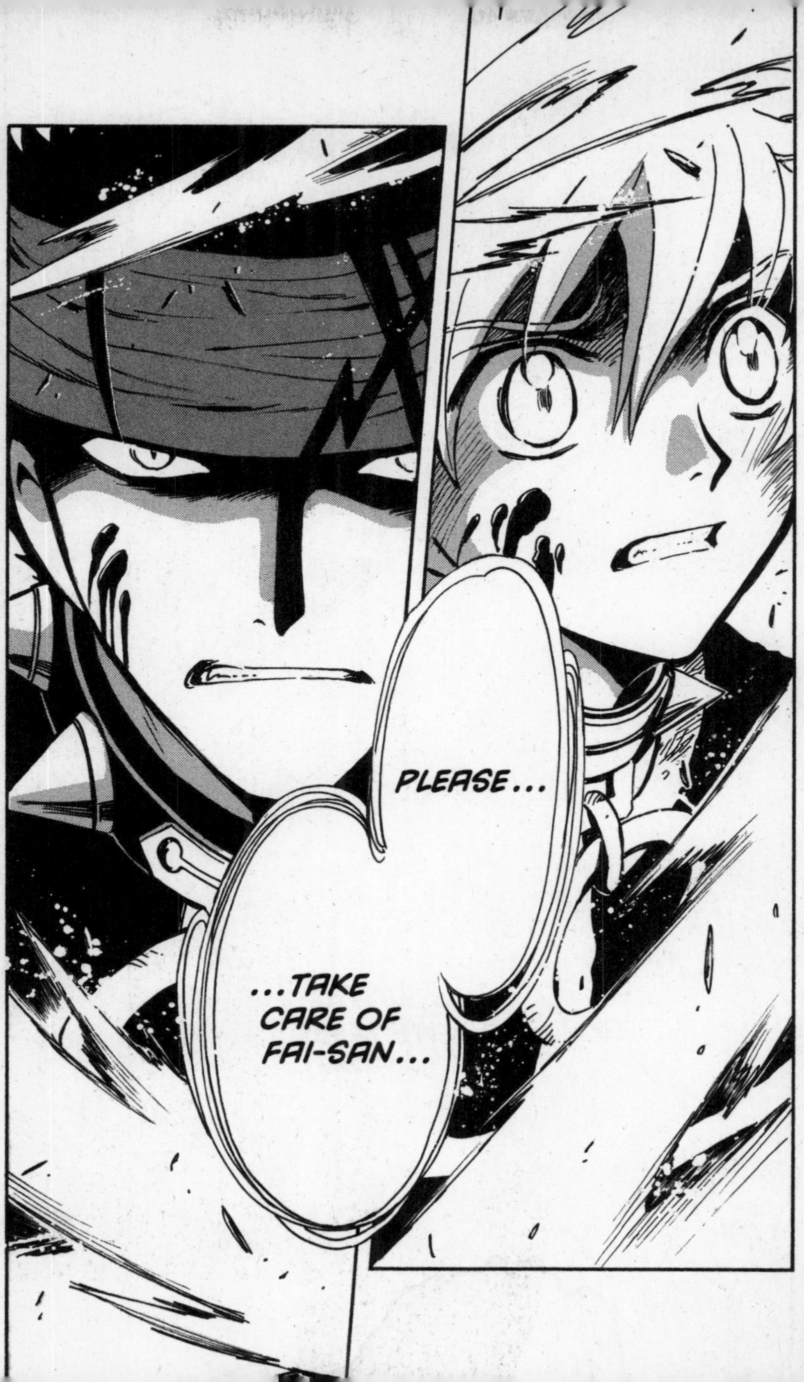
PLEASE...
...TAKE CARE OF FAI-SAN...

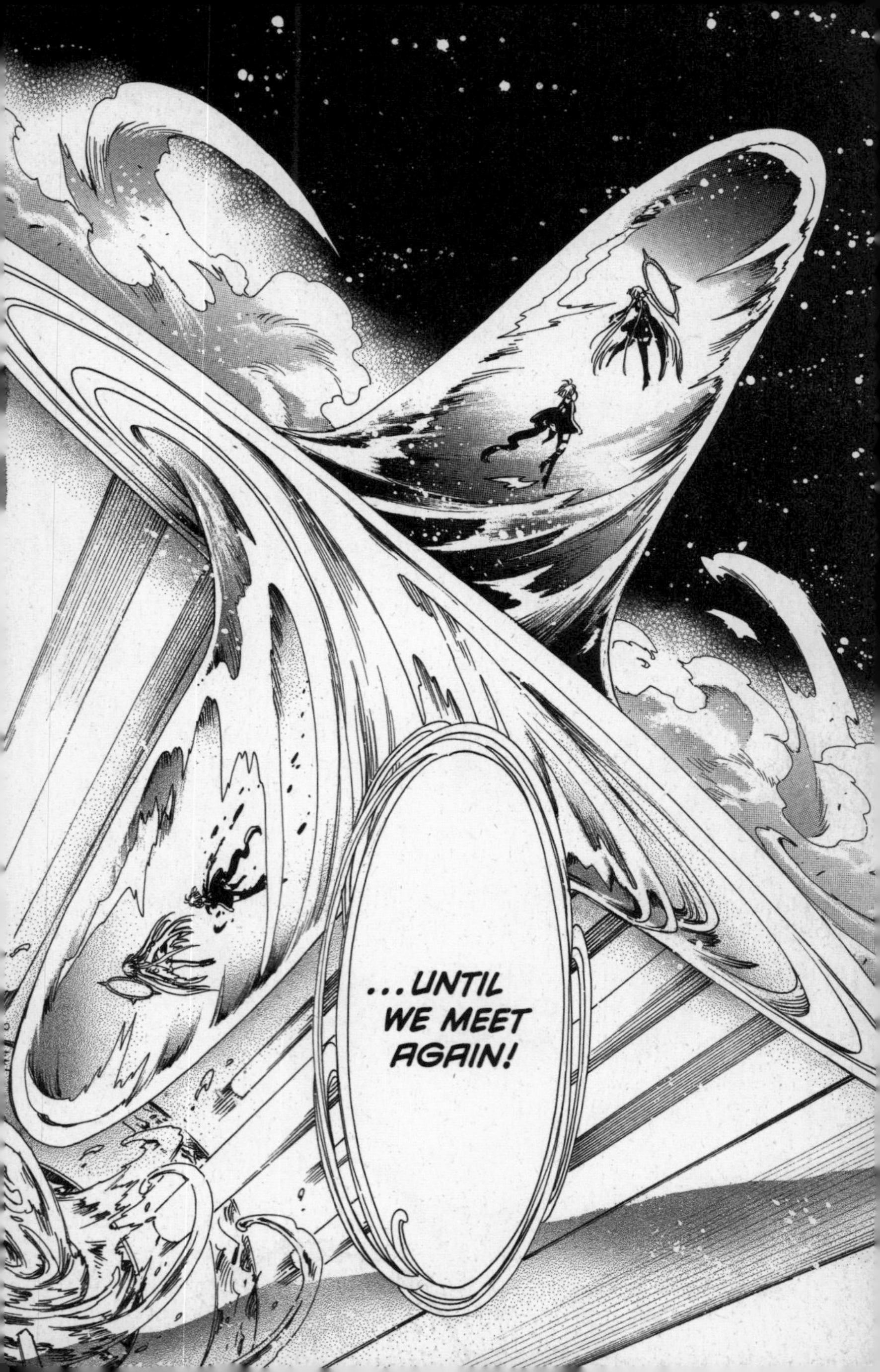
...UNTIL WE MEET AGAIN!

To Be Continued

About the Creators

CLAMP is a group of four women who have become the most popular manga artists in America—Nanase Ohkawa, Mokona, Satsuki Igarashi, and Tsubaki Nekoi. They started out as *doujinshi* (fan comics) creators, but their skill and craft brought them to the attention of publishers very quickly. Their first work from a major publisher was *RG Veda*, but their first mass success was with *Magic Knight Rayearth*. From there, they went on to write many series, including Cardcaptor Sakura and Chobits, two of the most popular manga in the United States. Like many Japanese manga artists, they prefer to avoid the spotlight, and little is known about them personally.

CLAMP is currently publishing three series in Japan: Tsubasa and xxxHOLiC with Kodansha and Gohou Drug with Kadokawa.

Translation Notes

Japanese is a tricky language for most Westerners, and translation is often more art than science. For your edification and reading pleasure, here are notes on some of the places where we could have gone in a different direction in our translation of the work, or where a Japanese cultural reference is used.

Fun Drunks, page 14

It's been noted by more than a few observers of Japan that the Japanese tend to have more fun drunks than other kinds such as depressed drunks, melancholy drunks, and belligerent drinks. Of course Japan has its fair share of other kinds, but more fun drunks seem to be found in Japan than in the west. If this is true, the Japanese custom of drinking together to form stronger bonds between colleagues—a practice that is used not only by businesses but also clubs, college groups, etc.—is probably the cause of all the cheeriness. The tradition of getting drunk with

THIS SYAORAN IS A FUN DRUNK.

colleagues has lost some of its strength in the last two decades as more workers begin to place a higher priority on family life over business or social concerns. But still, since nobody likes a mean drunk, Japanese people seem to make an extra effort to have fun when they drink.

I'll be back/Come back soon, page 33

What Sakura and Fai said in Japanese, *ittekimasu*, is a standard phrase said when someone from a household is leaving the home. It's usually followed (or preceded) by the person left behind saying, *Itterashai!* Translating this is a little complicated since English doesn't have ritual phrases of the same meaning. The translation tried to use appropriate dialog for the situation.

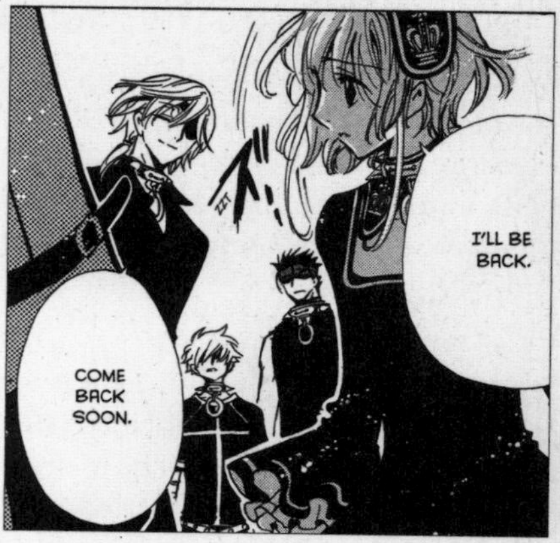
I'LL BE BACK.
COME BACK SOON.

I'm home/Welcome back, page 54

Just as prevalent in a Japanese household as *Ittekimasu* and *Itterashai* (see the above note) are the phrases used when one returns to a household. *Tadaima* is a phrase that means "just now," and is short for the longer phrase, *tadaima kaerimashita*, or "I have just now returned." It is followed (or preceded) by the person who stayed at home using the phrase *okaeri-nasai*, which literally means "come back" but translates better as "welcome back," or "welcome home." It is not unusual for the one coming home to repeat *tadaima* several times when meeting different members of the household.

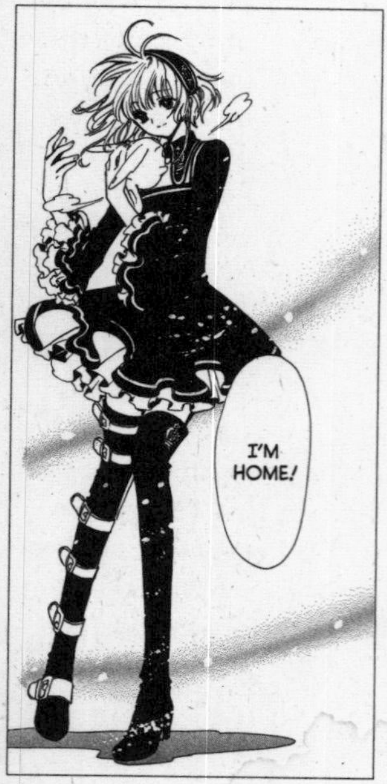
I'M HOME!

THANK YOU!

SYAORAN-KUN.

That Syaoran/Syaoran-kun, page 71

Throughout the past three volumes, since the addition of the Syaoran who was imprisoned by Fei-Wang Reed, the other characters referred to him by saying his name within a thick set of Japanese quote symbols. I've generally translated this as "that Syaoran," since the English phrase seems to contain a nuance of being left out of the group, which the quotation marks seem to express in Japanese. In this scene where Sakura finally calls him by name, it is the first time that Sakura's dialog did not contain the quotation symbols in Japanese. This seems to express that she now accepts him as a person in his own right, rather than simply being a look-alike of the previous Syaoran character.

The Automata, page 80

Although she isn't named in this volume, Eagle's "chess piece" is the Infinity world's version of Hikaru, the "Angel" battle doll of the main character Misaki from the world of *Angelic Layer*. In a strange mix of crossovers, Hikaru is named after Hikaru Shidô, one of the three main characters of *Magic Knight Rayearth* (since the character Misaki is a fan of the Rayearth manga). To complicate the crossovers, our three Mafia men, Eagle Vision, Lantis, and Geo Metro are also from the *Magic Knight Rayearth* world. One more interesting point is that the character of Chi first appeared in *Chobits*, which shares the same universe with *Angelic Layer*. Got all that straight?

183

KASUMI
かすみ

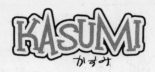

STORY BY SURT LIM
ART BY HIROFUMI SUGIMOTO

A DEL REY MANGA ORIGINAL

Exploring the woods, young Kasumi encounters an ancient tree god, who bestows upon her the power of invisibility. Together with classmates who have had similar experiences, Kasumi forms the Magic Play Club, dedicated to using their powers for good while avoiding sinister forces that would exploit them.

volume
1
KASUMI
かすみ
Story by
Surt Lim
Art by
Hirofumi
Sugimoto

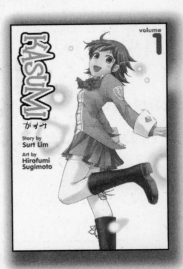

Special extras in each volume! Read them all!

VISIT WWW.DELREYMANGA.COM TO:
- Read sample pages
- View release date calendars for upcoming volumes
- Sign up for Del Rey's free manga e-newsletter
- Find out the latest about new Del Rey Manga series

RATING T AGES 13+

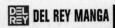

DEL REY MANGA デルレイ
The Otaku's Choice™

TOMARE!

[STOP!]

You're going the wrong way!

Manga is a completely different type of reading experience.

To start at the *beginning*, go to the *end*!

That's right! Authentic manga is read the traditional Japanese way—from right to left. Exactly the *opposite* of how American books are read. It's easy to follow: Just go to the other end of the book, and read each page—and each panel—from right side to left side, starting at the top right. Now you're experiencing manga as it was meant to be.